One Discipline, Four Ways

D0964499

One Discipline, Four Ways: British, German, French, and American Anthropology

FREDRIK BARTH

ANDRE GINGRICH

ROBERT PARKIN

SYDEL SILVERMAN

The Halle Lectures   *With a Foreword by Chris Hann*

UNIVERSITY OF CHICAGO PRESS / CHICAGO AND LONDON

The University of Chicago Press, Chicago 60637
The University of Chicago Press, Ltd., London
© 2005 by The University of Chicago
All rights reserved. Published 2005
Printed in the United States of America

14 13 12 11 10 09 08 07   3 4 5

ISBN-13: 978-0-226-03828-5 (cloth)
ISBN-13: 978-0-226-03829-2 (paper)
ISBN-10: 0-226-03828-9 (cloth)
ISBN-10: 0-226-03829-7 (paper)

Library of Congress Cataloging-in-Publication Data

One discipline, four ways : British, German, French, and American anthropology /
Fredrik Barth . . . [et al.] ; with a foreword by Chris Hann.
    p. cm. — (The Halle lectures)
    "The twenty chapters of this volume derive from a series of lectures titled Four
traditions in anthropology, which were organized to mark the inauguration of the
Max Planck Institute for Social Anthropology in Halle (Saale), Germany, in June
2002"—Fwd.
    Includes bilbiographical references and index.
    ISBN 0-226-03828-9 (cloth : alk. paper) — ISBN 0-226-03829-7 (pbk. : alk. paper)
    1. Anthropology—History—19th century. 2. Anthropology—History—20th
century. 3. Anthropology—Philosophy. I. Barth, Fredrik, 1928– II. Series.

GN17.O48 2005
306—dc22   2004024388

⊗ The paper used in this publication meets the minimum requirements of the American
National Standard for Information Sciences—Permanence of Paper for Printed Library
Materials, ANSI Z39.48-1992.

CONTENTS

Foreword / *Chris Hann* / vii

The twenty chapters of this volume derive from a series of lectures titled Four Traditions in Anthropology, which were organized to mark the inauguration of the Max Planck Institute for Social Anthropology in Halle (Saale), Germany, in June 2002. Our institute had begun its work in temporary premises some three years earlier, but no one wanted any rituals before we had moved into our permanent buildings. By linking the inauguration to the annual general meeting of the Max Planck Society, we ensured that a good number of our research colleagues would be able to join all the ministers, rectors, and other dignitaries who had played a role in the founding of the institute. But we were also determined to infuse our collective rite of passage with an anthropological dimension; hence the idea for a lecture series.

Our current research projects are overwhelmingly concerned with contemporary social transformation and are based on fieldwork methods, but the establishment of a large new research center with an explicitly international ethos seemed to us an excellent opportunity to take a fresh look at the history of anthropology. Because this was very much an exercise in ritual, we felt free to experiment and even to indulge in role reversals. We therefore invited Adam Kuper, best known as a historian of the discipline, to deliver a *Festvortrag* in the grand opening ceremony on a contemporary topic. (He chose to address controversies concerning the land claims of indigenous peoples, under the title "The Return of the Native"; for the published version see *Current Anthropology* for June 2003.) For the lecture series that preceded the inaugural ceremonies, we decided to approach four distinguished anthropologists who, although they had contributed to the writing of disciplinary history, were not primarily specialized in this field. Each lecturer was encouraged to adopt a basically chronological approach to a single "tradition" but was otherwise given an entirely free hand. Amazingly, everything proceeded according to plan, so that over a ten-day period an audience augmented by numerous foreign guests was treated to a splendid program.

Each lecture was a cocktail based on concentrated scholarship and variously shaken up with engrossing personal reminiscences, entertaining digressions, and deadly serious scientific, moral, and political criticism. For this publication we have decided to group each author's lectures together, although in the Halle delivery they were interspersed. Each lecture was followed by a brief question-and-answer period, and each cycle of four lectures by an extended discussion session. In this way, we continuously identified the multiple links between the four traditions and reminded ourselves of the obvious inadequacy of selecting only four, with a strong "Western" bias. There are now vibrant schools of anthropology on every continent. Given my own views on treating Eurasia as a unity, it was especially regrettable that our format left us no scope to consider the rich traditions of Russian anthropology, or more recent developments in China and India. Perhaps most important, we constantly questioned the very idea of presenting disciplinary history in this way. Space restrictions prevent us from including any record of these animated discussions in this volume, but the reader should be aware that they took place. The lecturers have occasionally picked up some of the key points in their revisions.

It seems to me undeniable that the diverse trajectories of anthropology (which, of course, we take as an umbrella concept, subsuming fields such as ethnology and ethnography, as well as folklore, museum studies, and so on) have indeed been deeply marked by their "national" settings, that is, by different intellectual contexts as well as different social and political environments. This is nowhere more evident than in East-Central Europe, where our institute is located. German scholars developed pioneering research agendas and coined numerous key terms in the eighteenth century, long before the forging of a unified German state. Here, as elsewhere in Europe, the anthropological field has been strongly marked by nationalism. Even where this legacy was later modified by the imposition of Soviet Marxist theories, the continuities remain substantial. These lectures are primarily devoted to four variants of the comparative enterprise of *Völkerkunde* rather than to *Volkskunde*, the study of one's own people, but we need to recognize that national frames have influenced both of these strands of anthropology almost from the very beginning.

Yet it also seems self-evident that at least some differences have been narrowing in recent decades. The very establishment of the Max Planck Institute for Social Anthropology (in German, *Max-Planck-Institut für ethnologische*

Forschung—literally, "for ethnological research") and my recruitment from Great Britain as one of the founding directors are small signs of these trends of convergence. Our institute respects differences in scholarly traditions just as we respect them in other fields. We have no wish to promote Anglo-Saxon domination or a bland uniformity of style; instead, we wish to encourage better contacts across all national and ideological boundaries. In short, we would like to foster cosmopolitanism in a field that, all in all, has been one of the less cosmopolitan up until now. João de Pina-Cabral, in a report on the Halle event (published in *Newsletter* 33 of the European Association of Social Anthropologists in October 2002), highlighted the diverse backgrounds of the participants and concluded optimistically that

> The moments of discussion . . . showed that, today, socio-cultural anthropology does share a common stock of knowledge and a set of mutually available working concepts and methodological formulations. These constitute a common, global framework for debate and intellectual fertilization that is claimed by anthropologists far beyond the boundaries of the twentieth century imperial nations. Might this not be thought of as a *fifth tradition* that, coming out of the imperial moment, provides us today with a largely globalised, non-national tool for scientific endeavour?

It remains for me, as the responsible host and project coordinator, to thank all four lecturers for coping with the limitations of the format, cooperating throughout the planning phase, performing heroically during our rituals, punctually supplying their revised texts for this book, and generally being a wonderful team.

Chris Hann
Max Planck Institute for Social Anthropology
Halle (Saale)
March 2003

Britain and the Commonwealth / FREDRIK BARTH

The Rise of Anthropology in Britain, 1830–1898

The field of study that became British anthropology arose on the fringes of a scholarly world that regarded other topics as far more important and interesting than the study of human social and cultural diversity. It faced an academic establishment that seems to have been most reluctant to welcome it as a bona fide discipline within the range of academic specialties worth pursuing in scholarly institutions. Under such circumstances, an account of the British tradition of anthropology cannot be restricted to an internal story of scholars wrestling each other over intellectual ideas, innovations, and orthodoxies: we must also take account of the interests and prejudices that prevailed in the larger society, to which these scholars had to accommodate, and of the particular organizations and resources in academic life that were available to them as the means of pursuing their goals.

Of course, much of British academia suffered under similar constraints. The small number of universities catered to the sons of the upper classes and were designed to provide them with a few years of culture and education before sending them on into the practical world. To the extent that curricula in the humanities looked beyond British topics, their focus was overwhelmingly on the Greco-Roman tradition, as part of a conscious effort to make that tradition foundational to British thought and civilization. Other scholarly specialties were pursued only as sidelines by the dons of these subjects or as hobbies by persons of independent income.

Inevitably, Britain's role in exploration, overseas trade, and colonial expansion during the nineteenth century led to a growing scholarly and public curiosity and interest in more global knowledge. Geography, zoology, and botany were in due course developed into the generalizing traditions of academic scholarship of the naturalists, and they produced epochal intellectual achievements, such as the theory of evolution. Similar developments did not take place in the humanities. Scholarship regarding the societies, languages, and cultures of the peoples of the growing empire and beyond its boundaries was pursued sparingly and in the particularizing mode of Orientalism, and outstanding studies such as E. W. Lane's *An Account of the Manners and Customs of the Modern Egyptians* (1836) and the honorable Mountstuart Elphinstone's *An Account of the Kingdom of Caubul* (1839/1972) failed to converge into a generalizing perspective that could become anthropology. While there was a large public market for serious travel literature, travel authors looked to history and geography for their wider perspective, and the lives of "savages" did not receive much serious attention.

Instead, the field that was to become anthropology arose out of the concerns of compassionate activists who were linked to a distinctive circle in British society: that of Nonconformists and especially Quaker philanthropists. The following discussion of the emergence of British anthropology leans heavily on a detailed and perceptive article by George W. Stocking Jr. on the origins of the Royal Anthropological Institute (1971). For a rich and detailed account of the whole period, see Stocking 1987.

Political figures among the Nonconformist and Quaker activists led the campaign against the African slave trade and the legality of the institution of slavery in the British colonies. When the abolition of slavery was achieved in 1833, this same group took up the situation of native populations in South Africa by spearheading the establishment of the Parliamentary Select Committee on Aborigines and subsequently forming the Aborigines Protection Society, with the motto *ab uno sanguine*—"of one blood." The goals of the society arose from the gross disparity its founders saw between Britons' behavior at home and their behavior overseas, that is, between the devotion to civil freedom and moral and intellectual improvement in England, and the "injuries we have inflicted, the oppression we have exercised, the cruelties we have committed, the vices we have fostered, the desolation and utter ruin we have caused" in colonial areas (Aborigines Protection Society 1837).

The Aborigines Protection Society provided the first forum for discussions and publications in which "authentic information concerning the character, habits and wants of the uncivilized tribes" (Aborigines Protection Society 1837, 4) was compiled and systematized, and thus the first point of growth for an anthropological perspective. Though the members shared the humanitarian sentiments, tensions emerged between those more strongly committed to evangelism as the self-evident course for the betterment of aborigines, and those who would give greater priority to the task of studying the aboriginal populations. This soon led to the separate establishment in 1844 of the Eth-

FREDRIK BARTH / 5

nological Society of London, with a full-fledged scholarly program to "in-quire into distinguishing characteristics, physical and moral, of the varieties of Mankind which inhabit, or have inhabited, the Earth [and] ascertain the causes of such characteristics."

Though its membership was miniscule (it had declined to thirty-eight pay-ing members by 1858); the society became a very contentious arena. Its core constituency was led by Thomas Hodgkin (1798–1866) and James Cowles Prichard (1786–1848), both Quakers who claimed as the premise for their moral and philosophical position the unity of blood embracing all of human-kind, and who favored as the explanation for human diversity the effects of environmental differences. Others, both within and outside of the society, fo-cused more on the anatomical differences between racial groups, and, influ-enced by some contemporary currents in French and German thought, they argued for the "diversitarian," that is, polygenistic, character of mankind and regarded racial differences as the cause of human cultural and moral diversity.

This diversitarian position was favored by James Hunt (1833–1869), a mercurial speech therapist who was made secretary of the society in 1860. Hunt pursued his racist views with energy and rancor, and in 1863 he broke out with his faction to found the separate Anthropological Society of London. Having articulated their diversitarian position before the publication of Dar-win's *Origin of Species*, these anthropologists shortly found themselves in op-position both to the humanitarian ethnologists and to the new Darwinians, who conceived of a single origin for the human species. Within two years, Hunt claimed more than five hundred members for his new anthropological society and had embarked on a career in which he pursued his polemics; cul-tivated flamboyant and notorious public figures like Sir Richard Burton, the scholar-explorer of African and Arabian fame and translator of sexually ex-plicit Oriental texts; and formed a dinner circle with his partisans under the name The Cannibal Club. Through such antics, Hunt brought about an im-probable alliance between the humanitarian ethnologists and the Darwinians, but it was touch and go whether he or they would prevail until 1871, when the alliance was victorious under the leadership of Thomas Huxley—and then only because of Huxley's adroit maneuver of co-opting the term *anthropology* and incorporating it into the name of the unified organization, now called the Royal Anthropological Institute.

The significance of this contorted microhistory should not be underesti-mated. Through it the humanitarian ideology of the founders of the antislav-ery movement and the Aborigines Protection Society and the premise of the unity of humankind were made foundational to the emerging discipline of anthropology; racist explanations of cultural differences had become compromised. Though not sufficient to secure a total and definitive rejection of racist ideas, James Hunt's excesses were long remembered in the Royal Anthropological Institute.

The scholarly achievements of this early generation of ethnologists were insignificant, but their ideology and perspective provided an enduring platform for British anthropology through their articulation by Edward Burnett Tylor (1832–1917). Tylor, the son of a Quaker businessman, was of the same class and ideology as the founders of the Ethnological Society of London. Because he had symptoms of consumption when he was a young man, Tylor was given a modest life pension by his family and was thus free to travel and study, joining the ranks of other enlightened amateurs and scholars. To improve his health he traveled extensively for a while in Mexico, where he was impressed by the cultural richness of native civilization. On his return to England he read widely and assimilated the many new impulses circulating in English intellectual life at the time, and he published an account of his Mexican travels. In 1862 he started to attend the meetings of the Ethnological Society, which drew archaeologists as well as ethnographers. Struck by the parallels between the tools of "savages" and the lithic industries that were being unearthed in Europe, and influenced by the surrounding climate of social evolutionary thought predating Darwin, members of the society speculated on the resemblance between contemporary "savages" and the lost races of primitive humanity. From this emerged a vision of the potential and global importance of systematic scholarship on "savages" that gave early anthropology as a discipline its defining topic.

With a small handful of likeminded scholars, Tylor proceeded to work out the issues and concepts for the new discipline and gave them a coherent formulation in his influential *Primitive Culture* (1871). Of greatest importance was his explicit premise of "the psychic unity of man"—a felicitously polysemous transformation of the ethnologists' abolitionist and humanitarian commitment to the equality and moral value of all of humankind. It introduced into anthropology a relativism with which to temper Victorian ethnocentrism.

In Tylor's hands the premise of psychic unity was the key to a reconstruction of the reflections that may have led primitive humans and contemporary "savage" people to develop the beliefs and insights they embraced. In the formulation of Andrew Lang, Tylor's junior and associate, the customs of other peoples could be seen as the product of reason like our own, working with knowledge imperfectly apprehended, and under stress of needs that it was the scholar's task to discover. Tylor saw this panhuman reasoning capacity as the motor that could generate the gradual change and overall progress he observed in human history. Finally, the premise of psychic unity may have fixed in anthropological thought the expectation of intellectual accessibility and resonance between anthropological scholars and "savage" populations that was later to come to fruition in the practices of participant fieldwork.

On this philosophical basis Tylor proceeded to specify the anthropologist's object: *culture*. "Culture, or civilization, taken in its wide ethnographic sense, is that complex whole which includes knowledge, belief, art, morals, law, custom, and any other capabilities and habits acquired by man as a member of society" (Tylor 1871, 2:1). This definition provided the foundations for the work of the first generation of British anthropologists.

Tylor sought to lay out a number of explicit methodological concerns. The first step in the study of civilization, he stated, requires that one fragment culture into its details and then classify these into their proper groups; this was an analytical procedure for comparative work. But what kind of elements should the scholar divide the object into? The "proper groups" Tylor envisaged had to do with uses and implicit functions. His was an apparently circular operation whereby the culture that was defined as an assemblage of institutions and customs was again disassembled into elements like those that composed the definition.

Only by establishing these groups, Tylor argued, is the scholar able to compare like with like and thus identify variations in cultural forms. To make sense of this claim, one clearly needs to introduce a premise that remains unstated: that the culture one analyzes in each particular case is a manifestation found in a particular place; it represents what is acquired by man as a member of a *local* society. The diffuse singular of *culture* and *society* in Tylor's definition facilitated his synthetic and evolutionary vision of human history, but it mystifies somewhat Tylor's ethnological ambition, which hinged on "adhesions" and "survivals" in particular local cultures. Thus Tylor's next step was to invite the analyst to search for adhesions in the properly classified materials—a discovery procedure to find empirical linkages between distinct cultural features that go together in the sense of regularly forming a syndrome in their local co-occurrences among peoples. But Tylor's concept of culture lacks clarity on the issue of the possible nature of linkage and integration among the different elements of culture, as on the question of cultural or social entities and boundaries. Lacking such perspectives, Tylor and his contemporaries felt unconstrained by any idea of structure and would compare cultural features or traits without reference to their context.

Discovering adherences or linkages was a step of analysis for which Tylor used global data, most famously in comparative tables showing the presence or absence of various institutions and customs among 350 different peoples. Tylor saw the empirical linkages as evidence of either general laws of human reason and association, or particular historical connections. These two alternative explanatory frames have persisted in the guise of "independent invention" and "diffusion" in the distributional studies of cultural anthropologists for almost one hundred years.

Finally, Tylor sought to bring order to the analysis of culture by means of his concept of "survivals," cultural features that were once useful and reasonable but have since persisted beyond their time through human habit or inertia. Thus many customs and superstitions of European peasants could be understood as evidence of past culture, just as the culture of surviving groups of supposedly less developed races could provide evidence of the prehistoric culture of primitive people—evidence from which the evolutionary stages of culture could be discovered.

Tylor's main substantive interest was in the sources and evolution of religious beliefs. Having lost his Quaker faith, he wished to demonstrate that religious belief did not arise from divine revelation, but was the product of people's own efforts to understand and explain the world. For this purpose comparative materials from earlier stages of cultural evolution were of particular value. As Tylor wrote in a flippant moment: "Theologians all to expose—/ 'Tis the *mission* of Primitive Man." He developed the concept of animism to describe the earliest and most basic form of religion, explaining that it arose from the "crude but reasonable" primitive idea that other bodies were animated by a life analogous to one's own, which extended to lower animals, trees, and even material objects. Two further sources of reflection by primitive man would be dreams and the sudden departure of life at death, spawning ideas of a ghost/soul. A wide range of reported ethnographic evidence was interpreted in these terms, and a logical sequence leading from the first inklings of animism to fully developed monotheistic religions was constructed.

Other scholars, working with similar speculative methods, pursued other paths. John F. McLennan (1827–1881), a Scottish lawyer, focused on the evolution of marriage and also developed a theory of how rituals arose from survivals. Thus, for example, the ceremonial enactment of bride capture as part of the marriage ritual—as was reported from various parts of the world— reflected a former practice under primitive conditions of indeed obtaining wives by capturing them. His *Primitive Marriage* (1865) laid out a scheme of development from primitive promiscuity, through group marriage and polygamy, to monogamy, and sought to construct by logic and functional reasoning a plausible stepwise course of such a development. Others, such as Andrew Lang (1844–1912), a classical scholar who supported himself by writing for the educated public, delved into interpretations of folklore and myth with similar method and purpose. The most famous of them all was no doubt Sir James George Frazer (1854–1941), a classical scholar who held a fellowship at Trinity College, Cambridge, and spent his life compiling and abridging his thirteen-volume study of magic and religion named *The Golden Bough*.

The work of this period in British anthropology has a number of shared features. It is all based on written sources, not direct field observation, conforming to the pattern set by the scholars of classics and history. Its questions were all conceived as questions of origins and gradual development, of the reconstruction of human history without or before the presence of documents. Its explanations remained trivial, since they could very rarely be falsified or demonstrated by factual data on the past and could therefore depend only on the inherent force of plausibility for their support. Yet the glimpses into a distant past and the exotic distant places these explanations presented must have held a strong appeal to many. Indeed, anthropological titans of the following generations, such as Bronislaw Malinowski and Claude Levi-Strauss, have borne witness to how their reading of *The Golden Bough*—perhaps the most vacuous work of them all, but frequently regarded as a model of graceful writing—was a major inspiration to them when they first encountered it as students.

The contributions of Tylor's generation of anthropologists were nonetheless of clear significance to the development of anthropology as a discipline. First, these writers started documenting for the first time the staggering diversity of customs and institutions practiced by groups of human beings living in the nineteenth century—a body of facts with enormous potential and philosophical and moral implications that still seem to me inexplicably unrealized or underexploited. Second, they started developing a descriptive terminology for some parts of this diversity, with technical terms like *animism, exogamy, matriliny, totemism, taboo,* and so on— representing a set of concepts that anthropologists have continued to use and have critiqued and expanded ever since.

Evolutionist British anthropologists read widely and exchanged ideas with cognate German, American, and French scholars. Their discussions and disagreements were remarkably acrimonious—perhaps precisely because their explanatory ideas were so flimsy and so often led them to construct entirely different accounts. Tylor's leading position among them may have been won by his exceptional reasonableness and decorum as much as it arose from the profundity of his scholarship. His *Primitive Culture,* nonetheless, was judged of a quality to lead to his election as a fellow of the Royal Society and in due course to a professorship at Oxford in 1896 and to knighthood in 1912. But well before that time, sadly, an early senescence seems to have reduced both his vitality and his effective influence. Despite his high reputation he never had significant relationships with students or junior colleagues. Throughout the entire period, anthropology as a whole remained remarkably fragmented and disorganized institutionally, with the meetings and journals of the Royal Anthropological Institute as the only significant institutional forum for the practice of anthropology as a discipline.

Tylor and his cohort shared concepts, methodological concerns, and logical standards, but though they were critical and searching in their scholarly mode, they seem to have felt only a vague disquiet over the secondhand nature of the ethnographic data on which they relied. The only remedy they sought on that count took the form of a Royal Anthropological Institute publication: *Notes and Queries on Anthropology, for the Use of Travellers and Residents in Uncivilized Lands,* the first edition of which appeared in 1874. Tylor was an influential member of the editorial committee, which hoped that by making such a publication available to interested explorers, missionaries, and administrators in the empire it might bring about improvement in the scientific quality of what they reported. Since the publication of that first version *Notes and Queries* has been repeatedly revised and republished, and in due course it has served apprentice anthropologists as a guide during fieldwork. But the generation of Tylor remained entirely what later British anthropologists have disdainfully referred to as armchair anthropologists.

2

From the Torres Straits to the Argonauts, 1898–1922

The first drastic initiative to enhance the quality of anthropological data came, not surprisingly, from a zoologist. Alfred Cort Haddon (1855–1940) hailed from a similar social and religious background as most of the scholars discussed so far, though he was a Baptist rather than Quaker. Showing no great interest in business, he was allowed to attend Cambridge, where he read the newly organized Natural Science Tripos in the 1870s and specialized in invertebrates. The influence of Darwin and his circle cost Haddon his religious faith but secured him a post in zoology in Dublin. After some years of teaching he obtained funds for an expedition to study the formation of coral reefs, which he chose to do in the Torres Straits between New Guinea and Australia in 1888. There he got along marvelously with the natives besides successfully doing his zoological work; he collected ethnographic objects to help defray his expedition expenses; and he tried his hand as an anthropologist, inquiring into legends, beliefs, and family customs of the various island tribes. (He had brought along *Notes and Queries!*) Though he published in zoology upon his return to Dublin, he also wrote papers on anthropological topics and continued to develop his anthropological interests. Taking great care to maintain his connections in Cambridge, and networking widely, he was finally able to launch a project to bring a group of trained scholars to the field in the Torres Straits, there to study the anthropology, psychology, and sociology of "savage" peoples by making careful inquiries in situ.

The group was formed by selection and happenstance. Haddon secured the participation of Sidney Ray, a linguistically talented schoolteacher in London who had assisted him in the islands ten years earlier. For a psychologist, he approached W. H. R. Rivers, a medical doctor who had just been appointed to a lectureship in physiological and experimental psychology. When Rivers hesitated, two of his students, Charles Samuel Myers and William

McDougall agreed to go. At this point Rivers changed his mind and signed on as well. Anthony Wilkin joined as an anthropological trainee. Finally, the young medical pathologist Charles Seligman successfully begged to be signed on, despite doubts about his suitability and health.

The expedition arrived in the Torres Straits in 1898. To his credit, Haddon was fondly remembered for his earlier visit by a number of the natives, and relations between them and the expedition seemed to go very satisfactorily for both sides. The group did a considerable amount of island hopping and worked together and separately for four to six months in the islands and on the south coast of Papua, as well as accomplishing some sideline researches in Sarawak. Yet in each locality a certain amount of focus and time was allowed, both jointly and separately as expedition members sometimes traveled individually or were left to linger and be picked up again later by the expedition ship. A few island locations did, by chance and because of individual interests, receive considerable coverage.

The resulting six volumes of reports, which were published over the next ten years and more, were, to be candid, of no great consequence (Haddon 1901–1935). Nonetheless, the Torres Straits Expedition has rightly been recognized in the British tradition of anthropology as a turning point. Seen in retrospect, it is indeed as if the seeds were planted there for the whole series of transformations that would follow in the next twenty-five years. I point to four major aspects of this change.

First, the very mode of scholarship was transformed. Until then, anthropology was advanced by scholars extracting data from books in their libraries and accumulating archives on similarities of customs or other matters that might interest them from all over the world. This they did entirely on their own terms: the anthropologists determined the categories and the relevance of the snippets of data they selected. This was James Frazer's scholarship par excellence—and he continued it till his death, as did many others. In the Torres Islands, on the other hand, information was extracted directly by the scholars themselves, from native informants who told them about their own local customs, beliefs, and so on, and such data were even supplemented by the anthropologists' own direct impressions of places, objects, and events in the communities. The massive screens of misinformation produced by intermediaries, misinterpretations, and ignorance were radically reduced. Admittedly, none of the Torres Straits ethnographers learned local language beyond a meager Pidgin English, and there was no clear awareness of the value of participation in native life for production of the data of anthropology. Yet such methodological improvements would soon follow, with something like inevitability. But what had already changed was that the anthropologists had been relocated so the lives of local people impinged directly on them. They were now among people who to an extent exercised their own volition, who operated before the scholars' eyes in their own native world, and who held authority as arbiters of the very facts that the scholars were seeking.

Second, these facts came clustered and linked in ways that were no longer under the control of the scholars. Data were interconnected with each other by virtue of their local association and separated from "similar" facts—similar, that is, as defined by the investigators' categories and archives—from everywhere else. The island-hopping anthropologist was led to make the most of his few weeks on an island by maximizing the amount of documentation he collected, however haphazardly, from a particular community and place. The object of anthropological investigation had come to be no longer culture generally, but particular local cultures.

Third, some new features of methodology also appeared—springing from a desire for comprehensiveness, detail, and exhaustiveness of coverage—especially the procedures that became almost fetishized as Rivers's "genealogical method." The investigators discovered that with a patient mapping of primary kinship relations—mother-of, father-of, born-of—a whole community could become known and mapped and connected, and many things, most strikingly the meaning of kinship terms but also all the manner of social groupings and distinctions in terms of descent, totemic identities, cult congregations, and so on, could be worked out.

A final result of the Torres Straits Expedition was that the two key figures in the next generation of British anthropologists were trained and inspired by their adventures with the expedition: W. H. R. Rivers (1864–1922) and Charles G. Seligman (1873–1940) were thereafter enrolled into the miniscule but growing cadre of anthropologists.

It is striking that Haddon of all people never realized what had happened. In his 1910 *History of Anthropology* he still insisted that the innovation introduced by his expedition was that of "bringing trained scientists to make their observations in situ." But Rivers and Seligman and, for that matter, Haddon himself were not scientists trained in anthropology with any expert skills in identifying phenomenal forms and accumulating systematic observations in that discipline. They were, on the contrary, amateurs in anthropology with some scientific training in *other* disciplines. What had happened was that the little island communities in the Torres Straits had *imposed* on them the new organization of primary data by locality and the realization of the complexity and internal connectedness of each local form of life. Rivers and Seligman were exposed to an intensive training experience in these respects and thereby became ethnographers of a new kind.

Parallel serendipitous developments were taking place in a few other regions: Franz Boas was gaining his intensive ethnographic exposure to an Eskimo community, a process that was repeated even more deeply among the Kwakiutl, and V. G. Bogoraz, L. J. Sternberg, and W. Jochelsen, who were Russian radicals exiled to Siberia and thus had too much time on their hands, were pursuing their own studies among local aboriginal peoples. Closer to the British tradition, long-duration studies of indigenous Australians were being pursued by Lorimer Fison and Alfred W. Howitt, who corresponded with Edward Tylor and also with Lewis Morgan. Their work was published in the 1880s, followed by publications by William Baldwin Spencer and Frank J. Gillen in the 1890s; all of these works contained the fruit of similarly rich and long-term exposure and data. But these authors were not of the scholarly elite. British scholarship was so inward looking and mesmerized by the intellectual supremacy of Oxford and Cambridge that though these Australian field studies provided ethnographic data and stimulated British thought, they could not set standards and become exemplary for the practices of British academic scholars. Indeed, Edmund Leach argues in a devastatingly critical essay that such snobbishness continued to impede the development of British anthropology until 1945, no less (1984).

Rivers and Seligman were clearly smitten with the excitement and productivity of ethnographic discovery after their few months in the Torres Straits. Rivers soon left for more fieldwork, this time in South India in 1901, where he spent five months among the Todas and produced a study of a most intriguing, intricate, and almost fairy-tale community. Many snippets of strange ethnography had already been accumulated about the Todas from the reports of travelers and adventurers. But in Rivers's hands Todas emerged as members of a complex community with a distinctive way of life, and so *The Todas* (1906) was long regarded as a model of what an anthropological monograph could be when based on the new, intensive field methodology.

Seligman managed to raise funds from a wealthy American patron to return in 1903 to New Guinea, where he covered a large geographical region. His work produced the massive documentation for *The Melanesians of British New Guinea* (Seligman 1910). In 1907–1908 he and his wife, Brenda Seligman, also an anthropologist, went to Ceylon and did a study of the Veddas, a scattered hunting-and-gathering population living in parts of the Ceylon jungles (Seligman and Seligman 1911). With government funds the Seligmans thereafter proceeded to break new ground: in three long expeditions to the Sudan they documented the highly diverse cultures of Arabic, Nuba, and Nilotic tribes in vast areas of the central and southern Sudan (Seligman and Seligman 1932).

Rivers, meanwhile, returned to Melanesia in 1908 and again in 1914, accompanied both times by Gerald C. Wheeler and Arthur M. Hocart. There he practiced more of his "intensive" ethnographic work, spending several months with Hocart on Eddystone Island in the western Solomons, but most of his data were collected during a series of shorter stopovers. The region of Melanesia had by then been much explored and was even considerably documented ethnographically, though it was an area of extraordinary diversity. The authoritative ethnographic documentation till then had been written by the distinguished cleric and missionary R. H. Codrington, who had long been stationed in the area working for the Melanesian Mission. Rivers followed Codrington's framework (Rivers 1914). Traveling with the mission vessel the *Southern Cross,* he covered a great number of localities, some of them simply by bringing a local native up on deck and using him for a couple of hours as informant before sailing on. Yet even this practice did, of course, produce a deeper knowledge of the whole region than any armchair anthropologist could ever have achieved.

In this way, both Rivers and Seligman progressively veered away from seriously intensive local studies and shifted to a regional scope in their empirical work. But there were other, younger recruits to anthropology who continued the new tradition of intensive studies. Rivers's junior companion Hocart stayed in Fiji for four years, supporting himself as a schoolmaster; Wheeler stayed for ten months in Bougainville. A. R. Radcliffe-Brown had already launched his career with studies in the Andaman Islands during 1906–1908, and then among the Kariera in northwest Australia in 1910–1912. Diamond Jenness worked for a considerable period on Goodenough Island in 1910 and later did extensive work in the Arctic. John Layard settled in for two years in 1914–1916, working on the "Small Islands" off the coast of Malekula in the present Vanuatu, islands that were hardly larger than two sandbanks but were occupied by tribes with elaborate kinship systems and graded secret societies. Stories circulated that Layard was wont to join the natives, wearing only a *namba* penis sheath in their dances and rituals.

Under Haddon's direction Gunnar Landtman, a Finnish student of Edward Westermarck at the London School of Economics, went to study for two years among the Kiwai of Papua in 1910. And W. Armstrong went to Rossel Island (one of Seligman's options that Bronislaw Malinowski had failed to choose) in 1919, where he sorted out a most elaborate native system of shell money. Thus there was a growing intensive fieldwork activity among anthropologists. The star fieldworker, of course, was to be Malinowski, who went to Mailu in the Gulf of Papua in 1914 for six months, and then to the Trobriands for two years during 1915–1918.

But first, we need to give much more attention to the various roles played by Rivers. Perhaps his most enduring effect on the British tradition resulted from his painstaking conceptual work on social organization. To describe the findings he turned up in Melanesia he developed an enhanced order and precision in the descriptive terminology required in kinship studies and the description of social groups, revealing the systemic features of various kinship terminologies, ideas of descent, forms of marriage and marriage exchanges between groups, and so on. This analytical work on what he called social structure laid the foundation for what was to follow in the work of several generations of British anthropology. In the 1912 edition of *Notes and Queries* he further expanded on the methodological guidelines for "intensive" and "concrete" field methodology; and his "genealogical method" set the standards of exactness and detail that were now required of field data. Rivers also retained his deep engagement with psychology, holding a chair in Cambridge in that field and developing therapies for treating shell shock during World War I. In his explorations of theoretical issues in the border zone between psychology and anthropology, he remained open and imaginative.

Unfortunately, however, Rivers let himself be sidetracked by what ended up being only a brief and fruitless diversion in British anthropology: "diffusionism," or the view that the key issues in ethnography were embodied in the task of reconstructing a global culture history of human migrations and cultural borrowings. During most of the years of his active fieldwork, Rivers had continued to think in the broad tradition of Tylor's evolutionist anthropology, but this framework did not deeply engage his actual work and thought; his real interests focused more on the precision and care with which he could describe substantive materials on social organization and culture.

Several factors may have led to this change. For the distributional materials Rivers was now accumulating in Melanesia, with its patchwork of myriad differences and similarities throughout the area, Tylor's evolutionist vision of broadly shared progressive change could contribute very little. Such materials seemed to require something that would help an anthropologist to understand the local dynamic culture history that had produced the particular local distributions Rivers was now mapping in the Melanesian region. About this time, Rivers became familiar with the writings of Fritz Graebner and others of the German school of diffusionists, and their theoretical modeling of distributional data. Finally, as a friend and colleague of Grafton Elliot Smith, Rivers was drawn into comparative speculation over parallels between certain culture traits in Oceania and in ancient Egypt—most strikingly, Rivers's finding that some Torres Straits islanders practiced mummification. The result was Rivers's 1911 conversion to diffusionism.

The diffusionist perspective as adopted in England was linked to a claim that ancient Egypt was the wellspring of all human civilization, a view elaborated by Grafton Elliot Smith (1871–1937) and William James Perry (1889–1949) in their grand "heliolithic" thesis. These were not new ideas, but they were enjoying a strong and romantic revival in some circles of British academia. Indeed, Seligman became entangled in another branch of this construction and tried to account for the diffusion of civilizing stimuli out of Egypt into sub-Saharan Africa in accordance with what became known as the Hamitic hypothesis.

There would seem to be nothing inherently implausible in the notion that technologies, religious thoughts, and other cultural ideas have been transmitted and diffused between peoples throughout history, or that human migrants have carried such materials with them in the extensive population movements into and between sparsely populated areas. A dogmatic evolutionist view that the same innovations and institutions were constantly reinvented independently in different localities because of the psychic unity of mankind, might appear less plausible. But there were two enormous disadvantages to the diffusionist enthusiasm. On the one hand, it invited a frenzy of unsustainable guesswork in all its particulars, there being no conceivable proof or disproof of any of its specific claims. Historical episodes of actual contact and stimulus might well have taken place despite the absence of positive evidence, while on the other hand even physical, material evidence of visits by distant strangers proved nothing as to the lasting cultural consequences they might have produced among the populations that experienced such contact. The explanations provided by a theory of diffusion were simply reformulations of the overt similarities observed between items of the global ethnographic record transformed into claims of connection. Wisely, the next cohort of anthropologists, led by Radcliffe-Brown, simply dismissed diffusionist speculations outright as being conjectural history rather than entering seriously into a debate on the particulars of their claims—thereby also removing all the evolutionist conjectures from the discussion.

On the other hand, and perhaps more ominously, the idea of historical sources of stimuli and migration all too readily became entangled with racist claims as to the genius of certain peoples and the backwardness of others as a function of their biological capacities. Fortunately the humane values articulated by the early founders of ethnology and incorporated into British anthropology through Tylor's assumption of psychic unity prevailed—thanks both to their greater human appeal and to the transparent absurdity of so many diffusionist assertions.

In this disarray of theories and methodological developments, Malinowski's perfection in the Trobriands of the new kind of fieldwork that indeed Rivers had championed became the shared founding principle of subsequent generations of British anthropologists. Several components of his method were already variously being tried by the small cohort of colleagues I have reviewed above, but their synthesis was Malinowski's creation and depended considerably on his personal talents. Malinowski became the formulator, epitome, and propagandist of the new kind of ethnographic data. The first chapter of his *Argonauts of the Western Pacific* (Malinowski 1922) gives a twenty-five-page presentation of his views, and the subsequent text is a demonstration of the benefits of their practice. It incorporates the lessons of the Torres Straits Expedition: the primacy of the local context and the fullness of the record that should be sought of all aspects of local life. Also, starting with the practice of the genealogical method, with its implications of specificity of data on social relationships, Malinowski expanded the same order of detail into a general demand for the "statistical documentation of concrete evidence," including household and village composition; land rights; exchanges and distributions; the dovetailing of ritual, technical, and economic activities; and so on.

Besides the crucial primary data that such documentation procedures provided, they also produced the inestimable bonus of enhanced personal familiarity with the people in a community, which moreover is self-reinforcing. It is here that we find the essence of Malinowski's field practice, generally but unclearly named "participation." Malinowski describes the transformation that such knowledge caused in himself and in his own attitudes. Living there in the village, he found that he started looking forward to important or festive events, taking a personal interest in village gossip and news, and so on. Participation in this sense was short on dancing with the natives and long on taking a personal and genuine interest in "events usually trivial, sometimes dramatic, but always significant" (Malinowski 1922, 7).

For such participation, of course, facility in the local language was particularly important. It was probably fortunate that these first-time and therefore less clearly structured, efforts took place among people who spoke a Melanesian and easily learned language. But there is no doubt that Malinowski also had a very special ability with languages. Audrey Richards tells an anecdote from the time Malinowski visited her in the field among the Bemba. On their first afternoon they took a walk along the village path. Meeting a group of people, Richards greeted them with a phrase, and they answered with a rather longer phrase. A few moments later, they met a young couple, who greeted them with the same phrase Richards had used. Malinowski immediately answered with a mimicry of what the previous Bemba group had answered—at which point the young Bemba couple looked rather upset and quickly left. Malinowski turned to Richards and asked, "What was wrong? Didn't I pronounce it correctly?" To which Richards could tell him "Yes, it was perfectly understandable. You said 'We are on our way to bury our grandmother.'"

Malinowski's considerable vanity and his often flamboyant style probably stimulated his willingness to enact the requirements of participant observation, but more so did his reflexive awareness of the nature of his field activities and the critical passion with which he pursued his work. We may note, for instance, that he chose to publish his "Confessions of Ignorance and Failure" as an appendix of *Coral Gardens* (1935). Likewise, no doubt inspired by Rivers's innovative statement of fieldwork conditions and procedures among the Todas (Rivers 1906), Malinowski often provided explicit and reflexive accounts of his own presence and activities during fieldwork in his texts on the Trobriands. He also showed sensitivity to the "amplitude of variation" (Malinowski 1929, 237) reflecting the tension between human individuality and the cultural constraints on performance.

Malinowski's posthumously published field diary (*A Diary in the Strict Sense of the Term*, 1967/1989) has been read by some colleagues as a shockingly compromising and undermining revelation that indicates a disconcerting gap between the ideal and the practice of Malinowski's fieldwork. In it he recorded a detailed, day-by-day account of how his time was spent, but also often misspent; it notes his frequent despair over poor field progress, his self-pity, his hypochondriacal complaints, and his elation and depression, and it is laced with harsh and demeaning outbursts against the Trobrianders, collectively and individually.

I believe these readings distort the content and value of the diary. Malinowski had considerable insight into psychoanalysis and into his own self, and he clearly used his secret diary both to monitor his own condition and to provide catharsis for pent-up emotion and distress. Any anthropologist who has seriously attempted to do this kind of intensive fieldwork must be all too familiar with the strains and moods that Malinowski's text reports, and with the subjective need to externalize and manage them. Indeed, rather than diminishing the nature and quality of his fieldwork methodology, I think the diary shows both the seriousness of purpose with which he pursued it and the personal costs such fieldwork entails. But there can be different opinions here. To anyone interested, I strongly recommend Raymond Firth's sensitive and informed reflections as set forth in his "Second Introduction, 1988" in the reissued, 1989 edition of Malinowski's diary (Malinowski 1967/1989).

Malinowski's 1922 account of Trobriand overseas expeditions forever changed British anthropology, and no doubt all other traditions of anthropology, but the change did not happen immediately (Malinowski 1922). Some anthropologists became instant converts; others remained unmoved. For a long time some practitioners of anthropology in Britain even continued with their armchair researches as before the Torres Straits Expedition, and others continued to travel to the field but kept their distance from the natives and essentially collected their data by "debriefing tribal chiefs," as the practice has sometimes been called. And it is not as if a change can be achieved by a wave of the magic wand. There are honorable social anthropologists in Britain today who have tried to engage in fuller and richer field participation but have not particularly succeeded and so choose to gather data mainly by other techniques. Malinowski's style of fieldwork requires so many simultaneous talents that few, if any, other anthropologists can fully emulate it, and surely no one can practice it with his aplomb and success: some of us are shyer; some are more modest; some are poor and slow language learners; and very few can match him in brilliance, swiftness, and intuitive grasp. Participant observation can only mean participating in the ways that any particular scholar is capable of.

The change Malinowski's example made in the discipline as a whole was to put pressure on all of us to move our work away from the provision of externalist accounts of institutions and away from the even more impoverished superficial registration of ethnographic details, and toward an effort to penetrate the mental attitude revealed in those details—in Malinowski's words, an effort "to grasp the native's point of view, his relation to life, to realise *his* vision of *his* world" (Malinowski 1922, 25).

Throughout the twenty-four years of disciplinary creativity and experience summarized in this chapter, the formal institutional framework for the discipline of anthropology remained almost unchanged—in other words, such a framework continued to be absent. Sir James Frazer had a visiting professorship for one year in 1907–1908 at Liverpool University and thus incongruously instituted the name, "social anthropology," whereby the British school was to become known, but he never taught successors. Tylor lived his quiet life at Oxford, making little intellectual and no instructional use of his position there. There is some very contrary historiography describing Haddon's role in Cambridge, but I judge all the evidence to agree with Leach's assessment that Haddon wielded little intellectual and no constructive institutional power there or elsewhere and that he was unsuccessful in his valiant efforts to change the institutional situation of the discipline (1984).

Only at the London School of Economics was a small foothold established that reflected the intellectual and scholarly change that was occurring. The Finnish scholar Edward Westermarck (1862–1939) held a post in sociology at the school beginning in 1904 that was converted into a chair in 1907 and that he turned into a three-way arrangement: the Easter term he spent as a sociologist in London; the next term, at home in Helsingfors as a professor of moral philosophy; and the winter, in Morocco collecting anthropological materials on marriage, though mainly within an evolutionist/historical theoretical framework. In 1910 he was joined by Seligman, who likewise spent a significant amount of time in the field. Neither of them was theoretically innovative; only Malinowski represented the new anthropology. Nonetheless, the department at the London School of Economics offered training and a provisional identity to a few recruits in anthropology, including Malinowski on his first arrival in England. Seen in retrospect, anthropology in Britain seemed poised on the brink of beginning.

3

Malinowski and Radcliffe-Brown, 1920–1945

The great shift in theoretical paradigm in the British tradition occurred in 1922 with the simultaneous publication of Bronislaw Malinowski's *Argonauts of the Western Pacific* (Malinowski 1922) and A. R. Radcliffe-Brown's *The Andaman Islanders* (1922/1948). These two works and their authors shaped the whole next generation of pupils and delivered the enduring premises for British social anthropology. Their shared position entailed the abandonment of the search for origins as historical explanations, and its replacement with the new requirement that the analysis of ethnographic data be achieved through an immersion into the details of how native action unfolds in the contemporary moment; that is, it required that the anthropologist search for understanding and explanation *within* the very object of study. Thus the new direction was a radical disjuncture from what had been the British tradition of Edward Burnett Tylor.

Bronislaw Malinowski (1884–1942) developed his analysis by means of a broadly conceived "functionalism": the contention that all parts of a local culture played a role in the workings of all the other parts and that each local culture constituted an integrated, complex mechanism whereby "Man" as an organism adapted to his external physical and collective environment. These premises are familiar and in some sense unavoidable to anyone who has since done intensive fieldwork; they represent the discovery that all those cultural details that at first seem both arbitrary and meaningless do indeed make sense, both in terms of the other practices of the local population and as a way for people to survive in the local environment.

The richness of Malinowski's Trobriand materials made it an impossible task to document this through a single magnum opus. Instead, Malinowski presented a series of vivid monographs written over the next thirteen years, for each of which he chose one particular major institution as the focus, describing it and the multiple ways that other parts of Trobriand culture impinged on it. The project was never completed and indeed never could be; a number of very significant institutions were never given center stage, to the frustration of many pupils with tidy minds.

Alfred Reginald Radcliffe-Brown (1881–1955) likewise found in the concept of function the means by which to shift the framing of anthropological analysis from questions of origin and history to questions of structure and interconnection. But his systemic vision was linked to his concept of society, and his interest and intellectual style were to press the analysis to a far higher level of abstraction than did Malinowski. The theoretical path Radcliffe-Brown followed toward his vision was longer—or perhaps only somewhat more documented and visibly reedited—than that of Malinowski.

Radcliffe-Brown's fieldwork in the Andaman Islands in 1906–1908 took place ten years earlier than Malinowski's in the Trobriands—yet his account of the work was not published till that epochal year of 1922. He had chosen the Andamans as a field site on evolutionist criteria, because it was imagined that their society represented the most primitive and elementary level of human life and because of the pygmy stature of their population: such "Negritos" were regarded as belonging to the most ancient stratum of humanity. The islanders practiced a hunting-and-gathering economy in dense tropical forest and lived in small bands, so they were much more modest and less enthralling in their cultural creations than were the Trobrianders.

A small British Indian settlement had been established on Great Andaman Island as early as 1789, but it was soon abandoned, then was later reestablished as a penal colony in 1858. Though the Andaman tribes had been stubbornly hostile—indeed, one small tribe still seems to be so—those closest to the settlement were slowly lured into contact, and their life and traditions had been much impoverished by the time Radcliffe-Brown arrived. In other words, they presented an altogether different case from the intact, self-assured Trobrianders. A significant part of Radcliffe-Brown's fieldwork in the Andamans seems to have been done among the hangers-on around the penal settlement. Despite the persistent efforts that he describes, he never developed facility in Andamanese languages, and most of the data were collected through a Hindi-speaking interpreter. His field techniques were essentially those developed on the Torres Straits Expedition, though he never fully succeeded in practicing the genealogical method, to his own and W. H. R. Rivers's disappointment. His total time with the natives seems to have been about ten months. Nonetheless, the thesis he first wrote on the basis of the materials he gathered won him a fellowship at Trinity in 1908.

Radcliffe-Brown thus had none of the advantages that Malinowski's rich and vivid Trobriand materials offered. But through lecture series given at Cambridge and elsewhere in 1910 he had the opportunity to rethink his till then evolutionary anthropology in sociological terms—much inspired by Émile Durkheim's writings on the division of labor and the rules of sociological method—and also to reflect on his Andaman Island materials in the light of the growing literature on social organization, totemism, and exogamy in Australia. This provided the perfect preparation for his next fieldwork effort, in northwest Australia in 1911–1912. Troubled by internal contention between the expedition members and probably thin in its purely ethnographic harvest, this Australian trip nonetheless yielded materials that were a perfect fit with the thrust of his theoretical thought. His paper "Three Tribes of Western Australia," published in 1913, provided the key for all his subsequent work on Australian social organization, which culminated in his masterful "The Social Organization of Australian Tribes" (1930–1931). Here he could deliver his promise: a clarified and systematic comparative analysis of one typological class of societies.

The Andaman Islanders, though published nearly ten years after Radcliffe-Brown had his analytical breakthrough on Australian social organization, clearly contains materials that were conceptualized and written before he acquired those insights. But besides much detailed ethnographic documentation of little relevance to social and structural issues, it does contain, in its chapters five and six, a resolution of the new issues that arise once one adopts a sociological perspective: the nature of the relationship between individually held sentiments and collective social action. In a few seminal pages, Radcliffe-Brown here introduced his conceptual framework for how we can understand "why the Andamanese think and act in certain ways. The explanation of each single custom is provided by showing what is its relation to the other customs of the Andamanese and to their general system of ideas and sentiments" (1922/1948, 230).

In these chapters Radcliffe-Brown outlined the procedure by which anthropologists try to identify the meaning of customs, the role of ritual in establishing collective sentiments and transmitting them across generations, and thus the functions of native institutions for the reproduction of society as a whole. Then, through a series of spare and compelling articles over the next thirty years, subsequently gathered in his famous essay collection, *Structure and Function in Primitive Society* (1952), Radcliffe-Brown developed and disseminated his position and thereby established the premises on which the work of the next generation of British social anthropologists would build.

Malinowski's concept of function was more directly linked to the idea of human needs. This link hobbled Malinowski's theoretical work throughout his life, but it also allowed him to attack the question of sentiments and values in a less abstract way than did Radcliffe-Brown, and thus to speak to topics of the greatest importance among European intellectuals in the 1920s and 1930s, especially the writings of Freud. Malinowski's books were widely read, a situation that he shamelessly encouraged with titles such as *Sex and Repression in Savage Societies* (1927) and *The Sexual Life of Savages in North-Western Melanesia* (1929) for offerings no doubt far more titillating to English readers then than they would be today in our permissive times. His view was that the fruitful approach to kinship studies involved observing the emotional and economic primary relations between members of the family. The wider kinship terminology, he argued, came about through the extension of terms from the core set of relatives with whom the child was in contact, and the experienced quality of those relations. On the other hand, he had little patience with what he chose to call "kinship algebra," no doubt a dismissive term for Radcliffe-Brown's approach.

The intellectual excitement of Malinowski's teaching at the London School of Economics in the 1920s and 1930s was deep and pervasive. His famous seminars drew participants from far and wide and provided the first historic opportunity for anthropologists to join in a forum where they could adventurously and imaginatively work to shape the new kind of anthropology. Yet the number of professional anthropologists remained so small and the institutional resources so pitifully limited, it is a wonder that the spark could survive. Malinowski's post at the London School of Economics dates from 1924, when Westermarck and Seligman—not themselves functionalists in any sense of the term—also were there. But the rest of English academic institutions were closed to serious anthropology, and the modest anthropological slots elsewhere were peopled by colleagues who were unchanged by the new ideas.

The anthropological posts at University College London were occupied by Grafton Elliot Smith and W. J. Perry. The American anthropologist Hortense Powdermaker, who was a young apprentice participant in Malinowski's seminar in 1925–1926, tells a breathless story of how she once responded to an invitation to meet with Elliot Smith and Perry in their University College offices. They asked her what the topic of her thesis was, and when she answered that it concerned the nature of leadership in primitive societies, Elliot Smith immediately asked: "And what is the origin of leadership?" When she intimated that she did not know and did not care, the two professors vehemently confronted her, and she hastily fled back to the London School of Economics to report there on her sally into enemy territory (Powdermaker 1966, 37). Such seems to have been the nature of contact between the two departments.

At Oxford, Tylor had held a titular professorship only, and when C. C. Marett was appointed his successor in 1908, he was listed only as "Reader of Social Anthropology" (Stocking 1996a, 172). Marett's main position and influence in Oxford depended on his fellowship and later rectorship at Exeter College. Exeter seems to have offered a modest refuge for students with anthropological interests, but such activities were probably tolerated only thanks to an understanding with the Oxford establishment that anthropology should not encroach on important studies like Classics and should be strictly limited to the study of past and present savagery. Thus Marett's role in anthropology at Oxford seems to have been no more than that of conducting a long and intellectually very passive holding operation. The handful of committed students were thus driven to seek inspiration at the London School of Economics.

Anthropology at Cambridge can only be described as a disaster. Rivers died in 1922, and the few Cambridge anthropology students with serious intentions drifted the London School of Economics while Alfred Cort Haddon continued to wield an inept and unfortunate influence at Cambridge. Haddon retired in 1926. His successor was T. C. Hodson, formerly of the Indian Civil Service, supposedly chosen because the main task of anthropology was to give supplementary teaching to colonial service cadets. When Haddon retired in 1936, a field of applicants sought what had by then become a chair. Among them were such outstanding anthropologists as Gregory Bateson, John Driberg, Raymond Firth, Daryll Forde, Reo Fortune, Arthur M. Hocart, and Audrey Richards. Haddon saw to it that the chair fell to J. H. Hutton, a former civil servant and ethnographer in India and organizer of the great Indian census. It seems impossible to avoid the conclusion that, as Edmund Leach argues so forcefully (1984), anthropology was not simply ignored, but was actively suppressed by a hostile Oxbridge establishment.

While Malinowski found his toehold in London, this left Radcliffe-Brown entirely out of the equation and set him on a long odyssey overseas as an expatriate that took him to chairs in Cape Town (1920–1925), Sydney (1925–1931), and Chicago (1931–1937) before finally returning him to England and Oxford in 1937. During his time abroad Radcliffe-Brown's was a lone but powerful voice that was of great importance to the intellectual development of the British tradition of anthropology through his publications and during occasional meetings at the Royal Anthropological Institute and international congresses. Of almost equal significance, he taught social anthropology and recruited a handful of persons who later were to play prominent roles in British anthropology. In South Africa he taught Isaac Schapera, whom he subsequently sent on to the London School of Economics, and he worked with Winifred Tucker Hoernlé, whom he had known and influenced in Cambridge and who carried the torch in Witwatersrand, not Cape Town and recruited further members of a growing cadre after he left South Africa. In Sydney he taught and provided a center for coordinating anthropological fieldwork in Melanesia and Australia, facilitating the work of such junior colleagues as Gregory Bateson, Margaret Mead, Reo Fortune, and W. Lloyd Warner, as well as his own students Ian Hogbin, A. P. Elkin, and R. Piddington; he also engaged Raymond Firth as a lecturer for a year after Firth's first Tikopia visit.

Radcliffe-Brown also played a prominent role in the broader field of politics. He was known as Anarchy Brown in his college days for his enthusiasm for P'etr Kropotkin, and his radical and anticolonial views had driven him from South Africa and led to conflicts with the establishment in Australia, which motivated his move to Chicago in 1931. There he had a strong impact on a group of American anthropological colleagues and students that included such leading figures as Fred Eggan, Robert Redfield, Lloyd Warner, and Sol Tax. Local lore among Chicago anthropologists further tells that every week Sol Tax brought his notes from Radcliffe-Brown's lectures to the Field Museum's Ralph Linton, whose influential text *The Study of Man* (1936) clearly reflects Radcliffe-Brown's ideas. Radcliffe-Brown's lectures on *A Natural Science of Society* (published only later, in 1956; see 1956/1964) were an ambitious and sustained statement of the position he held on social structure at the time and marked his growing estrangement from the more culturally and psychologically oriented functionalism of Malinowski. Radcliffe-Brown's strong presence lingered in seminars and student discussions for a long time after he left Chicago.

But the true motor of the British tradition in the 1920s and early 1930s was, naturally, at the London School of Economics, both because of the inspiration Malinowski provided and because it was the only institutional refuge for a self-proclaimed new and revitalized anthropology in Britain. Here the new generation gathered under Malinowski's arbitrary but fruitful tyranny, and from such theoretical roots sprang the next generation of innovative monographs: Audrey Richards's *Hunger and Work in a Savage Tribe* (1932); Fortune's "Manus Religion" (1935); Firth's *We, the Tikopia* (1936); Bateson's *Naven* (1936); Monica Hunter's *Reaction to Conquest* (1936); and

Edward Evans-Pritchard's *Witchcraft, Oracles, and Magic among the Azande* (1937). Note the breadth of substantive concerns these studies addressed: labor and economy, religion, kinship and family, ritual, culture contact and change, belief and cosmology. They also presaged the shift from Melanesian to increasingly African ethnographic materials for functionalist studies. Their common strength was a sound grounding in rich empirical data, and also an inquisitive and creative theoretical urge: in his seminars Malinowski was famous for demanding a *problemstellung*—a concept he claimed was untranslatable into English, but that embraced both the question that was asked and the manner in which it was framed. A practical necessity for this flowering of functionalist anthropology, in view of the hostility of the prestigious universities in England, were also considerable research grants from the Rockefeller Foundation for fieldwork to both Malinowski's Africanist and Radcliffe-Brown's Oceanist students.

With the adoption of a synchronic and sociological orientation in functionalist anthropology an almost complete rupture was created with the traditional scholarly foundations of the discipline. Some of the old ethnography could still be read as interesting, or at least informative, in its data, and a number of the descriptive concepts of kinship, social organization, and exotic beliefs were still useful or could remain so if revised, but the theoretical framework of Tylor and the evolutionists, not to speak of the diffusionists, was dead, and so the very history of the British tradition had to be reinvented and rewritten with new intellectual roots. Quite clearly the immediate and recognized wellspring was Émile Durkheim (1858–1917), but British ancestors were also found, most importantly Henry Sumner Maine (1822–1888). Maine's writings on contract, rights, and especially the concepts of the corporation and its associated estate were particularly compatible with Radcliffe-Brown's thought, and they were written into the core of the emerging structural-functional theory.

When Radcliffe-Brown finally returned to England in 1937 and took up the chair of anthropology at Oxford and Malinowski departed from London for the United States for a sabbatical at Yale in 1938, it is as if the whole scene shifted. The old bastion of resistance had fallen and Radcliffe-Brown could gather a small group of promising younger anthropologists around himself in the prestigious center of British academia. World War II intervened in Malinowski's plans. He chose to wait it out in the United States, and he died there in 1942. Suddenly the magic of Malinowski was no longer around, and a familiar yet new and inspiring teacher and intellectual leader had ascended to the peak of the academic establishment at Oxford.

The differences between these two figures were deep and pervasive, ranging from personality through basic scholarly style to the particulars of their concept of function and the anthropological theory it undergirded. Whereas Radcliffe-Brown worked narrowly and systematically to build a discipline of coherent concepts, methods, data, and theory, Malinowski had remained in the flow of ever-changing cross-disciplinary impulses, responding to world issues and cosmopolitan intellectual life in a continuing conversation with his students.

Firth, who probably knew Malinowski better than any other of his colleagues, wrote a posthumous evaluation of his work in which he cited his own words from a tribute he had paid Malinowski in 1942:

> To his pupils, Malinowski's stimulus lay in a combination of many qualities: his subtle power of analysis, his sincerity in facing problems, his sense of reality, his scholarly command of the literature, his capacity for integrating detail into general ideas, his brilliance and wit in handling discussions. But it was due to something more, to his liberal interpretation of the rôle of a teacher. . . . He and his students did not always see eye to eye. But one felt that he had a great store of wise advice, which he expressed in his own inimitably shrewd fashion. Whether he gave it soberly or flippantly, one knew that he was sympathetic, that he felt the trouble as his own. And if a crisis arose—because one could argue fiercely with him at times—he had a most disarming way of suddenly putting aside all emotion, and spreading the whole thing out on the table, as it were, for analysis of his own motives as well as those of the other person. It was this capacity for friendship and sympathy, going beyond the relations of a teacher to pupil, that helped to strengthen his attraction. (1957, 9)

In other words, Malinowski's contributions were multivocal and deeply inspiring, but theoretically ad hoc.

Compare this to Meyer Fortes's corresponding tribute to Radcliffe-Brown, which appeared in the preface to a collection of studies presented to him in 1949, when his leadership was at its apex: "No living scholar has had so decisive an influence on the development of social anthropology as A. R. Radcliffe-Brown. As a teacher he is unrivalled; and his writings are ranked among the classics of anthropology. His influence is due not only to the wide geographical range of his work as a teacher and field investigator, but also to his gift for imparting to students the thrill of new discovery and the desire to join the task of further research" (Fortes, ed., 1949, v). Here we are firmly back in a world where virtue lies in systematicity and progress is linear and cumulative.

Radcliffe-Brown wasted no time taking over as director of the British tradition. His immediate task was to bring about a shift in master concepts from culture to social structure. In his presidential address to the Royal Anthropological Institute in 1940, he responded to a suggestion from Malinowski that South Africa should be studied as an arena where two or more cultures interact:

> We do not observe a "culture," since that word denotes, not a concrete reality, but an abstraction, and as it is commonly used a vague abstraction. . . . What is happening in South Africa is not the interaction of British culture, and Afrikaner culture, Hottentot culture, various Bantu cultures and Indian culture, but the interaction of individuals and groups within an established social structure which is itself in a process of change. What is happening in a Transkeian tribe, for example, can only be described by recognizing that the tribe has been incorporated into a wide political and social structural system. (Radcliffe-Brown 1952)

We can recognize today that this statement contains a number of challenges and hurdles that British anthropology only slowly became aware of and to a considerable extent was unable to find adequate solutions for—and also that Radcliffe-Brown's conceptual scheme was not free of some reifications of its own. He also may have been carried away in his polemics against Malinowski's views only to find himself piling up objections to which he also lacked answers. Yet the program he envisioned was clearly radical and novel, and it affirmed the shift from talking culture to foregrounding social structure.

A vivid and influential step in Radcliffe-Brown's program to reshape social anthropology into a systematic, comparative sociology was delivered in a volume on *African Political Systems* (Fortes and Evans-Pritchard 1940). Here are the exemplary fruits of Radcliffe-Brown's new discipline, in both senses of the term. Malinowski had notably failed to give an account of the political system of the Trobriands, and he had never in the literal sense performed comparisons. *African Political Systems* was a comparative treatise on politics that unscrambled the structure of a number of ethnographic forms and established two elementary types, centralized state structures and stateless political structures. Though small-scale band organizations, as found among the Bushmen, were recognized in the stateless type, the interest focused on the segmentary lineage system as the prototypical stateless polity—because here was a stateless form that organized quite large populations, and, more importantly, this was the type of polity that was studied and described by Evans-Pritchard and Fortes themselves and that fitted remarkably well into the conceptual scheme embraced by Durkheim and Radcliffe-Brown. Adding to the excitement, the connections between these political forms and other major aspects of the societies that were thus organized were laid bare in highly precise language. Quite clearly major substantive and theoretical advances had been achieved, and they were to shape much British anthropological thought for several decades.

The war years were necessarily a transitional period during which little new anthropological research was pursued. Thus what had happened around Radcliffe-Brown in his first years at Oxford did not become as widely known and was certainly not as recognized and assimilated in academic circles as it deserved. It was only in the expansive postwar golden years that the full potential of these theoretical achievements became manifest, and only then that anthropology took a more prominent place within British academia.

4

The Golden Age, 1945–1970

With the succession of Raymond Firth to the chair at the London School of Economics (1944); Edward Evan Evans-Pritchard to the chair at Oxford (1946); Max Gluckman to a new department at Manchester (1949); and Meyer Fortes to the chair at Cambridge (1950), to be joined there shortly by Edmund R. Leach, a new generation of scholars, all born after 1900, took over the leadership of the main academic centers of Britain with their new anthropology. Each had been shaped by Bronislaw Malinowski and A. R. Radcliffe-Brown—several in a close apprenticeship to both of them at different times—and each brought a distinctive intellectual style and ethnographic knowledge to his post. But it has also been noted by many commentators that they and their peers long remained marginal figures in the British academic and political establishment, as their predecessors had been.

Briefly, Raymond Firth (1901–2002) was a New Zealander trained in economics who had gathered an exceptionally rich ethnographic corpus of materials from the small Polynesian outlier of Tikopia, as reported in his classic *We, the Tikopia* (1936). His tenure at the London School of Economics had started in 1933. Later he was joined there by Isaac Schapera (South African) and S. F. Nadel (Austrian). Edward Evan Evans-Pritchard (1902–1973) was an Englishman who had read history at Oxford and had done a series of field studies in the southern Sudan. By the time of his appointment he had already written the highly influential *Witchcraft, Oracles, and Magic among the Azande* (1937) and *The Nuer* (1940). Meyer Fortes (1906–1983) was a South African trained in psychology and had published the exemplary monographs *The Dynamics of Clanship among the Tallensi* (1945) and *The Web of Kinship among the Tallensi* (1949b). Max Gluckman (1911–1974) was likewise a South African and had done fieldwork in South and Central Africa. He had directed the Rhodes-Livingstone Institute during 1941–1947, and he quickly brought a group of younger scholars from that institute to his new department at Manchester.

These chairs of major departments had a great deal of power to control their junior colleagues and students, given the structure of academic institutions at that time. They also wielded influence through the Colonial Social Science Research Council, which had finally started to provide ample British funding for field research. The mainstream of British anthropology still bears their stamp.

The publication of Evans-Pritchard's *The Nuer: A Description of the Modes of Livelihood and Political Institutions of a Nilotic People* (1940) had already defined the direction for anthropological research in Britain—indeed it is probably the most influential monograph ever published in anthropology. To the new generation of anthropologists, especially those under the sway of Oxford, it became the model and prototype for all ethnographic studies. Its spare description and high level of abstraction were admired and emulated, even exaggerated by those who followed Evans-Pritchard. Although *The Nuer* discusses lineage organization in detail, closer inspection reveals that it gives considerable space to other themes as well. One is that of environmental factors, signaled in its subtitle's phrase "description of the modes of livelihood" and in its explicit launching of the term *oecology*.

From the seasonal rising and falling waters of the Nile, a pulsation was induced between settlement aggregation and dispersal, which Evans-Pritchard found reflected in the segmentary structure of the political institutions. But since Evans-Pritchard was clearly unfamiliar with any ecological theory, he had no way of generalizing an analytical approach to the study of such connections between environmental factors and politics. Thus he rested content with showing a homology of form, and he and his followers passed over what could have been an invitation to pursue analyses of human ecology in relation to society. Likewise, the concepts whereby the Nuer themselves treated such environmental constraints were noted and might have been explored to link up with a Malinowskian interest in culture. But such an opening to explore native cultural conceptions in the text was cut short by their displacement with the analyst's own abstractions of "oecological time" and "structural time."

Thus Evans-Pritchard made salient to readers and disciples the powerful structural abstractions of status and corporate group, disentangling the form of social structure from the confusing complexity of local life. It was this operation that dazzled younger anthropologists at the time and led to a spate of studies of "lineage societies." The conceptual operations were further spelled out in Fortes's masterful article "The Structure of Unilineal Descent Groups"

(1953). Here anthropology's inclusive and fuzzy idea of "kinship" as an organizational category was explicitly divided into a politico-jural domain and a familial-domestic domain, clearing away the underbrush to allow a coherent and new "structural-functionalist" analysis of what could conceptually be separated and abstracted as the distinctive politico-jural domain.

A similarly surgical but fruitful operation was performed by Evans-Pritchard's followers on the topic of witchcraft. One strand of Evans-Pritchard's classical analysis of Azande witchcraft—that is to say, of attention to the social distribution of witchcraft accusations—was abstracted from the broader philosophical exploration of witchcraft ideas and used to identify tensions within various local social structures (Evans-Pritchard 1937; Nadel 1952). Perhaps the appeal of these modes of analysis, particularly among young anthropologists writing up their first data, lay in the way unwieldy field materials could be cut down to size and given a tidy analytical framework by such drastic focusing operations. The results that these abstractions produced were clear, obviously insightful, and often surprising to the uninformed. A sense was created among anthropologists that our discipline was progressing and that it placed powerful analytical tools in our hands. But at the same time, the continuation of Malinowskian practices of comprehensive and detailed fieldwork maintained a creative dissatisfaction or tension about the discrepancy between all that the ethnographer had observed in the field and the relatively limited and familiar haul that could be made by a strict structural-functionalist's analytical net.

Thus the main current in the British tradition from 1940 to 1970 can be seen as a disciplined and often successful attempt to apply Radcliffe-Brown's abstractions and to expand their use into ever new and growing empirical fields. I will pursue this view by noting a few cases of such expansions, and also some of the ethnographically engendered dissatisfactions that provoked other questions.

The first generalizing venture was fielded and edited by Radcliffe-Brown himself in the comparative study *African Systems of Kinship and Marriage* (Radcliffe-Brown and Forde 1950). It pursued a systematic program to replace old, ego-centered views of kinship with the new group-focused perspective—that is, to analyze different forms of descent and to focus on the group structures they generated, not on the webs of interpersonal relations that the acknowledgement of kinship organized. This gave very satisfactory results within its own terms, but it also for a while constrained the theoretical imagination of leading British anthropologists in respect to how societies ould be constituted. There is a notorious case, briefly summarized by Marilyn Strathern (1992), in which Peter Lawrence returned from New Guinea in 1950 with a description of local organization based on bilateral kin relations and other elements that seemed to fly in the face of all the generalizations that the structural-functionalists had established. Fortes simply rejected out of hand the possibility of any such social system, and it took many years before Lawrence's data were accepted. Only slowly did a sufficient corpus of so-called nonunilineal materials and analyses accumulate to establish the group properties of bilateral kindreds to the degree necessary for modification of the orthodoxies.

Fortes later proposed to accommodate the fundamentally bilateral nature of all kinship to the framework of lineage and descent theory by introducing the concept of "complementary filiation" for the nondescent parental relationship, as in, for example, the role of matrilateral relations in systems defined by patrilineal descent (Fortes 1959). Leach, on the other hand, had already, in his analysis of his Kachin ethnography, developed a structurally more radical view in which he counterposed descent to affinity. He was thereby able to give a group-focused analysis of the political role of marriages in certain kinds of descent systems. This analysis was first presented in a brilliant early article (1951) and formed the empirical core in a celebrated monograph (1954) that in numerous ways moved beyond the paradigms we are presently discussing. But Fortes ignored this insight into so-called alliance systems when he wrote his article on unilineal descent systems (1953); this may have been one of the reasons for the rift that developed between the two colleagues at Cambridge and permanently divided that department. (There were other reasons, starting with Fortes's failure during the 1950s to wield the influence needed at Cambridge to secure Leach a position beyond a lectureship after Leach had left his readership at the London School of Economics to join the department).

A certain unease with what can broadly be called lineage theory emerged as a result of the gap that often appeared between the structures as they were logically and abstractly presented and what seemed to be the facts on the ground. Evans-Pritchard himself had documented the disparity among the Nuer between the supposedly corporate lineage groups he described (1951) and the residential communities that existed in actuality. In every village and territory a significant number of villagers turned out *not* to trace descent from the ancestor of the "dominant" clan; these villagers might be matrilateral kin, affines, or mere hangers-on. Evans-Pritchard resolved the question by claiming that, for the Nuer, the segmentary genealogy provided the conceptual model of territorial segmentation, and so the disparity was made moot.

Gluckman followed Evans-Pritchard's account but added the functionalist claim that the presence of persons in a community who held alien descent positions served the function of promoting peace. Especially if they were members by descent of the opposed group in a feud, their interest would be to prevent conflict, so they would engage actively to negotiate a settlement. From this could be derived a general thesis on the integrating function of crosscutting loyalties. But what was then the ontological nature of these lineage segments that made up the core structure of Nuer society according to Evans-Pritchard's description?

For those who wanted to understand the facts on the ground, a number of questions were left hanging: Why did people settle outside their descent territories at all? What were the embraced values that governed the fusion and fission of lineages or communities in collective political action? What might be the varied and opposed political processes at work in this disordered field of differently aligned persons? In short, what did the schema of situational fusion and fission describe? Did it represent the logical operations of classification, the loyalties of composite local populations, or the actual alignments and confrontations of agnatic groups of warriors in blood feuds? A term that was increasingly used by lineage theorists was taken from Evans-Pritchard's own text: descent provided the "idiom" in which segmentary relations could be expressed (1940, 212). Quite what that meant remained obscure: Are segments, as groups of real people acting collectively, produced by people's ideas of agnatic descent, or are they not? If not, what were the sources of group loyalty? For some the unease remained. Yet the lineage model was eagerly appropriated by many fresh returnees from the field.

Evans-Pritchard had also used his Nuer lineage schema, in basically unaltered form, to represent the social structure of bedouin tribes in Cyrenaica (Evans-Pritchard 1949). Yet these populations must have themselves conceptualized descent very differently from the way the Nuer did. Their lineages were, for example, not exogamous; they certainly practiced a different mode of livelihood without the seasonal pulsations of the waters of the Nile; and they used a different set of images to represent lineage segments: fathers and sons (or co-wives) rather than, as among the Nuer, hearths and doors to huts. In a series of careful and elegant articles Emrys Peters, a student of Evans-Pritchard who did fieldwork himself among the Cyrenaica bedouin, explored the empirical facts among the bedouin in regard to such issues as the political uses of matrilateral ties, the practice of feuding, and the tendency toward proliferation of segments on some levels of genealogy and not on others (Peters 1960, 1967). Though subdued in his challenge, Peters was driven to introduce a far more processual analysis that went well beyond lineage theory to give an account of Cyrenaica bedouin ethnography.

In my own study of Pathans in Swat (Barth 1959), I found a population where the agnatic descent system defined the territorial units, but where lineage segments never fused as politically corporate groups because they were vitiated by tactical political alliances—a situation that seemed to require Max Weber rather than Émile Durkheim, Henry Sumner Maine, and lineage theory for its explication. The power of lineage theory to extract its object from the complexity of social life and to deliver a generalizable set of characterizations of groups seemed increasingly questionable.

Evans-Pritchard himself had already moved on. In a Marett lecture delivered in 1950 he declared that a historical viewpoint was the only tenable position for a social anthropologist (Evans-Pritchard 1962). Godfrey Lienhardt, the colleague who was perhaps the closest to him, suggests that this may have been Evans-Pritchard's attempt to adjust to the climate of opinion among senior academics at Oxford (Lienhardt 1974, 301). Others have put it down to both his personality and his polarizing intellectual style, noting the way he had earlier broken with Malinowski and now wished to break with Radcliffe-Brown (Firth 1975, 8). The posthumously published collection of manuscript fragments "*A History of Anthropological Thought* (Evans-Pritchard 1981) certainly reveals in brief passages on Malinowski and Radcliffe-Brown a singularly harsh and ungenerous assessment of both. But the embracing of history had little effect on Evans-Pritchard's own empirical work, though it may have lent support to the reorientation of some younger colleagues. In mainstream British anthropology the structural-functional juggernaut moved on for a considerable time.

An attempt to grapple with dynamic analysis within the main structural-functional orthodoxy took its framework from a seminal article by Fortes (1949a). In it he analyzed the composition of Ashanti domestic units as the outcome of incompatible preferences, the relative force of which tended to change systematically through the life courses of women and men. As I have already suggested in the case of the emulation of Evans-Pritchard's witchcraft study, so also Fortes's Ashanti study was pursued in only one strand of the original analysis: the effects on domestic units of the progressive maturation of its members. His work thus led to the creation of a "development cycle" model for depicting such groups (Goody 1958). But this idea of a development cycle provided only a modest window to some new ways of thinking about process and form.

The attention to issues of individual and collective behavior, or choice and norm, however, was far greater in other branches of the British school, especially among Firth and his students at the London School of Economics. Here was a milieu with unbroken continuity with Malinowski's early days, where questions of economics and about the human exercise of individual choice remained persistently on the table. Firth also consciously sought to maintain the Malinowskian tradition of highly stimulating, open, and creative departmental seminars, and he took an ever pragmatic position toward the passing fashions and orthodoxies of the anthropological scene. During the 1950s he tried to accommodate major perspectives by counterposing social structure and social organization, the former referring to the major principles characterizing social forms, and the latter to the manifold ways in which individuals generate patterns as they navigate their lives and pursue their situational options. It was a framework that gave space to questions on the nature of values and allowed the anthropologist to explore the paradoxes of abstract principles and facts on the ground, of norms and purposes, of collective representations and individual actions. It provided an intellectual environment for many of the objections and misgivings that structural-functional orthodoxy raised, though in itself it offered no answers of comparable strength to those that orthodoxy delivered.

The department in Manchester had its own distinctive focus, often at the place of tension between functionalism and the study of conflict. Several members of the Manchester school also did creative and important work in conceptualizing and analyzing networks, to correct the imbalance that a restricted focus on corporate groups inevitably produced.

Manchester seminars also had their distinctive character: Gluckman had an unusual ability to wrestle directly with the ethnographic data of others as presented in their papers, and he used it with great skill during seminar discussions. What emerged under the label "extended case method" was the collective fruit of such skills. To visitors, presenting a paper at Manchester would always be a stimulating challenge; to regulars these presentations sometimes took on the character of a blood sport. "You could positively see him wilt," was the triumphal report I heard of one such session!

The whole Manchester group was driven in these years by the enormous vitality of the person of "Max" and his intrusive engagement with the thought, indeed the total lives, of all the members of the gang. On weekends they even ritualized their collective identity by rooting for the sports team Manchester United. The professional strength of Manchester also lay in its serious early attention to expanding empirical fields, mainly in urban Africa, but also in village India (Frederick Bailey), Norway (John Barnes), and at home in Britain (Ronald Frankenberg).

An anthropological romance of a kind occurred with the discovery and opening of the New Guinea Highlands to anthropological research. Here were large, varied, pristine, and spectacular native populations suddenly accessible to ethnographic study. Young anthropologists trained in the British tradition, based first in Sydney and later at the Australian National University in Canberra, grasped this new opportunity. Initial interest naturally focused on social structure, which at first was analyzed on the basis of lineage models. But as first-rate and rich ethnographies accumulated, the gap between lineage-theory assumptions and ethnographic data widened, and Barnes, who was chair of the Canberra department by then, raised the issue of how appropriate African lineage models were in the New Guinea Highlands (Barnes 1962). This proved liberating to New Guinea fieldworkers, but they did not pursue the opportunity to broaden the theoretical questions by candidly rethinking the appropriateness of the lineage models as they were used on the original African materials.

In due course, the clarity and precision that were gained in the analyses of social structures made space for new ambitions in the analysis of rituals and symbols. A celebrated step was provided by N. M. Srinivas, then at Oxford, who demonstrated that direct expressions of structural relations in family and marriage could be found in the idioms of Coorg marriage rituals (1952). The work of Victor Turner, then at Manchester, on the set of color symbols among the Ndembu, started from the same position and likewise aroused great interest. But Turner soon realized that Srinivas's approach represented a too literal and direct effort to equate symbols, meanings, and the anthropologist's structural models item by item. Consequently attention shifted to a broader framing of such analyses, increasingly based on theories of communication and in transformational thinking such as had already emerged in the work of Claude Lévi-Strauss—though Lévi-Strauss's influence only slowly penetrated into the British tradition.

A persistent disquiet arose among British anthropologists over the inability of anthropological theory to handle questions of social change. In Malinowski's cultural paradigm the issue was thought of as a matter of culture contact: mainly, the effects of ideas and the breakdown of cultural integration as a consequence of the intrusion of outside forces. In Radcliffe-Brown's structural paradigm, the very description of social change posed difficulties, since social structure referred so clearly and by definition to something enduring, with an internal functional interconnectedness. Anthropological analyses therefore always seemed to turn out timid and conservative, in favor of the existing structures—despite the relative political radicalism of most individual British anthropologists. The use of a synchronic focus and the literary device of the ethnographic present in anthropological writing helped to obfuscate issues of time and social reproduction. Even the tensions that Manchester colleagues sought to uncover usually seemed to resolve themselves without consequences for an analysis of change.

The argument was sometimes made that structural-functional models were equilibrium models, and had to be so by virtue of the simplifying assumptions necessary to describe anything as complex as functioning societies. To sugar this discouraging pill, the claim was made that these were "dynamic equilibrium" models. But the models of society that anthropologists delivered could rarely show how social forms were indeed the product of anything dynamic; rather, they appealed in circular fashion to institutional rules and culturally valued ideals to reveal a preexisting structure that manifested itself in its own image.

In Firth's paradigm questions of change were somewhat more tractable because it always acknowledged a role for individual choices and their aggregate consequences. Yet in his efforts to speak the language of his colleagues and his discipline, he found the issues hard to resolve on the theoretical level, and he continued to think it some kind of a mystery that the exercise of individual freedom should result in patterns of social behavior that showed the degree of stability that could be described as structure.

Edmund Leach (1910–1989), at Cambridge, was the senior anthropologist who most creatively wrestled with these issues. He was also the one who bridged the passage from the social structuralism of the period we have been discussing to a subsequent, post–1970 structuralist framework. In this lecture I treat only his thought on the constitution of real social groups and the determination of patterns of social activity as they are manifested among people.

In the space of a few years, Leach offered two positions, one in 1954 and another in 1961. (Once, in a seminar, when he was reproached for having changed his position, he stood up on one leg and declared that he found it very difficult to remain in one position for a long time!) The first position was developed in his justly famous monograph *Political Systems of Highland Burma: A Study of Kachin Social Structure* (1954). The dynamic of his account of the social groups that formed in a large population of Kachin hill tribes in Northeast Burma depended essentially on the explanation that Kachins subscribed to a set of ideas that were incompatible with one another in that the pursuit of them tended to undermine the preconditions of whatever manifest social structures they established. On the one hand, Kachin embraced political ideas of equality between small neighboring patrilineal groups; on the other hand, they embraced ideas of marriage and affinal relations that tended toward the production of hierarchy. With a careful collective management of marriage practice, local circles of intermarrying lineages could temporarily maintain equality, in a structure that the Kachin called *gumlao*. But the pursuit of individual ambition constantly threatened this condition and readily transformed it into a hierarchical structure, locally known as *gumsa*. However, the successful creation of hierarchy tended to precipitate rebellions, and thus to lead to the reestablishment of equality. If the hierarchy was successfully maintained against all odds, the group would eventually become ethnically reclassified as Shan, like the population of the surrounding Shan states.

In other words, any particular local arrangement tended to be unstable, and the social structure produced pervasive flux and change all over the area. The analysis successfully depicted the dynamics that generated this flux, and the changing social forms. Although critics objected that this was a very special ethnographic case, one might observe that every detailed ethnographic analysis depicts only a special case. To the other objection, that in the broader ethnographic area what came out of the dynamics was only an eternal oscillation between two overt forms, the answer would be that this was not entirely true and that it did not matter anyway. No one could deny that here was a successful analysis of dynamics and change whereby concrete social communities were undergoing transformations in a manner that could be described and analyzed.

The Kachin monograph was so rich in other content as well that it became greatly admired, but it was often misunderstood, and never emulated. As if to confound his readers further, Leach next produced an excruciatingly detailed analysis of the organization of society in a small village in the present Sri Lanka over the preceding seventy-year period (1961). In it he argued that whatever stability and determination of social form the village exhibited was the effect not of its inhabitants' bilateral kinship ideas or their marriage practices, but of the persisting physical layout of the village water tank, irrigation channels, and fields. He thus questioned the whole conceptual order that constituted structural-functionalism.

Leach cited Fortes for the conventional view: "The tendency towards equilibrium is marked in every sector of Tale society and in the society as a whole; and it is clearly the result of the dominance of the lineage principle in the social structure. . . . The almost complete absence of economic differentiation . . . mean(s) that economic interests do not play the part of dynamic factors in the social structure" (Fortes 1945, x, as cited in Leach 1961, 8). Leach argued that such a view reflected an a priori choice by lineage theorists to isolate and give primacy to kinship over all other constraints on social form. But both social groups and individual behavior were, he argued, far more determined by material circumstances in the case he analyzed, and would probably prove so in other cases as well if the analyst's perspective were widened. We have finally come full circle to the point where the founding premises laid down for structural-functional analysis and lineage theory were rejected.

The critique also raises a deeper conceptual problem that had surfaced in the thought of some American colleagues, including David Schneider: that of how to identify anything as substantively and inherently constituting kinship in its content when the matters that are transacted between kin are patently matters of labor, consumption, land, or politics. But Leach's argumentation is both so detailed and subtle and so dialogical that its general importance has not been widely appreciated. Indeed, one might argue that it also presented an unheeded lesson to the Marxist ambitions that blossomed in the quarter-century that followed by demonstrating how an empirical study of a society's material basis would need to be pursued in a dynamic anthropological analysis.

These two works by Leach emerged out of themes that had been raised within the discourses of structural-functionalism, but each in its own way led to a very differently constituted theoretical position. The rest of his work, on the other hand, really transcended structural-functionalism and established entirely new beginnings; it will be discussed, along with the work of Victor Turner, in the next lecture.

The Association of Social Anthropologists of the Commonwealth was established in 1946 and created for the first time a professional framework for the British tradition. It became a major arena for discourse on topics that were central to the academic work of social anthropologists and a major force in the intellectual life of its members. Yet there was a distance bordering on disdain that divided the handful of major scholars and professorial colleagues who directed British anthropology in this period. Still, some friendships and some conditions of mutual respect crossed the divides: I understood there to be, at least for a long time, close relations and respect between Evans-Pritchard, Fortes, and Gluckman; and there were close relations between Leach and Firth and between Leach and Schapera, and for a while a degree of mutual respect between Leach and Evans-Pritchard.

Though there was little love lost between most of the members of this great generation, only the maverick Edmund Leach let some of the intensity of his differences with his colleagues reach published form. Jack Goody has more recently revealed more of these divisions and pettinesses (1995). In public the seniors tended to act in ways to paper over their differences: they were largely measured in what they published on their disagreements and were positively protective of each other vis-à-vis juniors and students. Thus a semblance of scholarly harmony reigned, and even mild deviations by juniors were met with heavy sanctions.

The considerable unity of the British tradition from 1945 to 1970 was thus maintained both by carrot and by stick: the ideas it offered were exciting, and internal criticisms were stifled. But was this situation optimal to the flowering of a British tradition? I believe the situation had both its advantages and its disadvantages: it held anthropological discourse together and enhanced the performance of all, as in a circus troop; it created a shared universe of discourse and some shared theoretical achievements; but it also delayed critical work and reduced individual creativity. It is interesting to examine the publication that the founding generation put together at the beginning, when they wrote the 1949 collection *Social Structure* to honor Radcliffe-Brown (it was probably authored in the early forties, since it was intended for his retirement in 1946; Fortes 1949). Even excluding the submissions from non-British contributors, the essays in that collection are characterized by a riotous diversity, originality, and promise. (I am particularly partial to the article by Gregory Bateson on schismogenesis, to that by Firth on authority and the weapons of the weak in Tikopia, and to Fortes's aforementioned treatment of statistics, process, and form in his analysis of residence decisions among the Ashanti.) This kind of exuberance soon disappeared; by comparison, the various collections of essays that were published later are more orthodox, more predictable, and more uniform, and though in some ways they are more useful, they are distinctly less original. Perhaps the golden years of the British tradition were bought at a cost.

5

Enduring Legacies of the British Tradition, 1970–2000

Let me start with a note of personal bewilderment. Not having written or for that matter taught a history of anthropology before, at this point I meet a difficulty that I had not anticipated. In the chronological frame that all of us in this series of lectures have chosen, we have proceeded from a distant past toward events and persons more and more familiar and well known, whose world we have increasingly felt we could grasp because it became step by step more our own, though still we could view it with the added wisdom of hindsight. But at this point the story has caught up with my own personal trajectory to such an extent that my task now is one of telling about ideas and circumstances to which I have been an accessory, matters that today make up my present, a time that I cannot help but experience as contemporary.

Yet many of my readers, younger than me, will not share this change of perspective with me: to them I am still talking about a past that is not part of their direct experience. Even more bewildering, some such younger persons will now themselves intrude into my account; these are participants in our shared discipline who are nevertheless uninvolved in some of this enduring present that is mine. I did not know what a difference that makes to the telling of history. To escape some confusions of positioning, I have already chosen to sideline parts of my own work that might otherwise have been included in an account of the British tradition, as, for example, my work on transactionalism. In the following, I also avoid entering too closely into the circumstances of the work of persons younger than myself, and thus I will treat the period 1970–2000 in a somewhat more cursory fashion than the previous periods.

First I need to note an external event that changed the context for British anthropological practice: the student uprisings of 1968 that shattered institutional constraints and changed the relations of power and thus also the bases for authority within academia. Anthropologists were not themselves centrally involved in causing these events, but their world was permanently changed by them. I have suggested that the senior anthropologists of the 1940s and 1950s in Britain had vast discretionary powers over their juniors, autocratically controlling research grants and appointments, for example; and I have suggested that they used these powers to bolster their own intellectual authority. Their juniors understood how appointments were made and departments were constructed, and they generally accepted the seniors' direction. Edward Evans-Pritchard, at Oxford, seemed most clearly to wield this combination of intellectual and administrative authority. He did so with great force during his tenure, as demonstrated, for example, at a time when positions were desperately few and he gave a key post to Godfrey Lienhardt, whom he had picked before Lienhardt had even finished his undergraduate training and before he had done any research (Goody 1995, 81–82). After 1968 this kind of arbitrary power was wiped out and replaced by committee procedures, and students and junior scholars knew it, so they could no longer be as effectively disciplined.

A result of the former suppression of dissent can be seen in the posthumous collection of Emrys Peters's essays, published under the editorship of Jack Goody and Emanuel Marx (Peters 1990). In the 1960s Peters had published several seminal articles based on ethnographic materials from the Cyrenaica bedouin, performing a moderate internal critique and correction of aspects of lineage theory as it was then constituted. But this posthumous collection additionally contains four previously unpublished essays, probably originating around the same time, which go much further in their critique and revision. The book opens with a devastating assessment of Evans-Pritchard's monograph on the Sanusi as static in its assumptions and arguably deeply flawed in its account. Since this study had been heralded by Evans-Pritchard himself as an exemplary case of the kind of historical analysis that would replace structural-functionalism in anthropology, the importance of the critique can hardly be exaggerated. In the sixth chapter of the collection, Peters further provided a compelling analysis of the dynamics of politics, leadership, and group formation among the Cyrenaica bedouin, and thus an analysis of the social and political mode of operation of their lineage system. The analysis is innovative in both its substance and its theoretical assumptions, and it offers a resolution of some of the enduring strains in the orthodox lineage paradigm.

It is my judgment that the publication of these analyses at an earlier time would have contributed greatly to the advancement of our understanding of tribal politics, since they went a long way to bridge the gap between the formal segmentary descent structures and the political groups and networks that were generated on the ground among the bedouin. The timidity on the part of the author or the outright control on the part of his seniors that prevented the publication of these essays at the time they were written, when they would have resolved important questions that held back the thinking of numerous colleagues, we can only interpret as a reflection of the power relations within British anthropology. An opportunity was thus lost to enlarge and transform in timely fashion the established theoretical constructions of "the British school."

Another anthropologist who built on the shared British tradition but moved beyond it and broke new ground was Victor Turner (1920–1983). With extraordinarily rich and detailed ethnographic materials from the Ndembu in Central Africa and some impulses from psychoanalysis he developed an analysis of symbols from bases essentially foreshadowed in A. R. Radcliffe-Brown's analysis of sentiments among the Andaman Islanders (1922/1948). Rather than eschewing emotion and affect, as had been the rule in British anthropology for the previous thirty years, Turner sought to grasp the gravitas and meaning of dense symbols in various Ndembu rites, linking them to their social context and searching for the meanings and subjectivities they induced. In the course of the 1960s he wrote a remarkable series of studies of rituals of initiation and affliction among the Ndembu, as well as describing the activities of Ndembu shamanism as a native system of knowledge (Turner 1965, 1967, 1968). The lesson of these studies was to show the distinctive character of symbols: their multivocality, ambiguity, and force. Turner next used the early work of Arnold van Gennep (1909/1960) to develop and generalize the concept of liminality in fruitful ways (Turner 1969). But after he moved to the United States in the 1970s his direct influence on younger British colleagues was reduced.

The main shift in the theoretical climate within Britain toward the end of the 1960s occurred as a result of the work of Edmund Leach. Ever since he published his first articles on kinship structures, Leach had experimented with another kind of structuralism, one based on the exploration of highly abstract parallels and on modeling operations such as inversions, reflecting his engineering and mathematical mode of thought. When during the 1960s he turned increasingly from the study of social structures to the study of meaning, he did so by making use of highly abstract theoretical approaches to the structure of thought and communication. Claude Lévi-Strauss served him as a stimulus in a number of ways, as did the structural linguist Roman Jakobson, with whom he had personal contact in 1960–1961, the year he spent as a fellow of the Institute of Advanced Studies in Palo Alto, California.

Around the same time, Lévi-Strauss was also receiving some other, though ambivalent, attention in some circles of British anthropology, spearheaded by Rodney Needham at Oxford, where the ground for French structuralism had been prepared by the idealist leanings of Evans-Pritchard's thought on social structure, the teaching of Franz Steiner, and Louis Dumont's periodic visits. In 1963, the Association of Social Anthropologists decided to bring together and assess some of these ideas and to devote a future session to a series of papers concerning the work of Lévi-Strauss. Leach was belatedly brought in as the convener of the session. The resulting collection of essays, which appeared in 1967, came out highly diverse and interesting, but some of the essays were tangential to the work of Lévi-Strauss. Leach's introduction indicates as much. "If this book provides illumination," he wrote, "it will be because of the light it throws on the assumptions and attitudes of particular British social anthropologists rather than because of any consistent analysis of the work of Continental Europe's most distinguished living anthropologist" (Leach 1967, vii). Some of the behind-the-scenes frustrations and confusions arising from this session are discussed in Stanley Tambiah's biography of Leach (2002, 234–58). However, the outcome of it all was, in due course, to place modern, abstract structuralism strongly on the agenda of British anthropological thinking.

Leach's own pursuit of structuralism was widely explorative, intense, and, in certain respects, rigorous, and he applied it widely to social structure, art, architecture, nonverbal communication, terms of abuse, ritual, myth, and other areas. His analyses make use of a few logical operations derivable from communication engineering, mainly those involving binary oppositions, inversions and other transformations, the exploration of the redundancies of variations and contradictions, and the effects of mediators, that is, anomalous occupants of the "excluded middle" that is implied by a dichotomy (a dichotomy of the type, in Leach's formulation, "p is what not-p is not"). In the analysis of myth Leach further accepted Lévi-Strauss's license—startling from a functionalist viewpoint—to treat as one corpus an eclectic range of myths from different places. He further extended this freedom to his treatment of the whole biblical collection as a single text without regard to disparate historical periods. The spate of short and long essays from his hand, mostly in puzzle format with radical resolutions, has challenged, inspired, and indeed puzzled many younger British anthropologists ever since.

One pervasive difficulty in reading Leach's texts is to distinguish when he intends to present an idea as a part of a new and consistent set of theoretical premises, and when he is playing, improvising, and changing his positions. Coming, as the British tradition did, from an era of considerable philosophical coherence and orthodoxy, how was one to identify the ontological position Leach was embracing? One may ask: Are the quasimathematical abstractions of his structuralism intended as a supple set of instruments by which an objective analyst can pragmatically explore the logical relations of variables? Or are we offered an effort, as Lévi-Strauss claims, to uncover how all human minds always work? Or is there indeed a third alternative, as Tambiah (2002, 348–55) suggests, that accords these cultural forms a distinctive ontology?

I find that there are some most intriguing suggestions of a kind of third option in Leach's general text *Social Anthropology* (1982, 122ff.). Here he seems to grant individuals a private realm of individuality and self-constructed, purposeful rationality—but also a realm of taken-for-granted structures that we individually and voluntarily embody and enact. He notes, with an appeal to introspection into our own lives, how many are the things we simply take for granted in our practices: the physical layout of houses and settlements, the way food is prepared and meals are composed, our sense of what is the proper way to behave toward kin and neighbors and persons in authority, the kinds of clothes and the styles of language that are appropriate to different occasions, how occasions themselves are constructed and classified, and so on. But "these distinctive features of our own way of life are not of our own making. . . . Very little of our public behaviour is innate; most of us have only very limited creative originality. We act as we do because, one way or another, we have learned from others that that is the way we ought to behave" (Leach 1982, 128).

So far, so good. But then, I would like to know, how do these blueprints of conventions come about? Where and how do the forms arise? Perhaps not directly from the universal structure of each individual human mind, as Lévi-Strauss would have us assume, but rather from constraints in an interpersonal field or realm of communication, where a set of distinctive, aggregating processes generates the remarkable kinds of regularities that Leach's structural analyses uncover? If so, I believe that we need to identify and study these processes, not just continue to provide more examples of their patterned outputs in the substantive form of structural oppositions and contortions. But perhaps in advancing this criticism I am belittling major, basic steps of the analyses that Leach does deliver. Perhaps I am making an impatient demand for even more: a full and satisfactory theory that would provide all the answers.

Be this as it may, Leach's and Lévi-Strauss's writings on structuralism certainly left distinct marks on the work of a number of junior British anthropologists, starting with Nur Yalman's elegant *Under the Bo Tree* (1967)

and reaching on through the works of Christine Hugh-Jones (1979) and
Stephen Hugh-Jones (1979) and a number of others.

More pervasively, structuralism brought a sea change to British anthropology. To some, it was empowering. It allowed Mary Douglas (1921–) to pursue her fieldwork discovery of the ambiguous pangolin of the Lele and develop it into her mature analysis of animal categories in Leviticus, and also to
forever shape our understanding of dirt as matter out of place. More broadly,
it provided to many younger anthropologists a frame and a vocabulary for a
great variety of explorations of cultural data. But in the profession as a whole,
it also led to a rather undisciplined spate of "structuralism light": of insignificant exercises that involved stating a dichotomy, applying it to some fairly
superficial bodies of data, and leaving it at that. The trouble is, there does not
seem to be any agreement in current British anthropology on canons of just
what such analyses need to contain and spell out.

For an assessment of what was happening in British social anthropology
around 1970, the various effects of Marxism and the growth of feminism both
need to be considered. Inspired by currents on the Continent and in the
United States, feminism may have been the most fruitful and enduring of
the perspectival changes to enter British anthropological awareness at the
time. Despite the long and illustrious presence of individual women scholars
among British anthropologists, there were clearly a number of issues relating
to the lives of women and to questions of gender relations that had received
insufficient empirical and theoretical attention in anthropological thought.
New ethnographies have progressively been produced by a new generation of
anthropologists, most of them women, that remedy this relative neglect. At
the same time, the acknowledgement of such lacunae of ethnography and
theory also brought an awareness of the need for action and change to combat
discriminatory practices of our own within anthropology as a discipline. The
course of this change in British anthropology involved partisanship for and
against and questioning of both of the importance of gender theory and the
need for practical reform. Purely scholarly curiosity alone might never have
provided sufficient impetus to feminist research and theory without the re-
formist energy of some concerned women. But the outcome was never in
doubt, and the benefits to British anthropology have been significant and
lasting.

Contrary to the simplifications that are sometimes fostered, the work of
Karl Marx has been given considerable attention as a source of social science

thought in the work of several generations of British anthropologists, and it was particularly represented during the 1950s and 1960s in the discussions of the Manchester group and in London. But with the growing attention to Marxism among the other social sciences, among many French anthropological colleagues, and in the general student body in the heady years following 1968, neo-Marxism suddenly gained extra clout, as if it might offer a complete and alternative paradigm for anthropology. As a theoretical position it was also confounded with student power and the spirit of 1968, and in that context it had the effect of disrupting the dialectic of more nuanced transmission and critique between anthropology teachers and students. Ideas that were intellectually simplistic could be promoted by oppositional students with confidence in the progressive nature of their own political cause and the assurance of peer support. The result was a lowering of the quality of transmission and knowledge and some loss of rigor in critical thought. Despite the spurt of intense interest, the lasting effects of neo-Marxism on British social anthropology have been remarkably slight.

The general oppositional climate of the times also stimulated an internal political critique of British anthropology, most strongly articulated in Talal Asad's edited volume *Anthropology and the Colonial Encounter* (1973). Resonating with American misgivings over the complicity of some anthropologists in the Vietnam War, the volume raised the issue of how British anthropology, specifically in the period 1930–1960, had been affected by its accommodation to the context of empire and may even have become complicit in it. The issue was not new, but thus far it had not been faced with sufficient critical reflexivity, in part because accusations and innuendos raised bristles and sidetracked serious discussion. Asad's introduction pointed to several possible levels for examining the issues: First, to what extent had anthropologists served the colonial administrators in ways that enhanced the latter's powers, making the anthropologists actively complicit in colonial oppression? Second, had the power relations that prevailed between anthropologists as Europeans on the one hand and the colonial masses on the other distorted the anthropologists' practice of fieldwork, and thus distorted the view through the lens of anthropology? Finally, was anthropology at least involved in structural complicity because it was "rooted in an unequal power encounter between the West and Third World . . . that gives the West access to cultural and historical information about the societies it has progressively dominated, and thus not only generates a certain kind of universal understanding, but also reenforces the inequalities in capacity between the European and the non-European worlds" (Asad 1973, 16)?

Peter Loizus convened a seminar at the London School of Economics (LSE) where several prominent senior British anthropologists were invited to respond to Asad's volume (see Berndt 1997, the issue of *Anthropological Forum* that contains these papers and also Tambiah 2002:407–14, who provides a discussion of the seminar). I am unsure how much convergence and disciplinary consensus this meeting achieved among British colleagues, at the time or for the future, but I can offer a few reflections of my own. Asad's last point seems to me the most sustainable, as there can be little doubt that his view is correct: Western knowledge is constructed in ways that place distinctive forms of global power in the hands of Western state systems. But this same expansive power is, it seems to me, generated by *all* thought and intellectual activity within the Western tradition: the forms of expression and insight it creates are indeed globally self-reinforcing and empowering. The issue that this fact raises thus cannot be resolved in simplistic terms of culpability and blame directed against anthropologists, but must be addressed on a much broader and intellectually more demanding level. This important question should not be sidelined as political critique of the practices of a handful of anthropologists, but needs to be reframed it as a major topic of social analysis.

Asad's other questions touch on the very nature of the Malinowskian project. Malinowski's hope to grasp an other's "point of view, his relation to life, to realize *his* vision of *his* world" requires, to my understanding, a willed disempowerment of oneself in the situation of anthropological fieldwork (Malinowski 1922, 25). It involves the field anthropologist in an eternal struggle *not* to deploy his communicative and social capital from outside the group being studied, but to build his public social identity progressively on what he is able to construct within local society—those are the only social resources that can provide the basis for Malinowskian participation. It has been the purpose of British empiricist anthropology, and the continuing task of fieldwork, thus to try to correct the astigmatism of the anthropological lens. As one step in this direction, Malinowski is reported to always have advised his students, in the idiom of the 1930s, both to minimize contact with other whites, and to refrain from thinking about change and induced improvements of native life. So I read Asad's question to be: Was this demanding exercise actually practiced by anthropologists in the context of empire—and was it indeed possible to do so? It is surely a very difficult task to perform for a person in the context of a colony, and the requirement goes much deeper than a mere distancing from the local hierarchies of colonialism: it necessarily must involve *all* the fieldworker's various empowerments. Moreover, the task does not necessarily become easier in noncolonial situations.

I have myself done fieldwork as a citizen of a small and powerless country living among marginal populations in independent states. Yet people there would tend to ascribe external power to me: as white, educated, male, rich, with the ever-present option of exit. To forego the social uses of these resources while in a pressed learning situation where I am ignorant and inept by local standards is never easy and can never be totally successful. Yet the struggle is instructive: some degree of success is possible, and I discovered that most ordinary people are remarkably forgiving and generous, even if they are poor and of low status.

Did British anthropologists in colonial times nonetheless make significant use of the colonial establishment during fieldwork, and even covertly act as agents of colonial administrations? It is ironic that the Polish freethinker Malinowski and his ragtag band of radical, largely nonestablishment, even foreign disciples should be faulted for serving and aligning with the empire. Since doing so would have been counterproductive for their fieldwork efforts, it is not credible that this would have been their general practice. For those who made the physically and mentally demanding, honest effort to practice Malinowskian field methods, any such insinuation would no doubt have rankled. And the difficulties presented by participant fieldwork could cut both ways: an anthropologist's behavior in the field must have appeared so bizarre to white colonial persons of power as to be deeply compromising. Practitioners at the time reported on how they suffered from the resulting dissonance with colonial administrators (see Goody 1995, in his chapter on Meyer Fortes titled "Making It to the Field as a Jew and a Red"; also the discussion in Kuper 1999, chapter 4).

Most Malinowskian British anthropologists would probably have thought of themselves not as legitimate objects of radical criticism but as practitioners of a new kind of idealism and of solidarity with the not yet empowered—much as students working in cultural survival probably feel today. The more general issue for modern anthropology is how to nourish the ideal and importance, indeed urgency, of continuing the effort of intensive, participant fieldwork because the challenge is still with us: the prevailing lifestyle in our world today emphasizes personal comfort and safety, and instrumental efficiency provides the supreme measure of value and the validity of knowledge—all attitudes that can limit the field anthropologist's willingness and ability to take on humble commitments in unfamiliar situations. Many anthropologists today question both the practicality of and the need for such "old-fashioned" fieldwork. Yet the insights that underpin an anthropological view of humankind surely still require the reiterated experience of participating in the lives of other people on their own terms. There is the added danger that the current fashion of structuralist puzzle solving may not make that need sufficiently obvious to sustain the broad practice of such personally demanding efforts among novice anthropologists. More important than the critique of "colonial" anthropologists is surely a searching self-criticism of the tangled compromises of our own professional ethics and practices today—another theme that can easily be sidetracked by the thrust of Asad's intervention.

The old guard in British social anthropology generally kept aloof also from the legitimate nonacademic applications of the discipline. Raymond Firth and Edmund Leach both seemed to regard applied anthropology mostly as a matter of applying common sense to practical local issues; others seemed to have contempt for the very idea of practical applications. The obstacles were also deeply lodged in the theoretical state of the discipline. The tensions between the functionalist ideal of fieldwork, static theoretical models, and the fiction of unit societies made any hope for the use of British anthropology for practical purposes in the postwar world somewhat illusory, and the addition of Marxism and abstract structuralism hardly helped matters. The ambition of studying social change was tied to something like the writing of exotic histories and certainly not to "social engineering," as applied anthropology was contemptuously known. The present generation seems more prepared to make the attempt, but little intellectual work has been done to develop the theoretical framework on which to base such engagement, and the various efforts that are found depend on the thematic commitments of practitioners and not on an integrated view of the role of social anthropology in modern society.

The retirement from their chairs of the leading figures of the golden age of anthropology—Firth, Evans-Pritchard, Fortes, Max Gluckman—closed a chapter in the history of British social anthropology. Their successors, however gifted and productive, could never recreate the conditions of authority and intellectual leadership that had once prevailed, but some departments fared better than others through the years that followed.

At Cambridge, Fortes was succeeded by his student and colleague Jack Goody (1919–), who had by then long played a significant role in the department with his rich ethnographic materials from West Africa, making significant contributions to the topics of kinship, succession, and property relations. The effect of his assuming the chair was the relaxation of some of the prevailing constraints on the discipline and an opening of the way for a greater diversity of interests, both among his students and in his own work. Goody expanded the scope for comparative work by using historical data from large-scale, Eurasian societies, and addressed questions on the historical emergence of civilization, especially in his analyses of the effects of literacy on thought and society.

In 1984 Goody was succeeded by Ernest Gellner (1925–1995), who likewise focused on substantive themes that had not been central to the work of the preceding generation: politics and anthropology in the Soviet Union and Eastern Europe; thought and society in the Muslim world; and most broadly influential, the nature of nationalism and its historical development in Europe. Gellner was born in Prague, was trained at Oxford as a philosopher, and had been appointed to a post in philosophy at the LSE. He played a distinctive role as a critic of the linguistic turn in British philosophy with his celebrated book *Words and Things* (1959). By that time he was doing anthropological fieldwork in North Africa under the direction of colleagues at the LSE, and he chose to change his professional identity to that of social anthropologist. In due course a chair in "philosophy with special reference to sociology" was created for him at the LSE. At Cambridge he continued Goody's encouragement of diversification in topics and areas, and he was a trenchant critic of many of the currents that were sweeping through British anthropology. Himself of a positivist persuasion and opposed to both Marxist and postmodern fashions, in his own prolific work he was partial to logical models, substantive correlations and explanations of social facts, and synthetic accounts of history and change.

Marilyn Strathern (1941–) was brought from Manchester to Cambridge to succeed Gellner in 1993. Cambridge trained, with extensive field materials from New Guinea and later from England, and with a topical interest in exchange, kinship, and a broad set of feminist issues, Strathern has long been a highly productive and respected scholar. The department at Cambridge continues to play a central role in the life of British anthropology under her leadership.

Though Oxford retained its institutional prestige and attracted students and junior scholars of high standard, it was less successful in maintaining a succession of influential professorial figures. Evans-Pritchard retired in 1970. He was succeeded by Maurice Freedman, whose work on Chinese lineage systems had received some recognition and who came to Oxford from the LSE. But Freedman died shortly after assuming the chair at Oxford and had no lasting impact on the institute. He was followed by Rodney Needham (1923–), who held the chair from 1976 to 1990. Needham had done some early fieldwork in Borneo among Penan hunters and collectors, and later in Sumba in Indonesia, but his main interests were distinctly theoretical. He was early influenced by Lévi-Strauss, and his whole book *Structure and Sentiment* (Needham 1962) is an extended defense of Lévi-Strauss's position in a debate on the proper framework for analyzing matrilateral cross-cousin marriage that occupied an international circle of scholars at the time. His teaching also inspired young students at Oxford for a while. But due to local factionalism and partisan ruptures, soon after his appointment he chose to withdraw to All Souls College, where he pursued his writing but discontinued any active engagement with his local colleagues. The intellectual environment at Oxford thus seemed, from the outside at least, to have become increasingly fragmented and insular.

The department of anthropology at the LSE had, at the time of Firth's retirement in 1968, several coeval professorial posts, and it has continued to function as a significant center of British social anthropology. Among the colleagues there Maurice Bloch (1939–) has perhaps been the most productive and influential. Bloch did extensive fieldwork in Madagascar and was strongly engaged in the several theoretical phases of Marxism and structuralism. More recently the focus of his research has been to explore the cognitive bases for people's understanding and modeling of their own society. There are also other significant centers of research and teaching in London: The School of Oriental and African Studies, University College, Goldsmiths College, and Brunel University.

In Manchester, Gluckman was succeeded by Emrys Peters, whose work is discussed above. Marilyn Strathern led the department during the period 1985–1993, until she moved to Cambridge. The chair in Manchester then passed to Tim Ingold (1948–), whose research interests can serve aptly to illustrate how far the present generation of British anthropologists have moved the conventional boundaries of the discipline: his major fieldwork was among the Saami of northern Finland, not Africa or Oceania, and his topical interests have been ecology, evolution, and human-animal relations.

Smaller and newer departments have also appeared and have played an influential role. Distinguished among them has been The Queen's University of Belfast. Under the leadership of Ladislav Holy (1933–1997), who had done fieldwork in the Sudan, Belfast in the 1970s became a center for rethinking core theoretical issues on the nature of actions, norms, and representations, stimulating more dynamic approaches to the empirical study of social organization.

Thus, it seems as if everything has changed in the social organization of British anthropology over a few decades. British universities now have between them at least two dozen established departments of anthropology. No more is anthropology an internal conversation among a handful of professional colleagues in the Oxford-Cambridge-London-Manchester circuit. Thematically as well as theoretically, the work of contemporary British anthropologists has gained in diversity, including greater variety in policy engagements, advocacy, and applied work. Programs of anthropological filmmaking, of high quality, further ensure a wide public awareness in Britain of the subject and the discipline. And fieldwork is actively pursued in many new areas outside the former British Empire, in the Mediterranean, South America, Central Asia, and Eastern Europe. These gains have been achieved, one should recognize, in an epoch of marked decline in British universities generally, caused by shrinking economies and stifling regimes of bureaucratic regulation and oversight. Under such circumstances the performance of British social anthropology can be described as a show of strength.

But there is no denying that the work of British social anthropologists no longer commands the attention of international colleagues that it did during the epoch from the publication of *Argonauts* in 1922 and well into the 1960s. What might be the main reasons for this?

Inevitably, a gain in diversity must lead to a loss in distinctiveness. The hegemonic position of the British school in its heyday may not have depended on any striking consensus among its practitioners, but it did depend on the convergence of its members on a shared discourse: an unfolding history of debate, clarification of positions, and mutual engagement with a set of theoretical issues. This is distinctly less true in the field today. With the disappearance of such a shared focus there has been a loss of self-assurance as well as self-sufficiency. New ideas are less endogenously created and sustained: there is a vast flow of ideas from U.S. colleagues and less of the reverse, as well as a continuing influence from French authors—Pierre Bourdieu, Michel Foucault, and others—that does not seem to be matched by an equal attention among them to the work of British anthropologists. A similar trend is also visible in the relations between the disciplines within England: younger anthropologists look more to sociologist Anthony Giddens for theoretical developments than they do to their current anthropology professors. Though the British tradition has, of course, always been open to outside stimuli from a variety of sources, it used to show a greater strength for internalizing such stimuli, reshaping them, and putting them to uses that were dictated by British interests and concerns, and the results of this process would, in turn, feed into the thought of those who had been their source.

While ideas have flowed in, personnel have been leaking out. For more than thirty years there has been a distinct brain drain from Britain to the

United States. This reverses the previous trend, most visible in the 1950s, when many important North American scholars—Elizabeth Colson, Tom Fallers, Paul Bohannan, Laura Bohannan, and others—chose to work for extended periods in England. Since then, the significant movement in the other direction has inevitably reduced the vitality and authority of British anthropology departments.

But perhaps this diagnosis, though not unfounded, rests on a certain misinterpretation. During the sessions in Halle when these reflections on the major national traditions of anthropology were presented, the question was raised of whether we were not now moving toward a single and shared world tradition of anthropology. Perhaps we are not yet, but many of the signs I have summarized indicate that at least the British and the North American traditions are today finally merging. There is this evident flow of ideas from contemporary North American research to Britain, but there are also many important, accumulated achievements of British anthropology embedded in the work of North American colleagues. This modern anglophone anthropology, if such it is, is a much more diverse and embracing discipline than British social anthropology ever was; and with the unequal demographics and economic bases of anthropology in the United States and Britain, it is hardly surprising that it is the British tradition that appears to be assimilated and submerged, despite its strong historical foundations. But as this joint tradition is currently pursued in British departments, the selection of main topics and interests still reflects a certain legacy of the past and, indeed, provides the foundation for the international prominence of some branches of this emerging anglophone world tradition.

The German-Speaking Countries / ANDRE GINGRICH

Ruptures, Schools, and Nontraditions: Reassessing the History of Sociocultural Anthropology in Germany

Prelude and Overture: From Early Travelogues to German Enlightenment

It is a privilege to have this opportunity to discuss some insights and perspectives with regard to the anthropological legacies from the German-speaking countries between roughly the 1780s and the 1980s. This intellectual, academic, and institutional history features dramatic ruptures and transformations as much as it is also characterized by continuities and schools of thought. Sometimes these schools became hegemonic to such an extent that alternatives were marginalized without any chance to develop continuities of their own. In retrospect, quite a few of these former schools represent more a warning as to what is better avoided than a valuable tradition on which to build. I thus use *nontradition* in a double sense—to refer, on the one hand, to dispersed, hidden, and half-forgotten treasures with little continuity and, on the other, to certain schools with a lot of continuity that, however, do not represent any positive tradition today.

I begin with some wider methodological issues concerning how to pursue a historical assessment of German-speaking anthropology. I follow what George Stocking calls a presentist approach in the history of anthropology. This represents a certain contrast to a more historiographic emphasis, which would give as much priority as possible to historical contexts and to historical agents' intentions in these contexts. A presentist approach has a somewhat different purpose. It is much more explicitly rooted in the present debates and future tasks of anthropology, and therefore it examines the past more selectively. This inquiry combines such a presentist emphasis with a critical interest in reassessment. Present debates and future tasks in anthropology require that we do not simply summarize previous and established insights and opinions, but rather that we question those established, previous opinions that today seem to be one-sided: one-sided, that is, from the perspective of those presentist, critical, and internationally oriented positions that we need to strengthen and promote today.

Now, what are the basic implications of such a presentist stand, and what are the consequences of such critical interest for our purpose? Let me outline three such implications of this presentist approach and three consequences of the critical interest of this project.

The first implication is that I will primarily deal with those historical traditions that had consequences for sociocultural anthropology as perceived today in an internationally valid sense. My focus will therefore include some consideration of *Volkskunde*, or folklore studies, which today are part of sociocultural anthropology everywhere else except for the German-speaking regions and some other parts of Central Europe. Simultaneously, however, my focus will consider to a very limited extent philosophical anthropology, physical anthropology, and so forth.

A second presentist implication is rooted in the international, transnational, and global dimensions of today's anthropological discourses and debates. Particular emphasis, therefore, will be given to what is relevant with regard to today's strengths and weaknesses in international anthropology, including the retrieval of certain valuable local traditions that seem to be unduly neglected today. By contrast, less emphasis will be given to lovingly recapitulating those works that perhaps are still held in high esteem locally, but that have little significance for today's international anthropology.

A last presentist implication concerns the linguistic and temporal limits of examining the historical record of anthropology in German. Timewise, the discussion will lead up to 1989 and the fall of the Berlin Wall. With regard to space, I will confine myself to authors who were writing in German for institutions and audiences in what may be considered historically situated forerunners of present-day Germany, Switzerland, and Austria. Also, serious recognition is long overdue for those emigrants and refugees who received some of their initial cultural, linguistic, or academic formation in the German language before becoming important anthropologists elsewhere. I will not consider the much wider realm of all anthropology that was ever written in the German language as an international academic lingua franca of former times. I thus will exclude, for instance, the vast German-language anthropological literature written inside the czarist empire and by Dutch and Scandinavian scholars of former times for elite Russian, Dutch, and Scandinavian audiences.

The first critical consequence of the critical interest of my approach relates to the explicit embracing of the broad set of values that we all share today, notably secular democracy and humanism. From the outset this necessitates precise ideological criticism and careful, distantiated evaluation when dealing with a legacy that is so strongly related to pan-Germanism, colonial military annexations, clerical and nationalist ideologies, and the most aggressive forms of racist crimes.

A second critical consequence is a reassessment: Many, if not most, of the hegemonic traditions of the past, being very well documented in this part of the world, are still held in some esteem locally, though they are relatively ir-relevant internationally. By contrast, some peripheral or subaltern traditions never received any local recognition or, more importantly, never aimed at get-ting any such recognition from empire, church, or the Nazi regime. Yet from an international perspective, some of these subaltern works and traditions are today much more interesting than the traditions that were celebrated locally in their time. This includes some of the subaltern traditions that never gained any significant position in academic institutions. Certainly not everything that was neglected then is interesting now, and not everything that was recog-nized then needs to be completely discarded now. Yet at this time we need to carry out a thorough reassessment in this direction, in contrast to continuing the rituals of ancestral worship that have prevailed far too long and, in fact, did so until very recently.

A last critical consequence is a new consideration of the extremely hierar-chical nature of academic institutions in the German-speaking countries. On the one hand, this implies a somewhat stronger external political contextual-ization of intellectual developments than is perhaps necessary for other tradi-tions in anthropology: these hierarchical academic positions answered to wider political interests much more explicitly than academic positions else-where. On the other hand, this distinctly hierarchical tradition in German-speaking academia, which, of course, is not at all specific to anthropology alone, created an explicit internal emphasis on schools of thought and on intellectual genealogies.

Certainly such a presentist approach and a critical interest in the anthro-pological legacies in German will always require complementary historicist and historiographic efforts, which I do not offer here. I am situated in a transnational and global present, with an intellectual and biographical back-ground that is informed much more by specific Western European and U.S. traditions than by those from local German-speaking contexts. My presentist and critical approach definitely is positioned and selective, and it merely offers to be one among several possible alternatives. At the same time, this approach is presented as a serious alternative with the hope that it will encourage further debate, reflection, and research among two specific audiences: first, the young generation of future sociocultural anthropologists in the German-speaking countries and second, those in international anthropology who may become convinced, as I am already, that in today's global world anthropology is bound to become a polycentric and culturally diverse transnational intellectual project.

The German Enlightenment

In this lecture I assume that there was a German Enlightenment worthy of that name. This is not an unimportant matter; nor is it uncontested. A number of historians of anthropology prefer to follow Norbert Elias in portraying continental Europe's intellectual history along a different line (1969). In Elias's view, France was not only the primary center of the continental European Enlightenment (a position to which I, too, subscribe), but also, together with Scotland, its almost exclusive locus. In that exclusivist perspective, the sociohistorical dimension of the Enlightenment is tied to the concept of civilization, as opposed to the almost exclusively Romantic tradition of culture in the German-speaking countries.

My take on the issue is that this position is too simplistic. The opposition of a rationalist, universalist, and enlightened concept of French civilization to a Romantic, strongly relativist, and inherently nationalist German concept of *Kultur* contains a number of very serious flaws. Not least among them is a potential bias regarding the intellectual superiority of Western Europe in relation to Central and Eastern Europe. Even more importantly, such a simplistic opposition implies complete denial of a second point: the commitment to "civilization" meant a very high priority for the colonial mission. In fact, the universal mission of French "civilization" was to be a colonial one. Elias's simplistic opposition, therefore, is too uncritical of the French legacy of "civilization," and too critical of the German tradition of *Kultur*.

In line with more recent research on eighteenth-century thought, such as that of John Zammito (2002), I therefore argue for a nonexclusivist and nonsimplistic perspective here. There was an unfinished but distinct scholarly Enlightenment in Germany that became one of the great intellectual laboratories for the formation and rise of international anthropology. Inside the German-speaking areas, however, these great beginnings produced only very few local follow-up effects for anthropology. This was the case because in the German-speaking regions the Enlightenment ended before ever becoming politically effective: aristocratic political fragmentation managed to persist, and there was no single German state until 1871. From an international perspective, however, these historical beginnings in German in the eighteenth and early nineteenth centuries continue to serve as an early intellectual referent for the formation of anthropology in the modern era. Reflecting upon the early formation of today's global anthropology is impossible without consideration of German eighteenth- and early-nineteenth-century thought as one of its main sources.

Thus, in contrast to the exclusivist position, I propose to take a more nuanced approach here, pointing out that there was a strong current of intellectual Enlightenment in the German-speaking countries at first, both before and after the French Revolution. For political as much as for intellectual reasons, however, the Enlightenment legacy in German subsequently became confined to narrow limits.

This nuanced general approach allows us to focus on the intellectual tension zone between Immanuel Kant and Johann Gottlieb Herder as one of the very first laboratory spheres for the formation of preacademic, modern anthropology. One may either see Herder as Kant's opponent or perceive Herder's work as complementarily carrying out ideas that Kant, in his own vision of anthropology, had left still untouched. At any rate, it was the tension zone between their works, rather than any single idea of either one of them, that promoted the emergence of modern anthropological thought.

Different approaches to this issue favor different perspectives. For instance, more radical interpretations of both Kant and Herder claim to identify an exclusivist dichotomy between universalism and relativism, similar to the one-sided dichotomy imposed by some upon the French versus the German intellectual interaction. In such a view, Kant would be the universalist and Herder the relativist. By contrast, my understanding is that there are intersections and complementarity as much as opposition and contradiction between the works of the two men. Kant's emphasis on the abstract unity of humankind was confirmed by Herder, who complemented it with the notion of human cultural variations. In a way, Herder's emphasis on observation, experience, and local experiment posed a healthy counterbalance to abstract, deductive theorizing in the Kantian manner (Zammito 2002, 309–47).

The unity of humankind and its cultural variation thus were the central ideas that inspired and informed those major empirical projects that were constitutive of the Enlightenment period. These major projects are best exemplified by two genres of research, pioneering travel reports and early philological studies.

Enlightenment Explorers

The work of the Forsters, that is, father Johann Reinhold Forster and son Georg Forster, usually is considered to be the outstanding empirical contribution from the German language zone to the travel-report side of Enlightenment anthropology. This is underlined by the Forsters' active participation in James Cook's second expedition, as well as by Georg Forster's sympathies with the French Revolution and its echo in the Mainz rebellion (Heintze 1990). After their return from the Cook expedition, father and son took on different academic positions in the German countries. Georg entertained close relations to Göttingen, a leading scholarly center in its time, partly due to the British Hanover ties of its rulers. Although in his writing he pursued the hypothesis of multiple origins of humans, Georg argued for a universalism that simultaneously recognized local differences. Absorbing his reading of Kant and Herder, he thus supported an empirical and descriptive method that was open to the assessment of commonalities and differences among humans. There were no a priori hierarchies among human societies, Georg Forster maintained by criticizing Göttingen scholar Christoph Meiners, who saw Europeans as being on top of a global hierarchy (Heintze 1990). Georg died early while preparing his next trip to India in 1793. His father survived him for four years.

The Forsters' clear, largely unbiased, and rich travel reports, published in English (*A Voyage Round the World*, 1777) and soon thereafter in German, received wide attention in the scholarly circles of Europe. They subsequently influenced generations of travel authors. Moreover, the Forsters' collections of ethnographic objects lay the early foundations of what were to become several anthropology museums in continental Europe, in places ranging from Göttingen to Vienna to Florence. By consequence, a separate ethnographic collection was established in Vienna as part of the Imperial Naturalienkabinett in 1806. Thus for the early formative period of modern anthropology it is difficult to underestimate the Forsters' significance (Enzensberger 1979; Steiner 1977).

In spite of the Forsters' eminent influence, it would be one-sided to lose sight of their important contemporaries or of the precursor traditions on which they built. Justin Stagl, with whose opinions and judgments I usually do not agree, certainly deserves credit for having documented and analyzed the vast tradition of German travelogues that accumulated before the Enlightenment period (Harbsmeier 1995; Stagl 1995). Beginning in the late humanist era of the mid-sixteenth century, this body of literature comprised travel reports from various parts of Europe, as well as from North Africa and Western Asia. It also included books of guidelines for carrying out such trips and for observing and describing travel experiences properly. In addition, several missionary reports, published diaries, and travel accounts in German from Asia and later from the Americas, such as the Jesuits' description of indigenous life in Paraguay, were the theological counterparts of the Enlightenment tradition. Moreover, this body of literature also comprised more or less accurate armchair summary reports and conclusions, including Olfert Dapper's famous seventeenth-century maps of the world. So the Forsters' work was embedded not only in a Zeitgeist, but also in a solid tradition emanating from humanism and the scientific revolutions of the sixteenth and seventeenth centuries.

In addition, the Forsters' work was not unique in its time. A more recent forerunner was Peter Kolb (1719), whose description of Southern Africa and, in particular, of the Khoikhoi became a milestone source for ethnographic accounts of that region (Raum 2001). Thaddäus (Tadeo) Haenke was a native of Bohemia (b. 1761) who authored, during several decades of traveling, excellent descriptions of indigenous lives in the Americas (Montoya 1992). Carsten Niebuhr, a north German in the service of the Danish Crown, is another outstanding, albeit less known, example of these Enlightenment explorer-authors writing in German. His meticulous and sympathetic late-eighteenth-century accounts of several years of scientific travel in the Middle East and South Asia (1969) represent a rich and invaluable source for anthropologists up to this day. The overseas travel reports of Ida Pfeiffer, the first woman writing in this genre, who wrote a few years later, also belong to the late Enlightenment period (Habinger 2003). And last but not least, also belonging to the same Enlightenment genre are the subsequent works of Alexander von Humboldt, who had traveled with Georg Forster along the Rhine—that is, his monumental thirty-volume report on five years of travel (1799–1804) in Southern and Central America, and his less known travelogue on Russia and Siberia. In turn, Humboldt interacted with a number of Romanticist German travelers and explorers, such as Georg Adolf Erman and writer Adalbert von Chamisso, who continued this tradition of German travel reports on Siberia (Schweitzer 2001, 84–102).

Works like those of Haenke, Niebuhr, or by Humboldt were primarily empirical, descriptive, and factual before their authors resorted to any wider theoretical conclusions. (The work of the Forsters was an exception in this regard.) In general, descriptive and nonracist approaches still prevailed in these writings, which stand in marked contrast to what was to come a century later. Furthermore, these authors' reports rarely served any immediate, short-term colonial purposes, though economic interests did play a strong role in their expeditions. But the fact that Germany hardly existed at all in those decades from the late eighteenth to the early nineteenth century, and that these authors thus did not primarily bow to any expansionist colonial ambition, allowed for an empirical Enlightenment spirit to prevail in their works.

In retrospect, this empirical and noncolonialist Enlightenment record deserves explicit emphasis. We have become so used to automatically connecting the rise of anthropology to the rise of European colonialism that we often forget about this additional dimension. Now, however, we see that some of the finest early anthropological writing in German had very little to do with European colonialism. In order to set the record straight, I prefer a more balanced interpretation that places the rise of early modern anthropology in the contested, historical tension sphere between European mercantilism, early missionary and colonial ambitions, and scholarly Enlightenment interests.

Language Studies and First Concepts

Noncolonial, empirical research interests also prevail in the case of the second class of innovations of strong anthropological relevance in the German Enlightenment: the rise of philological studies of non-European languages. To be sure, philological studies of German represented a separate, much stronger tradition of their own. They had expanded in the seventeenth century, leading to the wide distribution of linguistic societies (Fricke 1993) that combined an inner egalitarian structure with an ideology of German language purism and, in fact, of "linguistic patriotism" (Garber 1996, 30). It was out of these earlier contexts that mathematician and philosopher Gottfried Leibnitz had already postulated in the seventeenth century a correlation between the structure of a language and the intellectual achievements of its speakers.

In late Enlightenment, however, Herder's writing also inspired philological studies of non-European languages to an extent. Johann Georg Hamann (1730–1788), one of Herder's teachers and early friends, had come from a philological background. In his prize-winning 1772 essay "On the Origin of

Languages," Herder posited that a culture's spirit was embedded in its language (1772/1966). He combined this view of linguistic diversity, however, with his basic emphasis on the unity of humankind. Hamann then broke with Herder because he thought that Herder remained too close to Enlightenment reasoning (Baudler 1970).

Based, again, on important precursors, Enlightenment philology represented a towering first climax in the compilation, systematization, analysis and translation of major non-German and non-European languages and works, ranging from Chinese, Sanskrit, and Hindi to Persian, Turkish, and Arabic. Among the great language projects of the late Enlightenment period, the rediscovery of Sanskrit soon gained priority (Gardt 1999, 270). Friedrich Schlegel stated in 1808 (in *Über die Sprache und Weisheit der Indier: Ein Beitrag zur Begründung der Alterthumskunde*) that Sanskrit represented an older period than Greek, Latin, German, and Persian, which he saw as its younger derivates (Windisch 1992, 57ff.). By contrast, Schlegel and others claimed that the monosyllabic pattern of Chinese might have prevented any further cultural and mental development (Schlegel 1808, 157). A hierarchy in terms of developmental potential thus was introduced between Indo-Germanic and other languages.

These great philological and textual projects were informed by a more or less explicit distinction between what were considered primitive and illiterate, Oriental and literate, and modern European cultures and languages. That distinction was inherited and reasserted from a much older tradition, but it now became refined to the extent that "Oriental" languages were documented, classified, and contextualized, and always placed in a position superior to that of "primitive" languages. In his *Philosophy of History* (1882–1824/1990), Hegel elaborated such tripartite visions into a paradigm. But contrary to late-nineteenth-century German-language anthropologists, the enlightened philologists loosened up Herder's fateful distinction between "natural peoples" (*Naturvölker*) and "cultural peoples" (*Kulturvölker*) because they clearly recognized Chinese and Arabic texts and authors as representing *Kultur.*

Johann Christoph Adelung (1732–1806) elaborated the notions of *Kultur* and *Kulturgeschichte* ("culture" and "culture history"). While Herder mostly had used the term *Kultur* in the singular form, thereby indicating a general capacity of humanity, Adelung began to use the term more systematically in the plural, *Kulturen,* in order to emphasize difference. As the leading authority for decades on linguistics, but also on "standard German" and "pure German," Adelung laid the foundation for a specific kind of comparative linguistics.

Despite all their limits, most of these philologists' works evidenced a profound respect and admiration of Asian and North African cultures. Barbara Frischmuth referred to one of the greatest in these fields, Friedrich Rückert, when she wrote that one had to be "verrückt wie Rückert," that is, as madly devoted as Rückert, to commit one's whole life to nothing but the study of Asian languages and literature.

Friedrich Rückert (1788–1866), who received his first training in Persian and Arabic under the Austrian Academy of Sciences' first president Joseph von Hammer-Purgstall in Vienna, became one of the great translators and mimetic poets in German (Windisch 1992, 89). He worked with Sanskrit and South Indian languages, Malay, Chinese, and many other languages, though his most outstanding achievements were translations from Persian, notably of the thirteenth-century mystic Jalal al-Din Rumi, and from Arabic, of Imru l-Qais, of the pre-Islamic period. Present-day experts have continued to praise Rückert's unique contribution in these fields (Schimmel 1987).

To my mind, these innovative philological results of Enlightenment and early Romanticist anthropology in German had lasting effects in the form of solid empirical description of ethnographic and cultural variation, as well as the intense mastering of foreign languages. It set standards for a future international anthropology, and in spite of all of its subsequent broken and twisted historical paths, it remains a particular strength of anthropology in German to this day. This is one part of a fragmented record with a potential that could be newly brought into transnational anthropological contexts of the present and from which inspiration can be gained. In these present contexts, solid empirical description and profound submersion into local languages often seem to be neglected.

If these were the key innovative empirical results, the theoretical and conceptual record of the German Enlightenment was much more ambivalent, but no less significant.

First and foremost, a number of authors in recent years, ranging from Han Vermeulen (1995) to Gudrun Bucher (2000) and Peter Schweitzer (2001), have shown that this period saw the first elaboration of the term *ethnography*. The term was associated with Göttingen and the works of historian August Ludwig von Schlözer (1735–1809) in the 1770s. Before becoming a professor in Göttingen, Schlözer had been an assistant in St. Petersburg of Gerhard Friedrich Müller, a scholar in czarist service who was to become one of the great founders of historical and ethnographic research on Siberia. Schlözer's intimate acquaintance with Müller's descriptive and synthesizing reports of Siberia decisively contributed to his own theoretical conceptualization in

Göttingen. In this context, the term *ethnography* originally was elaborated as an analogy to *geography*, together with the German counterparts to both, *Völkerkunde* und *Erdkunde*. The Enlightenment concept still saw *ethnography* and *Völkerkunde* as synonymous terms for one empirically based academic science of the world's cultures, languages, and peoples.

It was therefore only a later development of the nineteenth century that the meaning of *ethnography* became reduced to a descriptive one only and that simultaneously the field of ethnography became opposed to the theoretical field of ethnology. As a related development of the later nineteenth century, *Völkerkunde* also changed its meaning and became the overall concept comprising both ethnography and ethnology. This new, post-Enlightenment understanding of *ethnology* had already been emphasized by Johann Severin Vater. He had posthumously edited and expanded one of Adelung's major works, and he also pursued early linguistic "hierarchical relativism," which had been part of Adelung's and Schlegel's writing (Gardt 1999, 186–93). In turn, Vater and Justin Bertuch became coeditors in 1808 of the first specialized academic journal in these fields, the *Allgemeines Archiv für Ethnologie und Linguistik* ("General Archives for Ethnology and Linguistics").

Although these theoretical and institutional initiatives triggered few local follow-up processes in the German-speaking countries, they were nevertheless indicative of the creative and contradictory early laboratory atmosphere of those decades, and they were of important consequence elsewhere. One local consequence was the effect these conceptualizations had, indirectly, on Alexander von Humboldt's brother: Wilhelm von Humboldt's legacy continues to be praised as the foundation of holistic, interdisciplinary academic life in German. His first elaboration on the institutionalization of academic research, or *Wissenschaften*, initially conceived of philosophical anthropology as one of the fundamental fields for all *Geisteswissenschaften*, or humanities. As Louis Dumont has shown, that initial conception of the humanities was inspired by a certain awareness of cultural, ethnographic, and linguistic diversity in spite of its elitist and state-serving priorities. Yet in the concept as it then managed to secure the Prussian Crown's approval, even such limited emphasis on ethnography and anthropology was discarded for other priorities, those of history and philosophy (Dumont 1994, 82–144; Berg 1990).

At the same time, Wilhelm von Humboldt (1767–1835) further elaborated Adelung's and Schlegel's reasoning on linguistic relativism, most notably in his three-volume treatise on the Kawi language in Java (quoted in Windisch 1992, 82–85). By determining human thought, Wilhelm von Humboldt argued, any specific language constituted a specific "cosmovision" *(Weltan-*

sicht). Consequently it was unavoidable, in Humboldt's view, to assume a general hierarchy of cognitive potentials among languages (e.g., between "inflecting," "agglutinating," and "isolating" languages).

Wilhelm von Humboldt's hierarchical linguistic relativism was to have a certain impact on Franz Boas, and among the works of Boas's students, it would resurface in those of Edward Sapir and, more explicitly but with modifications, in Benjamin Lee Whorf's *Language, Thought, and Reality* (1956).

By the 1830s and with Wilhelm von Humboldt's work, the Herderian tradition came to be elaborated, but also twisted and specified toward an increasingly explicit relativism with a growing emphasis on mind and soul. For Herder, universalism and relativism still held a certain chaotic and contradictory balance with each other. For Wilhelm von Humboldt, however, the universalist dimension came to be much more limited and downgraded, whereas Humboldt's relativism now entailed an inner necessity, a mentalist focus, and an explicit hierarchy among languages and cultures.

Limited Consequences

This leads us to the limited consequences of Enlightenment anthropology in German. A key reason for the demise of intellectual and empirical Enlightenment projects in anthropology can be identified in political contexts and conditions. They prevented the development of any bourgeois revolution following the French model, instead stabilizing and reasserting aristocratic rule and political fragmentation. On the intellectual side these factors imposed strong limits on any further development of explicit secularization and instead strengthened pietism in the north and Catholic restoration in the south. This conservative aspect was further enhanced when after the Napoleonic Wars the so-called Holy alliance of the Metternich years crushed all local attempts at political emancipation. Taken together, these and other factors twisted the demise of Enlightenment anthropology in German into an ideological turn toward what I call a twofold introspection in the first half of the nineteenth century: first, an introspective priority for German rather than non-German topics, increasingly combined with, second, an introspective priority for spirit and soul rather than practices and facts.

Within this turn toward a twofold introspection, Herder's work increasingly became a source of inspiration for Romantic speculation and for early nationalism in Germany. Yet we need to be careful not to jump too hastily to conclusions with regard to Herder. It is true that his work subsequently served as legitimizing material for all kinds of German nationalists. In the decades to come, these would range from Romantic nationalists of the political left and right in the early nineteenth century to the most murderous nationalists of the right in the first half of the twentieth century in Germany. Herder's work, however, is not directly responsible for all the crimes committed in his name—as little responsible as, say, Karl Marx's work is for crimes committed in his. In fact, Herder's work is best understood in an ambivalent transitional context between the late Enlightenment and the early Romantic period.

To be sure, Herder's work left a contradictory legacy for anthropology both locally and internationally. His vision of humanity as existing in unity through diversity, *"in Einheit durch Vielfalt,"* however, did have a universalist dimension to it that was closer to Kant than staunch relativists and nationalists would have it. From the outset it was within this vision of unity through diversity that Herder's concept of *Kultur* was embedded. It emphasized language, customs, and mentalities in a particularistic manner, but it did not include any consideration of race or other allegedly eternal, timeless properties. In addition, Herder's concept of *Kultur* emphasized observation and experience. All these priorities later helped to inspire the rise of folklore studies, or *Volkskunde,* and, of course, of some early German anthropologists of the nineteenth century, such as TheodorWaitz and later the young Boas.

Moreover, Herder's emphasis on a people's soul, derived from his pietistic family background, strongly inspired the twofold introspection, together with his ethnocentric distinction between the German and nearby European *Kulturvölker* and most other *Naturvölker.* Later ideologists and anthropologists selected and upgraded these aspects from his work and placed the Germans on top of a hierarchy of very few *Kulturvölker,* with all so-called *Naturvölker* below them. If, however, Herder's work is assessed in its own time and, in particular, in relation to Kant, with whom he studied in Königsberg, it not only includes opposition to and contradiction of Kant, but also, at the very least, encompasses many elements that carry out some of the Kantian legacy, are complementary to it, or transcend it. As Zammito has shown (2002, 347–52), Herder explicitly attempted in the sixth book of his *Ideen zur Philosophie der Geschichte der Menschheit* (1784–1791) to combine an early evolutionist view of human history with the relativist practice of assessing each culture in its own right (see also Berg 1990, 65–66). This is remarkable—not because of Herder's early evolutionism (which looked down on some "primitive" cultures while admiring others as "noble," as was common then), but because Herder's universalist evolutionism imposed limits upon his relativism. Because it was based on universalist principles, Herder's relativism was prevented from reaching absolute or strong dimensions.

By definition, however, it is a strong relativism, in one or the other version, that is inherent to nationalism. There is no teleological necessity evident, therefore, that would lead from Herder directly to the ideologists of later nationalism. It seems that this ground was prepared by others, often by one-sided reference to Herder—who thus became instrumentalized as a legitimizing force for other purposes.

Herder's work and contradictory impact represent a challenging enigma and thus certainly deserve further consideration in their own right. It is still possible that future research might come to the conclusion that Herder's work involved a weak, or soft relativism, rather than the strong ideological version propagated by later nationalists. In that case, such a weak notion of an empirically based cultural relativism would add up to the more lasting achievements of late Enlightenment anthropology in German: together, that is, with the great explorers' travelogues, profound Asian language studies, and the elaboration of the first concepts of ethnography.

At any rate, the more devastating effects on German anthropology for the next few decades were emanating not directly from Herder's legacy but, to my mind, from the work of some contemporaries of his, who were much more explicit anti-Kantians than Herder himself. Philosopher Christoph Meiners, for instance, drafted his 1785 *Grundriß der Geschichte der Menschheit* ("Foundations of mankind's history") by treating humans' physical diversity as directly linked to their social characteristics. Moreover, he was an early advocate of the theory that intermarriage between members of different races would lead to degeneration. Meiners conceived of geographically determined cultural circles in ways that would later on inspire Friedrich Ratzel and Fritz Graebner, the founding fathers of diffusionism and culture circle theory. Forster already had criticized Meiners's antiuniversalist stand, which gave priority first to Germans and next to other Europeans. In Meiners's view, this was related to their distinct racial origins (Lowie 1937, 10–11). On the other hand, Meiners's contemporary J. J. Blumenbach in Göttingen was an early physical anthropologist who began measuring humans and searching for typical racial examples. In view of this empirical effort, his work may be regarded as a forerunner to that of the more liberal phase of physical anthropology in late-nineteenth-century Germany under Rudolf Virchow. In theoretical terms, however, Blumenbach emphasized multiple origins of the human race and hierarchical linguistic relativism.

As the first half of the nineteenth century approached, a substantially weakened Enlightenment legacy was already marginalized. Under the impact of political and religious restoration, philosophy lost its leading academic role, to history in the humanities *(Geisteswissenschaften)* and to biology in the natural sciences. A weak and dispersed Enlightenment legacy for anthropology in German merely lingered on: in some museum collections, in an emphasis on the meticulous study of foreign languages, and in some Enlightenment works that became classics. The twofold introspection eventually gained preeminence, promoting historicist folklore studies with nationalist leanings inside the German-speaking countries and, for non-Germans, encouraging a tendency to postulate historical or biological inferiority.

In German, Enlightenment anthropology thus became a nontradition with limited consequences. Nonetheless, limited consequences are not the same thing as no consequences at all.

2

From the Nationalist Birth of *Volkskunde* to the Establishment of Academic Diffusionism: Branching Off from the International Mainstream

This lecture covers roughly the period from the 1840s to the turn of the century some sixty years later. Here I will deal with three diverse but interrelated topics: first, the separate, broadly rooted establishment of folklore studies, or *Volkskunde,* inside and outside academia, which was paralleled by the emergence of specialized precursors to academic anthropology; second, the rise of the socialist theory of Marx and Engels in Germany and its explicit consideration of anthropological topics; and third, against this background, the first two phases of anthropology's formal academic establishment, which in one way or the other are both linked to the name of Adolf Bastian.

The Emergence of Folklore Studies and of Anthropology's Academic Forerunners

The political period between the failed, 1848 "large" pan-Germanic revolution and the 1871 "small" Prussian unification of Germany was the wider context for the separate emergence of *Volkskunde,* or folklore studies—separate, that is, from what became *Völkerkunde,* or ethnology/ethnography. In a sense, this was a logical continuation of the earlier turn toward a "twofold introspection," which by the 1830s had received new energy from philosophical and artistic Romanticism and from political nationalism. Before and for some time after the failed 1848 revolution, the twin currents of Romanticism and nationalism were broad, heterogeneous movements that comprised intellectuals as much as workers and businesspeople; they were movements with both left and right wings. Nationalism and Romanticism both favored a new focus on rural homelands. Romanticism embraced the domestic countryside because of its search for a retreat into the aesthetics of idyllic harmony. In turn, these new aesthetic values had a standardizing impact upon the new political movements of nationalism. As Hannah Arendt pointed out, the ideal life in the Romantic imaginary of nationalism in the German-speaking countries, as much as in most of Central and Northern Europe, was perceived as a return to a nation's alleged rural roots (Arendt 1958).

These conditions led to the broad and popular emergence of amateur and academic rural folklore studies. After the 1848 disaster of the revolution, this interest in folklore became even more widespread as a seemingly politically innocent endeavor. The great fairy tale collections and codifications by the Grimm brothers are an early case in point, and so are a number of related collections of proverbs, jokes, riddles, legends, and the like. Especially relevant as an early source was Jakob Grimm's language and vernacular dialect research, out of which originated the historical research of narratives (*historische Erzählforschung*) as one component in the formation of folklore studies, together with statistics and Wilhelm Heinrich Riehl's documentary practices as additional components (Köstlin 2002, 393, 387).

In a related development, folklore museums of what was perceived as traditional material culture were first set up, by local intellectual amateurs as much as by aristocratic rulers such as Erzherzog Johann of Habsburg in Styria. Teachers, clerics, and composers began to collect and codify folk songs, a preoccupation that soon entered the academic establishment of musicology as well. Likewise, the study of verbal testimonials of folklore became part of the academic establishment of German literature studies and also, to an extent, of history, which had gradually gained preeminence in German humanities, or *Geisteswissenschaften*. Particularly after Leopold von Ranke established the historiographic and historicist school of writing history, this field superseded philosophy to become the dominant force in the *Geisteswissenschaften* throughout the nineteenth century and thereafter (Zimmermann 2001, 38–61).

After the failed revolution and once Friedrich Wilhelm IV had become king of Prussia and Francis Joseph emperor of Austria, folklore studies thus became an integral part of German historicism—not as a separate field yet, but dispersed among various disciplines under historicist hegemony. Up to this day, *Volkskunde* (or European ethnology, as this academic discipline renamed itself recently) has remained strongly attached to historical methods and to the academic field of history. It will continue to be a certain strength as much as a substantial obstacle if, in the future, serious consideration is to be given to the integration of former *Volkskunde* and former *Völkerkunde* into one comprehensive field, that is, the German-language branch of international sociocultural anthropology.

In retrospect, the folklore studies of the formative historicist period in the German heartlands, inspired by Romanticism and overt or covert nationalism, appear somewhat less interesting than those folklore studies that were carried out in the southern and southeastern periphery of the German language zone, that is, in Switzerland and in the Habsburg empire. By contrast to what was to become Germany, these two political entities were quite diverse linguistically, religiously, and culturally. In the German heartlands both before and after the 1871 unification, nationalism increasingly was instrumentalized as a force serving dominant Prussian interests. By contrast, before and after 1848 folklore studies in Switzerland and the Habsburg empire had to deal with cultural diversity as a given. In the German-speaking parts of Switzerland and the Habsburg lands, nationalism of any kind was generally dealt with as a subversive, secessionist danger. This promoted the popular and academic emergence of a less nationalist and more interculturally oriented tradition of folklore studies in these southern and southeastern areas of the German language zone. In a way, they represented the most anthropological tradition of their time in folklore studies (Köstlin 2002, 379, 384).

A number of influential works from other fields emerged in these first phases of historicist academic dominance in the German-speaking countries. These were works by a few historians of religion and law and philosophers of history, none of whom followed the nationalist mainstream. On the contrary, they turned to wider, comparative issues with a historian's interest that still echoed some of the Enlightenment interest in the stages of humanity's development while already absorbing the growing number of insights into the world's cultural diversity. This was already foreshadowing in rich ways the international rise of evolutionism.

Three armchair scholars, Johann Jakob Bachofen, Gustav Klemm, and Theodor Waitz, represent this phase of advanced precursors to academic anthropology, inside the German language zone as much as internationally.

Das Mutterrecht ("Maternal law," 1861), by Swiss historian of law and antiquity Bachofen, certainly is the most widely known work from this group of three authors. Bachofen wanted to prove that humanity had gone through an earlier stage of "gynaecocracy," and for this he used a variety of pre-Hellenic and other sources that, in Bachofen's interpretation, contradicted theories of male dominance. His research questions and methods led Bachofen to distinguish in human development a "chthonic early period" of promiscuity from a subsequent period of "lunar motherhood" and matrilineal kinship, which was followed by patriarchy as the most recent stage.

Bachofen was a deeply religious, Romanticist evolutionist whose theses were profoundly criticized by scholars of antiquity whereas others with an interest in anthropology discussed some of his ideas with respect: Lewis Henry Morgan entertained a lengthy correspondence with Bachofen and quoted him in his *Ancient Society* (1877) as a source supporting his own ideas. Consequently, Friedrich Engels and Heinrich Cunow later included Bachofen in their own expression of appreciation of Morgan's work for advancing their materialist German evolutionism. In turn, their later opponents, such as culture circle theorist P. W. Schmidt, discussed Bachofen's work as well. Much later still, early feminist anthropology would continue to refer to his work. Although the once popular thesis of an early stage of matriarchy has long become obsolete, Bachofen can still be seen as a founding spirit of the grand evolutionist debates that intrinsically connected the study of humanity's history with that of the development of gender relations (Schröter 2001, 8–10; Heinrichs 1975).

Gustav Klemm, a librarian trained in history and philosophy, was a significant collector of ethnographic objects. In the first volume of his *Allgemeine Cultur-Geschichte der Menschheit* ("General culture history of humanity," 10 vols., 1843–1852;) he laid out the first visionary plan of systematic ethnographic collecting and museum display. This field soon would gain particular significance in Germany; in fact, Klemm's own collection became the basis of Germany's second largest ethnographic museum, in Leipzig. His interest in material objects was part of an emphasis on economic and material factors in conceptualizing cultural history, which he saw as a unified process passing through the three stages of savagery, tameness, and freedom. By reference to the legacy of Voltaire, Immanuel Kant, and Johann Gottlieb Herder, and by his criticism of Christoph Meiners, Klemm systematically included non-European cultures into his culture history. For contemporary German mainstream historians, this made Klemm even more of an outsider, since they regarded nonliterate peoples as not constituting part of history. The huge amount of ethnographic information in Klemm's work, however, led Edward Burnett Tylor in Britain, as the world's first holder of an academic anthropology chair, to use and quote it, and to characterize it as an "invaluable collection of facts" (Tylor 1865). Moreover, Klemm's holistic perception of culture had a direct influence upon Tylor's classic 1871 definition of the term, and Marx would use Klemm's emphasis on material conditions and refer to it as confirming his own views (Rödiger 2001, 188–92).

In his *History of Ethnological Theory* (1937), Robert Lowie portrayed Klemm and Waitz as two of three important pioneers who paved the way for the academic international anthropology of Lowie's times. He saw Klemm's work as a precursor to Tylor's and Morgan's evolutionism, and he portrayed Waitz's work with some justification as a forerunner to Franz Boas's humanist relativism and his own. (Lowie's choice of Meiners as the third pioneer of anthropology can only be explained with reference to the dominance of diffusionist and racist theories in the 1930s in Germany and Austria.)

The issue of racial differences and origins was one important divide between Klemm and Waitz. Waitz criticized the racist and supremacist worldview of his French contemporary Arthur de Gobineau (a founding father of twentieth-century racism), and he also rejected Klemm's rather curious and harmless version of the theory of phylogenetic origins. Waitz thus became the author to establish the monogenetic theory of a unified descent of races in German anthropology, a position on which Rudolph Virchow, Bastian, and Boas would be able to build soon thereafter. In addition, Waitz persuasively argued that humans' outward appearances and bodily differences could vary according to a plethora of factors, such as climate, food, descent, or marriage. Culture, therefore, was to be conceived not in terms of race, but rather in terms of history. In his *Anthropologie der Naturvölker* (6 volumes, 1859–1872, partly published posthumously by G. Gerland), Waitz conceptualized this as a process of civilization, an argument that he substantiated with an exemplary wealth of well-documented cases drawn from earlier travelers' reports, while criticizing colonialism and slavery as inhuman and detrimental to the process. Because he was an academic pedagogue as much as a philosopher, it was logical for Waitz to conceptualize the historical process of civilization not according to Klemm's emphasis on material conditions, but in terms of mental variety and progress.

During the last years of Waitz's life, the first volume of his magnum opus was selected by the London Anthropological Society as an outstanding work from the Continent, and it appeared in translation in Britain as *Introduction into Anthropology* (Waitz 1863)—in time to further convince Tylor that racial differences were not a decisive factor in sociocultural variation. Other evolutionists were less appreciative of Waitz's work. Among the Boas school, however, Waitz's first volume was recognized "as a worthy forerunner of Boas's 'The Mind of Primitive Man,' which closely parallels its argument" (Lowie 1937, 17), and it continued to be seen as a first great anthropological work among subsequent generations of Boasians, such as Ruth Benedict (Streck 2001a, 503–8).

It should thus be noted that the profound post-Enlightenment turn from philosophical to historicist paradigms, that is, from Hegel to Ranke, had a creative side effect. Apart from its main impact upon introspective folklore in the German academic heartlands, it also had some other, more creative implications for anthropological thought in its combination with early evolutionary thinking on the academic periphery. Hans Jürgen Hildebrandt, who is the key expert in this field, has shown that early evolutionary thinking in German anthropology-related scholarship primarily dealt with family, law, and myths and that it simultaneously reached out for anthropology. However, Hildebrandt contends, it remained too weak, and thus it could be kept out from the formation of early academic anthropology (Hildebrandt 1983).

Anthropological Dimensions in the Works of Marx and Engels

One will hardly find any reference to Marx and Engels at all in academic German anthropological books of the second half of the nineteenth century. Yet no matter how critical one may consider the work of Marx and Engels today, a presentist approach to anthropology in German cannot deny the profound and profoundly ambivalent impact of their work on our field in the decades subsequent to its completion. This ranged from the impact of their wider social theory to that of their narrower interests in core topics of anthropological concern. The effects of their work would later range from encouragement for the pursuit of critical research questions in new ways to quite the opposite, namely the legitimization of dictatorial state terror in the twentieth century.

From the presentist perspective of international anthropology, it might be much more useful and reasonable to discuss in additional detail the other great founders of social theory and sociology in German—such as Ferdinand Tönnies, Max Weber, Georg Simmel, and Sigmund Freud, and later Theodor Adorno, Max Horkheimer, and Walter Benjamin. Yet at this point historical accuracy gains methodological priority over presentist interests: the classic authors of German sociology began to attain influence among anthropologists in the German language zone only at a very late point. With the exception of some of the German functionalists of the Nazi era, it took German-speaking anthropologists until 1968 and later to engage with sociology. Before that, mainstream anthropologists in German would hardly ever have quoted any of these major sociologists.

In contrast to the efforts of Tönnies, Weber, Simmel, Adorno, and Benjamin, Marx's work had some influence on anthropology in German at a much earlier point. On the one hand, this influence was exerted in indirect ways upon mainstream anthropologists, who sometimes polemicized against Marxism for political reasons and defended their own views by contrasting them to it. On the other hand, an early subaltern sequence of materialist and Marxist anthropologists emerged inside the German-speaking countries even before the Nazi period. After 1945 some aspects of Marxism became codified in Communist East Germany, and it shaped that country's anthropology. These are the main reasons that in the present text I give priority to the discussion of Marx over that of the other founders of social theory and sociology.

It is now common knowledge that the failure of the 1848 revolution and its mixed national and sociopolitical agenda, plus the inability of post-Enlightenment Hegelianism to cope intellectually with this development, led Marx and Engels to search for a profound alternative, a way out of the impasse between aristocratic rule and bourgeois nationalism. Perceiving themselves as radical renewers of the German Enlightenment's best legacy, and inspired by French social theory and British political economy, they set out to develop what they began to call historical and dialectical materialism. Though the German Enlightenment had been prenational and therefore not yet transnational, it had certainly embodied wider regional influences. By contrast, this post-1848, antinationalist turn by Marx and Engels was a truly transnational moment in German intellectual development. After Marx emigrated to England, and particularly after he became acquainted with Darwin's work when it was published, the historical materialism of Marx and Engels became increasingly evolutionist in orientation. They thus left behind their earlier adherence to the tripartite classification of history as primitive, Oriental, and modern, as inherited from Hegelianism and philology, and definitively set out to embrace the most advanced scholarly knowledge of their time.

For our present purposes, it will suffice to point out the narrower concerns of Marx and Engels for core topics in sociocultural anthropology, core concerns that display a surprising continuity throughout their work. They initially maintained a variety of Hegelian visions about non-European cultures, imbued with notions about stagnation and backwardness for earlier stages. This changed to a considerable extent with Marx's article series on British colonial rule in India, in which he contrasted India's historicity and the subcontinent's creative potential for alternative development with the destructive reality of its colonial subordination. On this basis a number of studies preceding *Das Kapital* and some references in *Kapital*'s three (or four) volumes display a certain interest from Marx's side. While he primarily focused on capitalism and colonialism, he was also interested in the inner logic of certain precolonial agrarian empires of Asia in their own right, as differentiated from Mediterranean antiquity. Marx thus strove to combine a basically universalist social theory with a more particular classification of various types of society in history. In his late years Marx turned again to anthropological topics, now inspired by Darwinian evolutionism: in his reading of Morgan's *Ancient Society* and also in his interpretation of a number of other works such as those of Maxim Kowalewski (Harstick 1977).

Two points are evident from Marx's notebooks as published by Lawrence Krader: first, Engels omitted important insights when he used Marx's notebooks for his *Origin of the Family* (1891 / 1972) after Marx's death, and second, Marx's notebooks display a now refined and more elaborated interest in his earlier project of combining universal history with diverse, particular trajectories of social formations—all of which was spelled out more explicitly in the new evolutionist terms of the time (Krader 1976). To my mind, it is a credit to Marx and his openness and curiosity, rather than a strike against him, that he left this project open and unfinished. In its last form the project included reference to *Kultur* as a set of customs and concepts; it displayed not one but various trajectories of particular evolutionary directions of development within a universalist frame; and it included some recognition of variation in family and kinship forms and, of course, a systematic recognition of capitalist colonialism as a global force.

That was by no means a small achievement by the exiled Jewish revolutionary if compared, for instance, to the unsystematic and opaque work of Marx's contemporary Bastian, the founder of official academic anthropology in Germany's capital, Berlin. The impact of this side in Marx's work upon anthropology in German was to become quite heterogeneous in the twentieth century, and to an unduly large extent, it would be conveyed first of all through Engels's *Origin of the Family, Private Property, and the State.* Engels wrote that work for a popular audience of German workers and party officials, and therefore he had to simplify it. Yet it offered little more but a popularized version of Morgan's work, a few selected quotes from Marx's notebooks, and some of Engels's own ideas about the future dissolution of the family that would later become important for feminism and feminist anthropology.

Regardless of its enormous influence among organized Socialist Party members, first in the German-speaking countries and then internationally, Engels's *Origin of the Family* had a number of serious flaws. In it Engels proposed a far more unilineal evolutionary perspective than was inherent in Morgan's work and Marx's interpretations. Consequently he presented European capitalism as the hierarchical evolutionary climax insofar as he saw it as the necessary precondition to socialism (Gingrich 1999, 245–246; Godelier 1977). In addition to a much stronger ethnocentric bias than was evident in Morgan's and Marx's writing, in *Origin of the Family* Engels expressed some sympathy for the concept of natural selection (Auslese) through the evolution of kinship and family. Considering these populist tendencies and simplifications, I regard the overall impact of the work to be largely a negative one in intellectual life and for anthropology in German. On the other hand, some works that recorded Marx's later anthropological insights, starting from *Grundrisse* (1953) and ending with his ethnological notebooks, became available to a wider academic public only gradually, beginning in the late 1930s, often after having been hidden away for decades in Stalin's archives. As a result, the actual intellectual impact of the narrow portion of the work of Marx and Engels that did see early publication differed widely from the critical potential of Marx's overall anthropological notes and considerations.

The Beginnings of Academic Anthropology

On the formal and institutional level, the academic establishment of *Völkerkunde* went hand in hand with the formation of imperial Germany, an empire that was founded on the basis of decisive external Prussian victories against Austro-Hungary in 1866 and against France in 1871 as an internal unification process from above. During the very same years, the central formal moves for the institutionalization of *Völkerkunde* took place. In 1867, the Berlin Society for Anthropology, Ethnology, and Prehistory was founded, together with its journal, the *Zeitschrift für Ethnologie*, which to this day is one of the leading journals of the field in German. Both preceded the installation of the Royal Museum für Völkerkunde in Berlin in 1873. The museum's first director was Bastian, a trained physician who had worked for years as a ship's doctor. He was the first German to pass the habilitation (*venia docendi*) for *Völkerkunde*, in 1869. Very clearly, then, right from its late beginnings as the newcomer in European capitalist competition and colonial rivalry, imperial Germany, supported by its academic professionals, sought to establish an anthropology at its service on both central and regional levels (Penny 2002, 17–49, 163–214; Zimmermann 2001, 201–16).

Initially this new empire did not have any colonies overseas. Its great ambition for such colonies, however, was soon realized in Africa after the 1884 Berlin conference, and in Melanesia and some Chinese towns with German colonial acquisitions there (Zitelmann 1999). Meanwhile, the Habsburg empire's economic weakness and territorial coherence inside Europe did not allow for any other colonies overseas. An anthropological society had been founded in 1870–1871 in Vienna, and other precursor institutions to anthropology and folklore museums also emerged, not only in Vienna, Prague, and Budapest, but also in Ljubljana, Trieste, Krakow and Bratislava. A separate academic *Völkerkunde* committed to the study of remote cultures had not yet been formally established in the Habsburg empire, however. Instead, culturally diversified folklore studies continued to dominate, with some limited nationalist leanings in the German-speaking parts of the Habsburg empire and somewhat more explicit nationalism in that empire's other parts (Köstlin 2002).

Before and during Germany's colonial expansion, great exotic spectacles, or *Völkerschauen* (literally: "shows or exhibitions of peoples") were fashionable. Asian, African, and native American persons, often in sensational settings, were publicly displayed to German and Austrian audiences. These *Völkerschauen* had some cosmopolitan and liberal dimensions, inasmuch as they evoked and manipulated public curiosity about non-European cultures, and they sometimes enhanced an atmosphere of awareness of the world outside. Yet side by side with that, these spectacles also had the more important potential to stimulate support for belief in German superiority and for racism, and to mobilize support for imperialist and colonial ambitions. After the Berlin museum's establishment, German anthropologists actively cooperated with these *Völkerschauen*, most notably among them Bastian's close museum collaborator Felix von Luschan from Lower Austria (Penny 2002; Zimmermann 2001).

Intellectually and academically, three interrelated developments among German scholars were further promoting the formal and institutional establishment of sociocultural *Völkerkunde:* growing museum collections, recent book successes, and new travelers' reports. First, royal aristocratic and private collections of ethnographic items had reached such significant dimensions that leading circles of businesspeople and officials in many cities of the German language zone felt the urgent need to systematically reorganize them and make them public, a process that was facilitated by new concepts such as Klemm's focus on material conditions. The commercial and industrial Swiss center of Basel already had taken the lead in 1849, establishing the first anthropology museum in the German language zone, which to this day is one of the best. Eventually decisive private and public initiatives followed elsewhere: in Munich (1868), Leipzig (1869), Berlin (1873), Vienna (1876, as a natural history museum's department), and Hamburg (1878; Penny 2002, 163–214).

Among these, the museum in Germany's new capital, Berlin, soon was not only the largest in the German language zone: until the 1930s, it would be considered the largest ethnographic museum in the world.

Secondly, publications of works by nonanthropological armchair scholars like Bachofen, Klemm, and Waitz had received some attention and recognition, while at the same time these very general theories also stimulated a renewed interest in more concrete evidence. This, in turn, strengthened the conviction that the systematic study of human diversity should be taken over by professionals who were specialists.

Third, while Klemm and Waitz had based their armchair works on earlier travel reports, a creative new generation of German academic field experts already had begun their work: Heinrich Barth, a trained philologist and geographer from Hamburg, spent more than five years with British support in North and West Africa. His report was published in five volumes in 1857–1858. It became an invaluable, detailed source of ethnographic material and continues to be to this day. Barth's work was based on a splendid elaboration of the Enlightenment legacy of careful description and mastery of local languages: he spoke Arabic, Tuareg (Tamazight), Haussa, and several other languages. Moreover, his reports and his drawings focused on people's everyday routines, and they were based on intimate observation and careful dialogue wherever possible (Förster 2001). Barth thus became the widely respected founding figure of German research on Africa *(Deutsche Afrika-Forschung)*, which would continue to involve German anthropologists of very different directions throughout the twentieth century. Maybe even more importantly, because of his empirical methods and his writing, Barth can be seen as a very serious first forerunner to ethnographic fieldwork in Germany (Förster 2001).

Gustav Nachtigal, on the other hand, was a medical doctor whose three volumes of travel reports on North and West Africa (1879–1889) contained less ethnographic material. His strong involvement with the Prussian authorities and his support for a Prussian colonial engagement in Africa (albeit based on his humanitarian motives) made him an influential but less interesting intellectual figure within a wider spectrum of scholarship related to Prussia's growing imperial ambitions (Braukämper 2001).

The two central actors of this first phase of academic anthropology in German were Bastian, for *Völkerkunde,* and physical anthropologist Virchow. Both were political liberals, both had received their first academic training in medicine and the natural sciences, and both were committed to an empiricist positivism of a nonevolutionary kind that followed the model of the natural sciences. The meaning of *Völkerkunde* now comprised a theoretical ethnology that classified and generalized the results of a strictly descriptive ethnography (Buchheit and Köpping 2001, 19–25). It seems that the reasons for the antievolutionist orientation of German anthropology, so closely connected to state and crown, were distributed among three factors: Protestant pietism tended to reject an anticreationist theory of the origin of species and of humanity; Prussian nationalism displayed deep skepticism toward a new theory from rival Britain; and imperial hegemony provoked profound distrust of a theory that largely inspired Marx and Engels, the leading thinkers of the German labor movement, soon to be the largest and best organized in the world.

Anthropology under Bastian's and Virchow's guidance thus was anti-Darwinian, but it postulated the unity of humans in an encyclopedic, empiricist manner. In addition, the museum's establishment brought to perfection a deep split that has characterized anthropology in German ever since: a historicist folklore research examined the researcher's own culture, that is, German-speaking local cultures, whereas *Völkerkunde* researched other cultures. In the new colonial context, the natural science model for *Völkerkunde* led to a continued revitalization of Herder's notion of *Naturvölker*, or natural peoples. In fact, most authors favoring a tripartite model of history had already helped to maintain it: for the antievolutionist Bastian, exotic peoples had little or no culture and no history, and thus they could reveal the true nature of humans.

Within this frame, Virchow represented *Anthropologie*, which was the term for physical anthropology. Although he certainly was not an explicit racist himself, Virchow orchestrated the first large methodological debates that sympathetically reassessed early precursors such as J. Blumenbach and, worse, Christoph Meiners. Virchow also directed the first huge research projects in race studies of imperial Germany. Most important among them were the measurement debates in craniology and the systematic, countrywide measurement of millions of school children, the *Schulstatistik* of the 1870s, which resulted in the constructed, ideological identification of a long-headed, northern blond type representing an allegedly pure German race, and a short-headed, southern brown German type. By 1876 Virchow had concluded that according to relevant, separately collected data, German Jews represented "a quite respectable contrast to real Teutons" (Zimmermann 2001, 135–46).

Politically Virchow never argued that race differences implied differentials in behavior, and he never pledged support for racist practices. Of course, this raises questions of interpretation. Proponents of a teleological, or strong relativist, argument on the history of physical anthropology in Germany might be tempted to contend that from Blumenbach to Virchow German scholars in one way or the other already were preparing the Holocaust. If the very premises of such an argument are met with some skepticism, however, then Virchow has to be assessed as a contradictory figure rather than as a tool of his culture. According to the latter perspective, Virchow certainly gave in to the rising mood of anti-Semitism and racism in Germany when he singled out data on Jews from his *Schulstatistik,* for instance, and when he gave the authority of his name to debates and research by others in such directions. In the long run, these debates and projects helped to give racism in Germany a completely new, academic legitimacy. They created an established acceptance on which the German racism of the first half of the twentieth century could then build with its own schemes and projects, and with increasingly murderous ambition.

From a nonteleological perspective, however, Virchow was not an intentional precursor of subsequent perpetrators of racist crimes in Germany, but a political opportunist who absorbed whatever he thought served the promotion of his field and his own status in it. In this limited sense, both Virchow and Bastian were part of an academic generation that combined liberal democratic ideals with their own orientation toward career and status. The "overwhelming majority of German ethnologists and anthropologists were liberal champions of cultural pluralism during the imperial period" (Penny and Bunzl 2003, 2).

It was only toward the turn of the century that things changed considerably in physical anthropology. In an article in one of George Stocking's important collections on the history of anthropology, Benoit Massin (1996, 80) provides sufficient evidence to show that "the teaching of racial anthropology began in the later nineteenth century, while race hygiene (a distinct discipline) began to be taught in the first decade of the twentieth. In response to 'external' political agendas, there was a break in the liberal-humanitarian tradition of German [physical] anthropology at the turn of the century, and . . . this influenced the 'internal' development of the discipline." This perspective has two advantages. First, it allows us to better situate the key racists among German physical anthropologists of the next generations—such as Eugen Fischer, Egon von Eickstedt, and Otto Reche—in appropriate contexts that had less to do with Virchow than with the influence, after crisis, of Ernst Haeckel's Darwinianism, Mendelism, and biometry (Massin 1996, 122–24). Second, such a balanced assessment of Virchow's contradictory role also is helpful for understanding the kind of influence from German physical anthropology Boas would take with him to the United States for, after all, nonracist and antiracist purposes: before his emigration to the United States, Boas worked with Virchow and Bastian for a while at the Berlin museum.

Virchow's close associate Bastian and academic *Völkerkunde* from the outset were thus collaborating to a certain extent in this academic elaboration of Virchow's physical anthropology in Germany. Virchow and Bastian shared the monogenetic paradigm of the unity of humankind introduced by Waitz. On that basis, Bastian primarily pursued his own agenda in *Völkerkunde* proper. Klaus Peter Köpping is among those who have outlined Bastian's vast interests, ranging from detailed individual case studies to wide comparisons, from sharp observation to superficial speculation (Köpping 1995, 75–91). All of this was deeply hidden in Bastian's notoriously unsystematic and incoherent style of writing, particularly so in his late works, whereas some of his earlier ethnographic writing was more lucid, as Lowie (1937, 34) observed. Bastian owed his emphasis on description, local terminology, and, to an extent, analogy first of all to Alexander and Wilhelm von Humboldt and to August Comte, but it also reflected respect for the philological tradition. That legacy of the late Enlightenment and of positivism would be maintained and elaborated by Boas (Bunzl 1996, 17–78) and by that group of Bastian's younger German associates whom I call moderate positivists.

Bastian never clearly elaborated his own theoretical concepts, which limited their potential, yet buried inside his volumes and articles was his key concept of what he called elementary thoughts, or *Elementargedanken*, a concept that was profoundly connected to the rationalist vision of humanity's unity. He saw Völkergedanken, or people's collective thoughts, only as secondary derivations, or manifest configurations, of the universal elementary thoughts (Köpping 1995, 75–91). "His view was that all cultures have a common origin, from which they have branched off in various directions. . . . He was keenly aware of the historical connections between cultures" (Eriksen and Nielsen 2001, 21–22), a sideline of his work that the diffusionist wing of his students would make their main concern. These and related concepts of Bastian's work were inspired, to an extent, by his decades of travel on all the continents, but also by his acquaintance with the work of Leipzig psychologist Wilhelm Wundt. This indicates first an early and weak element of social science in early German anthropology that would return to the field some decades later. In addition, Bastian's crucial intellectual interaction with Wundt is particularly significant because Wundt also was of some influence for Émile Durkheim, who visited him in Leipzig, and for Bronislaw Malinowski, who attended his lectures there before going to Britain. Wundt's influence on anthropology, however, remained limited to his own lifetime (Streck 2001b, 524–31).

My assessment of Bastian is therefore not negative, and it is more differentiated than most recent writing about him (e.g., see Zimmermann 2001, 55–57; 207–13). His conceptual work did have some creative intellectual potential, and his empirical and descriptive emphasis encouraged his best students, who, after all, ranged from Karl von den Steinen to Franz Boas, to vigorously pursue fieldwork much further themselves. In intellectual terms I would therefore argue that by and large, Bastian's priority was ethnography of an encyclopedic kind and the elaboration of his own concepts. In this respect he can be regarded as a decisive precursor to the scholars of two international traditions. One of these traditions relates to Durkheim and has to do with Bastian's theoretical concept of elementary thoughts, which, Bastian held, were shared by "all humans." In Germany, Austria, and many parts of East Central Europe this idea was to completely lose out against Friedrich Ratzel's notion of origins, according to which influence diffused from a "few centres" of geniuses. In contrast to Bastian's elementary thoughts, Ratzel's key concept was humanity's *Ideenarmut*, that is, its "limited inventiveness," or "mental poverty." Some of Bastian's ideas nevertheless resurfaced in the French anthropological tradition somewhat later. Though in Germany the concept of elementary thoughts thus lost against that of "cultural circles," in France with Durkheim—presumably through Wundt's influence—the elementary thoughts idea had a successful comeback (Chevron 2003, 44–81, 300–90).

In my view, there were creative potentials in Bastian's work, notably in his emphasis on fieldwork and in some of his conceptual thinking. To some extent this potential for conceptual creativity and fieldwork also lost out because of Bastian's own shortcomings—that is, his incomprehensible writing style and his autocratic and excessive concern for collecting instead of systematizing and theorizing. In the last two decades of Bastian's life, this resulted in a growing split among Bastian's younger colleagues and students.

It is well known that Boas, who was born and raised in Westphalia, studied physics and then took an early interest in geography, which led him to carry out a one-year field sojourn on Baffin Island (1883–1884). His studies among the indigenous population there convinced him to reject geographical determinism, which included the views of "anthropo-geographer" Ratzel. When Boas returned to Germany from Baffin Island, he became one of Bastian's assistants at the Berlin museum, where he also was influenced by Virchow. In 1885 Boas worked on the museum's Jacobsen collection from the North Pacific and the Northwest coast of North America, and a year later he first met Bella Coola natives at a *Völkerschau* in Berlin. Both experiences in Germany decisively shaped the future direction of his early career in the United States (D. Cole 1999, 83–86). This was to become the second important international influence that came out of Bastian's work and training.

After Boas attained his habilitation with Bastian in 1886 in Berlin, he managed to establish himself in the United States. He took with him Bastian's antievolutionist orientation and empirical emphasis, with certain historical and moderate diffusionist priorities. Boas's intellectual luggage from Germany also included interests in local languages, physical anthropology, folklore studies, and, to an extent, moderate forms of nationalism. The rise of anti-liberalism and anti-Semitism in Bismarck's Germany certainly were part of the political side in Boas's wider motives for emigration. The saber-dueling student fraternity member Boas, however, had himself been no stranger to German nationalism before his emigration (D. Cole 1999, 38–62; Girtler 2001, 572).

At the Berlin museum and elsewhere in Germany toward the turn of the century, the other younger colleagues and former students of Bastian gradually broke up into divergent groups. One older outsider to the whole cohort was a contemporary of Bastian and Ratzel, Heinrich Schurtz, a Bremen museum anthropologist with great conceptual competency and an interest in socioeconomic matters. His most famous work, *Altersklassen und Männerbünde* ("Age classes and male associations"), of 1903, although written from the admiring perspective of a member of Prussian male associations, remains worth reading to this day.

Some of Bastian's students followed their former teacher, whereas others turned toward the teaching of Ratzel, with whom Schurtz was loosely associated as well. In reference to their theoretical priorities, I call these two orientations moderate positivism and historical diffusionism. The moderate positivists did not become as famous, but in retrospect I regard them as the far more interesting group of scholars. In their time, however, they became increasingly marginal as the historical diffusionists gained new hegemony in anthropology in the German language zone.

These moderate positivists remained somewhat more faithful than the historical diffusionists to the legacy of Bastian, who died in 1905. Most of them had gone through a solid and extensive fieldwork experience. Within their more specific areas of interest they systematized topics and fields of thought that Bastian had only touched upon. Now, at the turn from the nineteenth to the twentieth century, they began to display a certain affinity to the international intellectual mainstream. Domestically, however, they received much less attention than the historical diffusionists, whose leaders established new paradigms.

In November 1904, trained historian and Polynesia curator at the Berlin museum, Fritz Graebner, and the museum's Africa curator, Bernhard Ankermann, presented two famous lectures in which they called for a definite break with Bastian's school of thought (Hahn 2001, 137–42). They suggested instead a new priority for culture circles and for the study of cultural diffusion from those circles through history. Their notion of culture circles was inspired by the work of a young self-trained scholar and future explorer, Leo Frobenius, who later discarded the notion himself, and by that of Leipzig geographer and social Darwinist Ratzel, who until his death in 1904 had emphasized the study of diffusionist migration as a prime mover through "time and space." Contrary to later Boasian approaches to diffusion in the United States, Ratzel had almost entirely dropped the requirement that diffusion be empirically traced. For Ratzel, Graebner, and Ankermann, German diffusionism thus became a genius-centered, speculative history of cultural distributions.

In 1911 Graebner published an elaborated and systematized version of this new theory in his *Methode der Ethnologie* (Striedter 2001, 142–47). A new period of anthropology in Germany had begun. Those in the lead pursued a steady branching away from international mainstream developments in the field of sociocultural anthropology, and the group that was much closer to the international mainstream gradually became marginalized locally. The moderate positivists remained systematic fieldworkers and museum documentarists. The historical diffusionists, however, elaborated new schools that taught versions of genius-inspired-origin theory. In indirect ways at least, their view of humanity would become influential in much wider efforts that would prepare the ideological ground for Europe's darkest time, the long decade from 1934 to 1945.

If we look back at the state of anthropology in German before World War I, what we see deserves little praise and no celebration, but rather very thorough critical examination. Classical evolutionism had been largely marginalized from academia, while historical diffusionism and social Darwinism were on the rise, also academically. Folklore studies were about to become established as the historicist study of a superior, Germanic self, set apart from the study of the Herderian *Naturvölker*. German-language anthropologists' research was still strongly embedded in the objectifying forum of the exoticizing museums of an empire that was an aggressive colonialist newcomer. In short, anthropology in the German language zone had branched away from the international mainstream to such an extent that it seems quite appropriate to speak of the existence during the next forty years of a distinctively German anthropology that became German and pan-Germanic to an increasing degree by marginalizing those subaltern tendencies that managed to persist.

3

From the Late Imperial Era to the End of the Republican Interlude: Creative Subaltern Tendencies, Larger and Smaller Schools of Anthropology

Before and after World War I, new schools of anthropology began to establish themselves. To some extent, the growing influence of the two larger schools, in Frankfurt and Vienna, was counterbalanced by a smaller school and various subaltern tendencies.

After Adolf Bastian's death in 1905, Fritz Graebner (who died early) and Bernhard Ankermann (following Friedrich Ratzel), as well as Leo Frobenius in ways that soon were to become different from the methods of these two, established and expanded their new hegemony. Soon they were to be followed and overtaken by the ambitious Pater Wilhelm Schmidt and his disciples in Vienna. In the German language zone the dominance of these major diffusionist groups and schools lasted so long, even into the period from the 1950s to the 1970s, that they were able to write and rewrite their own history.

For example, the very first university lecture on the history of anthropology that I heard in Vienna, as an eighteen-year-old student in 1970, was given by one of the last remaining representatives of Schmidt's school. It started and ended with Graebner's and Ankermann's notorious 1904 Berlin talks, in that lecturer's view one of the profoundly glorious moments in the world history of anthropology. When I dared to mention at that particular lecturer's exam that my then hero Rosa Luxemburg had seen things somewhat differently than his lifelong hero Graebner, this former Catholic priest shouted at me during the exam, and I quote: "Only over my dead body will you ever become a professional anthropologist, if you ever quote that Polish, Jewish, communist *woman* again!" Which, in a way, is what actually happened: failing to get tenure, he chose early retirement and died a few years later. Meanwhile, I finished my studies and got a job at this institute after Walter Dostal became a full professor there.

The more serious implication of this anecdote is that well into the second half of the twentieth century the established narrative of many mainstream anthropologists in the German language zone claimed that the large schools were all that had mattered since 1904, except during the Nazi years, when the large schools were persecuted. Everything else in the history of twentieth-century German-language anthropology was repressed, forgotten, or distorted.

In reality, the three decades between 1904 (the year of the Berlin museum lectures) and the early 1930s (when the Nazis came to power in Germany) represented a much more heterogeneous and more interesting picture. To an extent this heterogeneity had to do with institutional growth. In particular, many chairs and most university departments of anthropology in the German language zone were established only after World War I. Through this institutional enlargement, anthropology in German became much more diversified, and the centers of debate gradually shifted from museums to universities.

This new heterogeneity was in evidence in at least three main intersecting clusters of professional activity: colonial involvement; innovative elements of ethnography and of economic and Marxist anthropology and the "anthropology of women"; and the development of the small and large schools.

Among the less well-known, moderate positivist group of Bastian's followers, one cluster was more or less directly involved in applied anthropology of a colonial kind. At the service of the collapsing empires of Germany and Austro-Hungary, these researchers were joining activities on the diffusionist side, such as those of Frobenius in 1918 and the SVD missionaries. This group was perhaps somewhat stronger than its counterparts in Britain, France, the Netherlands, and the United States, yet inside the German-speaking countries, its members represented only a minority in the profession.

Among the work of those moderate positivists who were less preoccupied or who were not pursuing such applied colonial endeavors at all, three kinds of substantial and valuable contributions to anthropology may be identified. First, a number of anthropologists made contributions to fieldwork and to economic anthropology. These included Max Schmidt, Theodor Koch-Grünberg, Karl von den Steinen, Ernst Grosse, Eduard Hahn, Alois Musil, and Julius Lips. Also, a second and third generation of authors inspired by Marx engaged in interactions with anthropology that became interesting and influential in various ways for the field. This work comprised some anthropological parts in Rosa Luxemburg's and Karl Kautsky's writings, Heinrich Cunow's efforts, and the formative phases of Paul Kirchhoff's and Karl August Wittfogel's work in Germany. Third, an early "anthropology of women" tradition was developing in German language, exemplified by the works of Hilde Thurnwald and Eva Lips. To an extent, these remain valuable and useful elements, elaborated as they are by a nonhegemonic, noncolonial, and not-yet-Nazi or non-Nazi anthropology of scholars inside Germany and in exile. Future research might show that the valuable elements are even more comprehensive.

Discussion of the small and large schools of anthropology in German requires a critical assessment of the very contradictory biography and work of Richard Thurnwald. Such an assessment has to appreciate his efforts aimed at opening up *Völkerkunde* toward sociology and British social anthropology, his quasifunctionalist analyses, and his emphasis on wider regional interaction. Likewise, his outstanding contribution to economic anthropology and the anthropology of law have to be considered. Thurnwald's own social Darwinism, his obvious personal status considerations, and the struggle with his adversaries from the big schools persuaded or seduced him, however, to become a responsible collaborator with the Nazi regime and to let his vision of anthropology be instrumentalized for its criminal regime purposes.

Before 1938 in Vienna, Wilhelm Schmidt's research group of Catholic priests, following Ratzel and Graebner, carried out such a dogmatic rule in their universalist search for the origins of monotheism that any alternative or contradictory evidence was suppressed. Simultaneously other, nontheological supporters of Graebner's ideas continued a similar culture circle orientation in German anthropology museums and departments. To an extent, these nontheological variants of culture circles initially resembled the culture areas of Boasian anthropology, as in Clark Wissler's work (Wissler 1917).

In the Frankfurt case, Frobenius's *Kulturmorphologie* introduced a mysticist vision of *Kultur* as a cyclical, organic whole, the innermost soul of which was called *Paideuma*. This vision represented a resurgence of a one-sided interpretation of Johann Gottlieb Herder's work inside German anthropology that was filtered through Romanticism and Edmund Husserl's emphatic phenomenology. In a way this was the mysticist counterpart in German to the somewhat more rationalist "key values" of Nietzschean patterns of culture in Benedict's work in the United States. After all, Frankfurtian cultural morphology and the strong-culturalist Boasian version shared some of the same roots.

Colonialism, Early Schools, and Moderate Positivists

Until the end of World War I, a smaller group of moderate positivists closely cooperated with German colonialism or engaged in applied research for German colonial interests. In this regard they followed the example of the majority among their colleagues, who were from the larger schools.

Notwithstanding the work of other contemporary authors, such as Michael Harbsmeier in Denmark (1992, 422–42) and Ingeburg Winkelmann in her 1966 dissertation from Communist East Germany, it is the great merit of Thomas Zitelmann (1999) to have meticulously documented and analyzed these intrinsic connections between German colonialism and a distinctive faction of German anthropology, particularly in East, West, and Southwest Africa, but also in Melanesia.

The leaders of what would soon become the Frankfurt and Vienna schools were substantially involved in late colonialism. This already became evident in 1902 at the German Reich's first colonial conference, which drew together different groups from all segments of society to coordinate and concentrate Germany's colonial efforts. From the side of sociocultural anthropology, participants included Richard Thurnwald, Wilhelm Schmidt, Hamburg museum director Georg Thilenius, and several others. Before and during World War I, these activities increased (Gothsch 1983, 208–9). Leo Frobenius, who would found his institute for cultural morphology at first in Munich in 1920, conducted a military mission for the German army in East Africa at the end of World War I and maintained some attention to reviving German colonial interests throughout his career (Ehl 1995; Zitelmann 1999). Wilhelm Schmidt, in Vienna, on the other hand, was the leading figure of a Catholic missionary order, Societas Verbi Divini (SVD), whose followers were anthropologists trained in Schmidt's culture circle variant of the field as much as they were priests and trained missionaries. To an extent, their anthropological activities depended on their missionary network and its intrinsic, albeit sometimes ambivalent, relation with colonialism. While representatives of Schmidt's group contributed to Germany's first colonial conference and later held high positions at the International Africa Institute in London, their practical colonial involvement remained limited.

Meanwhile, and independently from these early phases of the large schools, German physical anthropologists developed colonial interests of their own. Most prominent and notorious among them became Eugen Fischer, whose 1913 publication on the "half-breeds of Rehobot" was based on his studies in the German colony of South-West Africa (today Namibia). This book, *Die Rehobother Bastarde und das Bastardisierungsproblem beim Menschen*, picked up Christoph Meiners's old thesis that racial intermarriage led to "degeneration," and through field cases from Namibia he argued for policies based on

Mendel's Laws. This was a clear departure from Virchow (Mischek 2000). On the basis of this early colonial involvement, Fischer would later become a leading proponent of the Nuremberg race laws and of anthropology's involvement in Nazi crimes. Likewise, Otto Reche carried out his first major empirical "measuring" and "racial evaluating" in German colonial contexts, as the chief physical anthropologist in the Hamburg museum's 1908–1910 South Pacific expedition (Fischer 1981). As professor in Vienna (1924–1927) and Leipzig (1927–1945), Reche would later become another key proponent of merging sociocultural anthropology with a racist physical anthropology, which he would then put at the service of the Nazi regime (Geisenhainer 2002).

Among the sociocultural anthropologists, however, it was not only the two emerging large diffusionist schools whose representatives became active for colonial interests or profited from them. Several scholars from the loose group of moderate positivists also tried to be useful to German colonialism or to benefit from it. Moritz Merker (1904) is one better known such case. He was a German *Schutzoffizier* of Jewish background at the service of the imperial colonial army who wrote a fairly solid ethnography of the Masai that became a standard source for British and other experts. For the Middle East, the Austro-Hungarian Alois Musil, who will be discussed below, is an example. For Melanesia, the Hamburg South Pacific expedition analyzed by Hans Fischer (1981) and the German navy expedition to Melanesia brilliantly researched by Andrew Zimmermann (2001, 217–38), are other cases in point. A faction of the moderate positivist group among Bastian's students and elsewhere in the German language zone, pursued an applied colonial sociocultural anthropology. These activities were joined early on by the new Viennese Melanesia curator at the Berlin museum, Richard Thurnwald.

In addition, Max Schmidt deserves to be at least as well remembered as, though not confused with, Wilhelm Schmidt, the head of the Vienna school of culture circle theorists. Max Schmidt, originally trained in law, became an ethnographic expert on Paraguay and on Brazilian indigenous cultures, about whom he acquired great field experience. In 1918, he became a professor in Berlin, a position from which he sought early retirement in 1929 for professional as much as for political reasons it seems. He then emigrated to South America, where he died in 1950. Schmidt's economic theorizing did include appeals to colonial interests that largely went unnoticed. Nevertheless, his *Grundriß der ethnologischen Volkswirtschaftslehre* ("Foundations of anthropological economics," 1920–1921) is an interesting masterpiece in its own right.

Thus, a faction of positivists and virtually all members of the hegemonic schools profited from and worked for colonial German interests until 1918, more explicitly and more directly than did their counterparts in France and Britain. However, with few exceptions, like that of Eugen Fischer, these colonial contributions by German and Austrian sociocultural anthropologists remained fairly limited in substance and relatively heterogeneous as to their purpose and direction (Penny and Bunzl 2003, 23–27). In addition, applied anthropology in the German language zone received one further boost during World War I when several of its representatives in the German and Austro-Hungarian empires carried out linguistic, physical anthropological, and ethnographic documentation among prisoners of war (Mühlfried 2000). It has been argued that these studies of POWs during World War I constituted one of the most decisive fields by which linguistic and ethnographic inquiries were brought together with racial studies, much more closely than had been the case before (Evans 2003). Several anthropological institutions—though by no means all of them—subsequently strengthened the cooperation between *Rassenkunde* (racial studies as a subfield of physical anthropology) and *Völkerkunde* (sociocultural anthropology) after 1918. In view of this late colonial and World War I involvement of several anthropologists, the group of moderate positivists may be further differentiated into those with and those without any interest in being at the service of colonialism and the imperial armies.

There was among the group of moderate positivists a faction of anthropologists who for reasons of regional specialization or out of conviction had very little to do with colonialism or even opposed it. "German anthropologists . . . were far more likely to pursue their interests beyond the colonial reach of the Kaiserreich. Working on every continent, Germans thus produced the vast majority of ethnography on the indigenous peoples of Brazil and other South American states during the nineteenth" and early twentieth centuries (Penny and Bunzl 2003, 14).

The most respectable moderate positivist was Bastian's closest disciple, von den Steinen, who taught in Berlin and Marburg and who carried out and published intensive fieldwork in Brazil and the Marquesas Islands before he died in 1929 (Harms 2001, 446–49). Koch-Grünberg, perhaps the most resourceful South Americanist in his generation, also has to be mentioned in this context (Stagl 1999, 208). Konrad Theodor Preuss, a professor and curator in Berlin, is one who remained with this group for a long time. Eventually he preferred a version of Americanist functionalism, rather than following Graebner's and Ankermann's conservative diffusionist revolution. Carrying out years of solid fieldwork in northern Mesoamerica and in Colombia, he entertained a close intellectual correspondence, still largely unpublished, with his former museum colleague Franz Boas on matters of joint Americanist interest (Riese 2001, 366–71).

In addition to von den Steinen, Koch-Grünberg, and the younger Preuss, a number of other German anthropologists from the period are also interesting: Ernst Grosse (in Freiburg, d. 1927), Max Schmidt, and to an extent Eduard Hahn can be seen, also in an international sense, as one founding group of economic anthropology that came from various theoretical backgrounds, although all of them emphasized a positivist empirical legacy. U.S.-trained German scholar Jasper Köcke (1979) deserves the credit for having pointed this out first. By elaborating on the theoretical reasoning of some early precursors, Hahn was the first, at the turn from the nineteenth to the twentieth century, to clearly formulate the position that pastoralism can hardly evolve out of nonagricultural conditions. Hahn also differentiated between hoe cultivation and plow cultivation, a distinction that became important in African Studies and in the analysis of gender roles.

Other representatives of early German economic anthropology were Julius Lips and his wife, Eva Lips. Julius Lips later summarized some of his research on the Ojibwa under the theoretical concept of "harvesting societies" (1953). This quasi-evolutionary concept envisioned a possible transitional phase between nomadic foraging and sedentary agriculture. After 1945 economist Esther Boserup synthesized a good range of this economic anthropological research, particularly on Africa, in ways that allowed Jack Goody and others to draw on it (Boserup 1970). These key representatives among Bastian's moderate positivist successors in the German language zone were devoted field-workers, students of archives, and museum curators with little inclination toward theoretical speculation such as was common among their diffusionist adversaries. They were rooted in empirical work and skeptical against evolutionism but open to comparative conceptualization. In short, they were the local German branch of the best that international anthropology then represented.

Brigitta Hauser-Schäublin (1991) has shown that the first female anthropologists were close to this group—among them Hilde Thurnwald and Eva Lips. Although largely trained by their male partners, they soon became independent-minded authors in their own right. Thurnwald and Lips were still working within the more traditional framework of gender roles insofar as some of their basic research orientations did not differ too widely from those of their better established male associates. Moreover, both of these better known scholars also took care of their husbands' works after their death. Still, they also developed a number of original ideas of their own, notably Thurnwald on psychological anthropology. In particular, they made special reference to women's role in indigenous societies. Thus German contributions to international anthropology of that era occupied a second important realm in addition to that of economic anthropology. This was represented by what one might call today a first phase of gender studies, still under the more conservative paradigm of an anthropology of women.

Two relatively innovative groups can thus be identified among the moderate positivists, namely economic anthropologists and early scholars of women's studies. Most importantly, representatives of these groups introduced systematic fieldwork into German-speaking anthropology. One example, with which I am particularly familiar because it relates to Vienna and the Middle East, should suffice to emphasize this point about the fieldwork generation of moderate positivists:

While Wilhelm Schmidt was setting out to combine his armchair speculation on culture circles with his even more speculative postulate about the universality of monotheism, another Catholic priest in Vienna was doing exactly the opposite. Whereas Schmidt dogmatically searched for the origins of monotheism everywhere, Alois Musil sought the origins of monotheism not everywhere, but reasonably enough in the Middle East. Ernest Gellner (1995), in one of his last articles, called Musil the "Lawrence of Moravia," and indeed, Moravian-born Musil was an intelligence observer for the Habsburg Crown in the Ottoman Middle East. In spite of this engagement with imperial interests, yet also because of it, he was an excellent fieldworker, and was actually the first serious ethnographer of Northern Arabia. In fact, Musil followed the same Zeitgeist of empiricism, which had one of its centers in Ernst Mach's epistemological circle in Vienna, that also had influenced Malinowski's early years in Krakow and Leipzig. In view of Musil's impressive fieldwork achievements, one may well follow Gellner (1995) in locating one of the intellectual roots of ethnographic fieldwork in Central Europe at the turn of the century.

Before 1918 Musil had an important role at court as the Habsburg family's personal confessional priest. That position was much more important than the one jealous Wilhelm Schmidt later declared had been his own position at court: Schmidt would claim that he had been the last Habsburg emperor's confessional priest, but actually he had merely read a few field masses for him. That rivalry at the Viennese court was significant, between the Westphalian German priest Schmidt in his SVD missionary order, and the Czech-born Musil, whose academic working language until 1918 was German. Musil was the cousin of novelist Robert Musil, who was later to become the famous author of *The Man without Qualities*, a profound literary criticism of Austrian opportunism. Moreover, Alois Musil's mentor within the church was an influential, Jewish-born convert, the liberal Bishop Cohen. Thus the conflict between Schmidt and Musil had several dimensions: they differed, for example, on whether to research the idea of God through diffusionist, universalist speculation or through regionally focused fieldwork and history. Whether to promote pan-Germanism or to favor good intercultural relations between German-speaking, Czech, and Jewish communities was a second dimension. A third one was whether to promote a prefascist authoritarianism or political liberalism in a reformed monarchy (Gingrich and Haas 1999).

As might be expected, Schmidt won and Musil lost. After World War I ended with Austro-Hungary's defeat and collapse in 1918, Schmidt successfully drove Musil out of Vienna, where Musil still had been dean at the university. Musil had to go back to what was now the newly founded Republic of Czechoslovakia. It was this crucial move that paved the way for Schmidt's subsequent rise to monumental intellectual influence in the anthropology of the German-speaking countries. From then on, Schmidt managed to establish, inside the Catholic church and in German-speaking academia, his dogmatic school of culture circle theory. Schmidt hardly ever appreciated what others wrote on religion in German. By consequence, contemporary insights of high relevance for the anthropology of religion, such as those of Max Weber and Rudolf Otto (1917), were largely ignored by sociocultural anthropologists in the German language zone. In the course of his rise, Schmidt did not hesitate to also keep Sigmund Freud from gaining a position at the University of Vienna and to polemicize against psychoanalysis and Marxism in his more popular writing. (Freud, of course, became influential for international anthropology quite early. However, he had so little influence upon German anthropology before 1968 that discussing his work is beyond the scope of this overview.)

While Schmidt rose to power in post-1918 Vienna, Musil eventually retired to a Czech monastery. For years, he wrote books for children in Czech while compiling and elaborating his field notes from Arabia. These were to be published neither in his native Czech, nor in his academic working language German. Fortunately for international anthropology, an American sponsor had the German (and, to a smaller part, Czech) manuscript by Musil translated into English for its sole print publication. It remains a masterpiece of an ethnographic monograph based on extensive fieldwork (Bauer 1989).

If I were to recommend a basic reading list of good anthropology from the

German-speaking countries in that period, it would include perhaps Schurtz 1903 and some of Koch-Grünberg's writing. Yet my list would also point out the lasting significance of Musil's *The Manners and Customs of the Rwala Bedouins*, published in 1928 in New York.

Good anthropology thus increasingly emigrated out of the German language zone while it became suppressed within that zone. In the same year as Musil was expelled from Vienna, where he had spent most of his academic life, Rosa Luxemburg was murdered in Berlin. Musil's ethnography, based on fieldwork from before 1918, did not become available to anthropologists of the Middle East until the 1930s and 1940s, and Rosa Luxemburg's anthropological reasoning from the years 1910–1916 began to have an impact for a few anthropologists in German only in the mid-1920s, after which it was forgotten again. This, therefore, is the nontradition of good anthropology in German: forgotten, repressed, and noticed only after tremendous time lags.

Renewed Marxist Interest in Anthropology

Marxist encounters with anthropology in German constituted another peripheral tradition from that period. The social democratic mainstream, which basically gave in to nationalism at the 1914 outbreak of World War I, produced two noteworthy oeuvres of anthropological relevance. First of all, there was Karl Kautsky's *Die Agrarfrage* (1899), "the agrarian question," a classic oeuvre of Engels's junior collaborator who became the centrist leader of the social democratic movement in Germany and in German-speaking Austria. Kautsky's *Agrarfrage* at first had no influence at all on anthropology anywhere, and certainly not on folklore studies in his time, although both dealt with peasants and farmers in Europe. Yet by the 1920s and, to an extent, through Chayanov's work in Russia, its intellectual radiation gradually reached academia. After 1945 a whole generation of anthropologists dealing with peasants worldwide and in Europe, ranging from Theodore Shanin to Eric Wolf to James Scott, were inspired by it in direct and indirect ways.

Less important than Kautsky was another socialist party intellectual, Heinrich Cunow—the only one among Marxist anthropologists of that time who actually achieved a substantial career in academia. As director of the Berlin museum for *Völkerkunde* from 1919 to 1928, Cunow was a relatively uninspiring armchair synthesizer of some of the good economic anthropology writing in German of his time, and certainly he also was one of the very few anthropological evolutionists in German academia before World War II and the Nazi period, both of which are exemplified in his *Allgemeine Wirtschafts-geschichte* (Ulrich 1987).

As is well known in Europe at least, Rosa Luxemburg led the antination-alist wing of the German labor movement, which first became the Spartakus-bund and after her death, then evolved into the Communist Party. Because of her many disagreements with Lenin, her work was published very late and was not widely distributed by the German communists under Stalin's influ-ence. As far as I know, her anthropologically most relevant work, *Einführung in die Nationalökonomie* (1925/1975), was first published posthumously in the mid-1920s and then in 1974 in Communist East Germany.

The range of Luxemburg's study of the important anthropological works of her time was impressively vast, much wider than what would have been available for Marx from anthropology and sociology in his time. Luxemburg's reading list comprised, of course, Lewis Henry Morgan, Maxim Kowalewski, Henry Sumner Maine, Cunow, and A. W. Howitt, but also Edward Wester-marck, Grosse, von den Steinen, Ratzel, Max Weber, and so on. On the basis of her interest into which direction modern capitalism was taking, Luxem-burg also studied what kinds of societies capitalism destroyed and subordi-nated on its path to global expansion. Her particular interest was in market expansion and commodity circulation. Orthodox communists criticized Lux-emburg because, they alleged, she neglected production in favor of circula-tion. However, this focus on circulation seems to be a particular strength of her work today, in the light of current debates on globalization and trans-national flows.

The careful interpretations in her *Einführung in die Nationalökonomie* make her the one author who seriously continued Marx's sketches and essays on precapitalist formations and colonial expansion, which Luxemburg could only have known very partially then. Her observations on the dissolution of agrarian communities under the impact of market expansion deserve special recognition. In this creative continuation of Marx's anthropological efforts, with its absorption of some of the best German and international anthropo-logical literature of her time, her work became a true precursor to present de-bates in anthropology on transnationalism and globalization—debates to which she still can speak through her work, more than eight decades after her death.

In one way or the other, the Spartakusbund, these armed German revo-lutionaries from 1918, then became personally and intellectually influential for Julian Steward and his post-1945 cohort of neo-evolutionist, left-leaning anthropologists, ranging from Sidney Mintz and Bob Adams to Eric Wolf and Marshall Sahlins. One of two ex-Spartakists who are important in this context was Paul Kirchhoff. He left Germany in the 1930s while his interest in anthropology was still in its formative stages (but see Kirchhoff 1931 for one of his early anthropological articles in German), yet his critical Marxism was acquired during his Spartakus period in Germany. This helped him as an anthropologist to elaborate innovative concepts for hierarchical constellations, such as his now famous notion of "conical clans" (Sahlins, 1968).

The other former Spartakist of importance in this context was Karl August Wittfogel. In contrast to Kirchhoff, Wittfogel left Germany after he had already published some substantive work that dealt with key anthropological topics. These fields included China and the Asiatic mode of production, or what Wittfogel later would call hydraulic societies, but also traditional aboriginal society in Australia (1931, 1970). It was because of these intellectual orientations that Wittfogel, by the mid-1920s, began to criticize the completely mutilated Stalinist party politics' appropriation of Marx's legacy. To do so he used Marx's notions of the "Asiatic mode of production" and of "oriental despotism" as a critical tool against Stalinism. He was defending what at that time was still offering some plurality in creative materialist thinking. These conflicts contributed greatly to his decision to leave the Communist Party and emigrate to the United States. There he and his wife, anthropologist Esther Goldfrank, exerted notable influence on academic debates while collaborating in Senator Joseph McCarthy's drive against leftist intellectuals. Regardless of how his association with McCarthyism in the 1950s is assessed, I would argue that Wittfogel's defense of academic pluralism against Stalinism in the 1920s and 1930s was a courageous and admirable stand.

The Academic Schools

Inspired by the Bolshevist revolution in Russia, the Spartakus uprising was crushed by regular and paramilitary forces in Germany. Some of these rightist and nationalist paramilitary forces soon became an early recruiting field for the newly founded Nazi party in the 1920s. A short but active association with one of these rightist militia groups after 1918 was not detrimental to Thurnwald's academic career. On the contrary, these connections became useful in his exceptional and contradictory biography.

Richard Thurnwald became the leading figure of the small schools. By the early 1930s, he was not only the most widely respected anthropologist from Germany in international academia, he also had developed a mild political preference for democracy. If he had left Nazi Germany by the 1930s—which he had tried to do before giving up—or if, like Max Schmidt, he had at least sought early retirement to dissociate himself from the Nazis, anthropology in German might have moved in a somewhat different direction, and after 1945 it would have had a better, more "Westernized" legacy to build on. But Thurnwald stayed on, pursuing business as usual: although he had developed some intellectual distance from the Nazis, he nevertheless tried to prove his usefulness to them by publishing articles that advocated the acquisition of new colonial territory. In addition, he actively mentored his disciple Wilhelm Emil Mühlmann, who would become the most dangerous Nazi ideologist in German *Völkerkunde*. Moreover, Thurnwald substantially contributed to the academic promotion of some persons, like Ingeborg Sydow and Eva Justin, who actively helped—as was reflected in the latter's thesis—to send Roma, Sinti, and Jews to death in concentration camps.

Yet it is no coincidence that Thurnwald stands out as one of the best known anthropologists of all time from the German-speaking countries. Perhaps it is good that this will remain so for a while to come, given the inherent symbolism of his profoundly contradictory biography. Two of the field's greatest celebrities of their day, Alfred Kroeber and Robert Lowie, contributed to the 1950 festive volume that Thurnwald's wife, Hilde, pulled together for his eightieth birthday, and no less an authority than Sir Raymond Firth, in one of his great late interviews, spoke very kindly of Thurnwald, who, Firth said a few years ago, was the one great anthropologist he could think of who deserved more credit for his achievements.

So what were these achievements Firth mentioned so respectfully? First, much more clearly than the moderate positivists inside Germany, Thurnwald combined rigorous fieldwork with theoretical analysis, in which he followed more closely British and North American anthropology. To the moderate positivists, he nevertheless had some methodological affinity, whereas he stood in strong opposition to the hegemonic German historical diffusionists, his lifelong adversaries. Second, in combining fieldwork with theoretical analysis, Thurnwald emphasized the functioning of local systems in a manner that was similar to that of British social anthropology. For Pacific cases Thurnwald elaborated notions of reciprocity and redistribution that, through Marcel Mauss and Karl Polanyi, became part of our discipline's basic inventory. For several generations of European students, his name was thus almost synonymous with economic anthropology. Simultaneously, he emphasized regional interdependence between such local systems in ways that went beyond regional and culture area studies as pursued, for instance, in American anthropology. Finally, Thurnwald saw this regional interdependence and interaction as oscillating around movements of *Siebung,* that is, of "sieving" or competitive selection, a key term in Thurnwald's thinking that included sociocultural factors but certainly had some social Darwinist logic in it (Melk-Koch 2001). Without that social Darwinist edge (and perhaps if limited to the valid dimensions of regional economic and political rivalry), Thurnwald's conceptualizations might have become an even more influential contribution to international anthropology than they actually were before and right after World War II.

Thurnwald was very well received during his stays at British and American anthropology departments in the 1920s and 1930s, but he threw away this great potential for the dubious privilege of gaining even more respect inside Nazi Germany. One may speak of a tragedy, but it was self-inflicted. Thurnwald had all the potential at hand to bring the very best of anthropology from the German language zone, which intellectually was already on its way toward global marginalization, back into the anthropological mainstream.

From his native Vienna, where he had worked as a Habsburg legal expert, and from Bosnia, where he had served as a financial administrator, he brought with him to Berlin some acquaintance with the fertile, nonnationalist, and historical tradition of folklore studies of Austro-Hungary. After his anthropology studies in Berlin, where he worked as a museum curator, he went through experiences similar to those of the moderate positivists. While the latter sought to calmly follow Bastian's legacy, Thurnwald chose to explicitly fight the speculative diffusionists with new and partially original concepts that were strongly linked to contemporary British reasoning. When the Nazis came to power in 1933 in Germany and in 1938 in Austria, they shook up some of the hegemony of the speculative diffusionists, who often were racist all right, but usually not racist enough for the Nazis. This relative weakening of Thurnwald's lifelong adversaries and his own social Darwinist and organicist leanings seduced him to power and glory. He sought his chance inside the Third Reich, where he was a prominent anthropologist in Nazi Germany's capital Berlin from 1933 to 1945. The small functionalist school thus was to be upgraded during the Nazi years, at the cost of its own profound corruption.

During the 1920s, speculative theorizing by the emerging large schools of cultural morphology and historical diffusionism became so influential that serious professional doubts were raised by many of those who did not support these orientations wholeheartedly. Hamburg anthropologist Thilenius, for instance, complained in a letter to Franz Boas about this "somewhat dense theoretical atmosphere" when recommending his student Günter Wagner—

as an alternative—for fieldwork training under Boas's supervision (Mischek 2002, 29).

Among these large schools from the Weimar and the first Austrian republics, the one in Frankfurt is somewhat more interesting than the one in Vienna. We have seen that Leo Frobenius inspired the 1904 counterrevolution at the Berlin museum, but soon abandoned the culture circle concept. Influenced to an extent by the German philosophical phenomenology in Husserl's version and by prefascist historian Oswald Spengler, but also driven by some influence from his teachers Ratzel and Heinrich Schurtz, Frobenius elaborated what he called cultural morphology: an introspective, intuitive, *and* diffusionist conglomerate. Frobenius's cultural morphology has left its imprint not only among African "Negritude" thinkers, including Leopold Senghor, but also among some of his own disciples in Germany. In this late Romanticist, speculative, and yet fieldwork-oriented vision (and, to my mind, this is a somewhat mysticist vision, rather than a solid research tool), cultures are seen as organic wholes with a soul that goes through cyclical stages.

This space- and time-embedded soul, or *Paideuma,* is seen as moving a culture from its younger stages of *Ergriffenheit,* or "inspiration," and *Ausdruck,* or "expression," to its mature stage of *Anwendung,* or "implementation," until it reaches the final stage of *Abnutzung,* or "deterioration." This school's overt preference for the irrational and the aesthetic was criticized with much justification, since it corresponded to an opaque Zeitgeist mysticism in earlier fascism. In addition, the Frankfurtian *Paideuma* notion also encompassed everything that can possibly be said about a particularist and diffusionist notion of *Kultur* from the German language zone: it was and is genius-oriented, it largely depends on external stimuli, and it is introspective in the nonenlightened culturalist tradition that sought inspiration from Herder and Romanticism (Straube 1990, 151–70; Ehl 1995).

Frobenius died in 1938. His represents one legacy in Germany that still needs to be much more profoundly assessed than I can demonstrate here. We shall see, however, that Frobenius's assistant and successor in Frankfurt, Adolf E. Jensen, became one of the few anthropologists for whom the term *inner emigration* (that is, noncollaboration) during the Nazi years seems acceptable.

As for the so-called Vienna school, my conviction is clear: What nonanthropologists Max Weber and Rudolf Otto wrote in German about society and religion remains highly relevant for anthropology. What Wilhelm Schmidt wrote on that subject, however, has not stood the test of time. Wilhelm Schmidt's life and works have been assessed more critically by Edouard

Conte (1987) and Suzanne Marchand and, by contrast, in somewhat too friendly a manner by Ernest Brandewie (1990). We have already seen Schmidt's rise to power against Musil in Vienna, where he then transformed the 1912 chair for ethnography into the institute (1929) where I work now; the institute then became essential for his "anthropological counter-reformation" (Marchand 2003, 293).

Politically Schmidt was a Catholic fascist of the Franco and Mussolini orientation, which was in line with Austria's leading political forces before the Nazi invasion of 1938. Although he was an outspoken clerical anti-Semite and believed in a wider variant of Germanic superiority, he nevertheless refused to merge his theological variant of *Völkerkunde* with racial studies, which is why he insisted on the necessity of their separate institutional existence. This led him to have some late second thoughts about the Nazis' biologist and secular preferences. His 1937 *Handbuch der Methode der kulturhistorischen Ethnologie* built on Graebner's 1911 *Methode der Ethnologie* and codified his universalist, diffusionist search for older and younger culture circles. The meticulous and relentless scrutiny by which this armchair anthropologist summarized solid ethnographic knowledge and tried to cast it into his theory, notably in his twelve-volume *Der Ursprung der Gottesidee* ("The origin of the idea of God," 1912–1955) is breathtaking.

Schmidt and his close but much more moderate associate Wilhelm Koppers were taken seriously in their time, by Soviet scholars such as S. A. Tokarev as much as by Kroeber and Lowie in the United States—not to speak of Clyde Kluckhohn, who studied for a year with them in Vienna and wrote his dissertation on the "two Vienna schools" of culture circle theory and psychoanalysis. Schmidt mostly recruited German-born priests for the academic faculty and for the SVD missionary institutes in St. Gabriel (near Vienna), St. Augustin (near Bonn), and Fribourg (in Switzerland), that is, all across the German language zone. Notably, before 1938 Schmidt's school also relied on a strong network of like-minded professional supporters not only in neighboring domestic fields, such as archaeology through Oswald Menghin (Kohl and Gollan 2002), but also internationally, through associates in Portugal, Spain, South America, Italy, Hungary, and Japan. Under Schmidt's iron dominance, this school maintained a hermetic, dogmatic influence. Critics were silenced or destroyed while Schmidt became an influential public speaker and writer as much as a vicious strategist inside and outside academic politics.

Schmidt's best associates did fieldwork, mostly among peripheral and foraging societies, to support his theory that those who were most primitive also were closest to creation. For this reason, the theory held, the "most primitive"

had to display some form of monotheism. The field evidence and source material collected by Martin Gusinde, Paul Schebesta, Joseph Henninger, Koppers, and others does retain some value—not because it supported Schmidt,
but because, of course, it could not fully confirm his ideology. The extent of
this contradiction between ethnography and ideology was often suppressed,
so much so that when some of his associates rethought everything they had
ever written, they did so at a very late stage, long after Schmidt had died. This
was the case with Joseph Henninger, who was on my own habilitation committee a few months before he died himself and who had been Schmidt's
secretary.

Schmidt's ideological rigidity and his organizational terror thus created
desperation among his own followers and blind fury among his intelligent opponents. After the Third Reich occupied Austria and the Nazis took over the
Vienna institute in 1938, it was an easy task for them to oust Schmidt, Koppers, and the SVD from their anthropology faculty positions and to pose
themselves as liberators of local anthropology.

4

German Anthropology during the Nazi Period: Complex Scenarios of Collaboration, Persecution, and Competition

From a presentist perspective, the vast majority of sociocultural anthropologists in Germany were more or less active supporters of the Nazi regime. As in most other fields of academia and state employment, the Nazi takeover was met by little resistance and instead by widespread acceptance, collaboration, and support. This basic, presentist insight may not be very surprising for members of the international community of anthropologists. For local anthropologists in Germany and Austria, however, it took two, if not three, generations after 1945 to intellectually acknowledge and empirically demonstrate this point. Key essays and central text books in German that document and analyze the roles of anthropologists in the Third Reich are still few and fairly recent.

German anthropology in the Nazi period involved complex scenarios of collaboration, persecution, and competition (Dostal 1994). Assessment of the practices and discourses of anthropologists in the Third Reich reveals profound parallels to other academic fields of that period, though with a number of qualifications and modifications. The parallels to other state-sponsored academic fields concern institutional, intellectual, and individual continuity, integration, and support in a majority of cases, and persecution or emigration in a strong minority. The modifications and qualifications relate to the fact that for the regime's purposes, sociocultural anthropology was less important than some, but more important than other academic fields. In addition, Nazism regarded some of the large schools of German anthropology as not particularly useful for its purposes. This seduced many gifted anthropologists into competing against each other for regime favors, as they tried to prove even better how useful their work might be for Nazism.

On the basis of these premises, in the present lecture I discuss five topics. In the first section I outline key steps of anthropology's integration into the

Third Reich. Second, I give a brief overview of what is known today about anthropologists who were persecuted, including those who were persecuted by other anthropologists. In the third section I then characterize some main directions of anthropology in Germany until 1945, and in the fourth I raise the difficult question of accomplices' responsibility by giving some specific examples. In the fifth section I proceed to point out key effects of that period beyond 1945.

From Above and From Below: Anthropology's Integration into the Third Reich

Adolf Hitler had been inspired by, among other theories, Friedrich Ratzel's key concepts of humanity's "mental poverty" and of "living space" (*Ideenarmut, Lebensraum*). During his imprisonment in the early 1920s, he also made frequent use of physical anthropologist Eugen Fischer's coauthored standard text book on races, the so-called "Bauer/Fischer/Lenz." These key anthropological concepts, that is, mental poverty, race, and living space, thus found their way into *Mein Kampf*, the book in which Hitler publicly announced, in the 1920s, his program of "national resurrection" through dictatorial tyranny, warfare, and persecution of Jews and other minorities. Hitler's plans and programs were well-known years before he came to power (Braun 1995, 21; Byer 1999, 282).

Academic anthropology's integration into the Third Reich was a relatively smooth process, as was the case with many other fields of the humanities, or *Geisteswissenschaften*. The Nazi party had more active members among state employees and academic professionals than among other segments of society. Although party members were a minority even there, this stronger Nazi party influence and an elitist tradition of state loyalty were major reasons underlying widespread acceptance of, if not support for, Hitler's electoral victory in 1933 and his subsequent establishment of a dictatorship in Germany.

Since the 1910s and 1920s, leading German anthropologists had announced and published explicit racist and colonialist views, as part of either their political opinions or their academic beliefs. Eventually some of them became members of the Nazi party, while many more did not. Yet the explicit racism and anti-Judaism in the works of anthropologists like, say, Eugen Fischer, Wilhelm Schmidt, and Otto Reche certainly made an intellectual contribution to the rise of racist ideologies by making these ideologies look more respectable and by providing an aura of professional credibility to racism. This silenced the voices of those anthropologists who maintained nonracist or not explicitly racist views, at least for a while—until some of them joined the chorus as well.

During the prewar years of Nazi rule (1933–1939), anthropology thus went through an integration into the Third Reich that was instigated from above but simultaneously found support and collaboration from below. This smooth institutional integration was supported and complemented by certain continuities in the public sphere as well, where an adventurist and voyeurist exoticism continued to prevail. This popular exoticism included strong supremacist elements in a wider sense; explicit elements of Nazi ideology merely constituted a small part of it.

The wider spectrum of exoticist popular culture during the prewar Nazi years was presented in elements of spectacular Völkerschauen, stage, and museum shows, in film and music, and in the book market. Two successful anthropological works competed and flirted, at least through their titles, with this kind of voyeuristic exoticism: *The Sexual Life of Savages in North-West Melanesia*, translated by Bronislaw Malinowski himself, had come out in 1929 (that is, before the first Nazi-led government) in German, and 1939 saw the simultaneous publication in Britain and Germany of Christoph Fürer-Haimendorf's first big book success, *Die nackten Nagas* (1939). The military sections of that book were republished in German during the war in 1944—while the author was with the British in India—as *Der weiße Kopfjäger* ("The White Headhunter"; see Schäffler 2001). Widely popular anthropological books thus were part of a public sphere that contributed to the gradual integration into the Third Reich of some academic fields, like anthropology.

Inside this field, some prominent experts were quick to grasp the significance of the day. Very soon after Hitler had taken over, a group of leading German anthropologists wrote an official letter to the now imperial chancellor in October 1933, in which they celebrated Hitler's ideas and emphasized German anthropology's competence and willingness to help carrying out these ideas: anthropology, the letter said, was indispensable for strengthening Hitler's ideas of *Volk* (the people) and *höheren Menschentums* ("a superior type of man") by combining racial with cultural studies. The text was signed by cultural anthropologists such as Fritz Krause, chairman of the Society of Ethnology (Gesellschaft für Völkerkunde, the precursor of today's national professional association DGV, the Deutsche Gesellschaft für Völkerkunde), and Bernhard Ankermann, the 1904 cofounder of culture circle theory, as well as by physical anthropologists such as Otto Reche from Leipzig and Eugen

Fischer in Berlin. (Since 1927 Fischer had been director of the Institute for Anthropology, Studies in Hereditary Transmittance, and Eugenics at the Kaiser Wilhelms Gesellschaft, the precursor of today's Max Planck Society.) This unsolicited pledge of allegiance by top leaders of the field in Germany obviously demonstrated these leaders' eagerness to collaborate, but they probably did so with the uneasy thought in mind that studies on African and Melanesian cultures might not be interesting at all for a racist German Nazi government. Perhaps this is why, in a programmatic move, the letter was jointly signed by cultural as well as physical anthropologists. Whereas these two fields had reached a fair amount of institutional dissociation in most parts of the German language zone before the Nazi takeover, professionally and intellectually physical and cultural anthropology became almost inseparable during the Nazi years. This was the second programmatic message of the 1933 letter. For subscribers to a racist ideology like Nazism, a physical anthropology of their liking was bound to become a science of central importance. *Völkerkunde* quickly understood this.

In following years the Nazis tightened their influence on academia in general, and as much as on anthropology. A 1934 legal decree introduced political Nazi criteria for academic promotion to positions as senior lecturers and professors. In 1935 the Berlin Society for Anthropology, Ethnography, and Prehistory introduced an Aryans-only clause for new members, as did most other anthropological and academic associations in Germany of those years. In 1938 the same society excluded all its remaining Jewish members, among them Franz Boas in the United States. By that year, virtually all anthropologists with a Jewish background who had not already been forced to emigrate had lost their professional jobs in Germany (Braun 1995, 23, 27–29, 36).

While such legal and political repression and persecution increased control and instrumentalization from the side of the regime, collaboration and competition grew among those anthropologists who were in a position to maintain and improve their status. Within certain limits, theoretical academic orientations mattered surprisingly little among these shifting networks of collaboration, alliance, denunciation, and career-mindedness under Nazi conditions, as Doris Byer (1999) has shown. This is the substance of my introductory statement that the vast majority of German anthropologists were more or less active supporters of the Nazi regime. Among physical anthropologists, for instance, a dispute as to whether the origins of the Germanic race were to be found in the north (some Nazi party leaders favored this "northern thesis") or in the east (some non-Nazis like Wilhelm Koppers preferred this "eastern thesis") mattered little in political terms: Eugen Fischer, Otto Reche, Egon von Eickstedt, and Bruno Beger, who were engaged in this debate on one side or the other, all had strong institutional and financial support from various factions of the Nazi state and party apparatus, factions that usually competed among themselves.

Likewise, proponents of the various theoretical directions of sociocultural anthropology, with a few exceptions, were eager to gain regime support and to prove their usefulness, and they more or less successfully managed to do so. This is true for cultural morphology, one of the large schools, as long as the very popular Leo Frobenius chaired in Frankfurt: although his research expeditions were not particularly useful for Nazi ideology, the continuing professional presence of this glamorous and internationally known author added to the regime's image in the prewar years, in the German public sphere as much as internationally.

Functionalism in German sociocultural anthropology, on the other hand, went through a remarkable period of promotion and upgrading during the Nazi years. Functionalism had some of the internationally best known scholars in its ranks, most importantly, Richard Thurnwald, but also Konrad Theodor Preuss. Moreover, some of the most active Nazi party members among social anthropologists were functionalists: Wilhelm Emil Mühlmann, Günter Wagner, and Martin Heydrich were best known among this group. In Vienna, anthropology department staff member (since 1934) Christoph Fürer-Haimendorf, who became a leading member of the London School of Oriental and African Studies after the war, also was associated with this group because of his functionalist orientation and his secret Nazi party membership (since 1933) before he moved to the British side when the war broke out (Linimayr 1994, 64–67). In addition to Preuss, some others of the former moderate positivists now followed German functionalism more explicitly.

Culture circle theory, however, as the other large school from the interwar years, adapted itself to prevailing circumstances. In Austria, where a Catholic fascist regime followed Mussolini's and Franco's orientation until the country was occupied by Hitler's Germany in 1938, Wilhelm Schmidt's school continued to search for "original monotheism." Until 1938, this Vienna school increasingly came to be treated as an obstacle and minor rival to Nazi ideologists, who pursued pan-Germanism, as opposed to any separate Austrian entity, and biological racism, as opposed to Schmidt's theological creationism. After Austria's occupation in 1938, these Vienna school representatives, under their leader Wilhelm Schmidt, lost their academic positions in Vienna and emigrated to Switzerland. Meanwhile, inside Nazi Germany other representatives of culture circle theory had further elaborated this diffusionist orientation, but in Fritz Graebner's originally secular variant, without the Vienna school's theological premises. Walter Krickeberg and Hermann Baumann, both in Berlin, and Hans Plischke in Göttingen were the best-known representatives of this secular variant of diffusionist culture history in the Third Reich.

In institutional terms, the historical diffusionists were better established and held more full professorships than the functionalists. Besides, after Austria's "*Anschluss*" in 1938, diffusionist Baumann became Koppers's successor and a full professor in Vienna. In the same year, Leo Frobenius died, and Adolf E. Jensen, as his former assistant, became his successor in Frankfurt's cultural morphology school. Jensen was not a supporter of the Nazi regime, and although his marriage was not an easy one, he refused to divorce his Jewish wife, which inevitably would have meant her death in a concentration camp. For these reasons, Jensen was suspended from office, though he continued to direct an understaffed institute behind the scenes (Byer 1999, 417) until he and other staff members were drafted into military service.

At the beginning of the war a certain rearrangement in German sociocultural anthropology thus emerged as a result of "integration from above and from below." The two former large schools had gone through setbacks and were now less important than before, or their members had been exiled. Cultural morphology in Frankfurt was reduced in size and amount of professional activity, and culture circle theory in its theological version was expelled while its secular historical diffusionist version was promoted. Finally, functionalism was now more important that it had been, and it tried to overtake its rivals from the large schools.

Persecution and Emigration

Mainstream sociocultural anthropology thus became integrated to a very large extent into German academia under the Nazis, while its theoretical directions were going through a certain rearrangement of recognition and influence. Most of the few professional anthropologists with Marxist or materialist sympathies, including Paul Kirchhoff, Karl Wittfogel, and Julius and Eva Lips, were forced to emigrate or managed to escape before the war began. The Vienna school was another exception to the general rule of integration. Apart from these exceptions, mainstream anthropology was largely integrated into the Nazi system (Streck 2000, 9), though cultural morphology was left at the margins (fig. 1).

If this insight is accepted, then an assessment of any middle ground has to be cautious. Between rival networks of accomplices on the one hand and those who suffered from persecution or who resisted on the other, there was not much room left. Jensen certainly represented the best of these pieces of small middle ground. In my view, the roles of Koppers and Paul Schebesta from the Vienna school also may be assessed in this manner, in contrast to that of their leader, Schmidt, who is better regarded as a losing rival to the Nazis (Conte 1987).

Preuss, Boas's old colleague in North American studies, represents a somewhat more ambivalent case. He was forced into early retirement by the Nazis and apparently disagreed with their views. In his advanced years, however, he agreed to step in as substitute editor for the anthropology textbook *Lehrbuch der Völkerkunde* after the original editor, Leonhard Adam, was ousted because of his Jewish background. Under Preuss's name the *Lehrbuch* came out in 1937, and it became an anthropological standard reference text in Nazi Germany. Preuss died in 1938, suffering at least in part from the pressure and bitter arguments that accompanied the publication of this book. (These arguments later were to become known as the Krickeberg debate; Byer 1999, 394). Fürer-Haimendorf, who entertained the flirt between German and British functionalism as long as it lasted before he and his British wife decided to stay on in India, probably is best assessed as a middle-ground example as well (Gingrich 2005).

Preuss's case demonstrates that in these small pieces of middle ground, there were few who could, like Jensen, keep a fairly clean record. Others, like Preuss, suffered from persecution as much as they also became accomplices. Among the network of accomplices, there also were cases of occasional minor or major persecution; among those who were persecuted there may have been instances of occasional collaboration.

While the divide may not have been clear cut in each and every individual case, the evidence of persecution as a social and historical fact is more than clear. Anthropologists made crucial contributions to persecution, and anthropologists were among the victims of persecution.

Berthold Riese (1995, 210–20) and Thomas Hauschild (1995, 13–61) have provided a first survey of those anthropologists who were forced into emigration or were harassed, persecuted, jailed, tortured, or murdered. The more well-known persons among them included anthropologist of law Leonhard Adam, who managed to begin a new career in Melbourne, and Gerardo Reichel-Dolmatoff, who left Austria for the Americas to establish himself as a renowned South Americanist. Julius and Eva Lips, from Cologne, reached

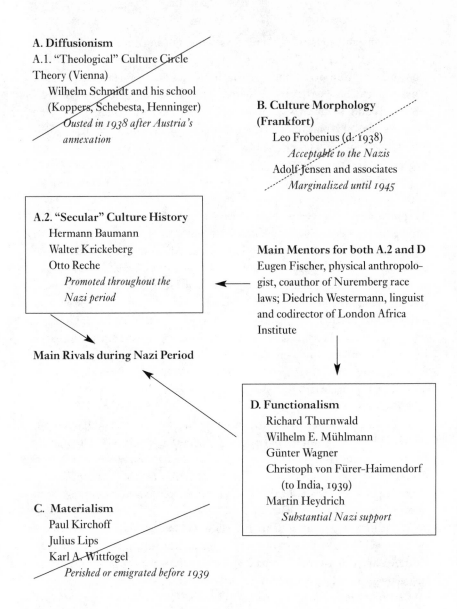

A. Diffusionism
A.1. "Theological" Culture Circle
Theory (Vienna)
    Wilhelm Schmidt and his school
    (Koppers, Schebesta, Henninger)
      Ousted in 1938 after Austria's
      annexation

**B. Culture Morphology
(Frankfort)**
    Leo Frobenius (d. 1938)
      Acceptable to the Nazis
    Adolf Jensen and associates
      Marginalized until 1945

A.2. "Secular" Culture History
    Hermann Baumann
    Walter Krickeberg
    Otto Reche
      Promoted throughout the
      Nazi period

Main Mentors for both A.2 and D
Eugen Fischer, physical anthropologist, coauthor of Nuremberg race
laws; Diedrich Westermann, linguist
and codirector of London Africa
Institute

Main Rivals during Nazi Period

D. Functionalism
    Richard Thurnwald
    Wilhelm E. Mühlmann
    Günter Wagner
    Christoph von Fürer-Haimendorf
      (to India, 1939)
    Martin Heydrich
      Substantial Nazi support

C. Materialism
    Paul Kirchoff
    Julius Lips
    Karl A. Wittfogel
      Perished or emigrated before 1939

Fig. 1. Theoretical orientations and their main representatives in German-speaking
anthropology (1933–1945). Solid slash indicates persecution and forced emigration under
Hitler. Dotted slash indicates gradual marginalization under Hitler.

North America exile, where Julius published his well-known anticolonial book *The Savage Hits Back* (1937). The Vienna-based specialist of African art and craftsmanship Marianne Schmidl did not manage to emigrate: because she was Jewish, she was forced to hand over her research notes to her academic supervisor, Otto Reche, before perishing in a concentration camp (Byer 1999, 291; Geisenhainer 2002, 201–20). Southeast Asianist Robert Heine-Geldern and ethnomusicologist Carl Sachs escaped to New York, and Sachs's associate Erich Hornbostel, to England. Several cases are still sealed because they might incriminate persons who died not long ago. The small group of anthropologists who actively resisted included the elderly Heinrich Cunow, former director of the Berlin museum (1919–1928), who was abandoned to helplessly die in his own Berlin flat (Ulrich 1987), and Robert Bleichsteiner, Vienna museum curator for the Middle East, who cooperated with organized opposition groups until 1945 and survived (Mühlfried 2000).

Main Directions of Anthropology in Nazi Germany

The shifting relations of power and influence among sociocultural anthropologists became evident in the so-called Krickeberg debate, which accompanied publication of the textbook edited by Preuss instead of Adam. Walter Krickeberg, a follower of Graebner's diffusionism, became curator for North America at the Berlin museum after his predecessor, Preuss, was forced into early retirement, not without Krickeberg's help it seems. When the Preuss textbook came out, an angry Krickeberg published a review in which he asked why the volume contained contributions written mostly by functionalists, members of a school that, he claimed, was close to the anti-German functionalist Malinowski in London and had Jewish sympathizers everywhere, not least of whom was the volume's former editor, Adam, who still had a contribution in the textbook. The book thus overrepresented an anti-German and pro-Jewish research orientation, Krickeberg claimed, and it misrepresented the good German tradition of historical diffusionism.

As a reviewer for the Berlin ministry, Hans Plischke, professor and museum director for anthropology in Göttingen, strongly supported Krickeberg's position (Braun 1995, 54–55; Kulick-Aldag 2000, 111–12). Richard Thurnwald und Wilhelm Mühlmann were quick to publish rejoinders. Mühlmann claimed that German functionalism was older than its British counterpart and that, moreover, it synthesized biological and historical reasoning. Thurnwald, in turn, pursued a less sophisticated intellectual argument by stating that Jews like Adam had published much more often with the historical diffusionists than with the functionalists as, for instance, Adam had on a previous occasion with Krickeberg's colleague Hermann Baumann. (Baumann wrote a quick apology for having published with a Jew, claiming that he had not yet known then that Adam was Jewish.) Moreover, Thurnwald added, the historical diffusionists were allies of the Catholic priest Wilhelm Schmidt in Vienna, who was not a friend of Nazi Germany. (Baumann nervously replied that he did not know Schmidt well.) The debate thus focused on whether functionalism or historical diffusionism was anti-Jewish and pro-German enough; it started with historical diffusionists' sinister critique of a functionalist textbook, and it ended with a fierce counterattack by functionalists.

Functionalism, thus, was moving forward to overtake historical diffusionism in Germany. The basic organicist paradigm in functionalism was more compatible with social Darwinism and with the biological requirements of academic racism. In addition, the functionalist preference for pragmatic analysis of the present as opposed to speculative theorizing about the past made it more useful for colonial interests. The nontheological variant of historical diffusionism, however, began to work hard to meet this challenge, and its representatives continued to control the larger number of academic and museum institutions. During the Nazi years each of these two competing orientations of German sociocultural anthropology thus worked eagerly in order to demonstrate its successful performance and public usefulness, both by effectively cooperating with physical anthropology and by carrying out colonial studies.

As for physical anthropology, throughout their careers some of its most prominent representatives had also pursued themes and interests that widely intersected with sociocultural anthropology, or *Völkerkunde*. Otto Reche, for instance, was among those who held chairs in both *Völkerkunde* and physical anthropology (in Vienna, 1924–1927, and in Leipzig, 1927–1945), and who taught, published, and trained in both. The move toward an intensified merging of physical and sociocultural anthropology during the Nazi years gave a unique opportunity to someone with this professional background who pursued the integration the two fields and was a Nazi member (Geisenhainer 2000, 83–100). During the Nazi years Reche transformed his Leipzig institute into a center for racial and racist anthropological theorizing, empirical research, and commissioned racial "evaluations" (Geisenhainer 2002, 196–366). Likewise, Eugen Fischer had early ethnographic training and fieldwork experience in Germany's colony of South-West Africa. During the Nazi years, he continued and intensified his integrating and merging activities in relation to sociocultural anthropology by supervising and mentoring *Völkerkunde* representatives like Dominik Wölfel (who presented elaborations about "White Africa" and "Black Africa"; Linimayr 1994, 243) and Hermann Baumann (Lösch 1997). These lines of cooperation show that as the older and more powerful school preceding the Nazi period, historical diffusionism had already established relations with physical anthropologists of long standing.

It is precisely for this reason that when the functionalists strove to gradually overtake their historical diffusionist rivals during the Nazi years, they also had to work much more intensively to gain a lead in relations with physical anthropologists. The functionalists thus were somewhat more ambitious, explicit, and ruthlessly effective in their integrative efforts toward Nazi Germany's key academic field of physical anthropology. In this regard, Mühlmann certainly has to be assessed as the most intellectual synthesizer of a racist biology with social Darwinian functionalism (Michel 1995).

By contrast, Günter Wagner's research interests had more of a practical political focus on applying such functionalist insights to Africa. In the early 1940s, his responsible participation in colonial planning and publishing activities served Nazi Germany's plans and ambitions in the reestablishment of a German East Africa colony, for which Wagner's former field site of Kenya already was envisioned as the northern part. In his writing of those years, Wagner—like everybody else who was active in this field for the Germans— argued for colonial policies that would have to differ from the British record by making more explicit recognition of differences between Europeans and Africans (Mischek 2002, 100, 175).

Compared to the more ambitious younger functionalists Mühlmann and Wagner, the aging Thurnwald already was more saturated academically. His own writing during the Nazi years on integrating physical and sociocultural anthropology was more a rhetorical than a substantial effort. Thurnwald did not refrain, however, from accepting and promoting PhD candidates who did applied research inside the Third Reich along the lines of merging social with physical anthropology under Nazi premises. A case in point is a certain Eva Justin.

Justin was a trained nurse and Robert Ritter's closest collaborator for years. Ritter had been director of the Reich's racial hygienics institute since 1936. In this position, his 1938 analysis of "Gypsies" as an "alien race" who should be either sterilized or eliminated became the basis for Himmler's Notification No. 12938 on "fighting the Gypsy menace," followed later by Himmler's orders of 1942 and 1943 to send "Gypsies" and their offspring to Auschwitz. Until 1944 the procedures that carried out these orders were based on criteria and assessments worked out by Ritter, his assistant Justin, and their team. Ritter and Justin, therefore, were responsible academic participants in the Nazi mass persecution of Roma and Sinti. Moreover, they were personally present when deportations of Roma and Sinti were organized, and they personally visited concentration camps.

At the University of Berlin in 1943, Eva Justin submitted her PhD thesis, *Lebensschicksale artfremd erzogener Zigeunerkinder und ihrer Nachkommen* ("Biographical destinies of Gypsy children and their offspring who were educated in a manner inappropriate for their species"), which argued that racial factors were so important among "Gypsies" that they could not be countered by social or environmental influences. "Gypsies" belonged to an "alien race" and were comparable to primitive foragers, she wrote. Her thesis was based on interviews with and observations among children and young persons who had already been selected for deportation, but had not yet been brought to Auschwitz because they were being made available for Justin's research first. Just like her career leading up to her PhD, so the research for her thesis was part and parcel of Nazi crimes against Roma and Sinti.

Eugen Fischer, then perhaps the Reich's most prominent physical anthropologist and racial reviewer, guided Justin through the process of her thesis review and her final doctoral exam. He and Ritter wrote the academic reviews for her first subject, physical anthropology, while Richard Thurnwald was the responsible reviewer for her second subject, social anthropology. No rule obliged Thurnwald to do this. For her final exams, Justin had to prepare for Thurnwald questions on the topic of foragers that picked up her thesis's theme. In his written academic review, Thurnwald acknowledged Justin's empirical work, whose gruesome context and background he must have been fully aware of, as "anthropological fieldwork" *(völkerkundliche Feldforschung)*. Although he criticized Justin's thesis for restricting its results to the empirical evidence only, this did not prevent him from grading her work with the best mark, "very good." After Justin passed her PhD, the children she had studied for her thesis were deported to Auschwitz, on 6 May 1944. When her thesis was published in autumn 1944, all of them were dead.

After the war cases were prepared against Ritter and Justin. In one case Justin was acquitted; the other charges never came to court. Ritter died in 1951. In post-1945 West Germany, Justin first became a psychologist for juvenile criminals with the Frankfurt police, and on that basis she later even acted as a consultant to courts in cases of compensation demands by survivors of Nazism (Gilsenbach 1988 a, b; Hohmann 1996a, 1996b; Reemtsma 1996 a, b). In the Nazi period the functionalist effort to embrace physical anthropology thus ranged from Mühlmann's theoretical synthesis to Justin's "applied" dissertation.

The functionalists also were active in colonial studies. This was true most notably of Thurnwald himself, since he had firsthand experience with colonial topics from his early sojourns in the Austrian colony of Bosnia and in the German colonies of Melanesia. Mühlmann contributed his insights for Nazi interests in Eastern Europe, while Wagner and Heydrich worked for Nazi ambitions in Africa. Yet by and large it seems that in colonial studies the historical diffusionists were equally active (Mosen 1991). While the famous linguist Diedrich Westermann supported colonial research by scholars from both directions, Baumann was the leading diffusionist figure in this regard.

Until the early 1940s the expansionist political and military plans of Nazi Germany's leaders definitely included a number of scenarios for Germany to become again a colonial power outside Europe. Most notably this concerned domains held by imperial Germany until 1918. After Germany's military defeat of France, however, these scenarios also included a new colonial alliance for Africa between Hitler's Germany and its vassal state, Henri Pétain's France. These scenarios and plans were the rationale behind serious material efforts that Nazi Germany mobilized for colonial research. Substantial budgets were established and funded, new positions were created, and military recruitment was waived for researchers involved in projects not only of racial and biological studies, but also of colonial studies. In both fields traditional academic institutions such as universities, museums, and the Kaiser Wilhelm Society were involved as much as new special purpose institutions created by Nazi Germany. These institutions ranged from Himmler's Ahnenerbe ("ancestral legacy") to the various colonial desks and offices of the Nazi state and party (Mosen 1991; Byer 1999).

From 1934 onward, sociocultural anthropology in Nazi Germany thus went through a smooth integration and gradual transformation. This process eventually included ruthless purging and persecution as much as a new internal redistribution of power and a shift of research priorities. Within these new priorities, an intensified merger with physical anthropology and a substantial effort toward colonial studies were top on the list. During the 1940s, when this process peaked, sociocultural anthropology's gradual transformation had reached quite a considerable extent—personally (by way of persecution and promotion), institutionally (by way of new funds and new sponsors) and in terms of content (by way of functionalism's new role, new priorities for colonial studies, and the merging of interests with racial studies). Other academic fields were transformed much more intensively to be sure, but the assertion that sociocultural anthropology was left out or forgotten by the Nazis simply is not justified by the evidence.

As serious and substantial as preparations for colonial efforts outside of Europe were, one should not overestimate them. Compared to the merger with physical anthropology and racial studies, and compared to those fields' practical involvement in Nazi Germany's colonial and holocaust program inside Europe, the colonial scenarios for Africa and Asia were politically lightweight. After all, the scenarios were never fully implemented in practice. This certainly was good for the inhabitants of those African and Asian regions for which Nazi Germany's colonial plans were designed. In retrospect, it was also good fortune for those German anthropologists who worked eagerly for this particular field that it never materialized.

During the Nazi years historical diffusionists like Baumann were ambitiously engaged in colonial research on Africa and other regions outside Europe. German Africa research *(Deutsche Afrika-Forschung)* had held a wide international reputation at least since the early twentieth century. All anthropological schools and research orientations had contributed to it: Frobenius's and Jensen's cultural morphology as much as Wagner's and Heydrich's functionalism, Schebesta's and Wölfel's Vienna school as much as Ankermann's and Baumann's more secular historical diffusionism. The reputation of German Africa research was held in such high esteem that, for instance, eminent German linguist Diedrich Westermann remained one of the two directors of the International Africa Institute and coeditor of its journal in London throughout the early Nazi years, until the war broke out. Before the war the Africa Institute's activities were not monopolized by British colonial interests alone, though Henrika Kuklick (1991, 194) claims otherwise. In his important recent analysis, Udo Mischek (2002, 45–61) has demonstrated the degree to which French and German interests also were involved at all levels of running the institute. Before the war, Schmidt and Schebesta, among other German anthropologists, also were on its governing body and executive council.

In a related instance, Günter Wagner, after returning from his North American studies under Boas and from his Hamburg PhD exams, had become a researcher for the London's International Africa Institute from 1933 until 1939. During that period he carried out his fieldwork in Western Kenya under Malinowski's guidance, and the books that resulted were published in English after the war (Wagner 1949–1956, 1954, 1970). Moreover, Wagner became a relatively close associate of Edward E. Evans-Pritchard and Meyer Fortes, to the extent that they insisted on his contribution being published in their soon-to-be famous *African Political Systems* (1940) even after Wagner returned to Germany and the war began (Mischek 2002, 46–79, 233). Wagner thus was probably the best trained social anthropologist Germany had throughout the first half of the twentieth century, and inside Nazi Germany he was the most anglicized among the strong group of functionalist social anthropologists.

When Hermann Baumann took over the Vienna chair in 1939, he faced serious challenges for historical diffusionism, but simultaneously he understood the opportunities before him. He could build his reputation on a reasonable fieldwork period in Angola (1930–1931) and on ensuing publications, among them a highly acclaimed analysis of African myths (Baumann 1936). As a mentee of Fischer ever since his young years in Freiburg, and of Westermann since his years at the Berlin museum, Baumann was promoted by two of the most powerful and influential scholars of these fields in Nazi Germany. Perhaps this encouraged his now notorious tendency to conspire against professional rivals and to point a finger at them. A member of the Nazi party since 1932 (Braun 1995, 41), Baumann had criticized Frobenius's cultural morphology in his widely quoted 1934 article in the London institute's journal *Africa*, saying that Frobenius separated culture from race in an unacceptable manner (Baumann 1934, 133–34). In the Krickeberg debate Baumann played a role in the pressures that led to Preuss's death in Berlin (Byer 1999, 394).

In Vienna, while teaching his courses dressed up and bearing the insignia of his party membership (Anna Hohenwart-Gerlachstein, personal communication), Baumann engaged in another conspiracy against a colleague whom he saw as a rival. That colleague was Hugo August Bernatzik, a professional photographer and trained freelance anthropologist. By the 1920s and 1930s Bernatzik had already published widely successful expedition reports with photographic documentation of unprecedented quality. This photographic work made Bernatzik a problematic early precursor to visual anthropology because he found and created his main audience in the public mass spheres of Nazi Germany. Bernatzik worked very hard as a freelancer to mobilize funds for colonial research that he would conduct by himself in Africa and elsewhere. There is no doubt that Bernatzik, who like his wife and coworker, Emmy, was a brilliant writer and lecturer, used explicit racist Nazi terminology in his various nonpublic attempts to raise funds, primarily through state and party offices and to a lesser extent with his popular writing. He certainly contributed decisively to mobilization for anthropology's part in the colonial effort outside Europe as long as it lasted (Mosen 1991). Yet identification of Bernatzik as the most prominent Nazi or the most efficient colonial anthropologist, as was common in anthropology circles after 1945 (with some echoes in later historiography), certainly was a profound misinterpretation based on postwar ignorance or on the apologetic search for a scapegoat.

Baumann was much more successful than Bernatzik in mobilizing support for colonial research. Behind the scenes their rivalry led to Baumann's active support of a campaign against Bernatzik in which some of the Bernatziks' work on Southeast Asia was denounced as a forgery. It was not until some years after the war that most sides cleared Bernatzik of these allegations; some of his relevant ethnography came out in English translation with HRAF Press after the war (1970).

Baumann spared no effort and saved no costs to get what he wanted during the Nazi years. There is no evidence available so far, however, that indicates that he was involved in ways similar to Thurnwald's substantial support for Justin's dissertation. After the defeat of France and the installation of the Pétain puppet regime there, Baumann and Bernatzik began to compete for French ethnographic sources from the colonial records in Paris and for the collaboration of French Africanists and anthropologists in their respective projects. The famous French names of those who collaborated in these two rival projects included, for an initial period, Michel Leiris and Marcel Griaule, and more extensively Jean-Paul Lebeuf, Henry Laubouret, and George-Henri Rivière. The Italian Vigini L. Grotanelli also collaborated (Braun 1995, 73–74; Byer 1999, 318–20).

For the sake of clarity, I emphasize that these men did not study children before they were to be sent to the death camp, nor did they, to my knowledge, directly and personally participate in any other activities of this type. Yet the two rival projects of Baumann and Bernatzik were part and parcel of Nazi Germany's colonial war effort against the Allies with the goal of winning territory and resources in Africa.

Through the Nazi military occupation in France Baumann acquired French colonial records and established collaborations that were to strengthen his own authority and reputation as a scholar. Bernatzik published his original project, which included two articles on Kenya and Uganda by Wagner, after the war in a German version that was more or less adapted to the postwar colonial period (1947). Baumann, by contrast, gave up the collective effort of an edited publication during the late war years. Instead, he focused on publishing in French a version of his German magnum opus in a fairly successful attempt to reestablish his international academic reputation for the post-Nazi years. His *Les peuples et les civilisations d'Afrique* (1948) thus became a classic of a sort.

This work and Baumann's other writings were by no means free of racist tendencies. Most importantly, they followed the dominant Hamitic paradigm, according to which tall, fair-skinned warrior groups from Africa's north and northeast (inspired, as the diffusionist Baumann claimed, by Mesopotamia) became the driving force in Africa's history by pushing southward and establishing themselves as the elites. In this perspective Bantu-speaking people were seen as subordinate to or as undermining the superior elites. For the latter process Baumann's Vienna museum associate Walter Hirschberg coined the term *negroization (Vernegerung)* to characterize the alleged racial-cultural corruption from below (Byer 1999, 112). Still, it has to be acknowledged that this Hamitic paradigm was shared by most European and American anthropologists of Africa until the mid-1950s; it thus represents nothing specific to Baumann's work or to anthropology under Nazism. Baumann's 1948 book used ecological, linguistic, historical, economic, and sociocultural criteria to outline nine cultural areas and twenty-seven "ethnographic" or "cultural provinces" (Baumann 1948) in Africa. Many experts argue that in this regard Baumann's work represented the best synthesis in its time of whatever overviews anthropology had to offer. Some experts who find cultural areas and zones still useful go as far as to indicate that in their broad outline Baumann's classifications of African cultural variety may even have stood the test of time. This part of the debate is best left to the experts of Africa and inside Africa.

In their practical involvement as accomplices of the Nazi regime, anthropologists thus sometimes were and sometimes were not part of the Nazi killing machine. Furthermore, a relatively heavy practical involvement with the Nazi political apparatus was in some cases (Baumann) not very explicitly apparent in these authors' core academic writing, whereas in other cases (Mühlmann) it was reflected in fully elaborated academic Nazi propaganda. This leads to the difficult question of responsibility.

Questions of Responsibility

I am neither a lawyer nor a moral philosopher nor a historian. I am convinced, however, that assessing the history of anthropology has to be a joint effort by lay historians who are professional anthropologists as much as by professional historians who are lay anthropologists, and both of these should be from local as much as from international backgrounds.

Out of these considerations an assessment of historical responsibility can build on some of the main insights of other research on the history of Nazism. These works by historians, political scientists, and law experts follow different theoretical and methodological priorities out of which one has to choose.

For German anthropology during the Nazi years, I have so far differentiated between networks of accomplices, small pieces of middle ground, and dispersed groups of victims of persecution and of those few who resisted. I have clarified that instances of persecution could occur among the networks of accomplices and that instances of collaboration may have occurred among those who resisted or were persecuted (Bleichsteiner certainly collaborated to an extent). On this basis, and building on the two final points of the last section, for this provisional discussion of historical responsibility of accomplices I differentiate three categories of such responsibility: First, some anthropologists made successful personal contributions toward the professional destruction or physical elimination of other persons, by denouncing them, by recommending that they lose their jobs, and so forth. Second, some anthropologists carried out applied research for Nazi purposes—research that in cases of responsibility in the narrow sense would benefit from the Nazi killing machine or contribute to it. Third, some anthropologists produced explicit propaganda for the Nazi regime and elaborated its ideology by using and abusing their academic and professional authority.

A scenario that takes us back to 1937 indicates how deeply the leading groups of German anthropologists were involved from the outset in Nazism's medium-term efforts.

Leading anthropologists were among the members of the German delegation to the peacetime conference of the International Union of Anthropological and Ethnological Sciences in Copenhagen in early August 1938. The official leader of the German delegation was Eugen Fischer, who was accompanied by his close disciple Othmar von Verschuer. Fischer had been the director of the Berlin Kaiser Wilhelm-Institute for physical anthropology since its foundation in 1927. He was also a key spirit behind the Nazi elaboration of the Nuremberg race laws. Until his retirement in 1942, Fischer and his institute staff delivered numerous "racial assessments" and evaluations during the Nazi years that were decisive for sending many to their deaths in concentration camps and elsewhere. Fischer and his institute carried out crash courses for SS doctors for their selection activities in the death camps. For his research

Fischer solicited body parts of inmates of prisons, hospitals, and concentration camps. Verschuer would become Fischer's successor at the Berlin institute in 1942. After the war Fischer, who died in 1967, became an honorary member of the German Society for Anthropology, an organization for physical anthropologists in West Germany.

Another member of the German anthropology delegation in Copenhagen who was not well-known then but would reach sinister fame soon was Josef Mengele. He was Verschuer's disciple and assistant. During the war Mengele would become the responsible doctor in the Auschwitz death camp, often personally standing on the notorious Auschwitz ramp, selecting countless incoming prisoners for immediate death in the gas chamber or for his experiments. After the war Mengele managed to escape to South America, and he never was brought to justice.

The Copenhagen delegation thus demonstrated to the outside world as much as to German academia that physical anthropology had gained official hegemony over the other fields, which were represented by prehistory (archaeology) and *Völkerkunde* (sociocultural anthropology). German sociocultural anthropology was represented in Copenhagen by its internationally most widely respected figure, Richard Thurnwald. His reputation counted with the international academic public. It was significant, but maybe more relevant for internal political cohesion, that Baumann belonged to the responsible inner circle of the delegation (Braun 1995, 53).

Eugen Fischer, an applied researcher and, already in 1937, a desk perpetrator; Joseph Mengele, a mass murderer of the near future; Herman Baumann, a historical diffusionist and Fischer's mentee; plus, last but not least, the flamboyant functionalist Richard Thurnwald: this was the core group in the official delegation of German anthropologists in Copenhagen (Linimayr 1994, 67f.; Braun 1995, 53). It shows how very close sociocultural anthropologists sometimes were, institutionally and symbolically if not intellectually or legally, to several central academic perpetrators of the Holocaust and war crimes. It should be added that although sociocultural anthropologists were close to these central perpetrators, they were not identical to them, but many of them knew and supported them.

This Copenhagen cast of characters corresponds fairly well to the three categories of responsibility I suggested earlier: Mengele and Fischer made personal contributions to the destruction of others; Fischer, Verschuer, and Mengele conducted applied research benefiting from or contributing to the Nazi killing machine, as did Thurnwald, to a lesser degree, by supervising Justin; and Fischer contributed explicit propaganda pieces for the Nazi regime. Apart from this, one may argue that at the time of the Copenhagen conference sociocultural anthropology had not yet found its leading Nazi propaganda activist. That would soon be solved, as we shall see.

Other actions of German anthropologists fit these three categories of responsibility. First, many of the "racial assessments" resulted in personal contributions toward the destruction of others. Physical anthropologists were the most responsible in this regard, but among them were some who promoted the merging with sociocultural interests (Fischer, Reche) and even some physical "experts" who were primarily sociocultural anthropologists (Heydrich).

While some anthropologists, like Justin, were actively involved in the persecution of Roma and Sinti, others contributed to mass crimes against Jews. In East Central Europe, two trained sociocultural anthropologists of small reputation sought to promote their careers by making practical contributions to Nazi Germany's murderous reordering of these areas: they were Anton Adolf Plügel, a Viennese disciple of Fritz Röck and Nazi party member since 1929, and Ingeborg Sydow, a student of Koppers and Frobenius at first, and of Richard Thurnwald later. Since 1941 both of them had been employed in the ethnological section of the Institute for German Eastern Works (Ostarbeit) in Krakow. They carried out empirical and conceptual studies for the "new European order" that the Nazi occupants pursued there. These studies included proposals for "ghettoising," in Plügel's words, "as a first basis to the final solution of the Jewish question." Plügel was drafted by the Wehrmacht in 1942, and Sydow left the institute in 1943 (Michel 2000, 160, 162).

One may further differentiate these "applied academic" activities from sociocultural anthropologists' security-related efforts for the Nazi authorities that unavoidably were harmful to others. One case in point is that of historical diffusionist Walter Krickeberg, whom I already discussed as American curator at the Berlin museum, the successor to Konrad Theodor Preuss, and the unhappy instigator of a debate. There is sufficient evidence to prove that during the Nazi years Krickeberg reported five colleagues to the authorities (Byer 1999, 394). After 1945 he was promoted even further to become the new director of the Berlin museum. Another case in point is that of functionalist Africa specialist Günter Wagner. At the beginning of the war, he had returned from the Britain to Germany, where he had taken office in the colonial political office of the Nazi party and in Joseph Goebbels's propaganda ministry. During the war he was responsible, among other duties, for censoring social anthropologists and providing publication permits for them (Mischek 2002, 84–113; Byer 1999, 303, 388). Wagner's direct collaboration with the ministry-sponsored "Anti-Semitic Action" in 1939–1940 is confirmed, but cannot yet be documented in detail. This unit was involved in early Nazi plans for mass deportations of Jews to Madagascar (Mischek 2002, 85–87).

Second, some of them conducted applied research for the Nazi regime in several central fields. One of them was racial assessments. Apart from Fischer and his Berlin institute staff, Otto Reche and his associates in Leipzig were heavily engaged in these activities (Byer 1999; Geisenhainer 2002, 236–306). Sociocultural anthropologist of Africa Martin Heydrich also may be referred to here: promoted from Dresden to Cologne in 1940, he became director of the museum and institute there. On several occasions he delivered professional racial assessments for the Racial Political Office. After the war he managed to stay on in his Cologne positions (Putzstück 1995).

Another central field of research involved "expeditions" that prepared for or supported the war. Cases in point were the German Hindukush expedition of 1935 (Mischek 2000, 134) and Walter Schäfer's team's mid-1930s expedition to Tibet (Brauen 2000). Supported by Himmler's *Ahnenerbe*, the Schäfer team explored whether Tibet was a potential war ally, whether its barley and its ponies could be used for winter war in Europe, and whether its high altitude allowed more reliable weather forecasts for aerial warfare. In addition, anthropologist Bruno Beger measured Tibetans to find a possible answer to the dispute over northern and eastern Germanic origins. During the war, Beger solicited skeletons from Auschwitz for comparison with this Tibetan data (Brauen 2000). Yet another field of applied research were was colonial studies, which the course of war prevented from becoming practically effective in most parts of Africa and Asia. The consequences of such colonial studies by Richard Thurnwald, Baumann, and Bernatzik for Nazi Germany therefore cannot be compared at all to those of racial assessments.

Third, sociocultural anthropologists engaged in "academic propaganda" for the Nazi regime. Until the late 1930s this could be carried out in a general supremacist and racist way, or in a more specific anti-Jewish manner, or both. It was part of anthropological museum exhibitions, successful anthropological publications on the popular book market, and so forth. Some of it came out of intention and conviction, some of it was opportunistic flirtation with what seemed fashionable, and some was merely fulfillment of a rhetorical minimum obligation. That wider academic racism, however, did not quickly lead to the emergence of an explicit pro-Nazi ideologist among sociocultural anthropologists (although Krause and others tried their best), as was shown by my examination of the 1938 Copenhagen delegation. Yet by that time, somebody was already working vigorously to soon fill this gap. That person was Wilhelm Emil Mühlmann (1904–1988), whom I regard as the most influential and most intelligent Nazi ideologist of academic *Völkerkunde* (see also Streck 2000, 9; Michel 1991).

Mühlmann, who had first studied physical anthropology with Fischer in Freiburg and Berlin, had finished his doctoral studies in social anthropology with Richard Thurnwald in Berlin. Emerging as Thurnwald's junior mentee, he shared his teacher's functionalist paradigms while preferring a wide interdisciplinary orientation over Thurnwald's emphasis on ethnographic fieldwork. Like his teacher and other German functionalists, Mühlmann saw social anthropology as basically connected to sociology, which reflected the aim to establish a German counterpart to the British model. Mühlmann, however, transcended this functionalist paradigm, by pursuing a much more integrative interdisciplinary orientation in two directions. On the more abstract and theoretical level, he sought to combine the sociological–social anthropological axis with philosophy, in particular with German phenomenology. On the more empirical and existential level, he sought to make physical and racial anthropology the profound basis of the whole interdisciplinary endeavor.

From early on, Mühlmann thus was central among sociocultural anthropologists in Germany in the effort to merge and integrate their field with physical anthropology. What had been outlined in the early 1933 letter to Hitler by other anthropologists was carried out by Mühlmann. His definition of race included sociocultural factors and accepted some aspects of racial assimilation. One of Mühlmann's first major books, his *Methodik der Völkerkunde* (1938) was conceptualized as the German functionalist alternative to the rival volume of similar title by Schmidt in Vienna (*Handbuch der Methode der Völkerkunde*), whose days were over from a Nazi perspective. Both books intended to supercede Graebner's outdated 1911 *Methode der Ethnologie* to become the new methodological standard work of the field in German. Mühlmann's *Methodik* and the Preuss-edited textbook thus were key functionalist signposts and indicators of social anthropology's gradual transformation and integration into the Nazi Reich.

By Nazi standards, Mühlmann's 1938 volume left few wishes unfulfilled. In its motto, the book celebrated Austria's annexation. As its central argument, the *Methodik* sharply opposed Bastian's "old" view of humanity's unity and instead pledged in favor of the study of racial differences. Moreover, Mühlmann specified that this was part of the necessity to bring about "a profound biological penetration" of the humanities and social sciences: This "integrative" and "interdisciplinary" orientation of anthropology, in Mühlmann's view, should provide Germany with new orientations in the world of "foreign peoples" that "surround it". Mühlmann argued in support of the Nuremberg race laws and against racial intermarriage, and he called for new colonial tasks. The rejection of Bastian's views from a half-century before was no side remark, but central to his argument. Most of the older functionalists, like Preuss and Thurnwald, had been trained as Bastian's disciples. By contrast, Mühlmann sought for a completely new paradigm that would radicalize the social Darwinism inherent in Thurnwald's concept of "sieving" (Siebung) by explicit subordination to physical anthropology and on the racist basis of racial differences. For this attempt toward a paradigmatic change, Mühlmann would need concepts centered around *Volk* (or *Ethnos* which he began to use as a term almost synonymous with *Volk* during the war), in which the racial and the social dimension would be brought together. It is hard to deny that Mühlmann's work represents the culmination of ongoing efforts not only to break with a past derived from Bastian or diffusionism, but also to establish a new synthetic paradigm that corresponded quite closely to the Nazis' program and ideology.

For these and similar efforts, Mühlmann received increasing support from Nazi authorities. He had been an early member of Hitler's paramilitary mass organization, the SA, and a Nazi Party member since 1935. In his 1939 habilitation he already argued that *Völkerkunde* should, by becoming an interethnic political sociology, include the study of large peoples. Thurnwald, Fischer, and Westermann endorsed Mühlmann's habilitation, whereas Preuss, in his review made shortly before his death, opposed academic approval on the grounds that Mühlmann would pursue a complete reorientation of the field. Preuss's assessment turned out to be correct. After one year in the army, Mühlmann was granted the waiver of war-relevant status with Rosenberg's personal approval so he could continue his anthropological work with a more and more explicit focus on the target area of Mühlmann's "large peoples," Eastern Europe. In 1942, Rosenberg, who would be the "Reich's minister for the occupied Eastern territories," organized an "Eastern conference of German scholars," in which Mühlmann participated, to pool together academic efforts for the Reich's plans in the East. Throughout this period Mühlmann's regional redirection of his anthropological interests and his new Eastern European focus led him to pay special attention to German minorities in those parts of the world.

It was in these contexts that he elaborated some of his key concepts of *Volkstum* (a "people's" existence rooted in race and culture), *Umvolkung* (either "Germanization" or, more generally, the transformation of a people through change in racial and cultural properties—the term, however, can also mean "being surrounded by other peoples"), *Überfremdung* (being "flooded" by foreigners), and *Volkwerdung* (the "emergence" of a new kind of people through such transformation). In Mühlmann's relevant writings of 1942–1945, as his biographer Ute Michel clearly has demonstrated, he also employed the term *Scheinvölker* ("fake peoples"). The term was borrowed from SS annihilation and extermination expert G. Teich, who had coined it for Jews, and Mühlmann further elaborated the concept. He used it to designate "half-breeds," "Gypsies," Jews, U.S. blacks, and people without clear ethnic features who were often denied assimilation. The term suggested intentional ethnic disguise and rendered academic credibility to racist discrimination and persecution (Michel 1995 and 2000).

With his Eastern European reorientation, Mühlmann thus intentionally sought to gain "applied" relevance for the region at a time when the Third Reich was preparing for and carrying out mass crimes of unprecedented dimensions in order to implement its plan for a completely altered demographic order under the hegemony of new German settlers and the old German minorities of Eastern Europe. Mühlmann therefore integrated his reorganized anthropological forms and concepts into the language and ideology of the Nazi party, the SS, and their extermination experts. In addition, he worked for the "application" of this new conceptual inventory in Eastern Europe when Nazi crimes approached their climax there. In short, Mühlmann has to be reassessed, and he may well be considered anthropology's Holocaust ideologist, and a colonial anthropologist as well, probably with more practical relevance for Eastern Europe than all the others had for Africa and elsewhere. After 1945 Mühlmann continued to be a highly influential figure in the *Völkerkunde* of West Germany.

Changes and Continuities

Some very important recent research has been carried out by anthropologists and historians on the role of sociocultural anthropology in the Third Reich. Most of it has been published since the 1990s in German. With few precursors from earlier years, this represents merely the first generation of research on this topic. Any summarizing statement thus would be premature.

On the basis of new evidence and disputed interpretations of it, that first generation of solid studies resulted in a number of healthy debates. One of these debates centered around Hans Fischer's 1990 thesis that *Völkerkunde* was relatively unimportant for the Nazi regime and that it managed to survive almost unaffected. Although this may have been so in some aspects for the Hamburg case that Fischer primarily examined, my own study here leads me to embrace the view of those authors, like Jürgen Braun (1995) and Bernhard Streck (2000, 8), who argue to the contrary. During the Nazi years *Völkerkunde* certainly was less important than some fields, such as the natural sciences, which were crucial for war production and Holocaust crimes. Through its merging with physical anthropology, however, it became more important than many other academic disciplines, including philological studies and several other historical fields. By institutional, financial, and staffing criteria, *Völkerkunde* as a whole did not experience a severe setback under the Nazis; rather it went through substantial processes of promotion.

A second debate centered around Peter Linimayr's thesis that during the Third Reich *Völkerkunde* was on the point of being radically transformed into a "Nazi science" (1994). Again, this emphasis on the discontinuities is somewhat more arguable for the Vienna case (before and after 1938) examined in detail by Linimayr, with its more drastic change of staff and orientation. Others, like Ute Michel (2000, 164), have countered Linimayr's argument by pointing out the general continuities before and after 1934 in German sociocultural anthropology. Here I have noted both the continuity of a smooth transition in 1933–1934 and thereafter, and the discontinuities evident in the new enhancement of colonial and racial studies culminating with Mühlmann. Which one of these prevailed, continuity or discontinuity, I leave to experts' further debate. What can be outlined at this point, however, are some of these changes and continuities in sociocultural anthropology that became apparent around the end of the war, with the defeat of Nazi Germany.

Compared to the general loss of lives and opportunities brought about by the Nazi regime and its war, the losses inflicted by, and on, social anthropologists seem moderate if not insignificant. Yet for a relatively small academic field, if we consider the long and still incomplete list of its representatives who were persecuted or had to emigrate, the losses were substantial. If the cases of Siegfried Nadel, Paul Kirchhoff, and Eric Wolf also are included in these considerations, then a dramatic prewar brain drain becomes apparent, from which any recovery was bound to be difficult.

In addition to those who emigrated or died in the war as civilians or soldiers (such as one of Jensen's associates, for instance), Nazism's seduction of competent anthropologists like Thurnwald and Wagner was a loss of a different kind, namely a deplorable selling out of skills and talents.

As the Allied Forces moved closer, the Reich's outposts were given up by those social anthropologists who held them for Hitler. The Krakow Institute was abandoned, Baumann fled from Vienna back into Germany, and several Nazi supporters (though by no means all) left East Germany for the West, when the Red Army arrived, or they were arrested by U.S. forces, as was Otto Reche. He would receive Austria's "honorary medal" for his "academic achievements" in 1965 (Geisenhainer 2002, 402–6). Some of those who had been institutional representatives of *Völkerkunde* and its neighboring fields during the Nazi years also left Germany altogether soon after the war: Some, such as Josef Mengele, went to South America to hide as the war criminals they were. Others with an incomparably less sinister record had the chance to pursue their academic interests under institutional conditions they found attractive—like Günther Wagner in South Africa and Oswald Menghin in Argentina (Kohl and Gollan 2002).

The majority of the more well-known scholars, however, not only survived, but eventually managed to reestablish themselves in their academic profession inside Germany. Rarely did they lose their academic credentials for good, although some (Baumann) did lose them for some time.

Under communist rule in East Germany, *Völkerkunde* began to go through quite a radical kind of transformation: a few re-migrants and party ideologists began to promote a dogmatically Marxist *Ethnographie* there. For *Völkerkunde* in West Germany and Austria, however, the transition out of the Nazi period was almost as gradual as the transition into the Third Reich had been. Because some key representatives of the old large schools had not been treated favorably by the Nazis, many of them took their second chance after 1945. Simultaneously, many of German anthropology's more prominent Nazi supporters were content with less important academic jobs now, although some managed to maintain their former positions (like Heydrich and Plischke) and a few even achieved promotion (like Krickeberg). To some extent, the overall institutional result became apparent in the few years following 1945. Thus, in West German and Austrian *Völkerkunde*, a major job rotation occurred: ex-Nazi supporters often had to step back into more secondary positions, whereas large school representatives often returned to key positions. Through this job rotation a substantial amount of personal continuity and some intellectual continuity prevailed. The chances for an overdue renewal of sociocultural anthropology were missed.

5

Anthropology in Four German-Speaking Countries: Key Elements of Post–World War II Developments to 1989

After 1945 a more rapid expansion of anthropological institutions in Switzerland, which had been spared the war devastations, contrasted to a very slow reorientation elsewhere in the German language zone. For the reconstruction of academic life in both West and East Germany (FRG and GDR, respectively), as well as in Austria, sociocultural anthropology did not rank very high on the list of postwar priorities. Financial constraints and political and intellectual factors were the main reasons why anthropology in these major parts of the German language zone took an extremely long time to reorient itself after 1945. Economically means were scarce at first for fieldwork and for institutional relaunches. Intellectually the return of the old schools in the West, that is, in the FRG and in Austria, did not stimulate any innovation; only a few emigrants (like Robert Heine-Geldern) were invited to return to academic positions, and the effects of the prewar brain drain began to be felt. Meanwhile, the establishment of the communist GDR did not trigger much enthusiasm there for a field that had been marginal even in the Soviet Union.

It took anthropologists of the German language zone one or two decades to fully understand how much the post-1945 world had changed for them in terms of language and status. Until the late 1930s, German had been a widely understood international lingua franca in academic life. After 1945, English became the only academic lingua franca in the West, and to an extent Russian became so in the East. Few anthropologists in the German-speaking countries were trained or prepared for this new situation linguistically, let alone intellectually. For all these reasons, anthropology from the German-speaking countries came to occupy a relatively self-contained world of its own, less isolated, of course, than it had been during the war years, but still cut off from the international mainstream to a greater extent than, say, sociology or philosophy in German. A whole generation of anthropologists had lost international status and reputation that only one or two decades before had been quite high. In the 1950s and 1960s, hardly any British or American editor of a major anthropology edition would invite a German author to contribute, like Günter Wagner had contributed to Meyer Fortes's and Edward E. Evans-Pritchard's 1940 volume. Those days were over now for a long while to come.

This changed to an extent with the social and intellectual upheavals of the late 1960s and early 1970s, which introduced a more intensified development of new directions in local anthropology as well. I trace this sequence up to the late 1980s. By then, the fall of the Berlin Wall created a new political and institutional landscape and accelerated an ongoing generational change.

The Return of the Old Schools

De-Nazification among sociocultural anthropologists in Germany and Austria has not been carefully studied yet. It seems safe, though, to state that in the West it was more of a symbolic and gradual than a substantial institutional and intellectual process. On the symbolic level, the term *Volk* eventually fell into disgrace because of its former central usage in Nazi terminology and ideology. Likewise, the term *Rasse* fell out of academic usage. During the next decades, many of the field's local institutions changed their name in German to include the word *Ethnologie* rather than *Völkerkunde*. (The museums, however, retained *Völkerkunde* in their names longer and more often than did the university institutes. In the GDR, the new label for the field was *Ethnographie* instead of *Ethnologie*.) Institutionally, this renaming was preceded or accompanied by a more profound development: the separation between physical and sociocultural anthropology virtually everywhere in the German language zone. Ever since this post-1945 separation, physical and sociocultural anthropology have been kept strictly apart in the German-speaking countries in terms of academic training, teaching, and research positions, which is in line with the general situation of sociocultural anthropology in Western Europe. With regard to the long-established separate existence of folklore studies, however, the immediate post-1945 years did not bring about any institutional changes in the German-speaking countries.

Symbolically and to an extent institutionally, post-1945 changes in sociocultural anthropology were thus more visible than they were on an intellectual and academic staff level. In this regard overall continuity prevailed in the West, while some specific discontinuities occurred as well. A few of those who had entertained intimate relations with Nazism maintained or improved their former academic positions after 1945 (e.g., Martin Heydrich, Walter Kricke-berg), whereas others (Wilhelm Mühlmann, Hermann Baumann) had to wait some time before they were allowed to reassume their profession. It is cer-tainly noteworthy that in the FRG and Austria, almost every single sociocul-tural anthropologist who at first was banned from academic life after 1945 be-cause of former Nazi involvement and then applied for reentry did receive that permission sooner or later.

The serious fall into international insignificance and the domestic intel-lectual stagnation of sociocultural anthropology in the German-speaking countries therefore cannot be reduced to international changes in post–World War II political and language hegemonies alone, nor to lack of local funds and the prevalence of other priorities. Unchallenged brain drain from the prewar years, combined with post-1945 personal and intellectual continuities had their share in this shift toward international insignificance and domestic stag-nation. Even though several from the pre-1945 generation of academic soci-ocultural anthropologists did sincerely reconsider their previous attitudes, and regardless of the fact that most from the Nazi-period generation now ob-tained less important positions than they had held before, that generation continued to be influential in academia and among students.

Over the next decade those who had been more explicit supporters of Nazism mostly reentered in minor positions, while the representatives of the former large schools returned to the center. Richard Thurnwald (d. 1954) soon retired; Mühlmann (d. 1988) eventually became a full professor in Mainz and then in Heidelberg; Baumann (d. 1970) reemerged as a lecturer in Frankfurt and Mainz before again becoming a full professor in Munich; Adolf Jensen (d. 1965) reassumed a central role in cultural morphology in Frank-furt; and Wilhelm Schmidt (d. 1954) and Wilhelm Koppers (d. 1961) returned to Vienna to reestablish culture circle theory there.

Simultaneously, an emerging Swiss social anthropology in German was treated for a while as if it were a theoretical suburb of Frankfurt and Vienna (to paraphrase Ernest Gellner). In Freiburg/Fribourg, for instance, Schmidt's Societas Verbi Divini (SVD) order maintained an important academic out-post (this was to change only in the 1980s). The SVD-led journal *Anthropos* also reemerged as one of the field's three or four leading journals in German. In Basel it took eminent textile specialist Alfred Bühler and his team a while to disentangle from cultural morphology and culture circle theory.

Until the late 1950s and early 1960s at least, the three main directions that had existed before, cultural morphology, historical diffusionism, and func-tionalism, continued to dominate in the West—that is, in the FRG, Austria, and the German-speaking parts of Switzerland (Gingrich and Dostal 1996). All these three traditions upheld an unchallenged notion of *Kultur* that, through several filters, went back to Johann Gottlieb Herder.

It has been said that Jensen's variant of cultural morphology may be interpreted as the intuitive West German parallel to the strong particularism pursued by Ruth Benedict and others in the Boas tradition of the United States. To an extent, Jensen's anthropology also can be paralleled to some of Marcel Griaule's (1938) conceptualizations and to those of Griaule's subsequent school. On the basis of his fieldwork in Africa and on the Moluccas, Jensen followed Frobenius in searching for a culture's innermost "soul," or *Paideuma*, in its cyclical stages. (*Paideuma* thus is also the name of another major journal in German.) This was a mentalist, or idealist, agenda that combined particularism with regional diffusionism. Jensen's 1948 book, *Das religiöse Weltbild einer frühen Kultur* ("An early culture's religious worldview"), and his 1951 *Mythos und Kult bei Naturvölkern* (with a short *Current Anthropology* version published in 1965) were relatively readable and well-meaning works that inspired a number of major and minor fieldwork projects among Jensen's students. These works remained relevant as far as they went—the ethnography was rich, but the interpretation was restricted by these very specific theoretical interests. One may conclude that Jensen's impact was a valid one ethnographically, but to my mind, it remained a mysticist and particularist theoretical influence.

By itself, this was nothing unique for West German anthropology; the same could be seen in France (Griaule) and the United States (Benedict). There, however, Griaule and Benedict each represented only one element in a wider spectrum that also included other, more future-oriented tendencies. Inside West German anthropology, the "wider spectrum" around Jensen included not future-oriented tendencies, but representatives of the Nazi past, such as Krickeberg, Heydrich, and Mühlmann. By its contrast to the work of Krickeberg in Berlin and of Mühlmann in Mainz, Jensen's anthropology looked progressive from a local perspective, but internationally it represented a relatively conservative, wider culturalist trend in Western anthropology. If we accept the parallel to Benedict and Griaule, then the most progressive forces were active elsewhere. This was, after all, the golden age of British social anthropology.

Historical diffusionism, by contrast, lingered on in more heterogeneous forms. Baumann continued with his Africanist and empirical diffusionist interests. In his case it is perhaps possible to differentiate, up to a certain point, between the man and his work. Elements of racist diffusionism were apparent in his major Africa publication, which was posthumously reedited by Baumann's students (Baumann 1975–1979). In spite of that, some experts hold that his empirical cultural circles remain an interesting point of reference. One might argue that they even resemble George Peter Murdock's 1959 *Africa*, but that they went beyond that in detail and erudition. If that were indeed the case—and although I am not an expert, I remain skeptical—then Baumann's Africa work and that of his disciples may be qualified as a modest version, for Africa south of the Sahara, of what the *Handbook of South American Indians* (Steward 1946–1949) represented elsewhere with sounder theoretical implications. In addition, in his 1955 *Das doppelte Geschlecht* ("Double Gender") Baumann pursued an innovative, lifelong sideline of his research that culminated in the publication of a final rich volume on the occurrence of ritualized gender transformation and its original context, which Baumann saw in complex societies. This book seems to have remained an interesting contribution to its topic as well.

Historical diffusionism's theological version under Schmidt and Koppers came to an early end when its two main proponents retired and died in 1954 and 1961, respectively. Koppers's successor, Josef Haekel (the first Austrian-born nonpriest in this chair since the institute's foundation), together with Robert Heine-Geldern (one of the few re-migrants from exile), his assistant Anna Hohenwart-Gerlachstein, and Walter Hirschberg, soon thereafter declared Schmidt's culture circle theory obsolete. The times of the closed SVD anthropological school were coming to an end, and the SVD order has completely changed its overall theological and academic orientation since then. Those who continued to work as anthropologists now would be able to elaborate more extensively that line in which the former Vienna school perhaps had been best: the systematic compilation of source material (Haekel, Joseph Henninger). This was not too far away from Vienna Africanist Walter Hirschberg's methodological elaboration of ethnohistory in the early 1960s, which postulated a descriptive historiography of local sequences as far as they could be substantiated by sources. Heine-Geldern, on the other hand, pursued his much more speculative diffusionism (for example, by supporting Thor Heyerdahl's boat expeditions to prove transpacific migrations to the Americas), which in turn stimulated contradiction and different orientations among his students Karl Jettmar and Walter Dostal.

After the late 1950s and early 1960s this new heterogeneity in Vienna, and a comparable situation in German-speaking Switzerland, stood in contrast to anthropology in the two Germanies. Whereas a more pluralistic landscape of anthropological work emerged already in the decade before 1968 in Austria and German-speaking Switzerland—where the two largest anthropology institutes of the German language zone are located—the situation in West Germany remained less pluralistic and more conservative for a longer period (Gingrich 1999a, 156–59).

German functionalism, for which Thurnwald had introduced the term *Ethnosoziologie*, received important new institutional support. In his last years Thurnwald managed to found an institute for *Sozialpsychologie und Ethnologie* at West Berlin's Free University, where another major anthropology journal in German, *Soziologus*, founded by Thurnwald, also came to be located. At this precursor unit of the present university institute, a former student of Thurnwald's, Sigrid Westphal-Hellbusch, soon became his associate. Under his supervision Westphal-Hellbusch had earned her PhD in 1940 and her habilitation in 1946. In 1959, she became a professor, and then the first female full professor of sociocultural anthropology in the German-speaking countries. On the basis of her extensive fieldwork and museum experience, she became an excellent ethnographic analyst of West and Central Asian societies, but also continued the tradition of early gender studies through the analysis of transvestites in Southern Iraq (Hauser-Schäublin 1991). This may be considered a strong point on the positive side of Thurnwald's very contradictory overall record: in the end, a small nonracist social science–based anthropological legacy managed to materialize.

Günter Wagner received his personal de-Nazification in 1948, for which Evans-Pritchard, Fortes, Daryll Forde, and Siegfried Nadel all contributed with written testimonies to the effect that he had been an impartial scholar before the war. Wagner rejected offers by Thurnwald and Diedrich Westermann to contribute toward the new institute in West Berlin, and he attempted to obtain a position in Britain, but failed at first. Shortly before his early death in Southern Africa he declined a substantial offer for a professorship in London, apparently both for family reasons and so he would be able to pursue "fieldwork opportunities" he had at hand in his new home: as an "assistant government ethnologist," Wagner had started to work for the Native Affairs Department of South Africa right at the time when the National Party came to government power and began to establish its now notorious racist Apartheid regime.

Like several other German sociocultural anthropologists in those years, such as Werner W. Eiselen, Friedrich R. Lehmann, Paul-Lenert Breutz, and Oswin Köhler, Wagner collected documentation and prepared reports for the Apartheid regime on African groups in South-West Africa (today Namibia) and South Africa. It is still under discussion whether these reports were of substantial importance for domestic politics in Southern Africa. Still, the

German connection in academic and applied fields of South African anthropology under the National Party's emerging regime is undeniable (Hammond-Tooke 1997, 113, 116; Mischek 2002). Inside that connection, however, the ideological and conceptual dimension probably was much more significant than the empirical side: a specifically essentialized notion of timeless neo-Herderian *Kultur* can well be traced in the nationalist and racist Afrikaner ideologies of those years. To some extent these views already had been inspired by early *Volkekunde* and *Ethnologie* courses at the Afrikaner-language University of Stellenbosch since the 1920s, with a relatively continuous usage of some of the German *Völkerkunde* literature there (Hammond-Tooke 1997, 58–69). Perhaps even more important for the history of anthropology is the fact that Mühlmann's notion of *Ethnos* became quite influential among leading academics and politicians of Apartheid South Africa, including Hendrik Verwoerd, the Department of Native Affairs minister and prime minister of South Africa until 1966 (Sharp 1980).

Throughout his post-1945 academic career, Mühlmann worked very hard to also transform his doubtless intellectual skill into a respectable academic record. For his post-1945 audiences, readers, and students, he rewrote and republished with new terminology many of those works he had written before 1945 (Seiler 2003). His book *Rassen, Ethnien, und Kulturen,* for example, first appeared during the war, and then after 1945 in a reworked edition (1964). In this case the title, in English *Races, Peoples, and Cultures,* was aimed at keeping an old terminology fashionable for new contexts. This book represented one of Mühlmann's continued efforts to theorize interethnic relations. The original, pre-1945 context of these and related efforts by Mühlmann makes me highly skeptical that this book can be regarded as a precursor to Frederik Barth's *Ethnic Groups and Boundaries* (1969), as some German-speaking anthropologists continue to argue.

Perhaps Mühlmann's most intelligent, but also most self-revealing post-1945 publication was his *Chiliasmus und Nativismus* (Mühlmann 1961). The first volume of this two volume-publication comprised library-researched case studies by Mühlmann's students on revitalist movements in South and North America, in Africa South of the Sahara, and elsewhere. The second volume, authored by Mühlmann alone, analyzed additional historical material on nativist and chiliastic movements, ranging from the early days of Jewish and Christian history to the sixteenth century. In his results and findings, Mühlmann argued that all these movements had emerged under conditions of external pressure and of asymmetric power relations imposed from the outside. In addition, Mühlmann suggested that they all displayed their adherents' aspiration to achieve a new and just order by following a leader to salvation and reestablishing a lost paradise. For that purpose they would mobilize to purge the present of its evils, an effort that inevitably resulted in sequences of mass action.

As interesting and persuasive as these insights may be, they include an implicit message that is less innocent than appears at first sight. Already in 1933, as a young man and active Nazi Party member, Mühlmann had written an article on Hitler's movement "as a participant," in which he characterized it as "chiliastic millenarianism." Against this background, one may acknowledge a self-reflexive dimension in Mühlmann's 1961 volume. The German anthropologist and ex-Nazi tried to assess, through the means and tools of anthropology, what Nazism had been all about. To that end, he returned to his 1933 idea. Characterization of Nazism as a very particular kind of revitalization movement actually is a useful hypothesis, as was confirmed in 1999 by Eric Wolf in his last book, *Envisioning Power*. Wolf, the Viennese Jewish refugee from Nazism who then became a highly decorated U.S. soldier in the war against Hitler, did not discard Mühlmann's revitalization thesis per se, but absorbed it for quite a different purpose (1999: 198, 281). He explored the contrasts and parallels between Nazism and two other societies, Kwakiutl and Aztec, in order to identify the logic of power and ideology under conditions that were specific for each case, thereby following a middle-range approach between relativism and universalism.

Mühlmann had something else in mind. In his 1961 volume, the legitimate dimension of self-reflexivity was combined with a profoundly apologetic second dimension. By studying chiliastic and nativist movements from virtually all cultural and historical spheres and by emphasizing commonalties more than differences in this endeavor, Mühlmann clearly aimed at a universalist rationale that was irrespective of historical and sociocultural context. The German anthropologist and ex-Nazi tried to explain, with the means and tools of anthropology, that phenomena like Nazism occurred, in one way or another, at all times and in all societies. Whereas Wolf would use a few selected case studies for "controlled comparison" (Gingrich 2002) in order to identify both parallels and differences, Mühlmann used universalist comparison to primarily emphasize commonalities and parallels. With this procedure, Mühlmann sought to strengthen the role of general patterns of human behavior, which is helpful indeed if one is interested in attenuating and downplaying the significance of particular contexts. He thus employed a universalist rationale to convey the implicit message that individual responsibilities and options are less important if seen through the lens of universal necessities.

It is evident that Mühlmann pursued an intelligent ideological opportunism for all seasons: in the Nazi era, he had launched his attack against Adolf Bastian's legacy and the universalist paradigm of the unity of mankind in order to promote his hierarchical and racist relativism. For the democratic purposes of 1961, he employed the universalism he had once fiercely attacked, in order to now demonstrate that Nazism was nothing exceptional, but simply normal human behavior under particular circumstances.

By the 1960s at the latest, many among Mühlmann's second generation of students sensed the biases and opportunistic priorities of their teacher. To an extent this also had to do with another of his influential books, *Geschichte der Anthropologie* (1948/1986). This history of anthropology presented a profoundly one-sided, apologetic, and Germano-centric perspective of the field's evolution. Republished several times until 1986, it was virtually the only textbook on the topic available in German. Many students could and did resort to English or French textbooks, or were recommended to do so by good teachers. Where this was not the case, however, three generations of German-speaking anthropology students learned the history of their field from a book by someone who had been most heavily involved with Nazism.

It was thus no coincidence that during the student revolt of 1968 and thereafter rebellious students of anthropology researched and asked questions about what their professors had been doing under Nazism. West Berlin was the main center of the students' revolt, but Heidelberg was one of its other important focal areas, and this was certainly so in anthropology. In 1968 the anthropology professor at Heidelberg was Wilhelm Emil Mühlmann. When revolting students accused him of having been an active accomplice of Nazism, Mühlmann chose resignation from office and went into retirement.

1968 and GDR Anthropology

The events of 1968 had different intellectual repercussions in the German-speaking countries than, say, in Paris, San Francisco, or New York. These repercussions were also different for anthropology in German than, say, for sociology or philosophy in German.

In the western part of the German language zone, protest against the Vietnam War combined with protests against the silence surrounding continuing local respect for old Nazis. Soon this also combined with protest against the Warsaw Pact invasion of nearby Czechoslovakia, in which, for the first time since 1945, a German army helped to occupy another country. In the course of these intellectual and social movements, innovative debates were taking place in some parts of West German academia. In sociology, for instance, a formerly exiled but now returned Theodor Adorno and his young assistant Jürgen Habermas engaged in the grand debate in Frankfurt about positivism (Adorno 1969). By contrast, the critical young generation of *Völkerkunde* students in West Germany had some spectacular success at first, but after a while they were largely silenced. After some time, the 1969 and 1971 meetings of the German Society for Völkerkunde (DGV) resulted in another stabilization of prevailing anthropological directions in West Germany. However, the more spectacular, short-term institutional changes resulted in the installment of the difficult and isolated U.S. Marxist Lawrence Krader in West Berlin and in Mühlmann's resignation from office in Heidelberg. Otherwise, changes were of a more gradual kind in the West.

Ironically, the events of 1968 seem to have had a much more positive effect upon our field in East Germany than in West Germany. Under Walter Ulbricht's late Stalinist regime until 1970, ethnography and *Völkerkunde* had very few possibilities. Some museum collections were reorganized, such as those in Dresden and Leipzig, and a very small cohort of anthropologists were employed. Most of them held political and ideological appointments and had no interest in fieldwork. Julius Lips and his wife Eva returned from U.S. exile to Leipzig, where Julius became director of the anthropology institute that was later named after him, and dean of the University of Leipzig. He then died early and was made into an icon posthumously with the help of his widow and the Party, which contributed to a number of questions that have been raised since then about the authenticity of some of his work.

A few among the first generation of trained ethnographers and their students in the GDR managed to carry out important archival studies, or even fieldwork under difficult conditions. Ingeburg Winkelmann, for example, completed work in 1966 on German imperial colonialism, and Irmgard Sellnow conducted motorbike-aided fieldwork in Ghana. Sellnow had received her training in West Berlin with Westphal-Hellbusch before the Berlin Wall was built in 1961. In the leading power group of the GDR's anthropologists of the 1960s, 1970s, and early 1980s, Sellnow was a rigid party ideologist, but she was also a selectively promoting and even protecting figure for younger anthropologists. Being a Marxist of conviction rather than of opportunism, with her Western training and her own fieldwork experience, she not only exercised political control, she also set certain professional standards, which cannot be said for many among her colleagues in the GDR then.

In the GDR the impact of the year 1968 was that the neo-Stalinist Erich Honecker forced the late-Stalinist Ulbricht into resignation in order to prevent developments going in a direction similar to those in Czechoslovakia. That new regime initially allowed for limited reforms in several fields of domestic culture and education. One of the results of that turn during the first Honecker years was a modest growth in faculty, staff, students, and research possibilities in the ethnography and *Völkerkunde* of the GDR.

Let me make it absolutely clear that the dominant development of the GDR's social and historical sciences was ideological distortion at the service of the regimes in East Berlin and Moscow. Several leading academics produced very little other than propaganda, and hardly any ethnographers were allowed to travel abroad without special permission. Many research results were internally censored before being academically accepted, let alone published, if publication was granted at all. Quite a number of decent scholars in our field suffered serious setbacks in their careers due to denunciation to the Stasi or because of political pressures from the Party.

In spite of these damaging and restrictive conditions, and in spite of the existence of power centers that did not favor academic results unless they were somehow useful for the system, some good work was accomplished. During the twenty years from 1965 to 1985 a number of authors managed to produce results that actually were quite remarkable.

The general climate that has come to dominate since German reunification tends to distort everything carrying the label "ex-GDR," and therefore most of these works are neglected. Some of these authors did the best they could under conditions that were much less favorable than those in the German-speaking west, and they deserve to be mentioned and appreciated in the record of German-speaking anthropology between the end of World War II and the fall of the Berlin Wall. Together with a number of Russian studies from that period, such as those by Anatolij Khazanov, Victor Kabo, and Igor Krupnik, these GDR ethnographers' and ethnohistorians' works represent the very best that was produced by our field inside the Soviet bloc.

GDR works worthy of appreciation include Wolfgang König's study of the Central Asian Achal-Teke nomads, a substantial piece in pastoral nomadism discussions (1962); Lothar Stein's monograph on the Shammar-Djerba in northern Iraq, which is a serious contribution to the anthropology of Arabia (1967); Ida Icke-Schwalbe's work in India on caste and class (1972); and Heinz Israel's study, based on the Herrnhuter archives, of Inuit history (1969), a work elaborating and complementing, in a way, that of feminist U.S.

Marxist anthropologist Eleanor Leacock. The quality and professional standards achieved in the GDR in spite of difficult conditions cannot often be found in West German anthropological works from around 1968.

Anthropology in the German-Speaking West after 1968

If history offers any answers for the present, which is a view that may in itself be contested, then the history of anthropology in German holds some more complicated, and a few clear answers. Among the latter, I identify two:

First, this history demonstrates how easily academic research can become corrupted and instrumentalized by political interests, whether on purpose or not. Colonialism, fascist authoritarianism, Nazism and Holocaust criminality, but also left party politics and Stalinist tyranny had their impact on sociocultural anthropology in different but important ways. The ensuing question can no longer be whether there was any such impact, but how anthropologists dealt with it in the past and, for that matter, how they might deal with political interests in the future. The history of anthropology in German shows that political engagement through academic means does not represent a safe answer at all. Instead, this history suggests that the pursuit of good sociocultural anthropology under responsible ethical premises has a better chance if it maintains a critical intellectual distance and independence from explicit political interests of whatever kind.

Second, the history of anthropology in this part of the world also provides a partial answer to its difficult current status in the new millennium. Anthropology in German has been marginal and somewhat secluded not just for reasons of globally shifting linguistic hegemonies after 1945; after all, locally there is more of a self-sustaining language market in German than in, say, the Scandinavian or Dutch cases. Furthermore, some German sociologists, such as Habermas and Ulrich Beck, have found an audience in English, so there must be more to it. Linguistic reasons are thus perhaps necessary for understanding the present of anthropology in German, but they are not sufficient.

The present status of anthropology in German is also informed by its history. The representatives of the large and small schools were in office until at least the 1950s and in some cases into the 1980s. These large and small schools display a number of merits on their record, but many more sinister achievements. If the last representatives of these schools tried to train their students according to their own priorities even into the 1980s, and they did, then they continue to exert some influence upon the present. The good news is that this influence has been fading to an increasing degree. It has rarely managed to renew itself, and alternatives have been adopted by members of the later generations. This was the lasting effect of 1968.

In the German-speaking West, the short-term changes brought about by the 1968 revolt had less of a lasting impact upon anthropology than had been expected: In Heidelberg, Mühlmann was succeeded by Jettmar, an empirically oriented historical diffusionist with a regional specialization in Eurasia and Central Asia. In West Berlin Lawrence Krader pursued his own Central Asian interests on the basis of a hermetic and speculative version of Marxism that had little impact elsewhere, except in the case of his edition of Marx's anthropological notebooks. In Vienna, museum director Hans Manndorff fell into public disgrace for alleged involvement with the CIA in Southeast Asia. More important were the medium-term consequences of the 1968 revolt for sociocultural anthropology in the German-speaking West.

On the one hand, these medium-term changes concerned the institutional and intellectual environment. In the aftermath of 1968, sociology, history, and philosophy were profoundly transforming themselves. In sociology such authorities as Habermas and Sir Karl Popper engaged in the debate on positivism *(Positivismusstreit)*. In the field of history new concepts and methods were introduced such as Hans-Ulrich Wehler's structural history and the "history from below" approaches. This created a new intellectual environment with a return impact, at first, on *Volkskunde* (folklore studies). Under the impact of the work of Hermann Bausinger and his students in Tübingen, German folklore studies were reinvented in a movement away from the nationalist study of folklore and toward a fieldwork-based ethnography of sociocultural processes at home. Eventually this was accompanied by a widespread change of name, from *Volkskunde* to *Europäische Ethnologie*. With two or three times as many university departments and museums as *Völkerkunde/Ethnologie* in the German-speaking countries, *Europäische Ethnologie* has managed to transform itself into a serious partner for sociocultural anthropology. In spite of continuing differences over certain methodological and topical aspects, potential for dialogue and cooperation has been growing ever since.

These progressive changes in several intellectual and institutional environments also encouraged changes inside the sociocultural anthropology of the German-speaking West. This was signaled at first by a number of influential new publications of the 1970s. Fritz Kramer and Christian Sigrist coedited their two-volume *Gesellschaften ohne Staat (Societies without state*, 1978), which, as a liberating alternative to Mühlmann's textbook, introduced several generations of German-speaking students, who at that time still had insufficient English language skills, to translations of the classic texts by Evans-Pritchard, Fortes, and their contemporaries in British social anthropology on Africa. In a comparable manner, Christian F. Feest published his *Das rote Amerika* (1976), in which he introduced readers to the histories and cultures of native North Americans and outlined American anthropologists' insights on them. Meanwhile, Georg Grünberg and Walter Dostal coedited Latin American anthropologists' and native representatives' texts from the first Barbados conference of indigenous representatives from the Americas, which Grünberg had co-organized (1975).

These and other publications indicated a new opening up of anthropology in the German-speaking West toward a more updated and engaged general orientation with a new emphasis on social science approaches and a nonspeculative writing of history. This was also reflected in a new series of institutional and generational changes. The anthropology museums of the 1970s and 1980s had to reorganize themselves for the new postcolonial era and managed to do so to an extent with the help of new media and by reaching out for new visitors.

Some of the best research skill and potential in anthropology in German began to reemerge after 1968 in the vast number of major and minor museums in the German-speaking countries. Solid regional and historical expertise was in evidence, and a number of subject specializations were reinvigorated in these museums. One case in point is that of the Basel museum, which, thanks to efforts initiated by Alfred Bühler and continued by Annemarie Seiler-Baldinger and others, became a center of global reputation for research on textiles. Another is that of the systematic handbook on material culture, *Technologie und Ergologie in der Völkerkunde*, a project initiated by Hirschberg, and continued by Feest and Alfred Janata (Hirschberg, Feest, and Janata (1966/1989). Visual anthropology went through a series of reforms after 1968 as well. A visual legacy that was as ambivalent as the written anthropological record in German was thereby eventually reassessed and found a new basis in the *Encyclopaedia Cinematographica* in Göttingen.

These were the main institutional changes in *Ethnologie*, as it came to be most commonly called in the German-speaking West. I conclude with a short overview of the main directions and representatives before 1989.

By the late 1970s and the 1980s, these main directions of *Ethnologie* had begun a transformation that led away from the three earlier post-1945 orientations of the old schools and on to the two main pre-1989 orientations, historical anthropology and social anthropology. Taken together these directions combined a few continuities with the legacy of the local past with more elements of a new heterogeneity that paved the way for the present.

Historical anthropology developed one of its strongholds in museums, where regional expertise and archival material promoted an earlier transcending of the speculative methods of writing history. This combined well with the important philological legacy in German, derived from Enlightenment. The humanities in German-speaking academia are richly endowed with specialized departments that come out of this philological tradition: Japanese, Chinese, Indian, and Tibetan studies; Arab, Turkish, and Iranian studies; and so on. Although still suffering to some degree from Orientalist limitations of the kind criticized by Edward Said (1979), these traditions and research records went through reforms of their own, while increasingly stimulating historical anthropology and being influenced by it. In particular, regional specialization and historical expertise gained new levels of quality for native South and North America, Africa south of the Sahara, the Middle East, Siberia, Southeast Asia, and Melanesia.

Whatever one may think about these highly specialized regional and historical competencies of German-speaking historical anthropologists in theoretical terms, they cannot be ignored as a solid empirical record. Whereas cultural morphology faded out only very slowly in Frankfurt itself (where Africanist Haberland continued to represent his personal past and the old school until the 1980s), the new heterogeneity in historical anthropology took shape elsewhere. In Bonn, Münster, and Vienna scholars like Feest, Oberem, Prem, and Köhler forged an Americanist ethnohistory with a strong focus on pre-Columbian and colonial history, often with a renewed affinity to the Boasian legacy. With a stronger diffusionist yet empirical emphasis Asian studies were pursued in Cologne, Heidelberg, Berne, Munich, and elsewhere by Jettmar, Johansen, Marschall, Vayda, and others. Particularly important anthropological research for Africa was continued in a more historicist manner in Hamburg, Munich, and Göttingen by Zwernemann, Raum, Fuchs, and Braukämper, and for Melanesia with a stronger sociohistorical focus in Hamburg, Göttingen, and Basel by Fischer, Schlesier, and Schuster. In addition, Hirschberg, his successor Wernhart (Vienna), and Szalay (Zürich) elaborated the methodological devices for an ethnohistory, while first initiatives on reassessing the discipline's history were offered by Brandewie (St. Augustin), Fischer (Hamburg), Feest (Vienna and Frankfurt), Stagl (Bonn), and Kohl (Mainz).

This newly heterogeneous historical anthropology in German often was closer to established notions of *Kultur,* but it had finally managed to break with other preconceived ideas, such as diffusion and, of course, race. Although English-speaking readers often would continue to perceive some of these works as too dense, and too introspective, most historical anthropologists of this generation managed to transform the heavy burden of German speculative historicism into a solid, updated skill, creating potentials for future contributions—to anthropology in the German-speaking countries, and then to the mainstream directions of international anthropology.

If compared quantitatively according to the number of institutional positions, historical anthropology was still stronger than social anthropology in the pre-1989 decade, whereas today the reverse is true: social anthropology has become a mainstream tendency in the German-speaking countries of the present. This gradual transformation already was indicated and anticipated when, long before 1989, social anthropologists took over the three largest university departments in Zürich, Vienna, and West Berlin. While *Ethnosoziologie* often continued to be the German term, social anthropology has also included due attention to economic and religious topics. In addition, a number of influential scholars who are primarily historical anthropologists (Schlesier, Johansen, Jettmar) also pursued social anthropology to some extent themselves and promoted it among their students.

In the second half of the 1980s, *Ethnosoziologie* in the German language zone already displayed three main directions that would further differentiate toward the present. First, development anthropology with some applied elements was more fashionable in those years than it is now. It retained its value through a strong emphasis on economics and social change. It was best represented by Elwert (West Berlin) for West Africa, Janata (Vienna) for the Middle East, and Löffler (Zürich) for Southeast Asia. Second, a comparative social anthropology was primarily pursued by cross-cultural data analyst Peter Müller (Zürich), "network" analyst Thomas Schweitzer (Cologne), anthropologist of art Benzing (Göttingen), and neo-evolutionist Middle Eastern expert Dostal (Vienna). These approaches stimulated methodological reflection and conceptual interest. Furthermore, comparative approaches received important inspiration from a new generation of feminist anthropologists, such as Hauser-Schäublin (Göttingen) and Nadig (Bremen). Third, structural anthropology was represented by India specialist Pfeffer (West Berlin) and by Himalayan studies specialist Oppitz (Zürich).

Unlike the historical anthropologists of their generation, these *Ethnosoziologen* of the German language zone had become more skeptical of an unchallenged notion of *Kultur.* Similar to their colleagues in historical anthropology, however, most among this new generation of social anthropologists also had overcome preconceived notions such as sieving, assimilation, and race. Some authors, like Janata, Elwert, and Dostal provided first steps for examining the field's past. These new social anthropologists of heterogeneous orientations were at first only rarely read by their colleagues abroad, though some of them are now, as are the more influential authors among the historical anthropologists.

By the 1980s social and historical anthropologists of the German language zone seriously had begun to assess the nontraditions of the past as a necessary precondition for moving ahead. *Ethnologie* in 1989 still was marginal to the international mainstream, but somewhat less so; it still remained a world of its own, but an interactive one—with windows and doors that were now wide open.

AUTHOR'S NOTE: Basic literature in English on the subject of sociocultural anthropology in German is still scarce. Elementary works include, in chronological order of the main periods the works cover: For the Enlightenment period, see Michael Harbsmeier's and Han Vermeulen's papers in Vermeulen and Roldàn 1995, and for the philosophical background, see Zammito 2002 and parts of Dumont 1994. On the nineteenth century, Lowie 1937 is still useful on Gustav Klemm and Theodor Waitz, whereas on the anthropological relevance of Marx, Godelier 1977 is best. For anthropology in Wilhelmine Germany, Penny and Bunzl 2003 and Cole 1999 may be consulted first, as well as the contributions to Stocking 1996b, notably those by Matti Bunzl and Benoit Massin. H. Glenn Penny's analysis of German anthropology museums in that period is excellent (2002), whereas Andrew Zimmermann's 2001 volume is useful and accurate but gives too enthusiastic a view of Fritz Graebner's and Bernard Ankermann's 1904 paradigm shift (Gräbner 1905; Ankermann 1905). For anthropology in German of the pre-Nazi period, readers might want to refer to Köcke 1979, Brandewie 1990, and Dostal and Gingrich 1996. For the Nazi period, one of the very few pieces available in English is Dostal 1994. There is no good overview in English of post-1945 developments.

Research for the present work was made possible first by my spring 2002 Lichtstern visiting scholar sojourn at the University of Chicago's Department of Anthropology, for which I thank its academic faculty and especially its then head, Susan Gal. Second, other important parts of this research were supported by the Austrian Science Fund's Wittgenstein Prize of 2000. For their research assistance, I am especially grateful to Sylvia Haas for her support throughout the overall project; to Christian Feest, Peter Schweitzer, and George W. Stocking Jr. for their critical comments; and to Maria Anna Six-Hohenbalken for her assistance in researching the Justin case. For her competent and engaged editorial work, I want to express my gratitude to Meg Cox. Finally, I would like to acknowledge that initial inspiration that came from Walter Dostal's courses of the late 1970s and 1980s on the history of anthropology in German. They were invaluable for me, as indeed for everybody who had the privilege to attend them.

The French-Speaking Countries / ROBERT PARKIN

Pre-Durkheimian Origins

A French Tradition of Anthropology?

Let me start with a rhetorical question: Is there a significant French tradition of anthropology? This may seem a strange question to ask at the start of a series of lectures dedicated to this very tradition. But in fact the French case involves a paradox that is not present in the British or U.S. cases, nor I suspect in the German one, at least to the same extent. It is, quite simply, that there has always been a clearer division of labor in France than elsewhere between those who have produced major theories and methodologies of significance to anthropology and those who have collected ethnographic data in the field (Adams 1998, 373–77). This is not to say that French anthropologists are unaware of theory or that they do not contribute to it—far from it. But France has no parallel to Britain's Bronislaw Malinowski, who at a key point in the development of his adopted national anthropological tradition invented enduring fieldwork methods, generated less enduring theories at least partly on the basis of them, and taught anthropology through both, thus inspiring generations of successors to follow his example of combining theory and practice.

As far as teaching and inspiring fieldwork are concerned, the nearest parallels in France are the two Marcels, Mauss and Griaule. However, there was a clear separation of roles between them. As many of his students and contemporaries confirmed, Mauss became very familiar with non-European peoples in the study, but the nearest he came to actually examining any of them closely was making a three-week trip to Morocco to study a cultic dance in 1909. His role was, rather, the teaching of ethnography in the light of Durkheimian theory in the interwar period. As for Griaule, although he exerted an influence of his own in France from the 1930s into the 1950s, not only over the practice of fieldwork but also with respect to attempts to link anthropology with art and literature, he did not combine his activities with more than the most superficial theory. Under his influence as much as that of Mauss, not a few French anthropologists down the years have taken a rigorously antitheoretical stance in preferring to stress ethnography rather than theory as the true basis of anthropology.

There is, of course, now a substantial body of excellent ethnographic literature in France, but it is not entirely clear why fieldwork proper got going so late there, really not until after World War II in any quantity or quality, despite Griaule's already controversial activities in the interwar period. One reason is that the dominant theoretical school surrounding Émile Durkheim remained close to the sociology of Europe until quite late in Durkheim's career, becoming significantly more anthropological only when Mauss took over from Durkheim after World War I. Indeed *anthropology* was a bit of a dirty word for Durkheim, since it conjured up memories of the nineteenth-century British school, whose interpretations of religion, at any rate, he was determined to challenge.

However, Mauss and Robert Hertz promoted the inclusion of non-European peoples in the Durkheimian project more vigorously, which in principle should have encouraged more fieldwork. Certainly those in Durkheim's group were increasingly aware that the British were well ahead of them in this department, if not in the realm of theory, and they took steps to do something about it. The main effort in this regard was Hertz's trip of six weeks to the Italian Alps in 1911, where he studied a Catholic cult dedicated to an obscure local saint, Bessu. However, this was not entirely approved of by his colleagues, who were always suspicious of anything smacking of folklore (see my third chapter), which is how ethnographic inquiries in Europe tended to be stigmatized at this stage, and even later (cf. J. Cole 1977; Abélès 1999).

This may have been another constraint on fieldwork: the Durkheimians were always very dismissive of Arnold van Gennep, whose fieldwork activities all over Europe were the very antithesis of the predominantly armchair anthropology of the Durkheimians, as I shall explain in the next lecture. Indeed, Hertz's brief trip was to prove the high point of Durkheimian activity in fieldwork before World War I. Leaving aside Mauss's even briefer trip to Morocco, only Henri Beuchat made any other such attempt, in trying to visit the Inuit. Polar explorer rather than academic, he perished in a shipwreck in the Arctic, taking whatever notes he had managed to collect down with him.

As a colonial power, of course, France had its share of amateur ethnographers—administrators, missionaries, military officers, and the like—but their work was as marginal theoretically as that of their counterparts in Britain, the United States, Germany, and the Netherlands. To begin with, the field studies that Mauss encouraged in the 1920s and 1930s were not long-term fieldwork in the indigenous language, but were more of the expedition variety, like Griaule's journey across Africa from Djibouti to Dakar or Claude Lévi-Strauss's travels around Amazonia. By and large, therefore, interwar French anthropology constituted an interim period between armchair anthropology and long-term fieldwork of the sort that had intervened in British anthropology under W. H. R. Rivers and his colleagues around the turn of the century, and of which the Torres Straits expedition is probably the best known. Although Griaule and his colleagues settled down with the Dogon during this period, Malinowskian fieldwork only really became established as routine in France after the war.

The question of the gap in France between theoretical development and ethnographic practice can be coupled with a further difficulty, namely that of pigeonholing most French theorists. While in the Anglo-Saxon tradition such boundaries are generally clearer, in France we have to ask: Just who among theoreticians can be counted as anthropologists, if anyone? Is Durkheim to be regarded as a philosopher or a sociologist, for instance; Lévi-Strauss as a philosopher or an anthropologist; Mauss and Pierre Bourdieu as sociologists or anthropologists; Foucault as a historian or a sociologist? As W. Y. Adams notes (1998, 377), there is also a great sense of personal commitment to a chosen line of theory in France, which shapes and identifies a theorist's whole career: the radical intellectual shifts undertaken by Rivers in Britain or Marshall Sahlins in the United States would be unthinkable.

One result of these factors is that while French ethnography, whose quality is generally first-rate, obviously does engage with theory, it often appears to be more concerned with the particular ethnographic analysis at hand than with comparative effort, let alone theory. This is often true elsewhere, of course; but while fieldworking anthropologists in other traditions do draw on other, nonfieldworking disciplines, they are left much more to their own devices in generating their own theories. And they are more inclined to do so directly from ethnography, including that undertaken by others. This is ironic, given the received wisdom in some quarters that the French are stuck with their fancy theories while the British cannot get beyond the facts: actually an awful lot of French ethnography is rigorously empirical and not at all theoretically ambitious (cf. Clifford 1983; Weber 2001, 479).

There are certainly French anthropologists who have successfully combined theory and practice in the Anglo-Saxon manner, like Louis Dumont (who taught at Oxford for four years in the early 1950s, in Edward E. Evans-Pritchard's heyday), Maurice Godelier, and other Marxists. Nonetheless it is clear that in France, fancy theories are not generally the preserve of ethnographers. Rather, they are generated by specialist thinkers who, though they may use it on occasion, treat ethnography as merely one tool among many in the construction of theories whose deductive nature is often all too apparent. When they do use ethnography, it is often simply to provide post facto support for theories they have already developed independently of it. In the case of Lévi-Strauss this is quite explicit, and for all Durkheim's emphasis on the facts, in practice the latter identified himself as a rationalist more often than as a positivist, let alone an empiricist.

In these lectures I shall focus mainly on the theorists who have been discussed more, but I shall address this disjunction between theory and ethnography in France when appropriate, and I shall also discuss leading fieldworkers at some length. In the rest of this opening lecture, however, I shall look at certain precursors of sociology and of anthropology proper in France, as well as the origins of the latter discipline in French museums and learned societies of the nineteenth century.

Montesquieu and Rousseau: The Prerevolutionary Origins of French Social Thought

If not in innovative fieldwork, then, France can certainly claim priority when it comes to ideas that have informed anthropological theory and practice. Indeed, it can claim a clear first in producing one early modern writer who combined an interest in the customs of other, exotic, and strange peoples with an attempt to systematize knowledge about human societies in a more or less objective manner, namely Montesquieu. Here I shall also discuss Rousseau, followed by Saint-Simon and Comte in the next section (see Aron 1968; Lukes 1973; Shilling and Mellor 2001; Swingewood 1984).

In general, all these figures were either producers or products of the Enlightenment, which dominated late-seventeenth- and eighteenth-century thought and is especially associated with France. By preserving a place for rationalism, the early-nineteenth-century reaction to the Enlightenment took a very different form in France than in Germany, where French rational universalism came to be rejected totally in favor of the increasing distortion, through cultural and racial discrimination, of Johann Gottlieb von Herder's doctrine of the particularity of cultures. This culminated in the irrational of

Nietzsche, the identification of leader and state through Hegel, and ultimately the racist crimes of Naziism (elsewhere in this volume Andre Gingrich discusses the post-Napoleonic fate of the German Enlightenment). Of course, France also produced the racism of Arthur de Gobineau and Paul Broca and the crowd psychology of Gustave Le Bon, both of which influenced fascist theory (cf. Neocleous 1997). In the long term, however, they remained marginal to French thought.

For our immediate purposes, what is significant is the influence that these earlier Enlightenment figures had on Durkheim, whose work and legacy are in many ways central to these lectures. Indeed, the notion of a collective, social dimension to human life through which the thoughts and actions of the individual are mediated to the point of becoming mystified, so that the social interferes in our direct consciousness of the world, is a consistent theme from at least Jean-Jacques Rousseau to Jean Baudrillard and Bruno Latour. Because Durkheim has so often been treated as the acme and fulcrum of this tendency, I shall proceed here in part by including his reactions to these early figures and the use he made of their ideas.

Montesquieu (1689–1755) has particular significance in the context of Durkheim's thought since he is the subject of Durkheim's Latin thesis, which has recently been translated again into English (Durkheim 1897/1997; cf. Lukes 1973, 279–82). A nobleman living in the perpetual crisis of French royal absolutism in the eighteenth century, Montesquieu produced his most significant work, from the point of view of later sociology, in 1748: his *Spirit of the Laws* (see Montesquieu 1949). At first sight this work does not seem to represent anything new, since it discusses the characteristics and virtues of different types of constitutions in a manner superficially resembling many writings from both antiquity (those of Plato and Aristotle, for instance) and the Renaissance (such as those of Machiavelli). Indeed, Montesquieu made use of similar though not quite identical categories, such as monarchy, democracy, and despotism. However, if we probe further, we find important, forward-looking differences.

Earlier writers tended to be judgmental and to explain constitutions with reference to human motivations, especially those of great historical figures, including legislators like Solon or Lycurgus; for the most part, Montesquieu left individual motivations out of his explanations. In general his accounts are not critical, though he sometimes suggested what he considered the best options in particular cases. Even more importantly, his interest in constitutions provided him with a basis for consideration of the types of society they were associated with. This led him to use a form of concomitant variation as an analytical tool. Thus republics, whether aristocratic or democratic, were actuated by the common good, whereas monarchies were subject to the separation of powers, and also of classes. The latter were the focus of different interests, though at least they produced conditions of freedom through their competition. Despotisms, on the other hand, consisted of just the ruler and an enslaved population. They were, he argued, more suitable for extensive Asiatic populations (such as those of Turkey, Persia, and China), whereas monarchies were of medium size and republics were small units, both being more suitable for the allegedly greater complexities of European societies. The latter were also Christian, not Islamic, Hindu, or Confucian, though Montesquieu distinguished between freedom-loving Protestants and authoritarian Catholics. In his overall scheme Montesquieu also included "savage" and "barbarian" societies, both of which lack a state, being associated with hunting and gathering and with pastoralism, respectively.

However, in considering the variable impact of environmental, especially climatic, conditions on societies and their laws, Montesquieu clearly invoked external, nonsocial factors of a sort that Durkheim routinely rejected. In his thesis on Montesquieu, Durkheim contended that Montesquieu confused a society's own ideological reasons for introducing laws with the objective circumstances whereby those laws had actually been introduced. He also discussed at some length Montesquieu's use of contingency to explain breaches of laws by the individual, which Durkheim preferred to treat as deviancy from social norms. Conversely, Durkheim noted approvingly that Montesquieu gave no consideration to individual free will, recognized that laws express social ideals, and was ready to think inductively at times, though the deductive reasoning characteristic of earlier thinkers was still apparent on occasion. Durkheim even claimed that his own differentiation between mechanical and organic solidarity was foreshadowed by Montesquieu's treatment of the republic and the monarchy, respectively, given the class distinctions of the latter and the lack of such distinctions in the former. Fundamentally, though, Montesquieu took significant steps forward in classifying societies into types that should be seen as integrated wholes that could be studied through their respective laws. He was also among the first to use a notion of sociological law that is distinct from the moral laws that societies impose for their own ends.

Another writer who had a strong impact on Durkheim was Rousseau (1712–1778), whom Stephen Lukes pairs with Montesquieu in his discussion of Durkheim's influences (1973, 282–88, 125–28). While Montesquieu was something of an apologist for the aristocracy he belonged to, his Genevan contemporary Rousseau, a hypochondriac and social misfit, would inspire numerous future revolutionaries and is often blamed for the French Revolution and all the mass totalitarianisms that followed it. Nonetheless Rousseau is perhaps famous above all for his advocacy of direct (i.e., not representative) democracy and his apparently contradictory suggestion that the individual's freedom was increased by it being given up to a higher social order. For Rousseau, although human beings were naturally social and cooperative, the institutions they created frequently enslaved them. The solution was for them to come together under a social contract that made them sovereign as a group. Only then were both justice and order possible, through the expression of what Rousseau called the general will. However, the general will was not a mere assemblage; it was greater than the sum of individual wills, which it both subsumed and replaced. To go against the general will was to go against oneself and therefore to limit one's own freedoms within society. Turning this negative perspective into a positive one, it is possible to detect a germ of Durkheim's later idea that to worship a god is to worship society, and therefore also oneself.

Indeed, Durkheim himself drew attention to this idea of Rousseau's as the expression of community values, since it had obvious parallels with his own notion of the collective consciousness. He also agreed with Rousseau's position that only social life was truly fulfilling for the individual and that it required the individual's self-effacing merger with the mass. However, he criticized Rousseau for positing a state of nature from which humans emerged to create society, although this was probably purely heuristic in Rousseau's case and not a piece of speculative history, as for Hobbes. For Durkheim, this amounted to denying the naturalness of society itself and made society seem artificial. Durkheim thought that Rousseau's society was the product of human reason and was created to serve the individual, whereas in reality it was external and logically prior to the individual. Nonetheless, he thought that Rousseau's embryonic pedagogy, especially in *Emile* (1762/1993), could be interpreted as recognizing the place of education in denaturing humans and thus making them a part of a greater whole that is society. Education was largely a matter of stimulating in the child a habitual resistance to the child's natural side in the interest of larger collective goals. Rather like Foucault later, Durkheim saw in *Emile* the inculcation of self-discipline through the objectivization of these collective goals, which then made external sources of discipline less necessary. Rousseau's ideas thus became a fundamental aspect of Durkheim's early teaching on education.

Saint-Simon and Comte: The Early-Nineteenth-Century Reaction to the Enlightenment

The defeat of Napoleon in 1815 brought about a reaction in France that was as much intellectual as political. The Enlightenment project of replacing religious mumbo jumbo with a rationalist individualism gave way to a counter-Enlightenment reaction that accepted the ultimate demise of conventional religion but did not accept the egotism that was now linked with the celebration of the individual. Many intellectuals of the early nineteenth century, especially in France, saw a need to preserve the spiritual essence of past religions, but in a secular, humanist form that would temper the selfishness of a world in which political stagnation was combined with entrepreneurial industrial development. They therefore began developing organic models of society that placed intuition above reason as a way of countering the individualism of the Enlightenment.

Cults of man had existed during the French Revolution, of course, but they appear to have become more prominent in later generations. One thinker who sought to propagate them as functional alternatives to the religion of the supernatural was Comte Claude-Henri de Saint-Simon (1760–1825), an eccentric aristocrat who, in works like *The Reorganisation of European Society* (1814) and *The Industrial System* (1821), railed against the immorality of individualism for its atheism as much as for its egotism (see Saint-Simon 1975).

For Saint-Simon, society was supra-individual and organic, hierarchical in the sense that it indeed required leadership, and religious in the sense that it could not function in a healthy way without some sort of cult that could be both a symbolic focus and a source of moral inspiration for the community. From his early nineteenth-century perspective, Saint-Simon saw industrial society as beneficial in most of these respects. Although in this new society merit was gradually replacing birth as the basis of leadership, there would still be both leadership and organic bonds between the different parts of society, as well as between the individual and society. To begin with Saint-Simon thought this was enough; only later did he also advocate a humanistic cult that would both celebrate this new form of solidarity and give it a moral foundation.

Although Saint-Simon's vision was hardly democratic, he saw industrial society as having at its basis what we would now call civil society, that is, units that were both independent of government and themselves linked together in free association through a system of division of labor. This represented a shift from previous regimes of direct authoritarian rule over subjects in European

society. His method was sufficiently positivist and rooted in a scientific historiography for him to be proclaimed a socialist by Friedrich Engels and both a
socialist and the true founder of sociology by Durkheim. The latter also appreciated his stress on the organic nature of modern society while criticizing
the exclusive focus on economic systems in his early thought.

Another thinker, Auguste Comte (1798–1857), went further than his contemporaries and sought to combine the sort of cult advocated by his precursor Saint-Simon with a new science that he at first called social physics,
following Saint-Simon, and only later sociology (see Comte 1973, 1988). Although Comte, rather than Saint-Simon, is popularly associated with the invention of positivism as both a term and a concept, he can hardly be described
as a neutral scientist who collected facts without rhyme or reason. Rather, he
was concerned to establish a scientific basis for the constitution of an acceptable society for the future. To this end the spiritual was to be united with the
scientific. Indeed, in accordance with the counter-Enlightenment program
outlined above, Comte saw the scientist replacing the priest as the source of
transcendence in society. A similar shift related to the role of elites, who were
no longer aristocratic warriors but the rising class of rich businessmen—predominantly industrialists, but also merchants. Comte believed that although
his own times were in flux, the scientist and the industrialist would ultimately
triumph over the soldier and the priest; it was sociology's task to underpin this
trend as the supreme science of all. In particular, sociology should undertake
the scientific collection and evaluation of sociological data that would dis-
courage excessive economic competition and ensure that the elite carried out
its social duties in relation to the rest of society. Like Saint-Simon, Comte was
not a democrat; he took elite rule in some shape or form for granted.

In being inevitable, this trend was also historical, and it represented the last
of Comte's famous three stages of human mentality as reflected in modes of
explanation for the human condition—a very nineteenth-century model. In
the first stage explanations were sought with reference to supernatural beings
modeled on humans themselves. In the second stage abstract forces like nature or the Durkheimians' later notion of mana were invoked as explanations.
The third stage was that of science, in which the earlier search for final explanations was replaced by the more modest observation of phenomena and
establishment of scientific laws. However, although the future triumph of
science was certain, like all advances it would be brought about not by reason
or intelligence, but by emotion. Comte often counterposed emotion and intelligence: while the first prompted change, the second consolidated change

by finding reasons for it. As the supreme science, sociology would embody those reasons.

There is thus a clear mystical aspect to Comte's work. He reduced even intelligence to the production of ex post facto rationalizations. Moreover, for Comte science was as transcendent as religion, since like religion it gave humans a reason for their existence, for their being bound to society and for society's rule over them, which it could also moderate. Unlike religion, however, it was grounded in the concrete, not the imaginary. Nonetheless Comte's science is unreal, since it is not a critical or even an experimental science, but dogmatic and final, again like religion.

Indeed, Comte created a cult of humanity under the impulse of his passion for a young Parisian woman, whose early death aggravated the mental illness he had always suffered from. The Great Being of this stillborn cult represented the embodiment of humanity and of all its achievements to date. Like Robespierre and Saint-Simon before him, Comte appeared unable to free himself from the forms of religion, even though he recognized that the message of religion had ceased to monopolize humans' thoughts or to produce their attachment to society. Comte's cult is a perfect example of Durkheim's model of ritual as society worshipping itself, except that here it was rather the whole of humanity that was both God and worshipper, not just single societies, and symbolic mediation was less in evidence. Unlike Montesquieu, then, or even Durkheim, Comte was ultimately not interested in the diversity of humanity. Humanity was one in spirit, and might ultimately become one in fact. The idea of social determinism in the sense of different social facts arising because of different social, including ideological, circumstances in different societies was not important to Comte, because history seemed destined to bring humanity to the same point sooner or later—another very nineteenth-century view, though in his case it made him critical of colonialism as hegemonic.

From Durkheim's point of view, Comte's sense of historical inevitability was relevant less for its possible accuracy—which Durkheim did not subscribe to—as for the absence, as in Montesquieu, of any reference to the free will of the individual or the role of great men. Comte asserted the priority of the social whole over the individuals that made it up, and he adhered to the sort of analogy between society and the biological organism that Spencer was positing in Britain in roughly the same period. This made Comte's account functionalist, like Durkheim's own. Comte also recognized the importance of studying a social phenomenon in its total social context and, unlike Montesquieu, he treated society as *sui generis* in that he refrained from invoking nonsocial factors to explain the social. But the most striking similarity is perhaps the centrality of religion in the work of both Comte and Durkheim: in particular, in being social, religion for Comte was also traditional and thus involved what we would now call social memory linking different generations.

Although the writers we have been discussing were closer to philosophers than to sociologists, more detailed sociological work based on interviews and other forms of direct field inquiry also emerged in embryo in the nineteenth century. The key figure here was Pierre Guillaume Frédéric Le Play (1806–1882), whose main work, a comparative study of family conditions and the links between family and occupation in 1855 (see Le Play 1982), grew out of his activities as a roving investigator of mines for the École des Mines in Paris, which took him as far as the Urals. Interested in the implications of technological innovation for social morphology and stability, he stressed the greater potential of the patriarchal family for providing the latter, at the same time identifying intermediate family forms, such as the stem family (parents, children, and widowed grandparent), that tended to undermine it. The migration of children away from the family home in industrial society was another source of instability, leading Le Play to stress the sense of place as a counter to it (see Brooke 1970).

The Nineteenth-Century Origins of French Ethnology: Museums and Learned Societies

The nineteenth century also saw the development of a distinct interest in ethnology in France, parallel in broad terms to developments elsewhere in Europe and the United States. As elsewhere, French ethnology was distinguished from sociology by its greater interest in non-European peoples; its basically evolutionary perspective; its confusion of race, culture, and language, yielding notions of racial as well as cultural difference; and the importance it accorded to material culture. The humanistic thought of the Enlightenment and its critical stance toward revealed religion also had an impact on these developments. In France as elsewhere the institutional structure that nurtured these early developments tended to be the museum and the learned society rather than the university.

An early abortive effort to launch an ethnological society was made in 1799, with the foundation of the Société des Observateurs de l'Homme. The society was dominated by naturalists such as Louis-François Jauffret and by the so-called Idéologues, who saw ethnology as a mainly scientific, positivistic discipline indulging in utilitarian explanations. Jean-Baptiste Lamarck was also a leading member. Among other things, the society promoted the issuing of ethnological questionnaires to travelers. It survived till 1804, when most of its members joined the Société de Philanthropie (see Kilborne 1982). The Société Asiatique and Société Géographique were both founded in 1822, and the latter in particular became a strong stimulus to overseas exploration.

Between 1839 and 1847 William Edwards, physiologist and theorist of race, and others founded the Société Ethnologique de Paris to study "physical organization, intellectual and moral character, languages and historical traditions" in what Han Vermeulen describes as a fusion of "ethnic and racial history" (1995, 50). In competition with this perspective was the geographical and linguistic orientation of the Société d'Ethnographie Américaine et Orientale, founded by Henri de Longpérier and others in 1859. The biological anthropologist Paul Broca and others set up a new Société d'Anthropologie in Paris the same year (that is, four years before the Anthropological Institute in London) to reflect a development away from a purely race-based ethnology to a more progressive anthropology uniting physical with social and cultural perspectives. A slightly later venture, set up in Hanoi in 1898, was the École Française d'Extrême-Orient. Sponsor of research and publisher of a major Orientalist and anthropological journal, it had a peripatetic existence after the ending of French involvement in Indochina and is now based in the former French enclave of Pondicherry in south India (Dias 1991; Dias and Jamin 1991; Karady 1981; Stocking 1964; Vermeulen 1995; Williams 1985).

The nineteenth century also saw the founding of ethnological museums in France. An early promoter of the idea was E. F. Jouard, who was to become curator of the Bibliothèque Royale in the 1920s. He consistently maintained that ethnological objects were of interest primarily for their scientific significance, not as works of art. But it was the opening of an ethnological museum in Berlin by Adolf Bastian in 1868 that finally compelled Armand de Quatrefages, Professor of Anthropology at the Musée d'Histoire Naturelle, and his student Ernest-Théodore Hamy to push for the establishment of a similar institution in Paris. This led to the setting up of the Musée de l'Ethnographie in the Trocadero in 1878, initially with a focus on pre-Columbian New World artifacts, supplemented later by interest in the French empire and in rural France. Hamy was the first curator of the museum, whose administration was continually hampered by underfunding and a lack of space to stage effective exhibitions or even to store things properly. He pursued a classification of objects that was based on function rather than either evolution or ethnographic area. Both he and Quatrefages had been associated with Broca in setting up the École Anthropologique in 1875, which sought to unite the study of humanity by combining physical, cultural, and linguistic aspects. However, Hamy himself wished to draw French anthropology away from biology and toward history and ethnography. His main activity consisted in seeking to prove the Old World origins of pre-Columbian civilization.

Existing institutions also provided a forum for academic anthropology on occasion. In 1855 a chair of anthropology was endowed in the Musée d'Histoire Naturelle, and teaching in anthropology was also provided by the medical faculty in Paris beginning in 1875. Both activities were sponsored by the École Anthropologique (Dias 1991; Dias and Jamin 1991; Jamin 1991b; Karady 1981; Williams 1985; Rogers 2001, 489).

By mid-century, therefore, in French anthropological activity there was already a split between ethnography (including collecting) and theory, which does not seem have been so clear-cut in either Britain or the United States, despite the division of labor between armchair anthropologists and fieldworkers in Britain. In the United States, at least Lewis Henry Morgan was beginning to spend his summers in the field, his winters in the study. By the end of the century, however, Durkheim and his group had grown used to reviewing ethnographic materials and incorporating them into their work, though they never got around to seriously collecting such materials themselves.

2

Durkheim and His Era

Émile Durkheim

If one theorist's name continues to dominate French anthropology and sociology to this day, long after his death, it is that of Émile Durkheim. His theory of social determinism, though out of fashion in other national social sciences, especially in the United States and Britain, is still influential in France, though it is often cited inexplicitly or only in a somewhat attenuated fashion. At various times Durkheim has been the darling of the republican left and the demon of both libertarians and the antirepublican right in France, quite apart from having had a distinctly mixed press in academia. The fact that he is cited less often these days indicates routinization of his ideas rather than their neglect or rejection. As I shall be arguing in my fifth lecture, even thinkers like Pierre Bourdieu, Michel Foucault, Jacques Derrida, and Jean Baudrillard, who all carefully distanced themselves from Durkheim, can ultimately be situated in the Durkheimian tradition. In addition, some French Marxists, especially Maurice Godelier, have deliberately sought to accommodate Claude Lévi-Strauss's structuralist development of the Durkheimian tradition to Marxism. Abroad, while U.S. anthropology was always closer to the German school that Franz Boas started out in as a student, twentieth-century British anthropology continued to be fascinated by the very French school that finally reduced the nineteenth-century British-school to the status of historical curiosities.

Born in 1858 into a rabbinical family in Epinal in the eastern French region of Lorraine, Durkheim turned away from Judaism in his youth, though many commentators have detected the influence of Jewish ideas in his thought. He went through the Paris system of higher education, then taught in a number of lycées before going to Germany for a year. While there he visited Wilhelm Wundt's psychological laboratory in Leipzig, which impressed him not so much with its contribution to psychology as with its collective mode of working—a practice that Durkheim and his colleagues were to adopt to some extent—and its use of historical and ethnographic evidence. From 1887 to 1902 Durkheim taught social science and pedagogy at Bordeaux, then transferred in the latter year to a post at the Sorbonne, where he remained for the rest of his career. For him the war years were characterized by his activities as an apologist for the French position on the war and were darkened by the death of his only son, André, on the eastern front in 1915. Émile Durkheim died, apparently of a stroke, in 1917 (Karady 1981; Lukes 1973).

The Bordeaux years saw the launch in 1896 of the journal *Année Sociologique,* which became the main vehicle for the intellectual development of Durkheim's new sociology. Indeed, Durkheim was not content to just earn a living from teaching, but set himself the task of establishing sociology, not so much as an activity per se in France, given the earlier work of scholars such as Auguste Comte and Frédéric Le Play, but as a university discipline in its own right. Despite much opposition, he fully succeeded in his task, having a profound impact on the development of both sociology and anthropology in France and elsewhere.

Durkheim was also politically engaged, not practically, but as a republican and parliamentary socialist intellectual who saw sociology as a way of creating a secular morality suitable for the Third Republic, the postauthoritarian state that he and other progressives of the time saw as threatened by rightist fanaticism and religious obscurantism. What Anthony Giddens supposedly was to Tony Blair in late-1990s Britain, Durkheim was much less equivocally and in much greater measure to Jean Jaurès and other leaders of the parliamentary left in France around the turn of the twentieth century. As in the case of Comte, therefore, sociology for Durkheim was program as well as science, and it even had a certain functional equivalence to Comte's cult of the human in providing a moral underpinning of the republican state's activities.

Durkheim's work in education should be seen as another aspect of this project. After the Jules Ferry reforms of the 1880s, education became mainly a matter for the secular republican state, not the church or other antirepublican bodies. It was therefore a primary arena in which the values associated with the Third Republic could be imparted to the youth of the country. Durkheim always saw education as a site for the social formation of the individual, not for the individual's own personal development. It was thus very far from the German idea of *Bildung,* an educational ideal serving precisely the latter. Durkheim's example spread beyond France, becoming a prescription for nation building in Kemalist Turkey (Kahveci 1995; D. N. Smith 1995), rather like Marxist theory did for many Third World postcolonial states later in the twentieth century.

In his treatment of the work of his predecessors, Durkheim focused especially on his precursors in social theory, such as Montesquieu, Saint-Simon and Comte. This is not to say that he was completely immune from the influence of other disciplines. Chief of these is perhaps philosophy, partly the Cartesian tradition of the isolation of mind as an object of inquiry, but also that of Kant as channeled through the French neo-Kantian philosopher Charles Renouvier, whom Durkheim famously proclaimed his "great master." Renouvier was a dominant figure in philosophy in the early Third Republic and shaped much of its official political doctrine. Steven Lukes lists those aspects that Durkheim admired in Renouvier, in particular his rationalism, his concern with morality and the need to study it scientifically, his rooting of morality in the social, and his locating of human dignity in social cohesion and social forces (1973, 54–77).

Lukes also traces to Renouvier Durkheim's modification of Kantian rationalism in the direction of the contingency of categories and thus their social determination, as forcefully demonstrated in both *Primitive Classification* (Durkheim and Mauss 1903/1963) and the later *The Elementary Forms of the Religious Life* (1915/1995). Although Durkheim was skeptical of much of Kant's own work, his fondness for dichotomies (individual–society; sacred–profane) can be traced directly back to the German master. Not all philosophy was congenial to Durkheim, however, as is shown by his long-running debates with the then dominant figure of Henri Bergson (1859–1941; see 1960, 1986), who advocated an irrational approach that linked consciousness, manifested in the nebulous form of the élan vital, or vital spirit, to external stimuli, and saw it as more accessible to intuition than to reason.

Two other influences of note, especially regarding Durkheim's work on religion, should also be mentioned briefly here. One is the historical sociology of Numa Denis Fustel de Coulanges, whose *Ancient City* (1864/1882) focused particularly on ancestor worship, treating it from the point of view of its place in society overall. The second is the ethnology of W. Robertson Smith, who associated the Arabian clan system with aspects of Semitic religions (1885, 1889)—an important input into Durkheim's theory of totemism as the original form of religion.

Durkheim turned his attention to religion in Bordeaux, and it was his main interest in his later years, when he was in Paris. His study of religion is the most anthropological in content of all his work, reflecting the expansion in published fieldwork monographs around the turn of the century, as well as Marcel Mauss's influence in stressing their significance to Durkheim. Durkheim's earlier books, dating from the 1890s, the *Division of Labour* (1893/ 1984), the *Rules* (1895/1982), and *Suicide* (1894/1951), all of which were published while Durkheim was still at Bordeaux, are by comparison more sociological in orientation. Although they are perfectly representative of Durkheim's thought, ultimately it is the overall theme of religion that represents his thought best. Durkheim came to see the sacred as equivalent to social ideology, and indeed to society itself seen as the embodiment of a set of values. God was simply society's representation of itself in symbolic form; in worshiping God, one was worshiping society, and through it oneself as a member of it. He later rejected his own early efforts to interpret religion, his major lasting statement being the last of the books he published in his own lifetime, *The Elementary Forms of the Religious Life* (1912/1995).

In this work and generally Durkheim was writing simultaneously against both philosophical rationalists and empiricists; against psychologists, with their focus on the individual; and earlier, against mostly British anthropologies of religion. It will be most convenient if we first address his criticisms of the nineteenth-century British school, which was characterized by two main tendencies, usually labeled evolutionism and intellectualism. Durkheim was opposed to Darwinian and British styles of evolutionism, but he also had his own evolutionary side, something that seems to me to be better developed in his work with Mauss, discussion of which I defer to the next lecture. As far as Durkheim himself was concerned, however, a consideration of evolution was occasioned by his need to oppose the no less extravagant accounts of the origins of religion that the intellectualists of the British school had come up with. They located these origins in the fear, wonder, or curiosity of primitive humans in primitive conditions when they were helplessly confronted with such imponderables as the forces of nature (whence nature spirits of various kinds) and the phenomenon of death (whence souls). In other words, though not lacking a collective dimension, religion was seen fundamentally as a product of the human mind and therefore of the psychology of the individual. This also entailed an emphasis on belief rather than ritual, despite the treatment, in the work of Tylor and Frazer especially, of magic as a set of ritual practices distinct from the purer form of worship that characterizes religion.

Durkheim was fundamentally opposed to this approach, since it required belief that humans in every generation must be going through the same experiences in order to maintain religion in being. No doubt religion did provide explanations for the imponderables, but there was more to it than the mere assuaging of individual emotions and satisfying of curiosity. Indeed, Durkheim rejected any place for psychology in the development of social facts, which he perceived religion to consist of. This was at least partly because humans were conditioned by the categories of religion rather than contributing to them themselves—in modern terms, they lacked sufficient agency to develop such ideas for themselves. Where, then, did these ideas come from? Durkheim's answer was that they came from society, which many have found to be a nebulous concept in this context. For Durkheim, however, any society had more or less identifiable sources of authority, however diffuse, and through them it used ideology, including religion, as a means of imposing its values on its individual members. These members included those sources of authority: Durkheim rejected the "crude Marxist" idea that ideology was simply an instrument of authority by the privileged over subalterns, since the privileged were no less affected by society and its ideology—in modern terms, they too had sociality.

Religion had four characteristics that enabled it to perform this social function. First, it was coercive: there was a strong element of compulsion backed up by sanctions ranging from mild disapproval to physical constraint. Second, it was general, in the sense that it brought together a collection of individuals on all of whom it has the same impact, at least externally. Third, it was traditional, in the sense that it existed before the individual did and would, broadly speaking, survive the individual. Fourth, it was external to the individual: only because of this could it act upon the individual. Nothing here made the slightest concession to the agency of the individual, who was not even society's cat's-paw, but its captive embodiment.

However, there was also instrumentality involved in relating the religious to the social. First of all, religious belief and practice gave expression to society's values through what were, in one of Durkheim's most famous phrases, "collective representations"—norms, symbols, myths, and values themselves. But they did not do this randomly: there had to be a specific occasion. For Durkheim, this was ritual. His contemporary, Arnold van Gennep, whom he ignored, saw rituals as being transitions between statuses and conditions, a perspective to which considerations of power have been added subsequently. Durkheim, however, stressed power more than transition. In his account, rituals were occasions of heightened social awareness at which all those present felt that they were one unified and ultimately undifferentiated mass. This was what made them an excellent opportunity to impart social values to the members of society. It was through ritual that knowledge was converted into power, which, for Durkheim, was basically the power of society over the individual, and the symbols used in the ritual masked this power.

Where the intellectualists thus stressed belief over ritual, Durkheim did the reverse. This can be criticized in its turn. A common remark is that there is a certain circularity of argument or, alternatively, a missing link in Durkheim's position. In opposition to the intellectualists, Durkheim insisted, reasonably enough, that rites were not a response to emotion but instead generated it. But if part of the ritual experience was to feel these emotions, and if these emotions were generated in the ritual, which represents the expression of the social at its most intense, what was it that compelled people to come together at a ritual in the first place? For Durkheim the answer was simply "effervescence," a kind of spontaneity of gathering that, it has often been suggested, suggests little more than a crude crowd psychology. However, Durkheim's view was of a congregation representing a community rather than of a crowd in Le Bon's sense. In addition, there was no reason to assume that those attending a particular ritual were all actuated by the same degree of emotional excitement in relation to it.

Here Durkheim is neglecting the fact that people do not lack sociality outside of ritual events but communicate with one another between them. One of the things communicated—even in gossip and so on—is knowledge about the correct type of sociality, including the necessity of ritual attitudes and associated symbolic values to that sociality. People also use their memories and unplanned happenings such as deaths to determine when rituals should be held. Rituals may heighten the sense of the social, but that does not mean that the latter is absent in ordinary time.

An example of what Durkheim means by seeing the social in the religious is his interpretation of totemism, which he sees both as the earliest form of religion and as a means of regulating marriage in Australian societies. Though his account of totemism is ethnographically deeply flawed, as his contemporaries quickly realized, it is nonetheless a perfect illustration of his doctrine that worship is in fact self-worship obfuscated by religious symbols that stand abstractly for society. In the early text *Primitive Classification* (1903/1963), Durkheim and Mauss suggest that in associating a natural species or phenomenon with a social group like a clan, totemism represents the modeling of the classification of the natural world on that of the social world, therefore giving priority to the latter. Thus the totem stands for the clan as an emblem. In addition, the members of the clan typically have a special, religious regard for the totem object that is associated with myths of origin in which it plays a part and with an obligation on clan members to avoid harming, killing, or eating it, especially if it is an animal. On ritual occasions, however, they are obliged to sacrifice the totem object and consume it.

On the face of it this is a typical ritual reversal, but consumption of a sacred object may also be interpreted as a means of becoming one with it. Because the totem stands for the clan, worshiping it in any form amounts to worshiping the clan itself and, by extension, worshiping its members, including oneself. And of course the clan is a social group, though admittedly not the whole of society itself. Direct worship will therefore be ineffective, since it will immediately be realized for what it is; it can therefore be challenged, and the ideology will be undermined. The totem therefore intervenes as a symbol between the members of the clan as, on the one hand, the subjects and, on the other, the objects of worship, obscuring the fact that they are actually one and the same. For Durkheim, realizing the fundamental categories of one's ideology frees one from it, making possible its contestation, opposition, and ultimately abolition. Religion prevents this from happening by using symbols to convey its message.

This links with another, more general problem in Durkheim, that of the relationship between society and the individual. One way of approaching this is again through his account of religion, and more particularly here the sacred. His focus on the dichotomy between sacred and profane is the most famous example of Durkheim's insistence on the human propensity to dichotomize, though there is not always agreement on what Durkheim meant by this particular case, nor whether it is even of value (cf. Evans-Pritchard 1965, 64–65). Actually, the sacred itself seems to me to present few problems: it is again the religious expression, in symbolic terms, of society's values. Indeed, if religion and society were coordinate for Durkheim, so were society and the sacred. Furthermore, what was sacred was also what was most likely to be given symbolic form in order to mask its true nature, which occurred especially in ritual.

As for the profane, Durkheim was not very consistent in his use of the word. Did it mean, for him, the mundane, that is, the religiously neutral, or did it rather represent the forces to which the sacred was vulnerable, like pollution and impurity? Certainly as the expression of social values, the sacred is threatened by the profane in the form of the world of individual interests and activities that violate society's injunctions. This may be seen as sin, crime, or the simple neglect of one's social duties. Here, at least, Durkheim allowed the individual some agency—but only an antisocial individual, one who had removed himself or herself from society by taking wrongful actions and must sooner or later make accommodation with society in order to survive, let alone prosper. His student Robert Hertz dealt with this more specifically in his work on sin, as I shall show in the next chapter.

Durkheim's treatment of the individual has repeatedly offended the liberal conscience as overly determinist. It is important to realize, however, that Durkheim was not thinking only, or even primarily, of obvious external constraints on the individual such as those exerted by the police and courts in modern societies or by religious authorities in more traditional ones: these rely on force; are often only too obviously the representatives of specific, dominant interests; and can be challenged or evaded both cognitively and physically. Instead, Durkheim's thought tells us that societies go beyond this in being moral communities that give us our values and our ideas of something—the sacred—that is greater than ourselves as either individuals or a mass of people. They therefore instill in us our sense of our responsibility to others, as well as the idea that living in society improves us both morally and physically. In addition, societies give us our basic categories whereby we map the world and understand both it and our place within it. We view the world through the categories society gives us, in a way that leads us to misrecognise a good deal of it.

Although there is constraint in these cases too, the constraint is moral and tends to be affirmed as proper: there is no attempt to resist or evade it. These values are affirmed for us through the emotional excitement generated by the ritual, as a consequence of which we internalize them operationally. In doing so we are projecting a notion of society as something above and beyond ourselves, but Durkheim was quite clear that collective representations exist nowhere but in the minds of individual humans. He contended that they become collective only through communication in a collective environment (cf. Ôno 1996; Mellor 1998, 2002).

One way of answering Durkheim's critics is by reflecting on the value of the individualism they hold so dear: for what else is this, ultimately, than a social value in its own right? If one can characterize a whole society, or group of societies like the West, as individualistic—with expectations that individuals should act as individuals rather than aping their peers, should think for themselves, should be self-reliant rather than dependent on others, and so on—then one can be pretty sure one is dealing with a social fact and not the aberrant practice of a few deviants. Yet Durkheim himself acknowledged social deviance and even saw benefits in it in terms of initiating necessary social change.

Durkheim had other reasons for limiting if not rejecting the agency of the individual in his own account of religion. Unlike the intellectualists, he did not treat religion as the illusion of frightened or curious primitives "reasoning from false premises." However, having thrown off any pretense to personal belief in his youth, he did not regard religion as theologically true either. Rather, its reality was social in that it gave shape and meaning to individual lives being led in a collective environment. It was also, like society itself, sui generis. Religion was not an explanation for the extrasocial, nor could any aspect of the extrasocial, such the individual's psychology or the physical environment, explain either religion or society. Religion was a social fact, and as such it could be explained only by other social facts. Durkheim laid down this fundamental methodological principle as early as 1895, in the *Rules of Sociological Method*. It meant that there was to be no compromise with the claims of psychology, philosophy, or the older style of anthropology in explaining the social. Only the new sociology could provide such explanations.

E. E. Evans-Pritchard remarked that Durkheim's explanation of religion works best for what the former calls closed communities, like those of the Australian Aborigines (1965, 55), material which Durkheim extensively though often inaccurately used to support his arguments in *Elementary Forms* (1912/ 1995). Closed communities or societies are typically characterized by religious unity and an absence of class, though there may well be status differences based on one's role as a religious specialist as well as on gender, age, and kinship position. As far as religious belief is concerned, there may be skeptics about this or that aspect of the religion—about the skills of a particular shaman, for example, or the effectiveness of a particular rite—but not developed alternative ideologies. What happens when we examine more structured, class-based, "open" societies in these terms? Religion per se often leaves the stage here, since it has become multistranded and is ultimately reduced to a matter of private practice in which the state does not have an interest. This was true of France in Durkheim's time, as indeed it still is. Durkheim's solution to this problem was to expand the notion of the sacred to cover secular values such as equality, individualism, and democracy, thus extending the notion of the religious into spheres that have nothing to do with the supernatural and that we might more usually describe as simply ideological or transcendent. In a sense, this was the final blush of secular cults in the manner of Comte or Robespierre, though Durkheim did not advocate them.

Durkheim had addressed the question of social solidarity in both closed and open societies as far back as 1893 in his French-language thesis, *Division of Labour in Society* (see Barnes 1966). Although religion was certainly already important to Durkheim's argument at this stage, so too was the type of social structure. Thus the typical tribe was divided into clans that depended on one another for wives but were themselves functionally equivalent, that is, functionally neutral: if one clan died out, this was without consequence for the society as a whole. These were societies with "mechanical solidarity." In addition, they had rather diffuse organs of control that nonetheless adhered to one basic set of moral and ritual values; as closed societies they therefore bound the individual directly to them.

Societies with "organic solidarity," conversely, were based on a division of labor, whether purely economic as in the Western capitalist system or principally ritual as in the Indian caste system. Given that the units in any system of division of labor are all specialized, they are all necessary to the functioning of the whole. Such societies were also characterized by social stratification, the embodiment of social authority in readily identifiable organs (the ruler, the state), and the existence of alternative moral and ritual perspectives, though these might be suppressed rather than tolerated. This is perhaps the most obviously functionalist of all Durkheim's major works, though religion too can be seen as having a function in demonstrating particular values to the members of society. Given especially his rejection of British evolutionism, Durkheim was led to functionalism by his internalist perspective that society was sui generis, that is, that social facts could be explained only by other social facts.

Suicide (1897), for which Mauss carried out a lot of the data collection, is exemplary of the Durkheimian approach and methodology in a different way. It is the first example of a number of projects produced by the Durkheimian school generally in which the respective author selected a topic that was seemingly explicable in terms of individual psychology, only to show that it actually had a social dimension too. Suicide was an obvious candidate, because it appeared to be a totally egotistical act. However, Durkheim not only noticed that suicide rates fluctuated markedly among different European countries and religious traditions, he determined that the act could be classified in different ways: as "altruistic" because of an excess of social feeling, "egotistical" because of a lack of social feeling, "anomic" when society failed to support the individual amid rapidly occurring crises, and so on. Other examples of this basic method were Durkheim's own work on education (e.g. 1979; see above), Paul Fauconnet's on notions of responsibility (1920), Célestin Bouglé's on ideas of equality (1899, 1903), Maurice Halbwachs's on memory and on what constitutes economic sufficiency (1912, 1933, 1999), Mauss's on the suggestibility of death (1979, 35–56) and bodily movements (1979, 95–123), and Hertz's on sin (1922/1994).

Durkheim's third important work from these early years is *The Rules of Sociological Method* (1895/1982), whose title is self-explanatory and some of whose key points we have already mentioned. One more ought to be discussed here. Although in the *Rules* Durkheim declared himself a rationalist and rejected both positivism and empiricism, his position on the familiar philosophical distinction between rationalism and empiricism is, strictly speaking, a neutral one, drawing on both rather than exclusively on one or the other. This is outlined especially clearly in Durkheim's short early piece on the philosopher Hippolyte Taine (1897/1997). Durkheim believed that Taine was the closest of all philosophers to his own position on this issue, though his own views had already been formed. Durkheim was certainly a rationalist in that he believed in the existence of logical links between ideas, but he thought that philosophy erred whenever it posited such links without being prepared to prove them. Empiricism was therefore also needed, to provide this proof. However, on its own empiricism was little more than the arid collection of facts: the logic of rationalism was required in its turn to order the facts and make sense of them. This entailed a new approach that only Durkheim's functionalist sociology with its interest in actual social facts, not speculative philosophy or a purely statistical sociology, could provide.

Arnold van Gennep: Folklorist or Proto-Anthropologist?

Criticisms of Durkheim began emerging almost as he wrote and have been added to greatly since. Arnold van Gennep (1873–1957) is one figure of particular interest in this regard because his work has clear significance for anthropology, though it has been neglected in France itself. Moreover, unlike most members of Durkheim's circle, van Gennep was a real fieldworker.

Born at Ludswigburg in Germany of mixed French, German, and Dutch descent and brought up in Savoy by his mother after his parents divorced, he, like Mauss, with whom he was roughly contemporary, lived a long life. Unlike Mauss, however, he was never in university employment apart from holding a chair at Neuchâtel, Switzerland, from 1912 to 1915, when he was expelled from the country for casting aspersions on Swiss wartime neutrality. He then returned to France to aid the war effort in various capacities. In later life he supported himself largely by making translations and taking up occasional posts of an administrative nature; he also undertook extensive fieldwork around Europe whenever possible. The latter activity was a deep personal commitment facilitated greatly by his gift for learning not only the main languages of Europe but many of their dialectal variants too. After 1920 he concentrated on France as an ethnographic area, producing, among other works,

ROBERT PARKIN / 181

the multivolume *Manuel d'ethnographie français contemporain* (1937–1953). His main concern was to reform folklore by converting it from a concern with archaism and survivals into a synchronic study more suitable for a true anthropology of France (cf. Belmont 1979, 1991; Needham 1967). Indeed, his work provided a sort of halfway house between antiquarian folklore of the classic type, with its reliance on theories of survivals, and the more holistic anthropology of France that was eventually to emerge after World War II (Rogers 2001: 488–89).

Van Gennep's ethnographic approach was put to good use in criticizing Durkheim, not directly on the basis of his own fieldwork experience, which was not in Australia, but because his own experience gave him an excellent grounding in the evaluation of ethnographic texts that Durkheim all too often, and obviously, lacked (cf. Lukes 1973, 524–27). Thus in his *L'état actuel du problème totémique* (1920), van Gennep claimed to have examined the same texts on totemism as Durkheim had and to have found them seriously deficient. This led him to add his voice to those of the many, especially Boas's student Alexander Goldenweiser (e.g., 1917), who thought that Durkheim's model of totemism was too rigid. Not all clan societies had totems, not all totems were associated with social groups, and not all governed the workings of exogamous marriage systems. Producing a whole theory of religion from one poorly reported ethnographic area was also wrong in principle, though the idea of an impersonal force (mana), which Durkheim claimed was involved in endowing totems with respect, corresponded to ethnographic realities generally. Van Gennep was also one of the first to make the criticism that Durkheim had reified society as a thing in a manner that completely ruled out individual initiative. Durkheim had also treated Aboriginal societies as simple and primitive on the basis of their technologies, whereas in regard to religious belief they were extremely complex and entirely modern. This point was taken up later by Lévi-Strauss, who defended Amerindian societies in particular against charges that they were primitive.

Van Gennep's ethnographic experience also informed his own books and articles, in which he expressed as much concern for the anthropology of religion as for folklore of a more traditional sort. One of his most extraordinary works is *The Semi-Scholars* (1911/1967), a series of fictional sketches poking fun at the academic establishment from which he was largely excluded. His most important and famous work, however, is undoubtedly *The Rites of Passage* (1909/1960), in which he uses rich ethnographic data to support a model of ritual process that has often been cited and sometimes modified, but never essentially criticized or surpassed since it first appeared. The structure he outlined was foreshadowed by Hertz's article on death (1907/1960), as well as by the work of Fustel de Coulanges (see Evans-Pritchard 1981, 188).

Essentially, wrote van Gennep, rituals are about transitions between statuses. Any ritual can be identified as having three stages, one to leave the old status, one to enter the new one, and a period of liminality in between. Since the liminal stage often suspends or changes normal social life in some way, it has been the focus of most anthropological attention. In particular, Victor Turner (e.g., 1969) expanded the topic with reference to the permanent marginality of *communitas* (hippiedom and the like), while Max Gluckman (e.g., 1963) introduced the notion of rituals of rebellion (especially by subjects against kings in Africa), whose cathartic processes were concentrated in this phase of the ritual. Hertz, in his article on death (see next lecture), showed that behavior in the liminal period could be more restricted than normal as well as more extravagant.

Van Gennep's model is obviously a structural one because he claimed that all rites in all societies had this threefold structure, regardless of the actual occasion. (Sometimes, he acknowledged, the liminal stage was very brief, almost vestigial, but, he insisted, it was always present). His is also a processual model, since rites occurred in time, changed from one phase to another, and changed people's statuses. Allying this protostructuralism to a processual view was a sophisticated move and was also quite an achievement for someone who had all too often been dismissed, by the Durkheimians especially, as a mere folklorist whose work was entirely without interest or value. There is certainly both structure and process in Durkheim's account of ritual, but its sense of dynamics pales into insignificance when compared with van Gennep's enduring model. As we have seen, Durkheim's focus was more on the use society makes of ritual to convey social information.

Saussure and Structural Linguistics

Jonathan Culler (1976) groups Durkheim, Sigmund Freud, and Ferdinand de Saussure together as three more or less contemporary thinkers who all stressed synchronic analysis in place of more traditional history in their considerations of the social, the psychological, and the linguistic respectively. Saussure's thought extended beyond the linguistic to semiology, or the study of signs in general, and was adopted into Lévi-Strauss's structuralism, Maurice Merleau-Ponty's phenomenology, and Jacques Lacan's psychoanalysis in the mid-twentieth century, as well as into Roland Barthes's more explicit semiology of images. Although Saussure was born in 1857 in Geneva, the city where he ended his career and died in 1913, he taught in Paris and Leipzig, and he wrote and lectured in French. A single work of Saussure is of interest to us here: the *Course in General Linguistics* (1983). Saussure's colleagues assembled the volume from students' notes on a series of his lectures and published them after his death.

One of Saussure's fundamental ideas involves the arbitrary nature of the sign, of the relationship between the signifier and the signified that composes it, and of the signified itself in terms of the difference in semantic space it occupies over time or between languages. This arbitrariness meant that signs could not be defined in terms of any essence, but only in terms of their relations with one another. Distinctions made by means of opposition were of fundamental importance. The famous example, though far from the only one, was that of voiced-voiceless pairs of consonants.

Another key idea is that of the division of language *(langage)* into *langue* and *parole* (grammar and utterance: the French words are often used even in translation), or its division into the rules of speech and the actual use of those rules by speakers of the language to produce a particular combination of sounds and meaning, including syntax. For the linguist, although *parole* was the immediately accessible source of data, it was arbitrary; *langue,* by contrast, was ultimately more important in representing the essential aspects of speech. This distinction can be mapped onto another famous binary opposition of Saussure's, that between the synchronic (the slice through a single point in time) and the diachronic (language as a flow through time).

As far as syntax is concerned, Saussure distinguished further between the paradigm or pattern of a sentence and the syntagmatic chain of words flowing through it. As for language generally, Saussure saw this as informing and directing individuals' thoughts and expressions, not as merely reflecting them as in earlier linguistic theories. In this respect, he identified in language a determining propensity that individual speakers obeyed while being barely conscious of it; he thus confirmed Culler's observation of a parallelism between Saussure, Durkheim, and Freud. This attitude is found again in the work of Lévi-Strauss and that of other successors in this line of thought (Culler 1976).

Rightist Social Science: The Crowd and *Anthroposociologie*

Although Durkheim's moderately leftist and prorepublican sociology acquired intellectual dominance, it was not without its competitors, and he argued against those competitors in his writings. Bergson's antirationalism was one current adopted by the political right. Another figure of note in this context is Gustave Le Bon (d. 1933), whose main theme was crowd behavior and crowd psychology (see Le Bon 1995).

For Le Bon any crowd of individuals, even a jury, was a site of the transformation of the rational into the irrational, as generally violent images and slogans took the place of reason and acted as a force for mobilization that could be exploited politically. Thus the orator temporarily replaced the official leader of society and governed the crowd in a way the crowd itself willed and accepted. Although Le Bon's crowd therefore threatened the social order, it was not itself anarchic. Le Bon saw in this model a reason for the failure of socialism, because it based its campaigns on rational arguments that the typical crowd will not listen to. He later acknowledged his support of Mussolini, who was directly influenced by his ideas. Another thinker, Georges Sorel, by contrast, saw in the crowd the very material for a specifically socialist revolution (cf. Horowitz 1968; Neocleous 1997: 4–8).

As Lukes points out (1973, 462–63), Durkheim's attitude toward the crowd was also positive, though in a different way: it was the effervescence that brought the crowd together at a ritual that promoted the religious idea. Durkheim therefore did not see the crowd as pathological and subversive like Le Bon did, or as revolutionary like Sorel, but—in the form of a religious congregation—as the foundation of orderly, conformist social life. Another turn-of-the-century rightist was Louis Maran, who advocated marshaling both anthropology and a rural sociology that romanticized the French peasantry in order to consolidate the French empire as an imperial project linking the colonies to metropolitan France. Increasingly influential in right-wing politics up to World War II, Maran ultimately fled to London after falling out with the Vichy regime (Richman 2002, 103).

Given the partial association of the term *anthropology* and its cognates with biological anthropology at the time, and even today in much of continental Europe, it is also appropriate to mention the international movement called, in late-nineteenth- and early-twentieth-century France, *anthroposociologie*, together with its leading figure, Georges Vacher de Lapouge (1854–1936). Essentially this was a French version of racial sociology combining Charles Darwin's theory of evolution (a marginal influence on French thought generally), Paul Broca's craniology, and Arthur de Gobineau's racism, and using race not only to explain the social, but also to condemn its influence. For example, social rules were criticized for interfering with natural selection to enable dwarfs and morons to survive; wars for eliminating the best elements in society, the

weaker ones being exempted from fighting; and professionalization for causing elites to reduce their rates of fertility. Humans were therefore considered
distinct from other species in allowing social selection to influence race. Because this was not a simple racial determinism, the credibility of the movement increased for a period, even among mainstream sociologists like Durkheim. Indeed, for a while the Durkheimians took the writings of this school
seriously enough to give them, and the school itself, coverage in the *Année
Sociologique* before Henri Hubert, Mauss, and others exposed it to their full
critical faculties. Apart from doing some informal teaching at the University
of Montpellier, which led to the production of his major work, *Sélections sociales* (1896; see also 1909), Vacher de Lapouge worked as a librarian rather
than an academic, though he had studied law and medicine (Llobera 1996).

It is notable that Henri Muffang, a minor and atypically right-wing
Durkheimian who initially looked after such studies for the journal, soon
broke with the Durkheim school, of which he had been a lukewarm member
at best (he had failed to join his colleagues in supporting Alfred Dreyfus, for
example). Other defectors were few, but they included Gaston Richard (see
Llobera 1985), Marcus Déat, and the Bourgin brothers, Hubert and Georges.
Déat's defection was partly a matter of the influence of psychology and partly
a matter of his desire to overcome the Durkheimian dualism between individual and society by invoking direct experience (Marcel 2001b, 48–49). Between the wars and under the German occupation, Hubert Bourgin indulged
in antisemitically inspired criticism of the Durkheimian project—which,
however, does not prevent his reminiscences from contributing many insights
to our knowledge of the history of that project (see Bourgin 1925, 1970). But
although the Durkheimian school was buffeted by such apostasy, the main
blow against it were the casualties of World War I, despite which it survived
to become central in the development of anthropology in the interwar period
and later, primarily under Mauss's guidance. I turn to these and some allied
developments in my next lecture.

3

Mauss, Other Durkheimians, and Interwar Developments

Marcel Mauss

Émile Durkheim's project was not a solo one, for he managed to attract a group of like-minded individuals, some of whom were equally brilliant. In this lecture I emphasize those who have had the greatest impact on anthropology in preference to others who are of equal interest generally but who remained closer to sociology or other disciplines (see Marcel 2001a).

Of all these figures Marcel Mauss (1872–1950) stands out as Durkheim's closest collaborator, his key lieutenant with respect to the rest of the group, whose work he often later issued on their posthumous behalf. Though certainly brilliant in his own right, he was important also in large part because he was the son of Durkheim's elder sister. Indeed Durkheim became something of a father figure to him: after Mauss lost his father at an early age, Durkheim had taken him fully under his wing. Born in Epinal in 1872, Mauss studied with Durkheim in Bordeaux and went with him to Paris in 1902. He taught entirely in Paris, first at the École Pratique des Hautes Études (EPHE, founded in 1886) with a chair in religions of "noncivilized" peoples (1902–1926), and later at the new Institut d'Ethnologie (1926–1940), which he co-founded, and the Collège de France (1931–1940). After World War I, during which most of the original group were killed and his uncle died, he trained a new generation of sociologists, anthropologists, and museologists, including Claude Lévi-Strauss and Louis Dumont, virtually single-handedly. He did no work in the last ten years of his life after being forced to retire by the Nazis, whose occupation was just as much of a shock to him as the losses of World War I. He died in 1950 (see Fournier 1994; James and Allen 1998; Jamin 1991d; Mauss 1968–1969).

Some scholars have detected a high degree of disorder in Mauss's intellectual work, as in his personal life. Eyewitnesses, such as Dumont, have commented on his style of lecturing, always vivid and inspiring, but apt to go off in any direction at any time; he would also pepper any social interaction, however casual, with ethnographically pertinent remarks. His enthusiasm for his work and his sheer scholarship cannot be in doubt, and his knowledge was truly encyclopedic. Certainly there is an absence of system in his writings overall, though taken separately each work is clear and coherent enough.

One of the reasons for this lack of system may have been intellectual (unless this was a post facto explanation on Mauss's part). In a review of his own career produced in 1930 as part of a failed first attempt to get elected to the Collège de France, Mauss referred to his preference for facts over theories (the review is published in English translation in James and Allen 1998), and he often rejected the idea of building a system in the manner of Durkheim. Actually, of course, Durkheim's system, such as it was, was enough for him, and he saw his main goal as developing his uncle's message and filling in the gaps by making use of the increasing amount of ethnographic data that was being produced, rather than breaking new ground. Thanks to the sheer range of his interests and his intellectual abilities, he did well at this task for someone who obviously had considerable difficulty with writing.

This is not to say that there were no differences in detail between the work of the two men, though Lévi-Strauss may have exaggerated them in trying to establish a modern, partly Maussian anthropology in France (see Lévi-Strauss 1987). Mauss certainly appears to us now as the more anthropological of the two, and he may have influenced Durkheim in arguing for the significance of anthropological materials in their work. Some have thought that his preference for facts over theory made him more positivist than his uncle.

There were certainly minor theoretical adjustments. Left on his own after World War I, Mauss came to doubt that the sacred was as universally significant as Durkheim had claimed, and instead he began to stress mana, a notion of supernatural force that he claimed was a symbol of social determinism. This was intended to replace the British intellectualists' concentration on spirits as the main symbols of religious belief (compare this to Tylor's well-known definition of religion as belief in spiritual beings). Later Mauss also regretted the extreme divide between magic and religion that Durkheim had taken over from his intellectualist adversaries and that Mauss and Henri Hubert had perpetuated in their own study of magic (Hubert and Mauss 1972); Mauss now preferred to talk of the "magicoreligious" instead. He also pointed out, with reference to Robert Hertz as much as to Durkheim, that humans not only dichotomize, they can produce classifications based on other numbers too, like the Zuñi of New Mexico, a favorite people of his, with their sevenfold classification of space (1968–1969, 2:145).

Mauss is also more closely associated with the idea of holism than Durkheim, perhaps unfairly to the latter. But certainly he insisted, in *The Gift* for example (1954), that in the study of any topic of sociological interest all the relevant social aspects should be taken into account and the topic itself should be properly situated within society as a whole. A connected point is that for the study of any topic, a particularly well-developed ethnographic example should be chosen, such as sacrifice among the ancient Hindus (Hubert and Mauss 1964) or exchange among Polynesians or, in the case of Hertz, secondary burials in Borneo (Hertz 1907/1960). Both principles were seen as an alternative to the cut-and-paste methods of past syntheses, exemplified most notoriously by the twelve volumes of James Frazer's *The Golden Bough* (1911–1936).

One relatively neglected similarity between Durkheim and Mauss is an emphasis on evolutionism. When Durkheim rejected the work of the nineteenth-century British school, he had to confront the question of the origins and evolutionary development of religion. In *The Division of Labour* (1893) he described a trend away from tribal ("closed") societies with a single moral and religious system toward stratified societies with several such systems and, further, toward modern, more diverse and ideologically more egalitarian societies in which religion had ceased to have a public place and had become solely the business of the private individual. Another trend was away from societies with mechanical solidarity toward those with organic solidarity, that is, away from "clan" societies toward "division of labour" societies. In both cases, there was also a sense of society becoming progressively more complex, as differentiation succeeded a prior unification.

This tendency was increased in Mauss, who explicitly declined to celebrate the demise of evolutionism in the 1920s. This evolutionism had already appeared in an article, *Primitive Classification*, coauthored with his uncle in 1903 (Durkheim and Mauss 1903/1963), which was concerned to relate classifications of the natural world with those of the social world. The fundamental point was that in the more "primitive" societies classifications of the natural world were based on those of the social world through, for example, totemism. However, in being set out as a series of situations, the work can also be seen as representing evolutionary stages. Again the Australian material comes first, because this is characterized by totemism—the earliest form of religion for Durkheim—in which there is a one-to-one correspondence between the two sorts of classification, and also because the Australians were seen as the earliest representatives of contemporary humanity. There is also a fusion between the two classifications: although the natural categories may have been based on the social ones, the two were also embedded in one another, since the clan was the totem as much as vice versa. After a series of intermediate stages, such as that of the "individual" totems of China, the link between the two classifications became completely broken in modern societies, where they were not even part of the same discourse of knowledge, biology being newly distinguished from sociology.

This habit of starting with the fusion of aspects and ending with their separation, especially in modern times, is quite characteristic of Mauss's independent work too, such as *The Gift* and his 1938 essay on the person (see 1938/1985; cf. Allen 1985; Parkin 2001, chap. 13). Although *The Gift* remains one of the most fertile and influential works in the whole of anthropology, it has often been criticized on various grounds. Firth (1929, 421) argued that Mauss misunderstood the nature of the *hau*, which may give the gift itself a sort of agency, but does not represent a part of the giver himself as Mauss claimed. But while Middle Eastern material also proves somewhat recalcitrant to Mauss's model, given the imperative to limit, or even avoid, exchange in many Arab societies (Dresch 1998), material on India supports it in respect to the giver's sins, which it bears, though not in respect to the obligation to give back (Parry 1986, Raheja 1988). Lygia Sigaud (2002) has argued that Mauss's contemporaries actually read into *The Gift* a stress on law, obligation, and holism: in her view it was Lévi-Strauss who began to emphasize reciprocity, a shift that has proved both fruitful and influential.

Mauss's famous place as a protostructuralist ought at least to be mentioned, since his work on the gift recognized the importance of relations and was to have a clear influence on the full development of structuralism by his pupil Lévi-Strauss. His abandoned 1909 thesis on prayer (see 1909/2003) was another instance of an apparently individual activity being shown to have social roots. Again there was an evolutionary dimension, ritual supplications by a collectivity being seen as becoming progressively individualized, as in Protestantism, for instance. But there was still a social tradition involved, and socially derived expectations of correct behavior even in solitary prayer.

Also of interest is Mauss's work on bodily movements as socially determined (1979, chap. 4). Dumont tells us that Mauss claimed to be able to distinguish an Englishman from a Frenchman simply by the way he walked (1992, chap. 7), and Mauss also argued that the bodily movements of Americans in the southern United States were basically the same regardless of racial difference and in spite of the long history of racial antagonism there. Then there is the essay on the suggestibility of death in the context of beliefs in supernatural attack, which had more impact in some societies than in others in actually causing such deaths because of the particular social and ideological circumstances in which the respective beliefs are located (1979, chap. 2). His work with Henri Beuchat on seasonal movements among the Eskimos stressed the different social qualities of winter and summer life (Mauss and Beuchat 1979), which clearly influenced Edward E. Evans-Pritchard's treatment of ecology in *The Nuer* (1940). The joint work with Hubert on sacrifice stressed that sacrifice was not just something being given up but a recognition of the power of the social (Hubert and Mauss 1964). And so on. For the sheer range and imagination of his writings, which are nonetheless still rooted in the fairly well-delineated model drawn up by his uncle, Mauss has few peers.

Robert Hertz and Henri Hubert: The Sociology of Religion

The approach developed by Durkheim and Mauss, and even some of the same arguments, are also present in the work of Mauss's friend and colleague Robert Hertz (1881–1915). If anyone is the great *regretté* of the Durkheim school it must be this man, whose brilliance impressed many and whose apparently great promise died with him in the French attack on Marchéville, which he led as an army officer in 1915. There is evidence from Hertz's letters of a mind in turmoil, of someone who could never convince himself that the cloistered life of academia was preferable to action to improve the lot of one's fellow citizens and of France itself. His origins, partly German-Jewish, partly Anglo-Saxon, and quite privileged, created in him an exaggerated desire to serve both the France where he was born and where he felt he belonged and the underprivileged working classes.

One of Hertz's greatest joys was being in the army in 1914 to 1915 with the men under his command, which he idealized as his absorption into a particularly disciplined example of the Durkheimian collectivity. While in the army he also recorded the songs and other folklore his men knew (1917). There are indications that if he had survived the war he would have deserted sociology to become an educationalist, like his wife Alice, who introduced the first kindergartens into France, and like Durkheim himself earlier in his career. Like Mauss and many other Durkheimians he was active in left-wing politics, being the main inspiration behind the Groupe d'Études Socialistes, a Fabian-influenced debating society that brought together academics (including Mauss and François Simiand) and left-wing activists to discuss issues of public policy (Parkin 1996, 1997, 1998). His tendency to somberness, referred to by Mauss and others, may be reflected in his work. Certainly he seems to have set himself the task of dealing with what Mauss called "the dark side of humanity" (1925, 24), that is, the negative aspects of social life, especially where that life is challenged in its essence and has to act to reconstitute itself.

This is apparent in Hertz's two best-known works, on death and on the symbolism of the hands, but it is also an important aspect of his own unfinished thesis on sin and expiation. The 1907 essay on death is at once an account of the phenomenon of secondary burials, of the structure of ritual (it may have influenced Arnold van Gennep, whose *Rites of Passage* came out only two years later), and of the exact place of emotion in funerals (see 1907/1960). The liminal period represented by the ritual was brought to an end by the secondary burial of the bones, a practice that Hertz discussed in relation to Borneo, though it can also be found in parts of modern Europe, for example, northern Portugal (Pina-Cabral 1980) and southern Greece (Danforth 1982). Hertz consistently represented death negatively, the function of the ritual being to overcome the breach that death has occasioned. Only later did anthropologists begin to see positive aspects in death rituals, which are often occasions for the reaffirmation of life, even its symbolic renewal (Bloch and Parry 1982).

In his 1909 essay on the symbolism of the hands (see 1909/1973), Hertz reversed the conventional physiological argument to contend that social determinism, in the form of a cultural preference for right-handedness, has an impact on the biological organism itself. At the end of the paper, Hertz praised modern educational attempts to move beyond handedness and promote ambidexterity. This involved overcoming the symbolic aspects of handedness by separating them from the use of the hands as a mechanical operation. In short, it is another example of the evolutionary disassembling of primitively fused notions that I identified above in Mauss.

Hertz's thesis on sin and expiation, or what he managed to write of it before his death (basically about 80 percent of the introduction), was published by Mauss in 1922 (see Hertz 1922/1994). Hertz intended this to be his major work; the articles on death and handedness, though he is better known for them today, were merely supplementary to it in his own mind, but the war and his own death prevented its completion. The fieldwork study he carried out in 1911 and 1912 on the cult of San Bessu, focused on a chapel built against a rock high in the Alps above Turin (see 1913/1983), was intended as part of a study of rocks and mountains more generally. Included here was his theme of projection from mountains, especially with reference to Hellenic mythology (e.g., the myth of Athena). Hertz also wrote an interesting if quite polemical pamphlet on depopulation in France, which he blamed on the middle classes, while also deploring the increase in foreign immigration into France that depopulation was encouraging (1910). Here we are confronted with Hertz the politically motivated intellectual, the Hertz of the Groupe d'Études Socialistes (the pamphlet originated in a talk given to the GES), rather than Hertz the pure academic.

The name of Henri Hubert is often coupled with that of Mauss. He was the latter's collaborator on studies of magic and sacrifice and lectured alongside him on ancient European religions at EPHE. He was also interested in ancient Celtic and German history and archaeology (1950, 1952). Hubert is now recognized as the author of a 1905 work on time (see 1905/1999) after a long period in which a quirk of publishing led to it being attributed to Mauss. Here too we find typical Durkheimian characteristics, especially discussions of the symbolic nature of time, its subservience to social agendas, the metonymic relationship between ritual days and the periods they are parts of (Sunday representing the whole week, and so on), and the separation of the use of time in symbolism from the purely mechanical measurement of it in the modern world in contrast to the fusing of the two in nonmodern societies—another example of the peculiarly Durkheimian model of evolutionism that I identified earlier.

Halbwachs and Other Durkheimians: Sociology in General

Another figure for whom time had some significance was Maurice Halbwachs (1877–1945), who for many years carried the flame of Durkheimianism at the University of Strasbourg before obtaining a much coveted professorship in the Collège de France in the middle of 1944. Tragically he was arrested by the Gestapo two months later and perished in Buchenwald the following year. Halbwachs is remembered today mainly for his work on memory (e.g., 1999)—a subject that modern anthropology has rediscovered—though he also took forward Durkheim's work on suicide (e.g., 1930) and contributed to the study of consumption patterns and other aspects of economics (e.g., 1912, 1933, 1999). Halbwachs wrote that memory, seemingly individual, is actually a thoroughly social phenomenon, since it is shared with others and prompted by our social surroundings. Furthermore, each generation modifies collective memory, adding its own input to what is already there. Memory is also influenced by age in the sense that becoming older draws us back to our traditions and thus to memory. Memory, then, is ideological and selective, reconstructing the past, and in important ways society itself, through its association with performative and reconstitutive rituals. Also, Halbwachs explained, in a complex society different social groups have different collective memories.

Phenomenological aspects have been discerned in the later Halbwachs. He developed an interest in social psychology, and he was not afraid to criticize aspects of Durkheim's work. This was especially true in the case of suicide, of which he identified rejection by others as a key cause. At root, though, he remained as wedded to the master's basic principles as anyone else in the group. He is also credited with having invented the notion of social space as a kind of analogue to Hubert's idea of social time, in which he may have been anticipated by the latter's Polish pupil, Stefan Czarnowski. This is different from the later use of the term by the French anthropologist of continental Southeast Asia, Georges Condominas (1980), for whom it is little more than a metaphor for social organization. For Halbwachs it is the social uses to which space is put and the social determination of spatial categories that are of interest.

Other Durkheimians can be dealt with more briefly here, since although they were part of the inner core of Durkheim's collegial circle in their respective lifetimes, they have had much less impact on anthropology as a whole. Célestin Bouglé (1870–1940) was one of Durkheim's earliest collaborators. He was already sufficiently formed in his rather psychologically oriented views for Durkheim to have to persuade him of the necessity of the new discipline of sociology. Once won over by Durkheim, however, Bouglé applied himself to studying notions of equality (1899, 1903), then examined the hierarchical caste system in India (1971), which he blamed on the Brahmans. His work on India, which recognized the importance of notions of purity and impurity in producing a caste system that involved both separation (of individual castes) and integration (of all castes into a system), considerably influenced Louis Dumont's later study of this topic (see my fifth lecture). Bouglé also studied the generation of social values (1969) and had a sustained interest in the sociology of Proudhon (e.g., 1912). François Simiand (1873–1935) was the economic specialist of the group (e.g., 1934–1942) and also published on the methodology of the social sciences (e.g., 1903). He showed that movements in the economy, of prices and so on, were not utilitarian but were structured by collective attitudes rooted in irrational bullish and bearish phases in the market and linked to a collective will to economic survival (see Marcel 2001b).

Paul Fauconnet (1874–1938), who had a legal background and built his academic career in Toulouse, also contributed to the discussion of methodological questions (Mauss and Fauconnet 1901), though he is perhaps better known for his work on responsibility and its judicial determination (1920; cf. Gephart 1997, Mauss 1999). In this work there is the familiar evolutionary sequence toward greater individuation in relation to society, which is reflected in the contrast between the malefactor's punishment in modern societies and his readmission in premodern ones. However, all regimes of justice are more concerned with establishing guilt than identifying motivation. As a Durkheimian, Fauconnet was keen to show the social nature of judgments, but he also emphasized the religious aspect, in terms of both the association of legal ideas with religious ideas and ritual practices, and the attribution of responsibility to the inanimate and the supernatural, and to animals and children in addition to mature adult humans.

Another Durkheimian with legal training was Emmanuel Lévy (1870–1944), who taught from 1901 to 1940 at Lyon, where he was also a noted socialist activist. As with responsibility, he saw both property rights and contractual obligations as being grounded in the belief of those immediately involved as well as in society more generally. Like Fauconnet, he identified religious aspects of these phenomena, but also distinguished the moral basis of such claims from the law, which was subject to rational calculation and imposed by outside authorities. With the arrival of the modern, capitalist, market-based economy, inalienable rights to possession were replaced by their alienation, being framed by notions of value, which shift according to what people are willing to pay. Here Lévy's activism enters the picture: capitalism constitutes a separation between rights (of the capitalist) and duties (of the worker), a rift that only radical movements such as socialism or syndicalism can overcome (see 1903, 1926, 1933; see also Frobert 1997).

Leading Non-Durkheimians of the Interwar Period

Some other figures from this period had an impact on anthropology, both in France and further afield, but were not strictly speaking, or even loosely speaking in some cases, part of the Durkheim group. The name of Maurice Leenhardt (1878–1954) was largely forgotten after his death until the 1980s, just after his major work *Do Kamo*, on New Caledonia, was translated into English (see 1947/1979). Born at Montauban in 1878, the son of a geology-teaching preacher, in 1902 he published his thesis on the so-called Ethiopian movement that had arisen in southern Africa as a response to racial discrimination (see 1902/1976). After studying theology and medicine, he went to New Caledonia as a Protestant missionary in 1902. His activities there are now often cited as an example of long-term fieldwork predating Bronislaw Malinowski, like whom he believed in living the life of the indigenous people as the only route to understanding their ideas and values.

While in the field Leenhardt sought to protect the local population from colonial abuses and promoted the founding of indigenous churches incorporating both local and Christian values. In this way he came to regard the local culture as both autonomous and valid in its own right. Intellectually he rejected his friend Lucien Lévy-Bruhl's distinction between primitive and modern forms of thought, which had an impact on the latter's own change of heart about this toward the end of his life. Nonetheless, an early student of personhood, a sense of which he derived from the person's consciousness of the body, Leenhardt thought that the idea of personality had been introduced into New Caledonia by Christianity. However, he excluded psychoanalysis as an explanation for personhood in favor of the holistic sociology and ethnography of Mauss.

Leenhardt was also interested in time, in the connections between myth and art, and in the integration of the notions of *kamo*, the living, and *bao*, the dead. In particular he pursued a phenomenological approach to myth, seeing it less as narrative in form than as a discontinuous series of "landscapes" or "periods" experienced by the individual, in which, rather as Lévi-Strauss later suggested (e.g., 1967), cultural, ecological, and cosmological realities are superimposed on one another.

In 1926 Leenhardt returned to France and tried to become involved in mission administration; his lack of success in that effort was a reflection of the bad repute into which he had fallen with his mission thanks to the supposedly subversive nature of his activities in the field. He published a broadly popular ethnography of New Caledonia, *Gens de la Grande Terre*, in 1937, and *Do Kamo* in 1947. In 1941 he succeeded Mauss in the chair of the history of "primitive" religions at EPHE, after a brief period beginning in 1935 when they had taught together; he was succeeded in the post by Lévi-Strauss in 1950. His first student while he was serving in this capacity was Michel Leiris. Leenhardt also taught at the École des Langues Orientales, was placed in charge of the Oceania section of the Musée de l'Homme, and set up the Institut Française d'Océanie at Noumea in New Caledonia in 1947. He died in 1954 (Dousset-Leenhardt 1977; Clifford 1982, 1991).

Another writer who came to prominence in this period is Lucien Lévy-Bruhl (1857–1939), a philosopher who was granted a chair in modern philosophy in 1908 and in 1925 obtained from the Popular Front government approval for the establishment of the Institut d'Ethnologie, which he entrusted to Mauss and Paul Rivet to run. Although he was almost contemporary with Durkheim, he survived him by over twenty years and only became significant for anthropology after Durkheim's death. Indeed, like Durkheim, Lévy-Bruhl turned to the study of so-called primitive peoples at a relatively late point in his career, around 1903 (e.g., 1923, 1912/1926; cf. Cazeneuve 1972). Thereafter they were his main interest until his death in 1939.

Lévy-Bruhl's position on "primitive" peoples was not a consistent one. Although he was careful not to identify himself too closely with the Durkheimians, like them he rejected the intellectualist positions that religion had its origin in the psychology of the individual and that all peoples shared a common mentality. He was strongly influenced by Durkheim's notion of collective representations, declaring that each society had its own socially determined mode of thought. He therefore considered modes of thought to be as useful as behavior for understanding the social life of other peoples. He is perhaps most famous, however, for his distinction between primitive and civilized mentalities, the former involving supernatural ideas, the latter logic. Primitive thought was thus "prelogical" and involved "mystical participations and exclusions" such that symbolized objects partook of one another's substance, appeared in two places at once, and so forth. These participations and exclusions also acted immediately on the perceptions of the primitive individual: for example, in seeing his shadow, the primitive individual believed immediately that it was his soul. Finally, they were themselves socially selected for the individual from a range of possibilities. This made prelogical thought noninnovatory and resistant to experience. Only later did myths and symbols enter history as mediating factors between experience and thought, at which stage the concept as a separate phenomenon also appeared. Prelogical thought was therefore conceptless—which makes it seem like a contradiction in terms (cf. Durkheim 1915/1995).

Lévy-Bruhl makes it quite clear that this distinction is a matter of the categories through which primitive people think, not of an absolute inability to think logically. Indeed, prelogical thought is characterized more by its greater tolerance for, indeed nonrecognition of, contradictions than it is by its nonlogical or antilogical properties. Other aspects of this mode of thought include the significance of mystical powers in indigenous ideas of causality; the lack of a separate sense of self (cf. Mauss 1985 here); and fusions between the spiritual and the material, the individual and the group, and the body and the mind, with the qualification that the body extends outside its physical boundaries to include things like hair, clothing, and footprints. Yet Lévy-Bruhl also recognized that not all the thought of the supposedly civilized is by any means logical: even scientific advances involve much intuition and following up of hunches rather than rational thought in the strict sense.

Lévy-Bruhl's attribution of different modes of thought to types of society seemed deeply problematic to his contemporaries. His posthumously published *Carnets*, or *Notebooks* (1949/1975) indicate that he eventually realized this himself. Under the influence of his friend Leenhardt, he now made more explicit the realization that the two modes of thought he had identified were found together in any society and were not separately the product of particular types of societies. He also shifted the emphasis in his description of "primitive" thought from the prelogical to the mystical, which he saw as more a matter of affect (especially fear) than intellect, thus moving back in the direction of the nineteenth-century Victorians. However, in applying the notion of participation to the relationship between humans and gods during ritual, he surely identified a basic aim of much religious practice.

It is conventional to dismiss Lévy-Bruhl's basic dichotomy today in the interest of maintaining the essential unity of the human species and of discouraging arbitrary and misleading constructions of the primitive that can all too easily become the basis of political discrimination. Those who have dared to revive Lévy-Bruhl's ideas explicitly, like Jean Piaget (1971) and Christopher Hallpike (1979), have often been condemned for perpetuating precisely such notions. Yet similar ideas survive in the intellectual undergrowth, partly because they correspond to a persistent but largely unspoken view among many anthropologists that "the West" is in some senses different from "the rest." Thus they emerge in other forms on occasion, as in Jack Goody's studies of the impact of literacy (e.g., 1977) and Dumont's distinction between modern and non-modern thought (1992; cf. Evans-Pritchard 1965, chap. 4, and 1981; Jamin 1991c). Although he was more prepared than many to take Lévy-Bruhl seriously, in his work on Azande witchcraft Evans-Pritchard (1937) rejected Lévy-Bruhl's position while partially returning to the intellectualism that both he and the Durkheimian tradition are conventionally seen as opposing.

Another significant figure of the time was Marcel Granet (1884–1940), who sought to incorporate Durkheimian insights and methods into his studies of China, where he lived from 1911 to 1913. Upon his return, he obtained a chair at the EPHE, taught at the École des Langues Orientales beginning in 1926, and was involved in the Institut des Hautes Études Chinoises. In his work he rejected conventional history in favor of the reconstruction and analysis of Chinese "civilization" (e.g., Granet 1930, 1953), using primarily historical documents in a manner that did not aim at the production of a flowing narrative but rather reflected the holism of his friend Mauss.

Granet was initially interested in the concept of honor in medieval Europe. From there he turned to China for comparative purposes, focusing mainly on the pre-Han period. This area then engaged the rest of his career. It led to a focus on feudal obligations in China, then on the family as an institution with which these obligations frequently came into conflict, and finally, by way of the family, on religion in the form of ancestor worship (1975). Like Durkheim, whom he discovered before developing his interest in China, he placed the emergence of ancestor worship relatively late in history, refusing, unlike the many evolutionists, to see in it an original form. Also like Durkheim, he identified an early conjunction between mystical and jural notions, and by preferring texts to informants' statements as his basic material, he echoed the Durkheimians' overall feeling that an overreliance on the latter produced only folklore and the misreading of myths of origin as factual history, not proper holistic analysis. Granet's notion of Chinese civilization as partly one of a distinctive mode of thought developing in historical time led him to stress continuities more than changes, as in conventional history.

Granet's examination of Chinese marriage systems (1939) had considerable influence on Lévi-Strauss's formulation of models of affinal alliance. One of Granet's students, Edouard Mestre, anticipated Edmund Leach in describing the Kachin system of asymmetric prescriptive alliance in his lectures at EPHE (Freedman 1975; Goudineau 1991).

Another figure of significance in this period and later was Georges Dumézil (1898–1986), one of Granet's students, whose work is occasionally seen as having served rightist agendas in the 1930s and even much later through its alleged suppression of the Jewish legacy in Western thought. After teaching history at the universities of Istanbul and Uppsala, Dumézil was appointed to a chair in the comparative study of the religions of Indo-European peoples at EPHE. Between 1949 and 1968 he occupied the chair of Indo-European civilization at the Collège de France (Charachidzé 1991). Dumézil called himself a historian, but he can also be considered an evolutionary structuralist for his identification of persistent representational structures going back to antiquity in Indo-European–speaking societies (e.g., 1968–1973, 1988). His comparisons thus include the peoples of India and Iran and the ancient Celts and Germans, as well as the ancient Greeks and Romans. As with Lévi-Strauss, myth was important to Dumézil, but conceptual triads replace the former's dichotomies in identifying the repeated division of functions between spiritual authority, secular rule, and wealth creation in both social organization and myth. Dumézil's work has spawned a veritable academic industry that has created a space for itself combining anthropology, history, and comparative philology, and it has inspired similar work based on other language families (Semitic, Tai, and so on). Dumézil's work was supported by that of the linguist Émile Benveniste, who used the Indo-European idea as a means of reconstructing and accounting for early Indo-European institutions, including those of European antiquity (1973).

Museums in the Interwar Period

Mauss's teaching informed two new initiatives for anthropology in the 1920s and 1930s. One was museological and focused on the Trocadero, which had been going through a long period of stagnation. Ernest-Théodore Hamy had died in 1908, to be succeeded by René Verneau, under whose administration the Trocadero declined still further. One feature of the Verneau regime, which ended in 1927, was the interest in *arts primitifs* that the museum stimulated among avant-garde artists of the 1910s and 1920s. Although for most anthropologists it was the scientific value of the artifacts that remained significant, this development raised their aesthetic profile in a way that Hamy was keen to encourage by mounting impressive displays whenever he had the funds to do so. Following the 1937 international exposition, in 1938 the Trocadero was converted into the Musée de l'Homme by Paul Rivet and Georges-Henri Rivière. The Musée went beyond Hamy's purely functional mode of classification and improved the sociological contextualization of the objects exhibited. The previous year, Rivière had founded the Musée des Arts et Traditions Populaires (MATP), including the Centre d'Ethnologie Française; it became a basis for the study of the new anthropology of France that was to develop after the war (Dias 1991; Rogers 2001; Schippers 1995; Williams 1985).

As well as inspiring artists, therefore, museums exerted a strong influence on French ethnography into the 1950s, as exemplified by some of Dumont's early work, particularly *La Tarasque* (1951), a description of a festival in southern France—Dumont was originally an employee of MATP. One result of this interest in museums and their artifacts was that diffusionism was current in France somewhat later than in Britain, emerging only in the late 1930s, fifteen to twenty years after its replacement by functionalism in Britain. Prominent examples of French diffusionists are Paul Rivet and André-Georges Haudricourt, the latter of whom I recall hearing lecture in Paris using a diffusionist approach as late as the mid-1980s.

Rivet (1876–1958) started his working life as a military doctor, in which capacity he accompanied a scientific expedition to Ecuador. While there he became interested in archaeology, linguistics, ethnology, and physical anthropology and also collected natural history specimens. He became attached to the Musée National d'Histoire Naturelle after returning to Paris in 1906. He then gradually moved over to conducting research on pre-Columbian Ecuador (e.g., 1912), and in 1925 he cofounded the Institut d'Ethnologie with Lévy-Bruhl and Mauss. He continued to be involved in museums, where he taught, as well as participating in the establishment of the new Musée de l'Homme in 1937 (Lévine 1991).

Haudricourt (1911–1996), born in 1911, was trained in botany and geography and in 1944 turned to the study of linguistics specializing in Slavonic languages. He made a number of research trips to Melanesia and the Far East between 1948 and 1973. These two aspects of his experience, his work in botany and linguistics, led him to pioneer the study of ethnobotany in France (e.g., 1943). A third interest was in tools and their relation to society (1987), his basic position being that tool invention was influenced by society rather than vice versa (Dibie 1991). Rivet and Haudricourt, therefore, both came from backgrounds in natural science but combined this with the disciplines of social science and the humanities in their mature work.

The link between museums and fieldwork was largely broken in the 1950s and 1960s with the arrival of Lévi-Strauss's structuralism. An exception was the MATP's continued support of the anthropology of France itself, as I explain in my next lecture.

Griaule and the Shift to Fieldwork

Mauss's other new initiative was fieldwork. The interwar period saw the development of ethnographic work in the French empire, which was itself at its height at this time. French Indochina, especially the central highlands, were occupied by non-Vietnamese, non-Khmer tribes. The history of anthropology in this area has been well described by Oscar Salemink (1991, 2003). Missionaries like Jean Kemlin had been active among the Bahnar since the 1850s, long before French pacification in the 1880s to 1890s. In the main, the missionaries' interest in understanding indigenous religions was in facilitating conversions. After pacification, the main interest of the authorities in these upland areas was the recruitment of the local tribespeople, or *moi* (literally, slaves), to work on rubber plantations and in the military. This in itself led to the production of anthropological studies of tribal societies, an early venture of this kind being *Les jungles moi* (1912), written by Henri Maitre, a colonial officer who was killed by the Mnong in 1914.

The major figure in this regard was Léopold Sabatier (1877–1936), who went out to Indochina in 1903 and soon became the French *résident* among the Rhadé. He served in this capacity until 1926, when he was sacked for persistently refusing to allow Vietnamese and French planters into the area in the interest of protecting the local population. Academically he is significant for having pioneered the production of a number of *coutumiers*, or accounts, of tribal "custom," each focusing on a different highland ethnic group. In effect these were colonial legal codes drawn up for the administration of local peoples, large-scale works whose ethnographic usefulness is generally diminished by the introduction of at least some French legal concepts and practices (e.g., Sabatier 1930; Sabatier and Antomarchi 1940). Nonetheless Sabatier's perspective was fundamentally one of cultural relativism combined with an implicit rejection of evolution as an explanation for social traditions, a position quite at variance with those of French planters, missionaries, and the generality of officialdom, for all of whom the local populations were basically savages in need of civilization.

Sabatier did have the support and cooperation of organizations like the École Française d'Extrême-Orient (EFEO), which drew up *coutumiers* of other groups in the highlands from the 1920s on and also carried out linguistic research. Although the Vietnamese language is actually related to many highlands languages, the EFEO's linguistic studies were used to support the more usual claim that highland populations were entirely separate from the Vietnamese. A specifically ethnographic section of the EFEO was created by Paul Lévy in 1937. Other institutions established in the region were the Institut Indo-Chinois de l'Étude de l'Homme, a joint venture of the EFEO and the medical faculty of the University of Hanoi set up to study ethnography and physical anthropology, and the Société des Études Indo-Chinois, founded in Saigon in 1880.

Anthropological survey work also went on in other parts of the French empire. Henri Labouret was the government anthropologist in Upper Volta (e.g., 1941), as was Louis Tauxier in the Ivory Coast (e.g., 1924).Maurice Delafosse was also active, producing works that put British ethnographic efforts in West Africa at this time in the shade (e.g., 1922; see also Goody 1995, 39–40). Delafosse was perhaps the major figure in this region before Marcel Griaule. Very familiar with Africa, he stressed in particular the historical contingency and social nature of inequalities between races. From 1901 he taught African languages at the École des Langues Orientales in Paris, as well as helping train colonial officers at the École Coloniale. He was also involved in another venture of significance to fieldwork, the founding of the Institut d'Ethnographie in the University of Paris in 1925 by Lévy-Bruhl, Mauss, and Rivet. He died the following year (Clifford 1983, 126–28; Jamin 1991b, 290).

Mauss taught regular courses on fieldwork and ethnography at the Institut, partly to colonial officers. This was a new departure in institutionalizing anthropology in French universities, though other subjects were also taught at the Institut, such as linguistics, geography, prehistory, and physical anthropology (Karady 1981). As in Britain, there was a sort of transitional stage of expeditions passing among many peoples rather than conducting long-term fieldwork with just one. The Torres Straits expedition of 1898 thus had its parallel in the Dakar-to-Djibouti expedition led by Griaule in the early 1930s, which was also concerned with the collection of artifacts; Lévi-Strauss's travels in Amazonia a little later in the same decade were in the same vein.

Marcel Griaule (1898–1956) was an influential but controversial figure in his own right from the 1930s into the 1950s. A student of Mauss, he had a definite enthusiasm for fieldwork, which he promoted as a scientific form of travel and exploration and as a sort of adventure that was also represented by his experiences as an aviator: he reportedly lectured at the Sorbonne in an aviator's uniform in the 1940s; and in 1943, as the first professor of general anthropology in France, he gave the first ethnology lectures there. In 1928, even before the Dakar-to-Djibouti expedition, he was in Ethiopia—which the later expedition also visited—doing fieldwork and collecting artifacts. The 1930s expedition had a very high profile, with companies like Citroën providing a lot of the funding. It was the period of *l'art nègre* and of enthusiasms for the primitive generally, on which Griaule the publicist fully capitalized to raise money for the venture. During the expedition the travelers spent time with the Dogon in Mali, starting an association that would last for the rest of Griaule's fieldwork career and would culminate in his renowned 1947 "conversations" with Ogotemmêli (1948/1965; see also 1938). Although the latter actually died quite soon after meeting Griaule, he is probably the most famous informant in the entire history of anthropology, and unlike that of Don Juan his existence has never been questioned.

Griaule would often use a range of assistants and colleagues at a ritual, placing them at different points in order to obtain an overall view of the activities of the different groups involved. Although influenced originally by diffusionism, he soon abandoned it in favor of an emphasis on what Clifford calls "synchronic cultural patterns" (1983, 122). He also stressed initiation rituals as an entry point into indigenous cultures generally, a principle that Germaine Dieterlin and other followers of his perpetuated. But although Griaule saw anthropology as multidisciplinary and fieldwork as involving the exercise of many different competences, his work was not very theoretical apart from development of the theory of fieldwork itself (see 1957). His tendency to reject theory may have had an impact, direct or indirect, on many later French anthropologists who stressed fieldwork and ethnography above theory.

Griaule has attracted criticism for the nature of his relationships with his informants, and the value of his reporting as anthropology has been challenged. He openly regarded fieldwork as inevitably involving unequal relationships of power in favor of the Western, white fieldworker. But far from reacting to this discovery with concern, as a present-day anthropologist surely would, Griaule seems to have reveled in it. He fully used his power as a white man over the local population in a colonial situation to extract from them not only information, but also artifacts and even skeletons from graves. In his view, encounters in the colonial situation were always potentially hostile, so he developed the habits of an interrogator rather than those of an inquirer, frequently using manipulative and forceful questioning to trick informants into revealing more than they really wished to.

Quite apart from the unethical nature of these methods, of course, the result of too much persistence may be answers invented on the spot. Such tactics and the staged and frequently theatrical nature of the activities he described—Griaule had a habit of setting up the situations he was examining rather than waiting for them to happen—as well as the closeness of his ties to key informants like Ogotemmêli, have led to accusations that his work was cultural production rather than ethnographic reporting. Certainly he relied greatly on translators and informants who were sympathetic to his project, which perhaps inevitably led to his essentializing the African past as "Africanism," as Jacques Maquet did later, and despite some cross-fertilization with the ideas of déraciné African intellectuals like Leopold Senghor and Aimé Cesaire. Nonetheless he held up the Dogon belief system as worthy of comparison with Christianity and other revealed religions.

Griaule worked with a range of colleagues, such as Leiris, who acted as Griaule's secretary, Dieterlin, and Delafosse, though not all of his colleagues remained followers. Dieterlin collaborated intensively with Griaule and published work on the Dogon under their joint names after his death (Griaule and Dieterlin 1965). She also did fieldwork with the Bambara (1951), her aim being to establish the existence of a pan-Sahelian mode of thought, a theme on which she later led a research team at EPHE and the Centre National de la Recherche Scientifique (CNRS). She was also interested in personhood (1973) and later collaborated with one of Griaule's students, Jean Rouch, in making films (Izard 1991). She continued to visit the Dogon until the year before her death, leading seasonal expeditions with colleagues rather than conducting long-term fieldwork alone, and she encouraged Franco-British cooperation among Africanist anthropologists (I. M. Lewis 2000).

Other students of Griaule's included the Belgian Luc de Heusch, a future follower of Lévi-Strauss; Griaule's own daughter Geneviève Calame-Griaule, who later became a sociolinguist (e.g., 1965/1986); and Denise Paulme (1909–1928). Paulme had trained in law, which may have given her an interest in social organization (including age grades) as well as in the ritual and symbolism that were a standard concern of this group; she also worked on oral literature. After taking part in Griaule's 1935 expedition, she produced a thesis on the Dogon in 1940 (see 1940/1988). Subsequently, with her husband, André Schaeffner, who pioneered the study of ethnomusicology in France, she did fieldwork with a number of other peoples in Guinea and the Ivory Coast (e.g., 1984). In 1958 she obtained a chair at the EPHE, where she set up the Centre d'Études Africaines (Jamin 1991a).

The Collège de Sociologie

Later in the same period, Michel Leiris (1901–1990) was involved in the short-lived Collège de Sociologie in France (1937–1939; see Hollier 1995; Richman 2002), which he founded with Georges Bataille (d. 1962) and Roger Caillois (1913–1978). They were all greatly inspired by Mauss's and Hertz's work on symbols and rituals, as well as by the new French ethnography initiated by Mauss, though only Caillois and Leiris were directly Mauss's students. Indeed, it was these two, together with Alfred Métraux, who led Bataille to add sociology to his existing interests in literature and philosophy. Leiris and Caillois also flirted early on with surrealism, but later broke with it; Bataille was never interested in that movement. The Collège de Sociologie itself was envisaged as a joint endeavor by scholars of similar intellectual and political orientation that went beyond normal academic cooperation: its founders were all strongly antifascist, and Bataille in particular had Marxist tendencies. This was reinforced by the creation of a journal, *Acéphale*, which was linked to a secret society of the same name.

Of this trio, Bataille seems to have dominated intellectually, and posthu-

mously he has become a guru of some modern cultural studies for his focus
on the irrational, including the violence and nihilism of the modern world
(see 1970, 1997). These also characterized the 1930s, of course, the period in
which Bataille was mainly active. Bataille's basic position was that the social
order that Durkheimian sociology sought to explain was ultimately less significant than the irrational, even self-destructive urge to violate the taboos that
protected that order. Indeed, the very existence of the taboo promoted precisely this irrational urge. And since this urge inhered in individuals, Bataille
supplemented rationalist Durkheimian sociology with a form of phenomenological collective psychology that was linked to ideas of will and power drawn
from Freud, Nietzsche, Hegel, and even the Marquis de Sade, who represented in an extreme form the violation of sexual taboos. Not only did this irrational urge replace the interdiction of taboos with their transgression, it also
represented a will to endanger what was sacred to society and to those who belonged to it, though this also released revitalizing energies.

Bataille was especially impressed not only by sacrifice, but also by the institution of the potlatch, described by Mauss, which, under the more general
term *dépense* ("expenditure"), Bataille saw as the basis both for society itself
and for subversive, antibourgeois currents in modern society, given the bourgeois stress on frugality. Using Hertz's paper on right and left, Bataille
stressed the left, or inauspicious sacred as a subversive force turning Durkheimian homogeneity into revolutionary heterogeneity, which modern capitalist, bourgeois society itself encourages by subordinating its other, the working class. Bataille also brought in Durkheim's notion of effervescence, seeing
in it revolutionary potential for both right and left in a reprise of Le Bon's
ideas. This is linked to the idea of sacrifice: one of the characteristics of the
modern for Bataille is that it posits universal ideas that demand constant
sacrifice, as in militarism (the sacrifice of life by the soldier), or the will of
modern mass movements to destroy class or racial enemies.

Bataille's work has been criticized for its slender ethnographic basis, which
hardly went beyond the rather superficial interest in the Aztecs encouraged
by Métraux, who asked Bataille to review an exhibition of pre-Columbian art.
More fundamentally, as Susan Stedman-Jones has pointed out, negativity, nihilism, and moral relativism are, even in the modern world, exceptional rather
than routine forms of day-to-day human conduct (2001). Bataille also offends
methodologically by confusing what one might call institutional nihilism—as
in his favorite example of the potlatch, where the apparently senseless destruction of property was socially required—with the transgression of social
taboos by individuals.

Caillois's work (e.g., 1950) was generally more equivocal, and his friend Bataille did not hesitate to criticize him for it. Caillois doubted the usefulness of the dichotomy between sacred and profane in modern society, which he saw as limited to cases of war and revolution and as no longer applicable to normal life, where sacrifice, especially of the destructive form that Bataille focused on, was more a matter of the individual's readiness to do without, not social imperative. After the war, Caillois would also counsel against romanticizing the primitive, which he claimed to discern in the new anthropology of Lévi-Strauss. Nonetheless, in a letter Mauss condemned Caillois for celebrating the irrationality that Mauss identified in Caillois's work, and no doubt in Bataille's work too (see Marcel 2001b). As with other commentators on the Collège de Sociologie, Mauss may have mistaken an intention to be objective about social life with a political program for how the group should be led: as already noted, the trio were firmly antifascist, and Leiris was to become famous for his antiracist, anticolonialist pronouncements, which did not spare his erstwhile mentor, Griaule.

A lot of the writing of this trio verges on the literary, and indeed merges with it in the work of Leiris, who eventually broke with Bataille and the Collège in July 1939. Initially he was inspired more by poetry than by any idea of anthropology as an academic discipline, and his earliest writings were published in the *Revue surréaliste* in 1925. This interest in surrealism dominated much of his work, despite his eventual break from the movement itself in 1929, and in the late 1940s he was mainly concerned with trying to reconcile surrealism with Jean-Paul Sartre's attacks on its allegedly voyeuristic passivity and refusal of moral commitment. Leiris also wrote on Africa, especially in *L'Afrique fantôme* (1934), a critique of Griaule's methods, in particular the latter's centering of initiation as an entrée into another culture for the anthropologist, as a representation of the crux of the culture itself. He rejected the rigid view that an exotic culture contained, or was, a kind of essence and insisted on including assimilated or Europeanized Africans in the overall account. He also disliked Griaule's aggressive methods of enquiry, arguing that the ethnographer should be an advocate for the exploited (Sartre 1948; Leiris 1950, 1968; cf. Boschetti 1985; Jamin 1991e; Robbins 2003).

After his break with Bataille, Leiris began to focus on the long-term anthropologically inspired autobiography for which he is best known (1968). Because of his criticisms of Griaule, Bataille, and others, he also stands out as an early skeptic concerning the validity and feasibility of the whole ethnographic process, of a sort that has become very familiar in anthropology since about 1980. This did not prevent him from becoming a director of research at CNRS in the 1960s.

Although the convergence, not to say confusion, of ethnography with art and literature in the work of both Griaule and the Collège de Sociologie was popular at the time, it is now little more than a historical curiosity. Of these figures, it is probably Leiris whose work has survived the best. As for Durkheim's intellectual lineage, its onward march was only interrupted, not ended, by World War II. Its continuation, explicitly with structuralism and implicitly in certain other schools, forms the main theme of my remaining lectures.

4

Structuralism and Marxism

Marcel Mauss's two most influential followers were Claude Lévi-Strauss (b. 1908) and Louis Dumont (1911–1998). The impact of his work on both of them was strong. Although Lévi-Strauss discovered Mauss only retrospectively after learning anthropology in the United States, he exploited Mauss's famous model of exchange in developing what he always considered to be the method, rather than the theory, of structuralism. Dumont's structuralism was always more contingent because, influenced by Lévi-Strauss directly as well as by Mauss's own teaching, he came to see the approach as most suitable for understanding both his south Indian ethnography and the Indian caste system more generally. But like Lévi-Strauss was also influenced by the notion of binary opposition, which was originally identified as a scientific puzzle by Robert Hertz. Dumont's achievement was to develop this notion, so fundamental to structuralism, in new directions.

Lévi-Strauss and Structuralism

Lévi-Strauss was born in Brussels in 1908. An early interest in geology led him to notice the survival of patterns from the past in surface landscapes that had themselves changed. This may be regarded as an early manifestation of a basic structuralist, Lévi-Straussian tenet, the distinction between enduring, constant deep structures and their variable surface manifestations. After studying law and philosophy and teaching in a lycée for a while, he lectured at the newly opened University of São Paulo from 1935 to 1938, which enabled him to undertake travels in the Brazilian interior, an experience that gave him some material for his later studies of myth and related topics. Lévi-Strauss never did fieldwork in the Malinowskian sense of long-term participant observation with a single group: his trips to Amazonia were more in the nature of the expeditions that intervened chronologically between armchair anthropology and long-term fieldwork in the development of both the British and French anthropological traditions. His work titled, even in its English translation, *Tristes tropiques* (1973), a union of philosophy, anthropology, and autobiography, represents this period of his career best. Among other things, we learn from it his dislike of fieldwork, which caused in him a temporary crisis over his ability to follow his chosen profession.

World War II brought Lévi-Strauss, in exile, to New York, where he encountered both structural linguistics through the agency of his friend and colleague at the New School for Social Research, Roman Jakobson, and the Boasian tradition, with its combination of antievolutionist, antiracist positions; reification of culture; and interest in common human mental patterns drawn ultimately from Franz Boas's involvement with Adolf Bastian in Germany. Lévi-Strauss's New York years were at least as formative in the development of his thought as French philosophy, from which he was to move even further away after his eventual return to France. His daily presence at the New York Public Library recalls, in some ways, Marx sitting in the British Museum Library in London a century earlier.

Although Lévi-Strauss was offered posts in the United States, his failure to obtain tenure at the New School for Social Research led him to return to Paris in 1947 to try and build his career there. Lygia Sigaud suggests that despite some false starts, he managed to establish his career by posing as Mauss's natural intellectual successor, a role Mauss himself saw him in (2002). Georges Davy took him on and became his supervisor, and in 1948 Lévi-Strauss was appointed *maître de recherche* at the Centre National de la Recherche Scientifique (CNRS) and then subdirector of the Musée de l'Homme. He taught at the École Pratique des Hautes Études (EPHE) from 1949 and then became director of studies there, taking over Mauss's and Maurice Leenhardt's old chair in the religions of noncivilized peoples the following year and immediately changing its name to the more politically correct religions of nonliterate peoples. In 1959 he was elected to the Collège de France on his third attempt; there he created the Laboratoire d'Anthropologie Sociale and in 1960 founded *L'Homme*, which quickly became the mainstream journal of anthropology in France (Sigaud 2002).

Apart from the influences he acquired in America, a number of other currents had an impact on Lévi-Strauss. There is more than a hint of early British intellectualism in his thought, though not of the evolutionism with which it was originally associated. This appears to be derived most immediately from

James Frazer, though Edward Tylor was a more explicit influence. Connected with this interest in the human mind is an awareness of Freud, which has drawn Lévi-Strauss close to psychoanalysis at times, though his idea of the unconscious is Saussurean rather than Freudian. Lévi-Strauss also discovered Hegelian dialectics and its Marxist development, which became useful to him as a way of relating not only deep structure to surface manifestation, but also deep structures to one another. Lévi-Strauss is not a Marxist, but he has said that he never writes anything without reading some Marx first in order to get his mind working in the proper dialectical fashion. He had already, of course, absorbed the fertility of the idea of exchange from Mauss's lectures. Putting all these strands together, he developed a view of structure as a set of relations rather than a matter of substance, as in the functionalist tradition). In Lévi-Strauss's notion of structure, the nature of the relations remains constant, however much the substances or entities they relate together—the content of the relations—varies from case to case, whether within societies or between them. And being unconscious, structures are uniform, being the location where cultures meet and can be compared.

Lévi-Strauss's interest in linguistics was perhaps the most important influence on his thought in general, or at any rate, the most widely applicable. The influence here relates to both the idea of structure as pattern and the notion of binary opposition that underpins structure in the first place. For the first, Lévi-Strauss drew from Ferdinand de Saussure (1960) the contrast between grammar and speech, grammar being a constant set of rules or patterning within which speech, a series of possibly unique utterances, is framed.

Utterances are transmitted in time, and the grammar one uses to make them is fixed for the period of the utterance (grammar is, of course, also subject to long-term historical change). Theorists offered concrete examples to elucidate this contrast between what are described sometimes in abstract terms as paradigms and syntagmatic chains, and sometimes as metaphor (an emphasis on similarity) and metonym (a chain relationship in which a part stands for the whole). One example, which is Saussure's, is the game of chess (and by implication all other games and sports), which combines a set of rules with the uniqueness of each game actually played, seen as a set of moves. Another is music, in which a standard harmony, fixed according to the rules of the day, is opposed to the fluidity and inventiveness of a unique melody. Yet another is the meal, with a fixed pattern of courses that is contrasted with the variety of actual dishes that might be offered in each course. In all of these the linear dimension of the message is subject to a set of rules, but also to more or less conscious selection within those rules. Though subject to analysis, the dimension of structure or pattern may not be subject to everyday consciousness at all.

Saussure's influence on Lévi-Strauss went further than linguistics per se, because Lévi-Strauss used linguistics to make a number of changes to the theory and practice of anthropology in France (see Johnson 2003). He suggested that anthropology should become a science like Saussurean linguistics, though of context-free culture rather than context-bound social structure, as in Alfred Radcliffe-Brown's alternative scientism. This led Lévi-Strauss to treat anthropology as a new subject separate simultaneously from the older style of ethnology in France, from sociology, and from philosophy. His de-centering of sociology was to bring him into personal conflict with Georges Gurvitch, the leading postwar French sociologist, while his rejection of philosophy was to create later intellectual disputes with Jean-Paul Sartre. Lévi-Strauss had a greater appreciation of history at this time, regarding it as the study of the conscious and anthropology as the study of the unconscious, both being needed for a rounded view of the human condition. However, Lévi-Strauss's structuralism does not need history, despite his later contrast between "hot" societies, which are aware of a linear history that they have accumulated, and "cold" societies, whose sense of time is noncumulative and is limited to the cyclical repetitions of myth.

The second idea that Lévi-Strauss took from linguistics was the semantic significance of voiced/unvoiced pairs of consonants (e.g., Jakobson and Lévi-Strauss 1962), adopted from the work of his New York friend Roman Jakobson and that of another Russian linguist, N. S. Trubetskoy. Thus the semantic difference between *sad* and *sat* is obvious to the speaker of English, who would nonetheless not be able to specify the phonological basis of this contrast, namely the voicing or unvoicing of the final consonant, without reflecting on it specifically. In other words, again we have a contrast between surface obviousness and deep obscurity as far as the typical social actor is concerned, as well as between many variables on the one hand and a common pattern of simple contrast involving binary opposition on the other. This focus on the binary opposition did not prevent Lévi-Strauss from identifying a third term mediating between the poles to resolve contradictions, especially in the analysis of myth, though not all oppositions lend themselves logically to this operation. All one now needs to arrive at his form of structuralism are transformations of narratives and other surface expressions of the cultural that are linked by a common pattern, for example, between myths in the same or different cultures.

These insights were worked out and demonstrated with regard to specific problems, such as exchange and its significance, in Lévi-Strauss's first major work, *The Elementary Structures of Kinship* (1949/1969). The main source of the notion of exchange was, of course, Mauss's work on the gift. Lévi-Strauss's contribution was to apply exchange to one of the contexts for which Mauss described it, namely marriage, in particular cross-cousin marriage, which itself is based on a universal incest taboo forcing men to give away their sisters in exchange (though not necessarily directly with another group) for others' sisters to be their own wives.

Some peculiarities of Lévi-Strauss's overall argument ought to be highlighted here. First, it is a type of contract argument according to which men came together to create society neither in obedience to a sovereign, as for Hobbes, nor in obedience to the general will, as for Rousseau, but simply for mutual support—a recapitulation of Tylor's "marry out or die out" argument. In this respect, it is un-Durkheimian. Second, at root this is a functionalist argument, and it is not Lévi-Strauss's only one: his treatment of myth as imparting social knowledge in symbolic form can also be seen in this light.

Third, both of these major bodies of work illustrate another aspect of Lévi-Strauss's thought—the conjunction between objective characteristics that apply to all humans as members of the same species, and the cultural variation whereby humanity divides itself up. At a certain level, Lévi-Strauss's structuralism depends on common human mental attributes that themselves are based on sheer physicality. Regardless of their cultural specificity, humans everywhere think in terms of binary oppositions because they share aspects of mind. This is because their brains are physiologically identical, which derives from the fact that they are all members of the same species. This is also where nature and culture meet. The incest taboo is a prime example of something located on the cusp of the transition between the two. The taboo is universal and therefore natural, in the sense that all human populations have a rule prohibiting incest. But it is also cultural, because the kin types to whom it applies vary from society to society. Humans also surpass it through exchange, specifically marriage—a social device that actually makes them social, since it allows them to leave incest as a mythically natural state behind them.

Lévi-Strauss's extensive studies of myth (especially 1964 and 1967) also illustrate his method. One of his differences from Durkheim is his focus on myth rather than ritual as the privileged location for both the anthropologist understanding culture and the native absorbing it (see Johnson 2003). For Lévi-Strauss, ritual is a performance based on a metonymic relation between a real sacrificial object and a nonexistent god and therefore on a false denial of the discontinuity between the objectively existing world and the imagined other world; it is also more notable for generating affective than cognitive meaning. Myth, on the other hand, being language focused on metaphor, and thus being like life despite its inversions of it, can be treated as an autonomous domain that provides the key to human thought through its resolutions of the false oppositions it sets up, which lead back to reality.

Lévi-Strauss makes a similar contrast between totemism and sacrifice, the former being an example of the nonutilitarian, context-free use of metaphor—the relation between objective systems of classifying the natural and social worlds—the latter being the false metonym of ritual just described. Myth is also persistent in its use of the repetition of mythemes, or basic events that have been symbolically transformed but adhere to the same structure. These repetitions have been compared to redundancy in information theory, that is, repetitions or other checks on the veracity of the received message, with which Lévi-Strauss is familiar (Johnson 2003). At the same time myth is like bricolage, or the improvised work of the handyman, since it systematizes its own random choices of material from the cultural and ecological inventories available to it by using an underlying structure. The focus on modes of thought at the expense of ritual action in Lévi-Strauss's anthropology, which involve denying the significance of effervescence in Durkheimian sociology, is the basis of one of his differences with Gurvitch, which led the latter to attempt to exclude him from the celebrations surrounding the 1958 centenary of Durkheim's birth.

It can hardly be doubted that myths have structures whereby they can be compared regardless of content. Contrasted with this constancy are the different characters and events that may be inserted into any of these patterns, depending on the myth and even the culture. The notion of binary opposition is again important here, not least because it actually shapes the mythical narrative by presenting one pole of an opposition at one stage of the narrative and the other pole at a later stage; such shifts between the poles of the various oppositions that appear in the myth are what move the narrative forward. Lévi-Strauss claims that those listening to the myth are subconsciously tracking the appearance and disappearance of these poles, linking them up as oppositions, noticing any mediations, and thus working out the symbolic meaning of the myth from the largely unfactual literal narrative.

This is the famous notion of a code that has to be unraveled, which stimulated Sperber's denial, in *Rethinking Symbolism* (1975), that people must decode symbols in order to arrive at concealed but vital social knowledge. For Sperber symbols instead *evoke* knowledge that the social actor already has.

But it is mainly by resolving contradictions symbolically rather than directly that myths complement ordinary cognition by allowing the unthinkable—for example, incest—to be thought. This fundamental opposition—between society as it might be and society as it is and must be —can be considered a Lévi-Straussian version of the Durkheimian insistence on society's shaping of individuals' thoughts and lives.

In general, Lévi-Strauss treats myth as exemplifying universal characteristics of human thought, indeed mentality. This is also illustrated by his short work on totemism (1963). In it Lévi-Strauss went to great pains to deny that totemism *does* anything, such as identify useful or dangerous species, as Bronislaw Malinowski contended. Rather, for Lévi-Strauss totems form a classificatory series parallel to the classification of the social groups they represent. Neither series is prior to the other. This is a denial, inter alia, of both Durkheim and Mauss's argument in *Primitive Classification* (1903/1963) that social groups are the model for classifications of the natural world, and of the functionalist position that totems are epiphenomenal to the social groups they represent. Rather, Lévi-Strauss treats the classification of totems as analogous to the classification of social groups and vice versa: Fox is to Bear as Clan A is to Clan B, and so on. Relations, not substantial identities, are therefore involved, despite much-discussed informants' statements such as "I am a cockatoo" (cf. Crocker 1985). In short, totemism is a mechanism of thought: in Lévi-Strauss's famous phrase, animals are "good to think," not "good to eat."

Totemism also plays a key role in what is perhaps Lévi-Strauss's most famous but also most difficult work, *The Savage Mind* (1966). In it we find even more strongly a focus on human thought and mentality that is entirely typical of its author. The work also contains a reply to the attacks of Jean-Paul Sartre (1905–1980) on the determinism of structuralism in the name of free will and personal moral responsibility. In replying to Sartre, Lévi-Strauss opposed the existential, phenomenological basis of Sartre's thought to the extent of treating philosophy as redundant to the new humanist anthropology Lévi-Strauss was seeking to create: in particular, Lévi-Strauss rejected the whole subject-oriented basis of French philosophy that dates from the Cartesian cogito. He also objected strongly to Sartre's neo-evolutionist political program of bringing Third World peoples into the Western orbit by extending Western values to them in an application of a version of uplift theory. For Lévi-Strauss this was simply ethnocentric, since it both devalued other cultures and denied them the right to be different. These sentiments had also informed his earlier antiracist statements, of 1950, which in 1951 UNESCO adopted into its own programs.

Some critics have charged that there is a certain circularity of argument in Lévi-Strauss's basic proposition of a duality between deep structures and their surface manifestations because concrete evidence is available only for the latter. Surface manifestations therefore have to not only account for their own existence, but also prove the existence of the very deep structures that are supposed to explain them. For Lévi-Strauss this is no objection to his argument. He is possibly the most deductive of all thinkers whose work has relevance to anthropology; his position is firmly rooted in the view that all humans share a fundamentally rationalist logic before they sort themselves into different cultures. It therefore does not matter to him whether the problem is approached from the end of generality or from the end of cultural, or superficial, difference. As Lévi-Strauss himself once remarked, whether he thought the myths or they thought themselves through him was immaterial, since at a deep level his mind was also the Tsimshian's mind, and the Nambikwara's mind, and the mind of every other human, regardless of culture.

For Christopher Johnson (2003), Lévi-Strauss's anti-Cartesianism extends to his authorial personality, or rather the lack of such a personality. Given Lévi-Strauss's own statements that he has no strong sense of his individual identity; that his books are written through, not by, him; that he cannot easily recall their content after they have been written; and that although he is interested in scientific developments, he has a "neolithic mind," like "old" or "cold" societies, it is easy to see an association between his view of himself as an author and his antiphenomenological, sociopsychological determinism. According to Johnson, it is unclear whether this is really the way Lévi-Strauss sees himself or whether this is a case of mere heuristic posturing (see also Badcock 1975; M. Lane 1970; Robey 1973; Jenkins 1979; Clarke 1981).

Structuralist Philosophy

Despite Lévi-Strauss's attempts to decenter their discipline, a number of highly eclectic philosophers in this period were influenced by structuralism, either Lévi-Strauss's or Saussure's or both, and in their turn played a part in the theoretical maelstrom of the 1960s and 1970s. Personally though not intellectually close to Lévi-Strauss, and a key supporter of the latter's candidature for a chair at the Collège de France, was Maurice Merleau-Ponty (1908–

1961), who taught at the University of Lyon, the École Normale Supérieure, and the Collège de France. Originally a Husserlian phenomenologist, Merleau-Ponty became an associate of Sartre's in the resistance in World War II, though he broke with him politically for a time in 1952 over the Korean War. This led him to move away from Edmund Husserl and nearer to Martin Heidegger, while his discovery of Saussure brought him closer to structuralism. His own phenomenology emphasized not only experience and free will, but also perception and the intersubjectivity of communication between individuals. Another influence on him was Jacques Lacan, though unlike Lacan, Merleau-Ponty stressed the conscious over the unconscious as a source of self-knowledge and understanding. Many have felt that he was prevented from producing a true rapprochement between phenomenology and structuralism by his often catastrophic misreading of his sources, especially Saussure (see especially Merleau-Ponty 1962; also Schmidt 1985).

Another phenomenologist, though also a Christian and anti-Marxist who was politically closer to the structuralists, was Paul Ricoeur (b. 1913), who shared certain ideas with Merleau-Ponty. Because of his politics, he had problems at the left-leaning Nanterre University, especially when, like Lévi-Strauss, he declined to join other intellectuals in the streets of Paris in 1968. Influenced initially by Husserl, as well as by Heidegger's concept of "preunderstanding"—in which prior knowledge informs all current understanding and therefore subjectivizes it— Ricoeur saw truth as being based on experience modified by intersubjective communication between individuals. He also adopted Freud's interest in dreams and symbols, but wedded this to the linguistic structuralism of Saussure to produce a view of language as the basic tool of culture, and indeed as culture. At first this meant symbolic language, but Ricoeur later incorporated ordinary language too into his interpretation. And because language is partly expression, motivation was for Ricoeur more conscious than it was unconscious, as Freud contended. In accordance with this, Ricoeur also stressed the creativity of metaphor in generating endless meanings and transformations of meaning. Some of his work directly reflected his religious and political beliefs. As a Christian, he criticized functionalist sociology and anthropology for reducing belief to ideology, rationalization, or social function. And although opposed to Marx's revolutionary program, he appreciated the latter's anticapitalism and his linking of political institutions with oppression and with the violent fragmentation of society into classes (see Ricoeur 1974, 1977; also Kurzweil 1980, chap. 4).

A third figure of note in this period, one who was even more controversial than Ricoeur, was Roland Barthes (1915–1980). Another eclectic, he now tends to be regarded as a sort of pop structuralist for his short and pungent pieces collected under the title *Mythologies* (Barthes and Lavers 1972), in which, like Jean Baudrillard, he exposed the subtexts of advertising and other media messages. Influenced initially by a combination of Marxism and Camus's minimalist *l'écriture blanche*, which he considered to contain the potential for social revolution, he then discovered de Saussure's linguistic structuralism, which he proceeded to apply to literary criticism. In this approach, the focus was on style as something independent of the author, superficially subjective but also rooted in specific cultures; neither the author's biography nor his period were of significance (compare this to Lévi-Strauss's readings of myth as nonauthored). This led to an interest in semiotics, in which the referent was ignored in favor of a sole focus on the signifier and the signified (the latter being the image of the object referred to, not the object itself). Another aspect of his work is the contrast between "readerly" and "writerly" texts, or between "just-so stories" and critical readings of text, terms taken up by many American postmodernists more recently. After the political disappointments of 1968, however, when Barthes and other leftists retreated from political action into writing, he gradually moved away from structuralism and semiotics, increasingly becoming bogged down in word games in place of criticism. For genuine intertexuality, we have to turn to Julia Kristeva and Jacques Derrida (see Barthes 1974, 1975; also Kurzweil 1980, chap. 7).

Postwar Ethnography: Against Theory

After World War II, anthropological work continued in what was left of the French empire until the liquidation of most of that empire by 1960. Much of this work was nontheoretical, even antitheoretical, in tone, reflecting the continuing legacy of Griaule's influence as a "pure" fieldworker before the arrival of structuralism. In the Vietnamese highlands, Sabatier's work, including the creation of *coutumiers*, was continued by missionaries, many of whom wrote extensive amounts of solid, unpretentious ethnography, like Jacques Dournes on the Sre and Jarai (e.g., 1951, 1972, 1977); Bernard Jouin on the Rhadé (e.g., 1949); and Paul Guilleminet on the Bahnar, Sedang, and Jarai (e.g., 1952). Like Leenhardt, Dournes, who also published under his Sre name of Dam Bo (e.g., 1950) and coined the term *Pémsien* (from "*P*ays *M*ontagnard du *S*ud-*I*ndochinois") for the highland peoples, later crossed the divide between missionaries and academics by becoming a professional anthropologist. This group was soon joined by professional anthropologists who had been trained at the Centre de Formation aux Recherches Ethnologiques (CFRE), which was founded by André Leroi-Gourhan and Roger Bastide in 1947 as a training school for anthropologists. Among early graduates were Pierre-Bernard Lafont, who worked among the Jarai (e.g., 1963), and Georges Condominas, who studied the Mnong Gar (e.g., 1965, 1977).

Condominas was initially sponsored by the École Française d'Extrême-Orient, the CFRE, and the policy-oriented Organisation pour la Recherche Scientifique et Technique de l'Outre-Mer (ORSTOM) to undertake an acculturation study of a Mnong Gar village in 1947 as part of a brief initiative to use anthropology to improve colonial administration. During this time he coined his own term for the Montagnards: *Proto-Indochinois.* Falling under Michel Leiris's influence, Condominas became skeptical of the value of this sort of research and opposed American involvement in Vietnam: the war and American resettlement policy effectively ended the existence of the Mnong Gar as an identifiably separate ethnic group. Maintaining a strong position of cultural relativism, he later became interested in comparative ethnolinguistics and ethnoscience in Southeast Asia. However, there is little theoretical depth to his work, apart from his notion of social space (see 1980), which is little more than a metaphor for social distinctions and organization. Back in Paris in the 1960s, he founded the Centre de Documentation et de Recherche sur L'Asie du Sud-Est et Monde Insulindien (CeDRASEMI), which briefly supported a journal (Salemink 1991, 2003).

André Leroi-Gourhan (1911–1986) was another figure who rose to prominence in Paris in the postwar period. He combined interests in social anthropology, paleoanthropology, and (especially after 1965) archaeology, focusing his research particularly on tools and technology and their implications for human physical evolution, human society in general, and religious belief and practice in particular. For him holism meant a combination of the human animal and human society, mediated through tools, of which he was an inveterate classifier (see 1943–1945, 1983). A student of Mauss and Marcel Granet before the war, he played a part in the transfer of the Trocadero into the Musée de l'Homme and carried out field research on the archaeology of the northern Pacific (1946). He taught at the Institut d'Ethnologie beginning in 1945, before founding the CFRE with Bastide. From 1945 to 1955 Leroi-Gourhan held a chair in ethnology at Lyon, from 1956 to 1968 chairs in ethnology and prehistory at the Sorbonne, and from 1969 until his death the chair of prehistory at the Collège de France (Bernot 1986; Cresswell 1991).

Another figure prominent at this time was Alfred Métraux (1902–1963), a South Americanist born in Switzerland, brought up in Argentina, and trained at the EPHE and the École des Langues Orientales. Like Lévi-Strauss, he passed the war years in the United States, in his case serving at the Bureau of American Ethnology and becoming an American citizen. Interested in archaeology, philology, and history as well as religion, he carried out research on Easter Island, in Africa, and among the Tupi-Guarani in South America, and he went to Haiti with Leiris in 1948. His main contributions were regarding the origins of colonialism in South America, myth, shamanism, and voodoo (e.g., 1940, 1942, 1958, 1959). He taught widely, at Tucuman (at which Argentine university he founded the anthropological institute), Berkeley, Yale, the University of Mexico, and the University of Santiago, as well as in Paris, where he was *director des études* at the EPHE from 1959 to 1963. He was also involved with UNESCO (which is based in Paris) from 1950 to 1962 as a permanent member running social science projects, which he is said to have administered conscientiously despite hating the paperwork involved, and he emphasized the merits of anthropology at every opportunity. He also became known for his highly informal style of lecturing, his view of his own writings as simply chronicles, and his view of himself as primarily a fieldworker, not a theorist. In one interview he suggested that humanity had made a mistake in proceeding beyond the Neolithic revolution, before which people were more content. This romanticized view of "primitive" society is also found in the work of his student Pierre Clastres (Bing 1964; Dreyfus 1991; Lévi-Strauss et al. 1964; Wagley 1964).

Another figure with limited theoretical ambitions but wide-ranging ethnographic experience was Lucien Bernot (1919–1993). He started out as a student of the Chinese language at the École des Langues Orientales, then Leroi-Gourhan found him a job in the Asia section of the Musée de l'Homme. Bernot then participated in an early anthropological study of a northern French rural community under the auspices of Lévi-Strauss (Bernot and Blancard 1953). In 1951–1952 he was with the Marma, a Tibeto-Burmese-speaking group in the Chittagong area of what was then East Pakistan (now Bangladesh), which he extended into a study of Burma in the 1970s (see Bernot and Bernot 1958; Bernot 1967a, 1967b). A pioneer, like Haudricourt, of ethnobotany in France, he also pursued interests in language and technology. He cofounded CeDRASEMI with Condominas and taught at CFRE, EPHE, and the École des Hautes Études en Sciences Sociales (EHESS) before occupying the chair of the *sociographie* of Southeast Asia at the Collège de France from 1979 to 1985. Skeptical of grand theory, he once remarked that while an ethnographic monograph could always be interpreted structurally, structuralism could never reconstruct the ethnography. Nonetheless, he theorized ethnography itself to the extent of claiming that it could only truly be successful insofar as it could be considered holistic in the manner of Mauss (Toffin 1995).

Theoretically Informed Fieldwork: French Marxist Anthropologists

Although many of these figures were openly skeptical of theory, it was Lévi-Strauss's influence that was central in postwar French anthropology well into the 1960s, and not only his influence on other structuralists, such as Dumont. This was the period when the impact of Louis Althusser's neo-Marxism began to be felt in France among younger anthropologists as well as among scholars in other disciplines (see Augé 1982, 65–77; Bloch 1983, 146–72; Kurzweil 1980). Although Althusser was not an anthropologist and vigorously denied being a structuralist, he recognized an affinity between Marxism and structural linguistics, as well as the difficulty of applying orthodox Marxist approaches to the study of precapitalist societies, which approximated Durkheim's tribal societies with their mechanical solidarity. Orthodox Marxism's treatment of anthropology as purveyed in the Soviet Union had not, in this view, gone beyond a doctrinaire acceptance of Morgan's phases of development, which other anthropological schools had long since relegated to the history of the discipline. In addition, despite French Marxist anthropologists' love of Morgan's anthropology and of Marx's own ethnological notebooks, it was clear that neither Marx nor Engels really understood precapitalist societies, though the anthropological materials available to them had been pretty basic. Althusser, like other contemporary Marxists, doubted the inevitability of the stages that orthodox Marxism still claimed. He therefore tried to dig deeper into Marx to find an analytical tool applicable to both class and nonclass societies. What he came up with was the mode of production.

A number of French Marxists were thus influenced by Althusser, among them Emmanuel Terray (e.g., 1972), Claude Meillassoux (e.g., 1981), and Pierre Philippe Rey (e.g., 1971). However, Maurice Godelier (e.g., 1977) stands out from the rest for his explicit attempt to reconcile structuralism and Marxism. Godelier had discovered anthropology in 1964 after brief flirtations with philosophy and economics, and he quickly became Lévi-Strauss's assistant, which exposed him directly to the still strong currents of structuralism. The early date and circumstances of this shift show that he developed his approach independently of Althusser, who was only just beginning to gain attention in the mid-1960s; certainly Godelier had his own direct impact on the issues the new Marxists were raising.

The basis of Godelier's attempt at bringing about a rapprochement between structuralism and Marxism lies in the similarities he detects between them. One obvious common interest between the two is in dialectics as a form of both setting out arguments and conducting analysis. But there is also a parallel interest in transformations, something Lévi-Strauss emphasizes particularly in his comparative studies of myth. These transformations are linked to an underlying structure, whether of forms of thought as in Lévi-Strauss or of modes of production as in Marx. These underlying structures are associated in both cases with the concealment, indeed mystification, of real social circumstances, whether defined as a general psychosocial determinism as in Lévi-Strauss or as relations of power as in Marx. Despite their concealed nature, structures themselves are real. In both cases, therefore, there is a clear sense that social actors are largely ignorant of the circumstances of their existence. This makes the actors' statements as informants only a starting point. From this line of reasoning both Lévi-Strauss and Godelier derive an antiempirical stance that can also be found in Marxism. From their points of view empiricism is impossible rather than wrong, since it falsely treats informants' statements as a more or less direct and final account of social reality. All that empiricists believe they are able to add to these statements is a more elegant and possibly comparative description, not analysis.

Any structuralist position also postulates that structures preexist their expression in social action. Marxists, including Godelier, therefore claim that empiricists do not actually engage in the neutral collection of facts and the inductive interpretation of them as they claim. Rather, they are motivated by a structure of their own making, one that finds expression in laissez-faire, liberal, bourgeois, live-and-let-live assumptions that conceal, whether deliberately or unconsciously, the real nature of power relations. Both Lévi-Strauss and Marxist anthropologists, therefore, prefer to proceed by deductively searching for examples to prove the existence of the structures that have already been identified and whose existence is explicitly seen as prior to their manifestation in the thought and actions of ordinary people. Logic ultimately underpins this approach, since structures inhere in all human minds (Lévi-Strauss) or in all social situations (Marxist anthropology).

Godelier goes even further, however, in moving away from Marxist orthodoxy toward a structuralist position. For one thing, he suggests that disruption to the social system need not come from internal contradictions, as in Marxist orthodoxy, but may be the result of other internal change or external influences. He also opposes the application of the notion of class to the analysis of precapitalist societies. Although such societies might have inequalities of gender, age, and kinship position, he contends that these are hardly classes in the orthodox Marxist sense, especially because a person's status in terms of the last two generally changes with the life cycle. This is not true of gender, of course, and Rey and Meillassoux in particular bring women into the picture as a subordinated quasiclass by considering modes of reproduction (in which women's reproductive powers are controlled by men through the kin group) alongside modes of production (in which, given class, some men control the productive or labor capacities of other men).

Second, Godelier, perhaps more than any of his Marxist contemporaries in France, has always been interested in the study of religion, which he sees as much more than ideological superstructure, as Marxist orthodoxy would have it. In his reanalysis of Colin Turnbull's material on the Mbuti, he suggests that the month-long mortuary rituals that are periodically held are not so much a mystification of the circumstances of social existence as a part of the mode of production itself, because they intensify the cooperation that is needed for the daily hunting that is itself part of these rituals, thus increasing the kill rate. Elsewhere he suggests that the Inca mode of production was actually organized by the religious institutions themselves, even though they divinized the ruling class in order to justify the extraction of economic surpluses from the ruled: in Marxist terms, that is, they were reproducing not only the ideological superstructure, but part of the economic base as well. Like that of Lévi-Strauss, finally, Godelier's analytic work does not require history, despite the importance of history to Marx and to certain other Marxist anthropologists, perhaps more particularly in Britain and the United States than in France.

The collapse of socialism in 1989 has done nothing to encourage Godelier to retreat from structuralism in recent years, and he fully recognizes that Marxism as what he calls a meta-theory is dead, though he continues to see potential in particular Marxist insights relating to power and subjection. By contrast, Terray, Meillassoux, Rey, and so on have always seemed closer to mainstream Marxism. They too, however, feel compelled to adjust Marxist orthodoxy to the demands of finding some sort of adequate Marxist interpretation for precapitalist societies. They all worked in West and Central African societies in which, as Meillassoux showed, a lineage mode of production had been disrupted by external impacts such as trade and the colonial economic system, with its emphasis on cash crops.

Rey, who was especially keen on the idea of lineage systems as class systems, conducted similar studies in the Congo and claimed that the actuality of power held by a man's mother's brother was masked by the attribution to his father of power that his father did not in reality enjoy. Meillassoux tried to use migration to link the domestic and capitalist modes of production, because migration provided a pool of cheap labor for colonial society and, after the colonial era, also for the former metropolitan powers. Terray rejected the notion of a single mode of production, such as the "lineage mode" that he found in Meillassoux and Rey, and suggested instead that one can speak of class only where there is a clear distinction between those who work and those who do not. However, he still saw the economic base as fundamental to the system and as involving both technology and social relations of production; he thus returned in part to pre-Althusserian orthodoxy.

Rey criticized Terray's position because it suggested social coherence and stasis where in reality there was likely to be flux and dialectical movement. Not even precapitalist societies are free from contradictions between the various relations of production and the ideological superstructure, from which Marx believed social change derived. This led Rey to the position that all societies, including precapitalist ones, are sites of class struggle; in the case of precapitalist societies, the struggle involves groups of elders as the ruling class. This not only reversed Althusser, it contradicted Engels too. Thus whereas Althusser's solution to this dilemma was to invoke the mode of production, and Godelier's was to call on structuralism, Rey's solution was to extend the central Marxist notion of class. Terray found reasons in Marx's work itself for rejecting this extension. However, Rey and Terray agreed that class is relative in these circumstances, as juniors gradually became elders through the life cycle. They also both saw kinship as part of the ideological superstructure rather than of the economic base. Godelier responded by arguing that it is both because, like religion, kinship can be a mode of production as well as an ideology. Meillassoux's attitude was still more radical: he denied that kinship has any material significance among hunter-gatherer societies (Bloch 1983; Augé 1982, 65–77).

Despite their differences, Rey, Terray, and Meillassoux have remained close to Marxist orthodoxy by using its own resources to find a way out of its contradictions. To that extent their work is mutually supporting. Godelier, by contrast, invokes an outside but not unrelated approach, that of structuralism, to the same end. In recent years, he has developed interests in gender and kinship (e.g., Godelier, Trautman, and Tjon Sie Fat 1998) and in the politics of Big Man societies in Papua New Guinea, where he has conducted extensive fieldwork (e.g., Godelier 1986; Godelier and Strathern 1991). He has recently revisited Mauss's *The Gift* (1999) and has also written on the body in editorial cooperation with Michel Panoff (e.g., Godelier and Panoff 1998), who has himself looked at labor in Melanesia.

Theoretically Informed Fieldwork: Structuralists, Psychoanalysts, Cognitivists, and Others

The early postwar period and afterward saw a considerable expansion of practical anthropology in the form of long-term fieldwork, including that undertaken by many of the Marxist anthropologists. Despite Godelier's attempted rapprochement, they were one source of criticism of structuralism. Another was the political events of 1968, which, apart from toppling de Gaulle, initiated a process in which the political attitudes and motives of intellectuals with regard to these events—especially those of scholars like Lévi-Strauss, who took no part in them—were increasingly questioned. At least as many of the anthropologists who came along in the 1960s and 1970s, however, were inspired directly by Lévi-Strauss; indeed many were his students. Prominent examples include Jean Pouillon, Pierre Maranda (who worked on, among other things, the history of French kinship terminology; 1974), Marc Augé, Françoise Héritier, and Philippe Descola.

Augé is the author of a short work attempting to reconcile the different schools of anthropology (1982), and more recently he has focused on modernity and postmodernity in the contemporary world (1995, 1999). Héritier succeeded Lévi-Strauss in his chair at the Collège de France, to be followed in her turn by Descola. Under Lévi-Strauss's guidance, Héritier studied the problem of Crow-Omaha, or semicomplex, kinship systems among the Samo of Upper Volta, pioneering the use of computers to handle complex kinship data (1981). She has also taken the study of incest further by focusing on the prohibition and occasional permission of simultaneous marriages to more than one individual who are themselves related to one another (e.g., marriage to both a mother and daughter; 1999).

Born in 1949, Descola has specialized in the Amazon, especially the Achuar, already better known as the Jivaro, though he has generally been more interested in Lévi-Straussian themes such as exchange, myth, cosmology, and the relation between nature and culture, nature being seen by the Achuar as itself having sociality. Descola has therefore been something of a pioneer in environmental anthropology in France (1994, 1996). He has taught in England and Latin America, as well as at the EHESS and Collège de France.

Another follower of Lévi-Strauss was the Belgian Luc de Heusch, who sought to combine structuralism with psychoanalysis (e.g., 1981, 1982, 1985) by interpreting, for example, the avunculate as the cultural expression of an underlying aggression that could be understood only by combining both disciplines (cf. Augé 1982, 38–39).

Coming from a more antistructuralist direction was Dan Sperber (b. 1942), a director of research at CNRS who has also taught at Nanterre and first gained prominence as the author of a forceful and famous critique of Lévi-Strauss's approach to symbolism (1975, discussed above), which drew on his fieldwork among the Dorze in Ethiopia. This developed into further work on cognition highlighting the significance of relevance as an incentive to communicate with others, the role of context in inference, and the place of implication and proposition in communication (see Sperber and Wilson 1986, written with the linguist Deirdre Wilson). Sperber has recently linked up with Maurice Bloch, a British anthropologist who has also developed an interest in cognition, to revisit the problem of the avunculate (Bloch and Sperber 2002).

Other projects of Sperber's include inquiring more generally into the nature of anthropological knowledge (1985) and putting forward an "epidemiological" interpretation of macrolevel culture based on the notion of a "contagion" of ideas that are transmitted and reproduced at the microlevel of interactions between people, a domain Sperber calls ecological (see Bloch and Sperber 2002). This is part of a positivist attempt to "renaturalize" the social by confronting anthropology with psychology and the culturally specific with the universal (1996). Sperber explicitly advocates this approach as an alternative to the traditional Durkheimian method of explaining social facts by means of other social facts (e.g., Bloch and Sperber 2002, 726–27). It therefore recalls superficially such approaches as methodological individualism, transaction theory, and Bourdieu's practice theory (on the latter, see the next lecture). However, the notion of a contagion of ideas and sentiments is also found in Durkheim.

The work of other writers was more specifically psychoanalytical in the tradition of Freud. Bernard Juillerat, a director of research of the Centre National de la Recherche Scientifique (CNRS), worked among the Mouktélé of Cameroon (1971) and the Yafar on the Sepik in Papua New Guinea, and claimed that it was the latter who led him to adopt psychoanalytical perspectives (1991, 1995, 1996, 2001). These insights are apparently limited to incest, under the false assumption of the universality of the nuclear family. Even Juillerat is guarded about applying Freud's ideas to myth, regarding them as too complex for this purpose. He has also revisited Richard Thurnwald's earlier fieldwork among the Banaro (Juillerat 1993).

Juillerat's interest in psychoanalysis followed similar earlier work by Georges Devereux, who was born in Hungary in 1908 but was educated in France. Devereux left France in 1932 to pursue a career in the United States. He undertook initial fieldwork among the Mohave of California and then, from 1933 to 1935, worked among the Sedang of the highlands of Vietnam (Devereux 1937), which led him into a brief involvement with the wartime Office of Strategic Services. He returned to Paris in 1963, becoming director of studies at EPHE. His most intense and longest-term ethnographic interest was in the Mojave, starting with his recognition of their tremendous psychoanalytical awareness and ending with the scattering of his own ashes on Mojave land after his death in 1985. Throughout his career Devereux argued for the complementarity of psychology and anthropology—an idea derived from the physics of Niels Bohr—but also their irreducibility to one another, rather than for either their antagonism or synthesis. Devereux described culture as a "standardized system of defences," an example being the role of the scapegoat as a possible vehicle for psychological projection. He was also interested in the interface between dreams, myths, and culture generally, accepting the universality of the unconscious as well as cultural difference. Finally, he anticipated Foucault in interrogating the practice of defining an individual's mental health by a standard of social normality (Devereux 1961, 1967, 1970; Deluz 1991a; Salemink 1991, 269; Xanthakou 1995).

Roger Bastide (1898–1974) was a schoolteacher before becoming a professor of sociology at the University of São Paulo in 1938. He served there until 1953. Returning to Paris, he became director of studies at EPHE, where his seminars especially attracted Third World students. In 1959 he was appointed to a chair in anthropology and religious sociology at the Sorbonne, and then he shared a chair in general anthropology with Leroi-Gourhan, with whom he founded CFRE in 1947. He became interested early in the psychoanalysis of Freud and Jung (e.g., 1950) and later studied Brazilian possession cults (1958, 1972), which he saw not as survivals or as manifestations of pathology, but as modifications of tradition that, although cathartic in part, were also subject to the strict observance of routine and structured practices. He was also among the first anthropologists to advocate, with regard to development work, that the developers be studied as well as the developed; he thus became a pioneer in the intellectual study of applied anthropology (1973; cf. Deluz 1991b). Other psychoanalytically inspired work was carried out by René Girard (especially 1972), who interpreted ritual as a form of sacrifice repeating a primordial act of violence involving the periodic expulsion of such objects as the scapegoat and the sacrificial animal.

Also active at this time and later were Georges Balandier (b. 1920), who developed new trends in political anthropology (1970a), using fresh perspectives on the impact of colonialism, especially in Africa (e.g., 1966, 1968), and what Augé considers a sort of critical functionalism (1982, 43 and 93–94). He initially studied postwar changes in French West Africa, comparing the experiences of the Fang of Gabon and the Ba-Kongo of Congo-Brazzaville (1970b). His perspective took into account both the sacred as a source of power and the significance of sources of disorder and instability in state and nonstate societies alike. Like Bastide, he was a pioneer in the anthropology of development and is credited with coining the term Third World. He founded the Centre d'Études Africaines at EPHE before being appointed to the first chair in African sociology at the Sorbonne in 1962. In the 1960s in particular his concentration on the untidiness of social life made him one of the most prominent antistructuralist voices in France, and like his ally the sociologist Georges Gurvitch, he rejected the distinctions Lévi-Strauss made between sociology and anthropology and between "hot" and "cold" societies. This was linked to his appreciation of history as something that anthropologists should take into account rather than be agnostic about in the manner of the structuralists (Jamin 1991b; Rivière 1991).

Another skeptic of structuralism was Éric de Dampierre, a French aristocrat who was associated with Nanterre University and died in 1997. A student of the sociologist Raymond Aron at the Institute of Politics, he was in Chicago among sociologists from 1950 to 1952, then studied the effects of colonial rule on the fertility of the Nzakara, a neighboring group to the Azande in what is now the Central African Republic, for ORSTOM. In 1962 he founded the Laboratoire d'Anthropologie et Sociologie Comparatives at Nanterre, and in 1986, the Société d'Ethnologie. Practically every year he visited Bangassou in Nzakara country to study the royal court, and he even managed to have a court bell returned to the Nzakara from the United States (see 1963, 1984). Apart from an inclination toward Marxism, it was his sociological background that made him skeptical of structuralism, and indeed of much else. Along with Leiris and Claude Tardits, he also cultivated interest in African literature (Bekombo 1998; Margory Buckner, personal communication).

In another direction altogether, Jacques Maquet used his own fieldwork in Africa to argue for the cultural unity of the whole continent (e.g., 1972), but he is perhaps better known for advocating replacing the anthropology of art with an anthropology of aesthetics by focusing on the symbolism of art rather than the social context in which it is produced, a curious retreat from conventional anthropology into essentialism, not to say minimalism (1979, 1986).

Another movement of a cross-disciplinary nature came to prominence in the 1950s and 1960s, namely the Annales school of history, which was explicitly influenced by anthropology. Founded originally at the University of Strasbourg in 1929 by Lucien Febvre, Marc Bloch, and Maurice Halbwachs, it survived the deaths of the last two at the hands of the Nazis when Febvre moved to Paris after the war and established himself at the Collège de France and EPHE. His student Fernand Braudel, who had held a chair at the Collège de France since 1949, was to become president of the Sixth Section of EPHE in 1963. Braudel stressed the importance of studying *la longue durée* in history and also introduced notions of holism from anthropology (see 1972). Many other historians of the school focused on regional rather than national histories of France—a nod in the direction of localized fieldwork in the anthropological tradition. Perhaps the best known example of such a history is *The Peasants of Languedoc* (1982), by Emmanuel Le Roy Ladurie, professor of the history of modern civilization at the Collège de France. Almost as famous is his *Montaillou,* a study of religious heresy in Languedoc around 1300 (1978; on the Annales school generally, see Burke 1989).

5

Practice, Hierarchy, and Postmodernism

The Post–World War II Institutional Structure of Anthropology in France

Many of the trends of the 1970s in Paris continued into the 1980s, to be supplemented and partly challenged by the arrival of new ones. By 1980, in addition to the three chairs of anthropology in Paris, there were also chairs at the universities of Aix-en-Provence, Lille, Lyon, Strasbourg, and Toulouse. Nonetheless, of the fifty-four universities and liberal arts colleges at the time, only eleven in the provinces and three in Paris offered courses in anthropology (including physical anthropology and prehistory). By the end of the century, this had improved to half the fifty-five such teaching institutions that now existed, and there were a total of around four hundred research and teaching positions in anthropology across the country. Such courses were not always taught by trained anthropologists, however, nor were they always recognized by the relevant ministry; indeed, the first degrees specifically in anthropology were awarded only in 1968.

Things were better in Paris, where the lead in both teaching and research was taken by the École des Hautes Études en Sciences Sociales (EHESS), the Fifth Section of the École Pratique des Hautes Études (EPHE), and the Collège de France. Many French anthropologists were effectively trained through the research and seminars held at these institutions rather than by means of any formal supervision, and there was a shift in pretraining background away from philosophy, which had been the focus in the past, to more "modern" subjects, especially sociology. Other institutions included Claude Lévi-Strauss's Laboratoire d'Anthropologie Sociale at the Collège de France; the Sixth Section of EHESS (now the Maison des Sciences de l'Homme, on the top floor of the EHESS building on Boulevard Raspail); the Centre d'Études Africaines; the Centre d'Études sur le Japon Contemporaine; the Organisation pour la Recherche Scientifique et Technique de l'Outre-Mer, or ORSTOM (a policy-oriented body that later became the Institut de Recherche sur Dévelopement); and the Centre National de la Recherche Scientifique (CNRS). Study of the anthropology of France continued at the Musée des Arts et Traditions Populaires (MATP), and that of material culture and ethnoscience at the Musée de l'Homme. The University of Paris X at Nanterre, outside the city to the west, also became significant for anthropology under Éric de Dampierre at this time.

CNRS and ORSTOM in particular were essentially for researchers (192 and forty researchers around 1980, respectively): teaching was limited, and in any case not required from researchers, and while posts were not terribly well-paid, in CNRS they were generally permanent. The existence of such institutions meant that research came to be uncoupled from teaching in France in a manner that made French anthropology's institutional structure unique, as well as the envy of anthropologists in other countries, though the French were apt to view anthropology as underresourced in France compared to the United States. CNRS in particular was associated with topically or regionally defined *laboratoires* and *équipes,* which were often interdisciplinary. An example was ERASME (Équipe de Recherche en Anthropologie Sociale: Morphologie, Échanges), formed in 1981 by Louis Dumont, then led by Daniel de Coppet. However, active collaboration beyond the holding of joint seminars and the editing of joint volumes was unusual. Rather, these teams brought together groups of very individual researchers linked by a common theme or area. ERASME was a partial exception here in that there was some joint writing as well as a common theoretical perspective, though some members were clearly more enthusiastic about the latter than others (see Barraud, de Coppet, Iteanu, and Jamous 1994).

Despite the activities of ORSTOM and the interest of Roger Bastide and Georges Balandier, applied anthropology was limited in France, being in general as disliked among professionals as among everyone else in this period. Intellectually, however, there was an increased interest in history, economics, politics, the environment, and the connections between anthropology and colonialism, adding to earlier concerns with human thought, belief, and social structure. This was not a one-way street: practitioners in these other disciplines—the Annales historians, for example—also began to take an interest in anthropology. Nonetheless, the general perception was that disciplinary boundaries were being maintained in this period. Except where mentioned above, there was little contact with museums, a change from the era before structuralism gave anthropology in France a strong identity that was separate from the study of material culture and any relic of evolutionary speculation. Anthropologists also began meeting outside these official forums: the first professional association of anthropologists in France was founded in 1979.

The anthropology of France itself also received a series of institutional boosts after 1980. Up till then, research on France had mostly been based at the MATP. In 1980, however, at the initiative of Isac Chiva, a colleague of Lévi-Strauss's at the Laboratoire d'Anthropologie Sociale, the Mission de Patrimoine Ethnologique was set up under the Ministry of Culture to further the anthropological study of the country. Since 1983 it has published a journal, *Terrain*, and books. Other centers with the same general aim now exist, including the Laboratoire d'Anthropologie des Institutions et des Organisations Sociales (LAIOS), the Centre d'Anthropologie des Mondes Contemporains (CAMC), the Laboratoire d'Anthropologie Urbaine, and, outside Paris, the Centre d'Anthropologie in Toulouse and the Institut d'Ethnologie Méditerranéenne et Comparative in Aix-la-Provence.

As is common in continental Europe, teachers and researchers in France are civil servants directly employed by the relevant ministry (of education or research) or the universities. Whether the universities' lack of institutional independence, which contrasts with most Anglo-Saxon practice, compromises intellectual independence is a matter of debate: probably on the whole it does not, though appointments to key posts very often have a significant political dimension. In general, it is probably fair to say that a degree of political constraint on academic appointments tends to be expected in France to an extent that would not be tolerated in the Anglo-Saxon tradition, in which academic freedom is reinforced by the formal autonomy of higher education. Nonetheless, no one doubts that there is true intellectual freedom in France: intellectuals of both the right and the left generally enjoy much greater respect and publicity than elsewhere, to the extent that not a few attain the status of media stars. Indeed, intellectual issues, including those of interest to anthropology, are routinely discussed in both print and broadcast media in a manner inconceivable elsewhere. This popularity extends to anthropology journals, which are regularly sold to the general public through bookshops. The leading anthropology journal is undoubtedly *L'Homme*, found by Lévi-Strauss in 1960, but also of significance are *Gradhiva*, *Journal des Anthropologues*, *MAUSS*, and a whole raft of regional journals. Of more general coverage are *Le Débat* and *Les Temps Modernes* (Picone 1982; Rogers 2001; *Current Anthropology* 1980; Casajus 1996; R. Parkin, personal data).

The Anthropology of France

The creation of new institutions specifically for study of the anthropology of France after the 1980s supplemented work that had already been going on at the MATP for over forty years, stimulated especially by Georges-Henri Rivière. Yet not even the founding of this museum in 1937 signaled the start of such anthropology. The background initially was, of course, folklore, which van Gennep sought to reform, especially in the interwar period (see my second lecture). Both he and Rivière are associated with an attempt to reconcile folklore and anthropology in the early post–World War II period. But the path of the anthropology of France has never been a straightforward one, as Robert Hertz's 1913 article on a French-speaking community in northern Italy illustrates (Hertz 1913/1983). As late as the 1970s, Marc Abélès reported that fieldwork in Europe was not taken entirely seriously, though it was considered suitable for women (1999, 405).

Attempts have repeatedly been made to bridge the gap between folklore and anthropology, and they have generally succeeded. The earliest such work after the war was the study of a cult in Provence, *La Tarasque,* by Dumont (1951), who had still not yet emerged completely from his chrysalis as a museologist to become a full-fledged anthropologist—indeed, an important focus of this work is the material culture associated with the cult. This was quickly followed by Lucien Bernot's cooperative effort with René Blancard on a village in Picardy that they called Nouville (Bernot and Blancard 1953). Their study examined the sense of community in the village and of difference from the outside world, as well as "objective" factors such as economics and the life cycle of villagers. But it is notable that thereafter both Dumont and Bernot built their careers through fieldwork conducted outside France, in more "exotic" locations in South Asia, though Dumont was later to return to the study of European ideologies, especially regarding values of individualism and equality.

Susan Rogers suggests that folklore continued to be significant in the anthropology of France into the 1970s and 1980s, given that anthropologists stressed the distinctiveness of the particular communities they worked in, which in part involved engaging with their particular histories, including what could be learned from material culture and oral literature (2001). However, grand syntheses based on survey-type studies plotting variations in time and space were replaced methodologically by long-term fieldwork in single communities in the usual anthropological tradition. Moreover, the study of material culture and oral literatures, as well as of historical documents, was supplemented by new concepts drawn from mainstream anthropology, especially in the context of kinship and ritual, which themselves helped draw the anthropology of France into the mainstream for a time. Thus Françoise Zonabend studied the history of a village in Burgundy in, for the most part, the twentieth century (1984), while Martine Segalen sought to establish a view of French rural life generally from documents going back into the nineteenth century (1983), and into the eighteenth century in a separate study of Lower Brittany (1985). Segalen built on these insights in a general work on the history of the family seen anthropologically (1986), in which she argued against the conventional view that families had decreased in both size and significance as a result of industrialization, urbanization, and other modern pressures: instead, they remained both varied and dynamic. She also looked anthropologically at contemporary society more generally (1989). Such work clearly converges with that of the *Annales* school of history.

As far as ritual is concerned, perhaps the leading work is Jeanne Favret-Saada's study of witchcraft in a rural area in northwest France, whose identity she concealed by calling the area the Bocage (1980). However, while on one level this work locates witchcraft beliefs in the overall system of local belief and practice in the classic holistic fashion, and even claims to see such beliefs as more useful than psychiatry for dealing with psychological strains, at another level it provides a picture of a community in more than just routine crisis, with younger priests refusing to "unwitch" the afflicted as their predecessors had done. Perhaps the fact that so many of these studies were on Brittany, with its "ancient" Celtic culture (see also Burguière 1975, a multidisciplinary, longitudinal study of a single village that was also studied by Edgar Morin [1977]), represents an unconscious search for the exotic within France itself.

Favret-Saada's work may therefore be a partial exception to Rogers's claim that French anthropologists of France itself were keen not to replicate the standard sociological view that French communities were disintegrating under the weight of manifold modern pressures, and that anthropologists were seeking instead to stress those communities' viability and integration in their own right. This led many to avoid rural, peasant studies altogether in favor of work in urban areas, on industry (e.g., Zonabend 1993, on a nuclear plant in Normandy and its relationship with the local community), among elites (e.g., Le Wita 1994, on the bourgeoisie) and on local politics (e.g., Abélès 1991, on Burgundy). But where there was rapid social change and movement, there were also limitations on the standard monographic format, which is why some studies were cooperative and often multidisciplinary projects involving a single village (see Zonabend 1991). However, these limitations have increasingly been shown to obtain in general anthropology too. There now can hardly be said to be a separation between anthropology abroad and anthropology at home for French anthropologists any more than for their counterparts elsewhere in Europe; and in some cases that separation is a good deal less among the French. Zonabend has drawn attention to the variation these studies have exposed in France, even between adjacent areas, making a global view of "French culture" deeply problematic (1991). This is both the strength and the inevitable outcome of the application of anthropological methods to the domestic scene.

Many non-French anthropologists have undertaken fieldwork in France too (see Delamont 1995). However, since van Gennep, who worked all over Europe, French anthropologists have been slow to work elsewhere on the continent, though this is changing (e.g., Vernier 1991, on kinship on Karpathos, a Greek island). More recently, Abélès (1992, 1996, 2000) and Irène Bellier (1995; Bellier and Wilson 2000) have undertaken work on the institutions of the European Union.

Lacan: Relativizing Psychoanalysis

Many fieldworking anthropologists (Roger Bastide, Georges Devereux, Bernard Juillerat, René Girard) were influenced by psychoanalysis, either in combination with or in opposition to structuralism. Apart from Bastide's and Juillerat's interest in Jung, most of the influence here emanated from Freud. Things began to change, however, with the work of Jacques Lacan (1901–1981), a practicing psychoanalyst who had a considerable impact on anthropology in France and elsewhere, exerted especially through his public lectures, which attracted audiences in the hundreds. Although Lacan's starting point was the work of Freud, he was vigorously opposed to the medicalization of psychoanalysis in the United States and projected a view of the discipline that was closer to philosophy and that stressed the enjoyment (*jouissance*) of therapy by the analysand rather than the aspect of cure. He rejected Freud's perspective that the disjunction between the individual's instinctive drives suppressed in childhood and the socially approved behavior learned as a replacement for them was subject to a cure: for Lacan, both were essential parts of the psyche, which was therefore always fragmented. Also, in place of Freud's link between psychological stress and frustrated needs, he posited desire that could never be requited.

Nonetheless, Lacan developed Freud's theory by stressing the alienating impact of the child's discovery that it is an individual separate from others and from the world in general. Conceiving itself as being linked with its mother in the initial, "imaginary" stage, the child then goes through the "mirror" stage, when the sight of its own reflection makes it aware of its self but not the world. This is followed by the "symbolic" stage, that is, the separation of the child from its mother by its father, the crisis whereby the child learns to associate the father's authority, expressed through language, with its own need to dissemble in order to cope with that authority.

Lacan was also influenced by Saussurean structural linguistics to suggest that the unconscious is not associated with randomness and chaos but is structured, and in addition that it is influenced as much by culture as by personal desires. This led him to take a relativistic interest in culture and its impact on the unconscious. He believed that the unconscious is only really knowable through language, which also leads us to relativism. One result is that how patients speak is as important for diagnosis as what they say. The mutual influence between structuralism and this form of psychoanalysis led to some cooperation between Lacan's and Lévi-Strauss's followers over the analysis of myth. Another influence from Saussure was Lacan's replacement of Freud's attribution of certain psychological conditions to the patient's confusion of word and thing with the doctrine of the confusion of the signifier and signified, which forms the essence of semiological theory. For Lacan, the unconscious is the realm of the signifier only: it is the conscious that links the signifier to its signified, much as Freud located the realm of representation in the conscious. But for Lacan, insofar as signifiers were linguistic, they are also unambiguously cultural (see Lacan 1968, 1977; also Kurzweil 1980, chap. 6; Ferrell 1996). Lacan's theories have been applied, inter alia, to the eruption of violence in Yugoslavia in the 1990s (Bowman 1994).

The influence of Lacanian psychoanalysis was particularly strong in the work of Félix Guattari, who teamed up with the Foucauldian philosopher Gilles Deleuze to extend Lacan's attempts to fuse psychoanalysis with culture, which ended in their rejecting Freud's Oedipal interpretation of the psyche completely. Instead, in a postmodern shift, they celebrated the fragmentation of the psyche—which Freud and even Lacan to some extent had seen as pathological—as liberating. Furthermore, although Freud and Lacan both focused on the nuclear family as the site of this fragmentation and conflict, Deleuze and Guattari pointed out that this social form was not universal, a consideration that reinforced the relativistic, cultural approach to psychoanalysis introduced by Lacan. They thus also sharpened Lacan's sense that culture intervenes in the unconscious, which is therefore not totally isolated in the psychic depths. As a consequence, behavior is rooted not solely in suppressed memories of childhood, as in Freudian orthodoxy, but in the world around us as well. Indeed, there is no disjunction between childhood and adult behavior for Deleuze and Gattari. They also criticized other currents, especially structuralism and Marxism. First, they opposed the universality of symbols asserted by Lévi-Strauss, suggesting that it was the efficacy of symbols that was significant, not their function or meaning. Secondly, they claimed that Marxism treated the working class as an undifferentiated and malleable mass, when in reality it was fragmented in many respects and capable of subversion.

As Marx said, one source of subversion is certainly contradictions within capitalism; but for Deleuze and Guattari this now meant not production, as for Marx, but capitalism's tendency to multiply desires for consumer goods in order to maintain itself in being (see also Jean Baudrillard, below). This actually opens up new spaces, which can then be used subversively (see Deleuze and Gattari 1984, 1988; also Augé 1982). This recalls the work of Julia Kristeva on the use of language to marginalize women, who may then react subversively from this position through their own writings. Insisting that gender is a social not a natural matter, Kristeva attacked the boundary dividing men from women and subordinating the latter to the former as a hegemonic structure that ought to be dissolved. This recalls Lacan's observation that the phallus does not separate men and women but joins them. In her psychoanalysis, she stressed not only the pre-Oedipal semiotic but also the mother in the Oedipal family, a continuation of the perspective of Melanie Klein rather than that of Freud himself (Kristeva 1980, 1988). In a different area entirely, she sought to identify the links between French identity and universal values (1993), as Dumont was doing from within structuralism.

Among other shifts introduced by Deleuze and Guattari was a reversal of the standard Morganesque evolutionary paradigm, a reversal that posited premodern humans as superior in "civilization." This attitude is also found in the work of a number of anarchist-inspired, antistate fieldworkers, especially Pierre Clastres and Jacques Lizot, who both worked on Amerindian groups. Clastres, who was born in 1934 and died in a car accident in France in 1977, was a director of studies and professor of the religion and societies of South American Indians at EPHE. A student of Alfred Métraux and Lévi-Strauss, he went out to Paraguay in the 1960s to study Tupi-Guarani groups, who were, as he saw it, at the point of social disintegration (1972/1998). This reflected the influence of Métraux, for whom social disintegration opened up the best view of a society. Clastres's anarchism led him to dismiss as ethno-

centric the idea that the state was an evolutionary necessity; instead, he developed a view of Amerindian societies as conflict-free, a perspective that has
frequently been found hopelessly romantic and unrealistic (e.g., Colchester
1982). Even for Clastres, however, leadership involved an exchange of benefits between the leader and the led—a point brought out by Lévi-Strauss in
Tristes tropiques (1973). Politics was therefore not superstructure, as for Marx,
but sui generis, thus giving Amerindian societies the option of rejecting
power and statehood: in the Tupi-Guarani case, wrote Clastres, this avoidance
was achieved through migrations that eased the population pressures that
would have made a state inevitable (1987).

Lizot's major work has been on the Yanomami, perhaps the most studied
people in South America. While the American anthropologist Napoleon
Chagnon has always been heavily concerned with delineating the structural
principles of Yanomami culture and social organization, Lizot is more purely
descriptive, for the most part eschewing theoretical extrapolations as much as
Bernot and Georges Condominas did. Nonetheless he stresses the weakness of
the political system, which both is caused by and causes the violence that the
Yanomami have become so famous for, and which he attributes largely to illicit
sexual relations. This implicitly contradicts Clastres's view of Amerindian society as conflict-free. Lizot also eschews Chagnon's materialist explanations of
warfare in favor of a structuralist view of it as a form of exchange tending toward equilibrium (1994). As with Clastres's *Chronicle of the Guayaki Indians*
(1972/1998), however, the descriptive, partly narrative style of Lizot's *Tales of
the Yanomami* (1985) verges on the literary, being mainly concerned to let the
ethnography speak for itself; neither book contains any references. Although
both Clastres and Lizot saw nonindustrial societies as affluent in relation to
basic needs, they have been criticized for disregarding the effect of European
contact: for example, Marcus Colchester argues that the supposed affluence
of such societies has a lot to do with the metal tools they have obtained from
Europeans (1982), while Bartholomew Dean has drawn attention to their des-
perate and extreme dependence on exploitative white farmers and "advocacy" anthropologists—that is, those supporting indigenous peoples practically in the latter's engagement with the modern world (1999).

Foucault and Bourdieu: Neo-Durkheimians?

Judging from the persistence with which anthropologists continue to cite them
today, of all the intellectuals that France produced in the postwar period, two

writers in particular seem to have had a longer-term impact on anthropology: Michel Foucault (1926–1984) and Pierre Bourdieu (1930–2002). Both can be fitted into the Durkheimian tradition, even though neither they nor their respective publics have ever been inclined to make this claim themselves. Certainly they both had their differences with this tradition as well as with one another, and Bourdieu in particular is best known for his theory of practice, with its nod in the direction of Max Weber.

There have been attempts recently to read Émile Durkheim and Foucault through one another, especially in a volume edited by Mark Cladis (1999) focusing on the themes of education and punishment. Cladis's British colleague Mike Gane had already written of Foucault's *Discipline and Punish* (1977) as a "delayed continuation of Durkheiman traditions" (1992, 4), and it is obvious that in a general way there are close parallels between Foucault's and Durkheim's intermediate theoretical positions, if not their methods, final statements, or fundamental approaches. Nonetheless Foucault was always an original thinker who preferred to cite other influences, especially Nietzsche, on power, and other German thinkers, as well Gaston Bachelard's resumptions of the Kuhnian "ruptures" between structures of knowledge that characterize the history of science (see Foucault 1978, 1979, 1984, 1985, 1997).

Throughout his career Foucault was concerned with deviance, with how it was defined socially, who in society defined it, and who cured it; often the same people and institutions were involved in all of these processes. In fact, any institution—hospital, clinic, asylum, prison, school, church, army unit, workplace, even Social Security office—could be seen as the site of discipline, control, and ultimately punishment by those who were often self-appointed social authorities over others, whom they subjectivized. Indeed, any kind of cure or remedy involved control and power by self-appointed experts, or at least specialists, over human subjects and ultimately their bodies. For Foucault, even the celebration of sexual difference and of what used to be considered deviance, like homosexuality, by self-appointed sexologists was in reality just another form of social control, in that it produced a standard against which "normal" behavior could be judged.

Like Durkheim, therefore, and also Marx, Foucault was concerned with the social foundations of control of the individual, and he linked deviance with what Durkheim called negative solidarity. As in Durkheim too, his individual humans lacked agency apart from the deviance that placed them outside society, and he was interested not just in the objective reality of social relations, but also in the collective representations that ideologically concealed that reality. Unlike Durkheim, however, who was generally positive about social order, Foucault deplored the control it entailed, seeing only the power it gave the few over the many, not the social solidarity it allegedly created for the benefit of all. At the same time, he regarded deviance not as pathological but as normal. This was partly because deviance was ideologically defined and could therefore never be fixed objectively: what was normal one day might be redefined as deviant tomorrow, and vice versa (as with the results of the sexual revolution). This meant that those whom society defined as deviants were in reality persecuted individuals suffering arbitrary exclusion. But there also seems to be a reference here to any society's invariable need to use deviance as a way of defining acceptable norms and providing itself with both a boundary and an identity. Given his negative attitude toward social control, Foucault's vision could ultimately only be one of despair. Although obscurely predicting the end of science, which had become, with law, the chief instrument producing discipline in modern society, he also appears to have believed that as long as humans were social, they would always be subjected to arbitrary regimes of disciplinary control of one sort or the other.

Society therefore defined both deviance and normality. But regimes of discipline were not just enforced from the outside—they were also frequently internalized by those made subject to them, who therefore came to discipline themselves. This situation was enforced in the modern world by the greater continuity and comprehensiveness of surveillance, now exemplified by the recent explosion in city-center security cameras as a modern form of panopticon. These disciplinary operations were conducted through what Foucault called structures, or codes of knowledge, whether religious, legal, or scientific, which were created by self-appointed experts in such a way as to appear both natural and neutral. In fact they were all, without exception, instruments of the power of control, arbitrary ideological devices that created the very deviancies they identified as requiring remedial action. This was as true of law and medicine in modern times as of religion formerly. Indeed ultimately, despite their rationalist pretensions, both law and science were as ideological as religion (cf. Comte). This applied equally to social science, and Foucault accordingly dismissed all other schools of thought in contemporary French intellectual life—Marxism, Lacanism, existentialism, and structuralism—as ideology.

Despite Foucault's vehement denial that he was a structuralist, however, there are obvious parallels in his work with that school, especially the notion of structures of knowledge whose ideological bases are hidden from subjects, but also the series of binary oppositions with which he worked, such as sickness and health, sanity and insanity, and anarchy and discipline, as well as doctor and patient, teacher and pupil, overseer and worker, judge and prisoner, and so on. Foucault not only approached language as yet another structure, he used the language of structuralism, such as *signified* and *signifier*. On the other hand, unlike Lévi-Straussian structuralism, Foucault's methodology was largely historical, both in the intensive use he made of actual documents and in the changes he tracked between different historical structures of knowledge that were separated by Kuhnian and Bachelardian "scientific ruptures." But above all, his condemnations of power and the structures it used were radical, perhaps more so even than Marx's or Rousseau's, and anthropologists have been deeply influenced by his stress on the ideological nature of even their own structures of disciplinary knowledge. Among other things, Foucault was among those responsible for the postmodern tendency to view the anthropological project as hopelessly flawed and therefore impossible because of the inevitably unequal relations of power between informants and the anthropologists who insist on speaking for them (Cladis 1999; Kurzweil 1980).

Some of the issues raised by Foucault also occur in the work of Bourdieu, especially his studies on education in France, which he saw as a means of reproducing social inequalities in each generation, right up to university level. Although education is represented as a neutral activity providing equal opportunities for all, Bourdieu saw it as a bourgeois instrument of power and of social and political inclusion and exclusion based on the continued accumulation of the right sort of cultural capital, from which the lower classes frequently excluded themselves voluntarily. The "symbolic violence" this involved as an alternative to direct coercion resembles the obfuscating use of symbols in Durkheim's theory of religion, its ideological naturalization of power reminds one of Marx, and its internalization of ideology by those disadvantaged by it recalls Foucault. Conversely, some of Bourdieu's later, not dissimilar work on notions of taste as both constituting cultural capital and providing a basis for deciding who has it draws Bourdieu closer to Weber's interest in the differences between class and status (see Bourdieu 1984, 1988, 1990a).

Bourdieu himself, born in 1930 into a petit bourgeois family in a peasant society in southern France, can be said to have bucked the trend in respect of the hegemonic aspects of education that he himself was to describe. Indeed, his view has been challenged recently by Deborah Reed-Danahay (1996), who showed how people in one community in rural France acted to subvert the metanarrative of the educationalists in their midst.

Despite his rather humble origins in terms of possession of the requisite cultural capital, Bourdieu rose to become the leading sociological guru in France in recent decades and remained so right up to his death in 2002. He has always been difficult to classify, suspended as he was between Marx, Weber, and Durkheim in a world largely but not wholly of his own making. His four years in Algeria, partly in the army, gave him a taste of anthropological fieldwork (1962, 1979), which informed his later writings. Although his actual ethnography on Algeria was unexceptional, he was to do further fieldwork in his home area in the Béarn, all of which he later incorporated into his theoretical writings along with the findings of various sociological surveys, often undertaken in cooperation with his colleagues or his students (e.g., Bourdieu and Passeron 1979 and Bourdieu et al. 1999, which documents the conditions of subaltern groups in contemporary France).

Bourdieu's critics have tended to find his forays into data collecting superficial and unsystematic. Nonetheless, fieldwork was important to his work. Algeria showed him that the *pieds noirs*, or French Algerians, were as much trapped within the conflict as the Arab population, which led him to oppose both Franz Fanon and the French left on the issue. This and his early political opposition to Stalinism should signify a need for caution regarding others' later attempts to claim him for Marxism, but Algeria was perhaps also an early demonstration to him of the social constraints on individual agency. He rejected Sartre's existentialism while accepting the need for a reflexive sociology that is aware of ethical issues (on the latter point, see Bourdieu 1990a; also Wacquant 1989; Robbins 2003). He flirted early on with structuralism, during a period exemplified by his famous analysis of the Kabyle house (1979), before moving away from a close association with that school.

Bourdieu's best-known work, and certainly the most influential in the long term because it is generally applicable, is that on practice (1977, 1990b). It can be seen on one level as his attempt to reconcile structure and agency, like Weber and Talcott Parsons before him and Anthony Giddens since. Yet in many ways Bourdieu was at his most Durkheimian here, since he contended that social realities were not only objective and independent of human agents, they also escaped humans' consciousness at the same time that they limited their agency. Bourdieu's chief innovation was in respect of how they did this. Eschewing the notion of rules as not corresponding to the way social epistemologies were ordinarily expressed, he introduced a number of other terms, partly inventing a language to do so, much of which remains obscure.

One of these terms is *doxa*, which refers to the more or less taken-for-granted aspects of social life, which are believed and enacted unreflectively, even habitually, though they have their origins in social example, if not always socialization as such (a term Bourdieu disliked). Another is *practice* itself. Practice is based on *doxa*, of which it could be said to be the enactment, though it also involves a degree of improvisation, as what Bourdieu calls competencies—in proper social behavior, that is—are presented to others and tested. If all this seems like tightrope walking, the habits associated with *doxa* actually aid the production of competent social performances that an excess of conscious reflection might have inhibited. Finally, there is the difficult notion of habitus. Bourdieu seems to mean by this a combination of cultural precedents and what he calls unconscious dispositions that social actors call on for social practice, and that therefore link *doxa* to practice. While there is no free agent, therefore, sociality consists not in the laying down of rules by a possibly obscure social authority, as in Durkheimian functionalism, but in the strategic improvisations of individuals using, generally unconsciously, what they have already rather diffusely learned about acceptable social behavior to guide them through existing social situations.

This is perhaps more realistic if one accepts that even in the most highly institutionalized of societies, and despite those societies' long-term educational trajectories, relatively little of the enormous inventory of acceptable social behavior that people acquire is actually formally inculcated into them by schools and similar institutions, or even in the home. Rather, we learn by doing, and by offending others with our doing—by practice, in other words, rather than by being presented with rules. This is still quite a long way from Weber's methodological individualism, in which social agents themselves create society through interpersonal negotiations, whether tacit or explicit, over the right forms of social behavior. Certainly Bourdieu was always vehemently opposed to rational choice theory, which dominates so much sociology today, yet that he believed neglected the social dimension of action, especially the fact that both interests and the appropriate strategies whereby to pursue them were equally socially determined. Practice enables rather than constrained, and this gives people a degree of agency; but they can only exercise agency within narrow limits, which are socially determined.

Louis Dumont: Linking Ideology and Practice through Hierarchy

Bourdieu is not the only thinker to have produced a reasonable reconciliation of ideology and practice from a perspective that is generally Durkheimian: the same applies to a self-acknowledged Maussian, if not Durkheimian figure, Louis Dumont. Compared with his other main mentor, the structuralist Lévi-Strauss, Dumont was a late starter. Born in Salonika, Greece, in 1911, he evidently ended his youth as something of a dropout. After drifting through a series of casual jobs, in 1936 he eventually found work at the MATP as a back-room boy. A growing interest in the exhibits drew him back to academic study, an important part of which consisted of Marcel Mauss's lectures. Dumont spent his war years not in exile, like Lévi-Strauss, but as a German prisoner of war, though his imprisonment was interspersed with periods of leave to study Sanskrit in Hamburg with a German professor, Walther Schubring, a specialist on the Jains.

It was India as much as Lévi-Strauss that converted Dumont to struc-turalism, since he thought that this approach explained his Indian material best (see 1986). But he also had direct exposure to British empiricism through his four years as a lecturer in Oxford (1951–1955), where he replaced the Radcliffe-Brownian functionalist M. Srinivas —he referred to his Oxford ex-perience as "a second training." Dumont then returned to France, then pro-ceeded to India to undertake fieldwork in the north, with which he was ap-parently less satisfied and about which he published little. In 1957, now back in Paris with a chair in the sociology of India and later in comparative sociol-ogy at the EPHE, where he remained until he retired, he launched the im-portant journal *Contributions to Indian Sociology* with David Pocock, the aim being to draw the anthropology of India away from its various folkloric, evo-lutionist, and functionalist origins and onto the path of structuralism, a ven-ture obviously modeled on the *Année sociologique*. A related concern was to promote the study of caste—earlier anthropologies of India had stressed instead the tribes, a minority of the population, which had become the focus of evolutionist speculations.

All this was but a preparation for Dumont's most famous and influential work, *Homo Hierarchicus* (1966/1980), a general anthropological account of the Indian caste system that discusses its hierarchical nature and the Durk-heimian subsuming of the individual by the social. This led to a long-term comparison of India and the West, the latter being represented by the con-trasting values of egalitarianism and individualism (1992), which culminated in his last major work, on German ideology (1994). In 1967 Dumont set up the Centre d'Études de l'Inde et de l'Asie du Sud, and in 1976 he established ERASME, a CNRS research team studying mainly exchange and mortuary ritual from a cross-cultural perspective. He died in 1998 (Allen 1998; Galey 1982; Toffin 1999).

Dumont's career thus reversed the earlier Durkheimian project of Céles-tin Bouglé (see my third lecture), who began studying Western notions of equality before turning to India. Bouglé never visited India. He certainly un-derstood it less well than Dumont, and he blamed all its alleged problems on the Brahmans. Few anthropologists have capitalized more fully than Dumont on the principle that studying another society teaches us a lot about our own. As for structuralism, Dumont's was always more culturally specific and less universalistic than Lévi-Strauss's. His work on kinship was also more in line with that of other fieldworkers in that he identified, in the Dravidian case, a constant structure to the terminology from variations in actual marriage rules and practices. This was still structuralist, not least because of the importance Dumont placed on affinal links between groups, but it was ethnographically more rooted than Lévi-Strauss's model in many respects (1983).

Dumont's development of Lévi-Strauss's structuralist motif of binary opposition into what the former called hierarchical opposition offers a means of uniting ideology and practice from within structuralism (see Parkin 2003). Dumont initially applied this revised form of binary opposition to the relationship between Brahman and Kshatriya in Indian society. A more familiar example may make clearer just what was involved (see Dumont 1992, 119). In pre–politically correct times, the English word *man* had a double meaning. On one "level," to use Dumont's term, *man* was simply opposed to *woman* as its opposite. On the other level it stood for the whole of humanity and included *woman* (as in *mankind* and so on). On this latter level, in other words, *man* encompassed its opposite, *woman*.

Clearly this went along with a whole set of circumstances in which things male were seen as ideologically more important, of higher value, and so on, than things female. On the level involving encompassment, moreover, women were simply invisible, thanks precisely to their encompassment. It was only on the level of distinction that the category of woman appeared at all. The two levels were thus different in kind. They were also ideologically unified into a single structure: they did not simply represent different contexts in which first one pole of a binary opposition then the other was prominent. The contexts produced by reversing one of Lévi-Strauss's binary oppositions were equivalent, in that moving between them simply involved reversing the polarity of the opposition. When moving between Dumont's levels, on the other hand, one was moving between a superordinate situation of the encompassment of one pole by the other, which caused the latter to disappear, and a subordinate situation in which both were present because both were distinguished. To return to India, the Brahman thus either stood for (encompassed) the whole of society in its relations with the cosmos in rituals in which only he was evident, or he appeared alongside the Kshatriya as subject to the latter's authority, but only in a subordinate (secular, nontranscendent) situation in which the Kshatriya is dominant.

The application of hierarchical opposition to the egalitarian West is one way of relating ideology to practice. Dumont gave practical activities their due place while characteristically subordinating them to the level of ideals—we have already seen this in the discussion of the Brahman-Kshatriya relationship in India. But the level of ideals and values always encompasses that of practice: although the former may be reliant on the latter for its fulfillment, the latter is ideologically subordinate, sometimes even ideologically unrecognized. It is only when the pragmatics of providing for religious activities, or the morally compromised nature of the world of practice, becomes a focus for discussion that practice is at all evident, and then only at the subordinate level of distinction, not the superordinate level of encompassment. I therefore suggest that Dumont's name should be added to the list of those who have attempted to combine practice and agency with ideology, including, in the most recent period, Giddens and Bourdieu; in the middle distance Parsons; and originally Weber.

Dumont has left his own legacy in the form of younger scholars in France, such as Cécile Barraud on Indonesia (e.g., 1981), Dominique Casajus on Niger (e.g., 1985), Daniel de Coppet (1933–2002) on the Solomon Islands (e.g., 1985), André Iteanu on Papua New Guinea (e.g., 1983), Raymond Jamous on North Africa and Muslims (the Meo) in India (e.g., 1981, 1991), and Serge Tcherkézoff on East Africa and Samoa (e.g., 1987). All of them were at one time members of ERASME, and in their various ways they have taken Dumont's teachings on hierarchy and opposition further in their own ethnographic writings. (The work of this group, and of Dumont himself, is described in detail in Parkin 2003; see also Barnes, de Coppet, and Parkin 1985; Barraud de Coppet, Iteanu, and Jamous 1994; and de Coppet and Iteanu 1995.)

One key proposal, of which a joint text is an attempted demonstration (Barraud, de Coppet, Iteanu, and Jamous 1994), relates to how we should compare societies while remaining in the Maussian tradition of holism. Mauss's own comparisons tended to have an evolutionary dimension: as I discussed in my third lecture, a common strategy he used was to compare the holistic aspect of a particular social phenomenon (such as exchange or the person) with different stages representing the gradual unraveling of that aspect in world history. For Barraud, de Coppet, Iteanu, and Jamous, it is the nature of holism itself that should be the basis for comparison. Accordingly, in this joint text Dumont's model of hierarchical opposition provides a way of comparing the ultimate or transcendent values of different societies, which are identified by the application of the model in each case.

Dumont has also inspired a large part of the distinctly French school of

South Asian anthropology, though Madeleine Biardeau's anthropological account of Hinduism as a civilization shows that his influence has not spread everywhere through this field (1989; also Biardeau and Malamoud 1976). Among other French anthropologists of India are Charles Malamoud (e.g., 1989; Biardeau and Malamoud 1976), Marie-Louise Reiniche (1979, on a south Indian cult), Jean-Claude Galey (e.g., 1989, on kingship), Serge Bouez (e.g., 1985, 1992, on tribals and Bengal), Marine Carrin-Bouez (e.g., 1986, on tribals), and Denis Vidal (e.g., 1997, on violence). French anthropologists of Nepal include Olivier Herrenschmidt (e.g., 1989), Marc Gaborieau (e.g., 1978; also work on Muslims in Nepal in particular), Gérard Toffin (1984, 1993), Anne de Sales (e.g., 1991, on shamanism and Maoism in Nepal), Alexandre MacDonald (who is of Scottish birth but was trained in France and is resident in Paris; e.g., 1983, 1987), Giselle Krauskopf (1989), and Bernard Pignède (who died young, in 1961; see 1993). That not all such works were focused on traditional forms of the exotic is shown by Gérard Heuzé's work on tribal miners (1996) and by the Belgian Robert Deliège's works on untouchables (1997, 1999; also 1985, on tribals). Not all of these anthropologists engage directly with Dumont's ideas, either critically or supportively, and in general their work fits in with what we can now identify as a French tradition of theoretically aware but rigorously empirical ethnography. South Asia has its own French journal, *Purusartha*.

Poststructuralism: Deconstruction, Simulation, and Postmodernism

It seems that structuralism had hardly established itself when it began to come under attack on a number of fronts. Among the challenges to structuralism were psychoanalysis, phenomenology, and what might be called ethnographic essentialism, such as that of fieldworkers Bernot and Condominas, all trends that date from the 1950s. Even so, the former two trends were also affected positively by structuralism, with which, indeed, they sought to combine. But the term *poststructuralism* tends to suggest other approaches, starting somewhat later, which sometimes seem to extend structuralism as much as contradict it. The deconstructionism of Jacques Derrida, the simulation of reality through images posited by Baudrillard, and the postmodernism of Jean-François Lyotard have all had an impact on the dissolution of anthropological structuralism, though they use much of its language and many of its ideas. None of these theorists can be described as anthropologists, and none of them have generally engaged with anthropology more than superficially.

Jacques Derrida, who was born in Algiers in 1930 and died in 2004, taught philosophy at both the École Normale Supérieure and Yale University after completing his education partly at Harvard and serving in a teaching position at Johns Hopkins University. In Paris he later became involved with Tel Quel, a group of radical intellectuals from a number of disciplines. Influenced by a range of other figures, including Friedrich Nietzsche, Sigmund Freud, Martin Heidegger, Edmund Husserl, and G. F. W. Hegel, he also engaged with the work of Jacques Lacan and Jean-Jacques Rousseau, as well as, from a skeptical though not entirely detached point of view, with Lévi-Strauss's structuralism. One of Derrida's fundamental observations regarding structuralism is that although it treats each text as unique and invariant, texts are not discrete units but have internal contradictions, as well as a tendency to refer to one another through what Derrida calls intertextuality. Given also that every reading of the same text is different, each text is neither integral nor bounded but actually represents a series of different texts based on these different readings. This aspect itself represents an additional dimension of intertexuality that is not merely a matter of cross-referencing between texts over time—that is, it is not purely historical.

Derrida's self-imposed task is therefore to "deconstruct" what are conventionally termed texts in order to expose the context in which they are written and in which they acquire and convey meaning. For him meaning is context dependent, even context defined, and rather like Foucault, he thinks in terms of the restraining influence on behavior of the regimes of knowledge expressed in texts that see themselves as truth-determined and therefore tend to avoid self-criticism (in the professions, for example, as well as in intellectual inquiry more generally). Although the language in which these regimes are imparted is self-contained and self-referential, it is never neutral. It is, however, ultimately social, existing outside of and imposing itself on the individual. One of the ideas Derrida takes from structuralism is therefore that aspect of binary opposition that evaluates the two poles of an opposition differently—an idea that recalls Hertz and Dumont rather than Lévi-Strauss. In terms of regimes of knowledge, a binary opposition can be set up in such a way that that one pole represents approved knowledge (science, for example), whereas the other pole represents what is disapproved and potentially subversive (here, perhaps, magic). Despite being marginal, magic defines science by determining the latter's boundaries. This again reminds us of Foucault, even though Foucault rejected Derrida's work as mere posturing.

But Derrida goes beyond this in his work of deconstruction to focus on the circumstances in which criticism takes place, in what is a meta-level of explanation and discourse. In the first place, criticism typically deconstructs concepts by focusing on their origins rather than just their present state, in such a way that the "trace" of the origin is always evident even after it has become absent. But the trace also constitutes the origin as its opposite, since it is only through the trace that we discern the origin.

One aspect of Derrida's theory is a notion of otherness that, despite Derrida, actually involves structuralism, reference elsewhere being made partly to the opposition of signifier and signified, which for Derrida are interchangeable. Furthermore, deconstruction is compelled to use the language of that which it wants to abolish, since it has not yet been able to develop an alternative language. Although criticism automatically places the concepts being criticized "under erasure"—that is, it tolerates them provisionally pending their abolition—for lack of an alternative form of discourse, this removal is always being "deferred" and never achieved, in a process of infinite regression. One clear example, not referred to by Derrida, is the necessity for antiracist activists to use conventional racial categories in arguing for those categories' falsity and redundancy. This idea leads to the most famous example of Derrida's use of puns as a heuristic device: criticism involves both *différence* ("difference") and *différance* (a Derridian neologism meaning "deferment"), a pun based on the double meaning of the French verb *différer* ("to differ; to defer").

Derrida's deconstructive approach extents to the footnotes in a text, which, he shows, are often used as a semiconcealed space to qualify and even contradict, almost shamefacedly, the assertions made in the main text. Those assertions, in being both intended by the author and acknowledged by others to constitute the privileged arguments and discourse, constitute the superior pole in another unequal binary opposition. Yet another opposition Derrida plays with is that between a preface and the text to which it relates, the former being an overcondensed exposition of the latter, but also involving a lie, because it is generally written subsequently to the text. In the Freudian language adopted by Derrida here, while the preface seems to engender the text, it is actually the text that is father to the preface, which, as its son, may reject the text by contextualizing it (see Derrida 1976, 1978; also Spivak 1976).

The work of Jean Baudrillard (b. 1929) has generally been concerned with media and the impact of its images on our perceptions and behavior; it thus recalls some of the work of Roland Barthes. The modern world is saturated with images to such an extent that media such as advertisements, film, and television have become caught up in a loop in which images ultimately refer only to one another, not to any reality. Modern media are intensely self-referential in the sense of being obsessed by the circumstances of their own (re)production. Perceptions of reality thus become filtered through images in such a way that we now live in a world of what Baudrillard calls simulation. This is hardly new, given the long history of plays about actors and references in theater to the circumstances of theatrical reproduction. Images also produce a sort of code whereby we define ourselves and distinguish others in a manner recalling Bourdieu's ideas of how cultural capital is created.

For Baudrillard the term *simulation* does not suggest any sort of replication of reality, nor even its distortion, but has become sui generis, as in computer virtuality. In addition, media now creates reality as much as it documents it, as when riots are sparked by the presence of TV cameras, or when TV producers themselves set up situations that are then reported as "reality"—that is, media provokes behavior that might not otherwise have taken place. Indeed, the arrival of interactive TV has now enabled viewers themselves to take part in the creation of the media images that constitute the simulation.

However, Baudrillard rejects the Marxist idea that images manipulate our behavior because this imposes a false disjunction between the makers and consumers of images. Instead, whether we make images or consume them, we are all socially conditioned to respond to simulation (a remark one could imagine Durkheim making). Baudrillard was certainly influenced by Marx early on via the revisionist French Marxist Henri Lefebvre, but now he sees contemporary capitalism as involving the production and consumption of images rather than products—as in the past and as in Marxist orthodoxy. Images are intended to create endless desire, not satisfy needs. For Baudrillard consumption has replaced politics, especially as it has absorbed even radical political images, such as that of Che Guevara, as money-making products. Linked to this is his idea that we do not actively resist images as we might an argument or an oppressive system, but that at most we ignore them—a position that ought to be revised in the light of contemporary anticapitalist movements' explicit opposition to advertising. There is also a psychoanalytical aspect to Baudrillard's work. Although advertising images make explicit a number of the supposedly unconscious dreams and symbols of Oedipal theory, they stimulate unconscious drives toward sex and death, though in advertising the latter is subsumed more safely under violence in general. Finally, consumption is rooted in the primal sense of lack, as well as exploiting the human responsiveness to symbols (see 1968, 1970, 1975, 1988a, 1988b, 1993; also Poster 1988).

Jean-François Lyotard (1924–1998) is generally credited with coining the term *postmodern*, in a report on the state of scientific knowledge for the Council of Universities in Quebec (1984). Postmodern style itself is supposed to have started in architecture as playful, vernacular, eclectic designs took the place of the severe utilitarian designs of the modernists. It was later transferred to literature and other genres, with popular and subaltern cultures being celebrated in order to subvert the modernist notion of high culture. Later still, social scientists discovered it as a tool for theorizing about the multistrandedness of much contemporary life, including such elements as multiculturalism, globalization, hyphenation of identities, and the decentering of hegemonic structures of all sorts (colonial, capitalist, gender-based, racial, and so on). In short, postmodernism celebrates chaos not order, fragmentation not unity, variety not uniformity, relativism not standardization, and equality not hegemony.

In the above-mentioned report Lyotard was reviving earlier studies by the philosopher Bachelard (1934, 1953) on the circumstances in which science is produced, and in particular on the contrast between the scientific view of objective knowledge and the actual, frequently contingent constitution of that knowledge by scientists acting as a community sharing common values. Bachelard was also interested in progress in science, seeing it as involving "epistemological breaks" rather than gradual change (cf. Kuhn 1970).

Lyotard himself focused on how scientists no longer regarded their work as permanently valid, as a cure for all the world's ills, or even as a comprehensive and integrated account of how the world works. There are a number of reasons for this, including uncertainty principles in science itself, controversies among scientists, an appreciation of the damage science has done to the environment and to whole populations through warfare, and the short-termism and muddy compromises of much scientific research, dependent as it increasingly is on funding agencies that have agendas of their own. Bachelard and Kuhn both pointed out that science is a product of the social in both conception and practice. At all events, science could no longer claim to be what Lyotard called a metanarrative producing an incontrovertible truth transcending all relativisms; this was a piece of deconstruction that recalled Derrida and Foucault. Indeed, Lyotard approved of the breakdown of the Enlightenment project and celebrated instead liberty, transparency of knowledge and of how it is constituted, and minor acts of resistance and subversion of the sort described by Scott among Malay peasants (1985). Accordingly, he was opposed to the creation of new metanarratives out of the experience of postmodernism, believing that the oppressed should be allowed to speak for

themselves, not through intellectuals claiming custody of particular knowledge regimes—like, traditionally, anthropologists. An increasing number of
anthropologists have adopted this view, perhaps mainly outside France.

Also active in the field of the sociology of scientific knowledge has been
Bruno Latour (e.g., Latour and Woolgar 1986), who suggests that the very
idea of modernity has proved to be false as a form of practice (Latour 1993).
In particular, science's claim to have revealed nature is contradicted by its
constitution of it in the laboratory, thus eliding the difference between distinguishing nature and society ("purification," which science depends on) and
confusing them ("translation" or "mediation," the latter a term also used by
Bachelard). In short, given that the laboratory is as much social as it is scientific, and given the principled intolerance of scientific thought for such hy-
brids between the natural and the social, which it has created itself, ideological modernity has never, in fact, existed. This recalls Dumont's identification
of the nonmodern thought that continues to lurk in the modern, which is connected with a similar sense of contradictions inhering in the latter but not in
the former. In another direction, Carsten (2000, 31–33) and Bouquet (2000)
have recently suggested applying these insights to the distinction between social and biological kinship.

Concluding Remarks

Although many of the postmodern and deconstructive currents that have be-
set anthropology since the 1970s have their origins in French intellectualism,
their impact on anthropology may have been less in France than elsewhere, as
more than one commentator has already remarked (e.g., Clifford 1983, 130–
31; Godelier 2000; Weber 2001; Rogers 2001). Rogers points to the absence of
reflexivity or autobiography as themes in French anthropology (Bourdieu's
stray remarks on the necessity of the former are quite exceptional in this regard), an anthropology that has also not attended greatly to ethnicity, which
elsewhere has come to be seen increasingly as a matter of shifting context and
hybridity. Rogers also argues that French anthropology and ethnography per
se still tend to be holistic and synchronic in orientation, stressing Maussian or
structuralist coherence rather than the fragmentation of the postmodernists.
These are perhaps methodological principles rather than theoretical ones, reflecting the ethnographic essentialism of many French anthropologists. Often
multidisciplinary in orientation, such writers are not ignorant of theory so
much as they are skeptical of it, or rather, they are focused on facts, empiri-

cism, and practice. This is for the most part a homegrown skepticism owing little or nothing to British or any other example. As for the study of folklore, although it has generally been theoretically unproductive, it ultimately merged with anthropological fieldwork on French soil to create a tradition of study that now extends to modern institutions.

Although multistranded, the French school does draw considerable theoretical unity from the precepts laid down for sociology in the 1880s by Durkheim, applied to anthropology by himself and by Mauss thereafter, and developed by Lévi-Strauss through structuralism after World War II. This influence can be detected even in the work of those authors who at first sight appear to reject these precepts. Thus writers like Foucault, Bourdieu, Baudrillard, and Derrida all have talked of the internalization of ideologies and images in a manner that recalls Durkheim's interpretation of symbols in a ritual, not to mention Rousseau, while Godelier has highlighted the similarities between Marxism and structuralism. Indeed, many so-called poststructuralist thinkers extended structuralism as much as criticized it, thanks to the persistent tendency to think in terms of binary oppositions even when the intention is to deconstruct them, or at least to deconstruct the inequalities they are seen to represent. There are thus continuities from Rousseau through to Baudrillard, mediated by major figures such as Durkheim and Lévi-Strauss.

The Lacanians also asserted the influence of culture on the unconscious, thus denying, as did Durkheim, the possibility of psychological determinism of culture or society. In other respects, although not to the same extent as the Durkheimian tradition, psychoanalysis has been a significant influence on French anthropology, reflected not only in its underlying presence in structuralism, but also in the more direct influence of Freud, to a lesser extent of Jung, and more recently of Lacan himself. Lévi-Strauss's use of psychology is, however, collective rather than individual, a matter of basic modes of thought that underpin superficial cultural variations. Lévi-Strauss's use of this generalized psychology in combination with a Tylorian view of culture and Saussurean structuralism enabled him to complete Mauss's work of establishing anthropology as a separate discipline in France as Durkheim had established sociology some sixty years earlier. In that sense Lévi-Strauss is the second great innovator, after Durkheim, of significance to French anthropology, and in my view he should join the triumvirate of Durkheim, Weber, and Marx as a fourth founding father of social science.

In its separation of theory and practice and of teaching and research, and in its considerable theoretical continuities and its relatively late institutionalization and turn to fieldwork, French anthropology can claim true distinction as a national anthropological school. Yet although this school has remained true to French intellectual traditions more widely, it has not been isolated. Modern French social thought has drawn on German hermeneutics and phenomenology and on British empiricism as well as on its own more rationalist and universalist traditions; it has also spread its influence abroad, not only to Britain, where it has perhaps been dominant, but also to America and Germany. France therefore fully deserves its status as one of the world's leading producers of social thought and ethnographic practice.

The United States / SYDEL SILVERMAN

I

The Boasians and the Invention of Cultural Anthropology

My task, to trace the history of anthropology in the United States in five lectures, is a daunting one, if only because of the sheer size of the field. There are today perhaps twenty thousand people in the United States practicing anthropology in some form or professing to be anthropologists. Their work and interests cover an enormous range, and they have behind them over a century of antecedents, themselves equally varied. To do justice to all of them is beyond my reach. I therefore propose to tame my subject with several provisos.

First, while American anthropologists come in at least four varieties (the subfields of cultural or social anthropology, today less often called ethnology; physical or biological anthropology; archaeology; and linguistic anthropology), I will concern myself primarily with the cultural/social variant, given this institute's emphasis. However, I will have occasion to refer to others of the subfields, and I hope to explain why American anthropology has this peculiar configuration and why some of us, at least, think it still serves us. (I use the adjective *American* only as a shorthand for *United States*, not to refer to the entire Western Hemisphere.)

Second, I will try to provide a sense of the major currents and developments in the field, but I will do so from my own perspective and will emphasize those that I consider the most significant or the most interesting. Since the American tradition is the youngest of our four traditions, with a shorter history but more to report on for the twentieth century, I will begin at a later point than my colleagues and will concentrate on the century just past. My organization of the five lectures follows a more or less chronological sequence, but after the first two I will back up in time to consider a particularly American interest in the anthropology of complex societies, which I trace into the 1970s. The last two lectures will move forward from that decade.

Third, I will not treat this history as a sequence of disembodied ideas ("isms") but will try to connect them with the story of institutions and social relationships and the external circumstances that affect these. It is in such institutional and social contexts that ideas emerge and have their effects. Although my picture will be partial, privileging what I know best, I hope it will provide a flavor of American anthropology as a social phenomenon.

Finally, I do not propose to present this history as an orderly progression built upon a systematic accumulation of knowledge. I do not think that is the way the history of any discipline works, and I have no interest in reshaping the past into a triumphal account of American anthropology moving onward and upward through the twentieth century. Much of our history has been marked by dissension and contentiousness, not all of it polite. While one might reproach our ancestors and colleagues for their ad hominem lapses, I think it is through such dissension that we learn the most. I will therefore frame some of my comments around controversies and conflicts. I hope that by the end I will have persuaded you that we are a lively if unruly bunch and that American anthropology continues to thrive on its peculiar mixture of passionate commitment and disagreement.

Beginnings

The standard textbook sketch of the beginnings of American anthropology looks something like this: Its father was Franz Boas, who trained the major figures of the first half of the twentieth century. With Boas came the anti-evolutionist critique; historicism of the trait-distribution variety; and the institutionalization of anthropology in university departments, museums, and professional entities. With Boas too came the four-field structure, which was initially a methodological device for the study of American Indians but then became entrenched under a theoretical rationale. And from the beginning, with Boas, there came the use of culture as the core concept—in opposition to the societal and social-structural emphasis of British social anthropology, to ethnology in A. R. Radcliffe-Brown's disparaging sense, and especially to explanations based on race or biology.

All this is true enough, but the history of American anthropology was not a systematic unfolding, controlled and unified by a school made up of the followers of Boas, to the exclusion of other voices, who were guided by a tidy theoretical framework. It was instead an arena of debate, conflict, and differences of many kinds—theoretical, social, political, cultural, and institutional.

The American anthropological landscape into which Boas inserted himself was neither vacant and awaiting his influence, nor without potential competitors to him. Our first question, therefore, is where to begin. Issues that would become central themes in anthropology once it was professionalized had been debated by politicians, men of letters, and scientists of diverse stripe at least since the early nineteenth century: issues such as the origins and cultural status of the Indians and what that meant for the westward expansion of the frontier; the significance of racial differences and how that bore upon slavery policies; and the nature of the new immigrant groups and the question of their proper place in society. There were travelers who collected artifacts and ethnological information on Indians, philologists who described or speculated about American Indian languages, phrenologists who carried out anthropometric studies, and amateur archaeologists intrigued by the mounds of the eastern United States and the Pueblo ruins of the Southwest; and there were learned societies in which these interests were pursued. In the post-Darwinian era, interpretations generally followed evolutionary schemes of one sort or another.

From our perspective today, Lewis Henry Morgan was the most important of the nineteenth-century gentleman scholars. A lawyer who had become acquainted with the Seneca tribe by representing them in a land dispute, he acquired an interest in Iroquois kinship (1851) and went on to publish a large comparative study of kinship systems (1870) that, some have argued, marked the invention of the anthropological notion of kinship. Morgan then used kinship as an entry point into a broader theory of social evolution, which he laid out in *Ancient Society* (1877). This work came to the attention of Marx and Engels and was to play a strategic role in American anthropology in the mid-twentieth century.

As the westward expansion pressed on, there were practical as well as intellectual motives for gaining knowledge about the Indians. The one-armed Civil War hero and explorer John Wesley Powell, an indefatigable compiler of Indian languages and customs, was appointed to head up both the U.S. Geological Survey and then, in 1879, the newly established Bureau of American Ethnology. At the bureau Powell was largely responsible for professionalizing the study of American Indians within an evolutionary interpretive framework. The ethnologists of the bureau, some of them carrying out adventurous fieldwork on the frontier, continued to plot a different course from that of Boas. Indeed, one of the criticisms of Boas has been that he neglected—even erased from anthropological memory—such antecedents and competitors, including Morgan, as he pursued his project of building the new discipline.

Institutional anthropology began in the museums as well as in government agencies. The National Museum of the Smithsonian, the Peabody Museum at Harvard, and the American Museum of Natural History in New York (AMNH) were all founded shortly after mid-century and soon established archaeological and ethnological divisions to gather and care for collections. They also instituted research; the AMNH Jesup Expedition of 1894, for example, preceded and was more explicitly anthropological than the Torres Strait Expedition mounted by the British. At about that time, the World's Columbian Exposition in Chicago, that great world's fair of 1893, gave rise to the Field Museum. The key figure in developing anthropology in the museums was Frederick Ward Putnam, who went on to set up the first academic departments as well, at Columbia, Harvard, Chicago, and Berkeley. It was through Putnam, who became Boas's mentor, that Boas found employment first at the Chicago exposition, then at the AMNH.

Boas had entered the anthropological scene in 1883 when he went to Baffin Island, in the area of the Central Eskimo, to carry out a geographic study and ended up an ethnologist. Returning for a year to his native Germany, he worked under Adolf Bastian at the Royal Ethnological Museum in Berlin. He later transposed the notions of Bastian and Rudolph Virchow to his treatment of culture in the American context. After another field trip, this time to the northwest coast of North America, Boas decided to settle in the United States, where he took up a series of editorial and museum-curatorial positions. He achieved his foothold in American anthropology when, around 1895, he acquired an institutional base at both the AMNH and Columbia University.

In the last decade of the nineteenth century the center of gravity of American anthropology was in Washington. The men of the Bureau of American Ethnology, the Geological Survey, and the National Museum formed the Anthropological Society of Washington in 1879 and instituted the *American Anthropologist* a decade later. The journal remained in Washington until 1902, when it was transferred to the newly created American Anthropological Association (AAA). (The American Ethnological Society, which was based in New York, actually predated the more influential Washington society.) The Washington establishment was dominated by an evolutionary tradition, as were most of the ethnological writings and museum exhibits of the day.

Boas found not only the evolutionary tradition to contend with but also a typological, racialist physical anthropology, which was spearheaded by Aleš Hrdlička at the National Museum (and later by Earnest A. Hooton at Harvard). Soon to be allied against Boas as well were archaeologists at Harvard's Peabody and at the Carnegie Institution of Washington. Their brand of archaeology, essentially descriptive and long denying human antiquity in the

Americas, was at odds with Boas's historicism. Still another player on the anthropological scene that Boas struggled against was the eugenics movement led by Charles B. Davenport.

These forces, which were almost as strong at Harvard as they were in Washington, came to be known as the Washington/Cambridge axis. Their opposition to Boas at Columbia and to the Boasians who soon fanned out across the country marked a continuing fault line, and relations between the factions were not friendly. They fought over dominance of the National Research Council and other sources of research funds, control of the AAA, editorship of the *American Anthropologist*, and appointments in the newly founded departments. The division was theoretical, counterposing evolutionary to historicist models, racialist to cultural determinism, and fixed types to plasticity; it was a cultural divergence, with predominantly old-American WASPs on the one side and the immigrant, often Jewish, Boasians on the other; and it often corresponded to political differences around issues of immigration policy, race relations, nationalism and isolationism during World War I, American Indian separatism and assimilationism, and other matters.

Boas and the Boasians up to World War I

In the 1890s, Boas began publishing critiques of evolutionist thinking, such as his famous article on "The Limitations of the Comparative Method" (1896); he meant by *comparative method* the specific procedures followed by the evolutionists. He used each critique to point to alternative emphases, not always doing so consistently. Although he did not produce a systematic theoretical magnum opus, by the time he published *The Mind of Primitive Man* (1911b), a book written for a lay as well as a professional audience, the outlines of a paradigm were clear.

Boas's paradigm made the empirical study of what were thought to be the rapidly disappearing native cultures the priority for anthropology; fieldwork was key to such study, although that generally meant the debriefing of elders and the recording of texts rather than the participant observation of later ethnography. It saw the four subfields of anthropology as complementary means for the study and historical reconstruction of nonliterate cultures. It emphasized language, both in its insistence upon working with texts in the native languages and in its view that language was an entry into mental states of the natives.

This paradigm marked a shift in the concept of culture. It defined culture inclusively to encompass material, social, and symbolic realms; this superficially resembled Edward Burnett Tylor's definition, but Boas intended something quite different. His paradigm used *culture* not as a synonym for *civilization*, as Tylor had done, but now in the plural sense, emphasizing the diversity of cultures and seeing cultures as contexts of learned human behavior. (In this it stood in contrast to the psychology of the time, which stressed instinct.) This notion of culture also called for a stance of cultural relativism, the idea that it is necessary to understand cultures in their own terms and their own historical contexts before attempting generalizations. The Boasian paradigm offered a strategy of historical particularism as the alternative to the orthogenetic evolutionism it criticized—that is, the view that cultural progress consists of an unfolding of predetermined stages of development. While diffusion and contact among cultures were seen as the primary historical mechanisms, in time the strategy made room for an interest in how cultures were internally patterned, an interest that grew out of diffusionist studies themselves because such patterns affected the way traits were adopted in a contact situation. That shift also entailed an increasing concern with the relationship between culture and the individual.

Boas's paradigm asserted the relative autonomy of cultural phenomena. Key to his approach was his separation of race, language, and culture, which he insisted were distinct phenomena and subject to independent causation. This view shaped his pursuit of physical anthropology, which was less a focus on biology as such than a means of challenging the racial typologies of the day with their assumptions of fixity in the mental as well as physical attributes of races. Boas questioned the fixity of even the classic anthropometric traits in his study comparing head measurements of immigrants with those of their American-born descendants, which demonstrated the plasticity of those traits, presumably in response to environmental conditions (1911a).

In this paradigm one sees the two threads of Boas's thinking, which were picked up by his students in different ways and between which he himself shifted: the historical, which was concerned especially with traceable processes that could account for the distribution of culture traits; and the psychological, which included both mentalist interests in what makes individual minds different in different cultures and integrationist concerns with how traits fit together. These two threads corresponded roughly to Boas's two epistemological sides as well, the historical and the scientific. In general, the first generation of Boas's students, those trained before World War I, emphasized the first thread; however, they differed sharply among themselves and with Boas on what was meant by culture history and how it should be studied.

The second generation, who studied with Boas in the 1920s, picked up the second thread, seeking principles of synchronic cultural integration and individual enculturation. A third generation, at Columbia during the 1930s, combined the two threads, but their return to culture history took the form of a focus on actual events (as opposed to historical relationships inferred from trait distributions), including native responses to external conditions and attention to the larger contexts in which native cultures were embedded.

As an institution builder, Boas made great strides. Beginning with Alfred Kroeber, who received his PhD under Boas in 1901 and went on to build the anthropology department at the University of California at Berkeley, Boas's first generation of students established departments around the country: Robert Lowie (joining Kroeber) at Berkeley, Frank Speck at the University of Pennsylvania, Fay-Cooper Cole and Edward Sapir at the University of Chicago (and later, Sapir at Yale), Melville Herskovits at Northwestern University, Alexander Goldenweiser at the New School for Social Research (where he taught Leslie White and Ruth Benedict), and others. Most of these departments incorporated Boas's four-field model of anthropology, although Boas himself (and Columbia) concentrated mainly on ethnology and linguistics. Much anthropological research at the time was still based in museums; Boas fostered the professionalization of museums and placed his students in key positions (such as Clark Wissler at the AMNH). Boas was also active in creating professional associations, including the AAA in 1902 (although he did not become its president until 1907); in founding journals; and in ensuring anthropological representation in national organizations. He was, moreover, a frequent commentator on public issues such as nationalism, race relations, education, and eugenics, not as part of a specifically political program but in the conviction that anthropological knowledge would itself point the way to societal solutions.

Although Boas's students are often spoken of as Boasians, there were strong differences among them. (It must also be said that Boas himself was self-critical, often changing his views and retracting earlier opinions.) Within the first generation, they differed with regard to how the Boas program should be followed. George Stocking Jr. has drawn a distinction between the strict and the rebellious Boasians (Stocking 1974, 17). Among those in the first category were Lowie, Leslie Spier, Herskovits, Wissler, and Speck. The second category included Kroeber, who pursued his own brand of historicism, and Sapir, who took a direction that focused on the individual and developed linguistic approaches that were increasingly at odds with Boas's. Stocking also sees a third category, evolved Boasians, among them Benedict and Margaret Mead.

Paul Radin was another rebel. Almost a polar opposite temperamentally to Boas and even more so to Kroeber, and staunchly critical of their distributional studies and statistical methods, Radin's main concern was with the worldview of "primitive philosophers." A theme of his work was the way recurrent figures such as the shaman and the mythical trickster revealed universal truths about primitive society and its contrast with civilization (e.g., 1927). For Radin, history resided in human experience; he pioneered a life-history method centered on individual experience and published an autobiography of a Winnebago Indian (1920). Then there was Goldenweiser, who was allied with Sapir and Radin on some issues (like them, for example, he accorded to individuals a creative influence on culture) but disagreed with each of them on other matters.

The divisions within the first generation of Boasians reached a crisis point with Kroeber's publication of "The Superorganic" (1917), in which he proclaimed the absolute independence of cultural phenomena from the organic, a category that included biology, psychology, and the individual. Culture was "an emergent level" distinct from these "lower" levels. Sapir led the critical charge, insisting that the locus of culture had to be in the individual (1917). Others in the group lined up on both sides, each side accusing the other of betraying Boas's intentions. A few years later Sapir set off another firestorm by rejecting the "technical, ethnological" idea of culture of most of the Boasians and proposing instead a theory of culture as the "spiritual possessions" of a group, which was an elaboration of Boas's notion of the "genius of a people." In this Sapir offered the first statement of "cultural integration," which he saw as a patterning of values. He drew a contrast between integrated "genuine" cultures, which were harmonious, vital, organic, and attuned to individual creativity, and "spurious" cultures—hybrid, discordant, and artificially imposed upon individuals (1924).

But these dissensions in the Boasian camp were minor compared to the challenges to Boas by his many adversaries. Anthropologists outside his circle resented his dominance of the discipline, and his public outspokenness made him anathema to the senior administration at Columbia. His enemies lost no opportunity to attack him. Their chance came when Boas opposed United States entry into World War I, not because he was pro-German (as was charged) but because he was a lifelong pacifist. Then in 1919 he published in *The Nation*, a popular magazine, a letter titled "Scientists as Spies," deploring those unnamed people who, he claimed, used the cover of anthropological research to work as government agents (he had in mind the Carnegie archaeologists). The Washington-Cambridge alliance used the letter to have Boas censured by the AAA and removed from several key positions. His excommunication, however, did not last long.

The Interwar Period

Kroeber and Sapir were the most important of the first-generation rebels. Kroeber, who after Boas's death in 1942 was the undisputed grand old man of American anthropology, was to remain a power until his death in 1960, producing an enormous corpus of work (which amounted to over seven hundred items) and organizing research in all the subfields. Kroeber carried forward the historical side of the Boasian paradigm but with his own twists that increasingly diverged from Boas. His overriding interests were in cultural forms, pattern cohesion, and cultural creativity. These he pursued through formal historical methods, emphasizing classification and quantification. Beginning by looking at culture traits in their particularistic matrices, he went on to seek organizing patterns among traits, using a method he called conceptual integration. He initiated the culture-area approach for sorting out the ethnologically significant regions of native North America (1939), then moved on to write about configurations of culture growth and growth cycles and eventually "style" (1944, 1957). He aimed for grand syntheses, from his comprehensive Culture Element Distribution project to his delineations of broad civilizational processes guided by a concept of progress.

The Culture Element project ended in a fiasco that is revealing of Kroeber's personality. During the 1930s Kroeber had initiated this ambitious series of studies, which he thought would yield a definitive analysis of cultural processes in western North America, and he had set a dozen or more of his students to work on it. Then, at an AAA meeting, he suddenly announced that the studies were a failure, since they had not elicited any patterns. People who had invested years of work and collected masses of data were devastated (Gene Weltfish, in Silverman 1981, 60).

In a sense Kroeber was more Boasian than Boas himself in that for him explanation consisted only of within-culture processes, to the exclusion of external factors. For example, his culture-area typology recognized environmental factors (which he took as givens) but stopped short of suggesting environmental causation. Similarly, in his famous studies (with Jane Richardson) of changes in women's fashions over the course of a century, he at first tried to correlate the changes with social unrest but soon gave up that effort in favor of a quantitative analysis, from which he concluded that cultural forms obey an inherent rhythm of variation (Richardson and Kroeber 1940). As we have seen, Kroeber also went further than Boas in his assertion of cultural determinism in the concept of the superorganic, from which (unlike Boas) he excluded any role for the individual or for psychology. He did not hesitate to challenge Boas directly, as when he accused him of not being interested in history at all. Boas shrugged off the attacks. He had never been an admirer of Kroeber, once having said of him, "He never thinks anything through" (Lesser 1981, 29).

Sapir was less an institution builder than Kroeber, but he had a profound influence through the force of his brilliance. After spending fifteen years at the Canadian national museum in Ottawa, Sapir taught briefly at Chicago and then moved to Yale. He had been attracted to Yale because of the opportunity for collaboration with compatible psychologists (among them Harry Stack Sullivan), but once he arrived he found that the interdisciplinary Institute of Human Relations had been taken over by a behavioral psychology and an evolutionary sociology that were antipathetic to him (Darnell 2001, 130–32). Still, his years at Yale, which were cut short by his illness and early death, had a major impact on the development of anthropological linguistics through his training of an important group of students who specialized in American Indian languages.

By about 1920 Sapir had come to loggerheads with Boas over what were the appropriate models for both linguistic and cultural change; it was a conflict over the very definition of history. Applying the methods of philology to American Indian languages and going on from there to develop historical reconstructions of cultures based on linguistic evidence, Sapir emphasized the genetic relationships of languages over diffusion. He even used such forbidden terms as *origins* and the notion of "archaic residues" from a common historical past. Sapir was increasingly interested in the relationship of culture to the individual, proposing that culture was not just a constraint but that individuals bent cultural givens to their own ends; in this view, he also tangled with his close friend Benedict. Sapir's disputes with the Boasians moved him closer to linguistics; at first he was an ally of Leonard Bloomfield but then diverged from him. Since Bloomfield was the major force in linguistics as it developed into an autonomous field, Sapir came to be somewhat marginalized in those circles as well.

Even as Sapir disputed Boasian linguistics and culture history in what was spoken of as a conflict of New Haven versus New York, he remained the guiding figure of such second-generation Boasians as Benedict and Mead. Anthropologists who are not linguists perhaps know Sapir best for his collaboration with his student Benjamin Whorf on what became known as the Sapir-Whorf hypothesis. Their idea was that the semantic structures of different languages (especially their grammars) are fundamentally incommensurable and that they shape the way language speakers perceive and classify the experienced world. The next step (which Whorf took) was to see these linguistic structures as having consequences for thought and for culture, such that each language is associated with a distinctive worldview. The hypothesis was highly influential for a time, but it came under increasing criticism and fell into disrepute by the 1960s, only to rise again in a recently renewed interest in linguistic relativity (see, e.g., Gumperz and Levinson 1996).

It was during the 1920s that the second generation of Boas's students came of age. Diffusionism and trait-list historicism were becoming old hat, and the psychological/integrationist thread in Boas came into prominence, influenced now by psychoanalysis and Gestalt psychology. Those who followed this Boasian strand, reshaping it as they went along into what became known as the culture-and-personality school, included Benedict, Mead, Irving Hallowell (a student of Speck), and Clyde Kluckhohn. Ralph Linton, from the Harvard line, joined in this tradition, which he merged with an influence from British social anthropology. Among those in this school, there was virtually no interest in history. The historicist Boasians continued alongside this strand, often highly critical of it, but even they tired of formalism and increasingly forged links with the comparative and functionalist movements that were being introduced into the United States from Britain. For example, Lowie, always a vigorous defender of Boas's historical agenda and a tireless critic of evolutionism, was one of the earliest of the Americans to write a general work on social organization from an analytic, comparative perspective (1920), and he later picked up the culture-and-personality theme with a study of German national character (1945). Even Kroeber was affected; as we have seen, his concern with culture areas and distribution studies increasingly shifted to cultural configurations.

Boas seems to have mellowed by that time; now he was Papa Franz to his circle. This cohort of his students included a substantial number of women (some of whom began as his secretary); he chose their research topics and secured funds for their fieldwork, but he rarely found jobs for them—none of these women achieved a regular academic position during his lifetime. Benedict became his administrative right hand, but she was passed over for his chair on his retirement and did not become a full professor at Columbia until two months before her death.

The 1920s were a time for romantic, "warm and fuzzy" ethnographies emphasizing coherence and communality. The Pueblos (such as the Zuni) provided the first instances, but the type case soon came to be Mead's Samoa (1928). Mead made her maiden field trip to Samoa in 1926 in the spirit of Boas's scientific side. She had decided that she wanted to do fieldwork in Polynesia, and Boas had agreed reluctantly. He selected for her a research topic he thought was consistent with her age and persona: the relative strength of biological puberty and cultural patterns of adolescence. Given the Boasian belief in cultures as diverse contexts for human development and behavior, the study would question the general assumption in the United States at the time that adolescence was inevitably stormy because of biological, hormonal givens. Mead thought that if she found a single negative case, it would disprove what was taken to be a universal. The study was also a pursuit of Boas's psychological interests, an attempt, as he said in the foreword to her book, "to enter the mental life of a group in a primitive society" (1928).

Mead's Samoan work was probably the first American ethnography in the holistic, Malinowskian sense, based upon participant observation. It also opened up several new niches for anthropology, including new interests in the Pacific, in adolescence, and in sex roles. Moreover, after Mead acceded to her publisher's suggestion that she add a chapter on implications for American society, the book became a touchstone for what would soon become her special public role.

It was Benedict, however, who carried Boas's integrationist interest to its ultimate expression. She had been influenced by Sapir's views on culture and the individual, but while his emphasis was on the individual, hers was on culture. Benedict's own forays into Pueblo ethnography and her connections with Ruth Bunzel, Reo Fortune, Mead, and others provided the background for what became the Ur-configurationist document: her *Patterns of Culture* (1934). (Boas, in an ambivalent introduction, acknowledged that the "old" interest in historical reconstruction had given way to the problem of integration and to efforts at "deep penetration into the genius of the culture," but he warned that the idea should not be taken too far [1934, xv].) Each culture, Benedict wrote, selected and elaborated upon certain portions of the "arc" of human possibilities; each culture could be seen as a "personality writ large," integrated around certain dominant themes. The different cultures described were likened to psychological syndromes, and the individual's fate—whether to become admired and successful or to be defined as abnormal—depended upon the fit of his or her personality with the values underscored or disparaged by the culture.

This was cultural relativism at its height. That concept may be understood in either a weak or a strong sense. In its weak sense, it was a basic premise of Boasian anthropology—and has been of every other anthropology since then: the idea that cultures and cultural processes must be understood in their own terms in the first instance, apart from the observer's ethnocentric standards. In the strong sense, cultural relativism sees cultures as incommensurate, each particular to itself and comprehensible only in terms of itself. This strong kind of relativism did not die with Benedict; it has had a resurgence in recent decades.

Cultural determinism is still another matter. Neither Boas nor any of his students believed in "absolute cultural determinism," as Derek Freeman charged when he launched his critique of Mead's Samoa study fifty years after the fact (1983). Freeman's claim was that Boas had ordered Mead to find a nonstressful adolescence in Samoa, in accordance with his own convictions, and that all of America had bought into her account, launching a half-century of permissiveness. (If any of the Boasians was vulnerable to Freeman's charge, it was Kroeber, who had argued that cultural phenomena were sui generis, but Kroeber's studies of basket designs and clans did not feed Freeman's ire.)

Boas's anthropology was premised on the interaction of biological and cultural phenomena, and he championed four-field anthropology partly on that basis. However, he was also continually battling against racial determinism, especially the belief that the "races" had different mental capacities. He used the weapon of a cultural determinism that insisted that behavior and mentality were products of learning within specific cultural settings. Boas began making public statements on race as early as 1906, and it is said that his last words as he collapsed and died in Claude Lévi-Strauss's arms were about race.

Mead's point, and that of other anthropologists of her time, was the fundamental lesson of cultural variability. It was cruelly distorted by Freeman and some other latter-day critics, but it is a message that anthropologists have had to return to again and again throughout the twentieth century: from the responses of Boas's circle to Nazi ideas about race and eugenics, to the multiple reappearances of racialist claims in books like *The Bell Curve* (Herrnstein and Murray, 1994), to the misuses of "culture" as justification for ethnic violence. This task for anthropology is still with us.

The 1930s were a time of Depression and Depression-era politics. New Deal programs offered support for anthropological studies in the United States, and fortunately so because there were virtually no positions in universities or museums apart from those already secured. During these years and up to the end of World War II, most anthropology was carried out under governmental auspices rather than in academia. After passage of the Indian

Reorganization Act of 1934, which sought to reverse earlier assimilationist policies and encourage greater tribal autonomy, many anthropologists were employed in the Indian service. Major archaeological projects were launched. Anthropologists were also hired to do studies of race relations and of rural communities.

Radical politics were common, especially in New York, and this third generation of Boas's students was more politically engaged than their predecessors. This was reflected in their research projects, which often started out as formal Boasian studies but then incorporated economics and history—history that now meant the real contact experiences of American Indians. Among this group were Oscar Lewis, who wrote on the effects of the fur trade on Blackfoot culture (1942); Bernard Mishkin, who analyzed rank and warfare in Plains Indian culture (1940); Jane Richardson, who studied law and status among the Kiowa (1940); and Alexander Lesser, whose study of culture change as revealed in the Pawnee Ghost Dance hand game (1933) has become a classic; as well as Gene Weltfish and Irving Goldman. Lesser headed a field-training expedition among the Kiowa in 1935 that resulted in a series of dissertations from similar perspectives, such as Preston Holder's on the role of Caddoan horticulturalists in Plains culture history (1951) and Joseph Jablow's on Cheyenne involvement in trade relations in the early nineteenth century (1951). Lesser himself was the author of several daring efforts to show that culture history was compatible with other theoretical approaches, such as functionalism and evolutionism, and he was among the first to challenge notions of primitive societies as isolates, offering the concept of "social fields" as an alternative (1961). Scorn was heaped on him for each of these efforts.

Several members of this Boasian generation became critics of the romantic ethnographies of the 1920s. They challenged the depictions of integration and harmony, seeing instead dissension, inequality, and strife in the so-called harmonious pueblos and in other settings that had been described in idyllic terms. Notable in this connection were some of the women trained by Boas, especially Bunzel and Esther Goldfrank.

When Boas retired in 1936, the president of Columbia was determined that Boas not name his successor, and Linton was appointed to his chair. The Linton/Benedict antipathy was legendary, and it went on for the whole decade of Linton's stay at Columbia. After Benedict died, Linton boasted that he had killed her using magical charms he had acquired during fieldwork in Madagascar—charms that he still carried around in a small leather pouch (Mintz 1981, 161).

Linton's appointment was a double blow to the Boasian tradition at Columbia, both marginalizing Benedict and drawing anthropology into an interdisciplinary "social science," the notion of which the Boasians abhorred, as they did that of behavioral sciences. Linton's orientation to social science was already evident in his book *The Study of Man* (1936), one of the first textbooks in anthropology, in which he introduced such key concepts as status and role. His interest coincided with the ascendance of social science in the United States, fueled by new funding sources, such as the Social Science Research Council (established in 1925), and the foundations created by the Rockefeller family. Linton led the way among anthropologists by linking up with acculturation, a key paradigm favored by the funders, and embarking upon an interdisciplinary initiative around that theme.

At Columbia Linton picked up the culture-and-personality interest that had been developed by both Mead, with her focus on enculturation, and Benedict, whose emphasis was on the arc, the array of cultures with distinctive personalities, but Linton took a different direction. He organized a seminar with the psychoanalyst Abram Kardiner, which began in 1938 and continued for several years. Anthropologists returning from the field presented psychological data they had collected, which the seminar analyzed to draw inferences about the culture. Among the ethnographers who participated were Linton with data on the Tanala, Kluckhohn on the Navajo, Cora DuBois on the people of Alor, Carl Withers on Plainville (a town in the American Midwest), and Francis Hsu on a Hunan village. This collective effort produced models for the interaction among culture, child rearing, and individual personality, and it yielded such concepts as basic personality structure, giving a major impetus to that emerging field. The list of seminar cases indicates another trend of this period in American anthropology: its tentative expansion beyond the American Indians into new ethnographic terrain in Africa, Asia, and Oceania.

By this time, anthropology had gained a significant public profile, thanks especially to the popular books by Mead and Benedict. Mead, at first feted as the girl scientist among the savages, expanded her role as a commentator on American culture from the perspective of a trained observer of the exotic. Her basic message was cultural relativism, which was to earn her blame, or credit, for a period of permissiveness in American attitudes toward sex, child rearing, and other cultural practices. She also widened her ambitions for anthropology to play a larger part in national policy, and she moved increasingly into the political arena.

A sense of Mead's faith in the power of anthropology can be gleaned from a letter she wrote to Eleanor Roosevelt in August 1939. Speaking from her "field experience of simpler social systems" and referring to some psychoanalytic writings, she offered a thumbnail sketch of Hitler's psychological make-up. She then urged Mrs. Roosevelt to tell her husband that he could "divert [Hitler] from an undesirable course towards a desirable one" by putting the Führer's acts "into a moral setting" and redirecting his desire for glory to an effort to build world peace (Yans-McLaughlin 1986, 194–95). A week later, Hitler invaded Poland.

Outside of Columbia and the Boasian outposts, American anthropology was taking other courses in the 1930s. The Washington/Cambridge axis continued on its separate way. Physical anthropology remained dominated by typological approaches. An alternative emerged in the form of human biology, but it was only with the new synthetic evolutionary theory in biology of the early 1940s that a more dynamic physical anthropology came to the fore. In archaeology, the new stratigraphy of the Southwest and the Folsom discovery laid to rest the long-standing skepticism about the antiquity of humans in the Americas, and the descriptive emphasis gave way to more problem-oriented work.

The University of Chicago was always a world unto itself, and it was now the seat of a major new influence on American anthropology, namely the sojourn there by Radcliffe-Brown from 1931 to 1937. Radcliffe-Brown's impact, combined with a unique Chicago tradition of urban sociology, created a permanent base for a particular brand of anthropology, strongly social structural in theory and oriented to the social sciences. (Later, this emphasis would lead to the near eviction of archaeology, primate studies, and physical anthropology from the department.) Fred Eggan and Sol Tax tried to bring the Radcliffe-Brownian and Boasian traditions together in their American Indian research, but with only mixed success. Radcliffe-Brown's stay, and Malinowski's parallel visit to Yale soon thereafter, injected British social anthropology into the American discipline, with lasting effects. Among other things, it gave *ethnology* a certain archaic ring; the term *cultural anthropology*, which underlined both the centrality of the culture concept and the distinctiveness of the American tradition, was increasingly preferred.

Other forces were brewing in the 1930s whose impact would be felt after the war. Two Boasian renegades were cultivating new agendas: Julian Steward (a student of Kroeber and Lowie who was influenced also by V. Gordon Childe, then in residence at Berkeley) was working on the archaeology and ethnology of the Great Basin and exploring environmental and ecological relationships. Leslie White (a Boasian by way of Goldenweiser, Sapir, and Cole) was doing Pueblo ethnology but beginning to work toward a theory of the evolution of culture, invoking that bête noire of the Boasians, Morgan. Both would be heard from before long.

World War II

After Pearl Harbor American anthropologists, like most Americans, were eager to join the war effort. Their problem was the fact that no one in government paid much attention to them, and they had to prove their usefulness. Many then and future anthropologists were in the military, which led them into a host of new areas of the world. In many cases they would return to those areas after the war to do research. Scores of anthropologists were recruited to do social analysis at the ten Japanese detention camps. A number of anthropologists were based in the offices of Strategic Services or War Information doing intelligence work, while others taught language and area courses for the military, contributing their knowledge of exotic places that were now suddenly strategic. Later these experiences would help build the burgeoning area-studies programs in the universities, as well as anthropological databases like the Human Relations Area Files at Yale, which began as a compilation of anthropological data on the Pacific for use by the military.

The most specifically anthropological engagement with the war effort was the enlisting of cultural analysis for potential use in psychological warfare. Mead and Benedict were in the forefront of a group of anthropologists who used their skills to provide cultural depictions of America's enemies and allies. In a series of studies of "national character," they applied approaches from the culture-and-personality movement of the 1930s and developed methods for analyzing inaccessible cultures—what they called the study of cultures at a distance (see Mead and Métraux 1953). They had their greatest impact with their advice on how the allies should deal with the Japanese emperor at the end of the war. The war solidified American anthropologists' engagement in policy arenas and with government agencies; this marked, among other things, the beginnings of applied anthropology.

The end of the war was a watershed for American anthropology. A new generation came into the discipline, including many hard-bitten veterans whose studies were financed by the GI Bill of Rights. There was a demographic explosion in the field and an opening up of jobs—not many at first, but certainly more than during the Depression years. This growth was matched by an expansion of interests, approaches, and theories. In 1946 the AAA was reorganized, having come to a compromise to resolve the long-standing contention over whether it should be a society of professionals or should be more inclusive. Two classes of membership were instituted: there would be fellows, who had voting rights and could hold office, and nonvoting members. After much debate, it was also agreed that it would remain an association of the four fields; although increasing specialization was already challenging disciplinary integration, the winning argument was that a larger, united body of anthropologists would be a stronger force in dealing with funding sources and policy makers. In this reorganization, the largest of the fields was now called cultural anthropology, an affirmation of the shift away from ethnology that had been taking place over the years. Anthropology was ready for a new era.

2

Postwar Expansion, Materialisms, and Mentalisms

Anthropologists returned to their work after the interruption of the war, and new students—among them the many veterans supported by the GI Bill— filled the classrooms. American anthropology was at the beginning of an expansion in numbers, institutions, and intellectual currents that would continue without pause for the next quarter-century. The year 1946 was a turning point for two major institutions: at Columbia it marked the arrival of Julian Steward, who ushered in a vibrant development of materialisms; and at Harvard the sociologist Talcott Parsons established the interdisciplinary Department of Social Relations, which would be the cradle of new mentalist approaches in cultural anthropology.

As the Iron Curtain descended over Eastern Europe, the Cold War replaced the hot one just ended. The Office of Strategic Services, through which so many anthropologists had joined the war effort with cultural analyses of national groups, became the Central Intelligence Agency. Responses to the Cold War affected American anthropology in two ways: on the one hand, McCarthyism cast a pall of nervousness and suspicion over academic life, and in a few instances, led to harassment and expulsion from jobs; on the other hand, as the government embarked on projects to "develop" the Third World and make it safe for capitalism, it turned to social scientists and provided them with funds for research and institution building.

Neo-Evolutionism and the New Materialisms

In anthropology, the Boasian paradigm was challenged from within by Leslie White and Julian Steward. Both had started their professional lives as uncontroversial historical particularists—White's PhD dissertation was on "Medicine Societies of the Southwest," based on fieldwork at Acoma Pueblo, and Steward's was a distributional study with psychological overtones on "The Ceremonial Buffoon of the American Indian." Both went on to challenge the Boasian stricture, shared by most American anthropologists at the time, against overly hasty generalization and especially against evolutionary schemes. They did so in quite different ways, but their combined impact was to bring into anthropology a new interest in explanatory models of culture and cultural development, models that gave priority to material conditions.

White continued his Pueblo ethnology throughout the 1930s, but he also began to publish a series of statements leading to a theory of the evolution of culture and redefining anthropology as a science of culture, which he called culturology. The reaction in the field may be gauged by White's recollection of a meeting of the American Anthropological Association (AAA) in 1939 at which he defended Lewis Henry Morgan against his mistreatment by the Boasians: "I presented a paper . . . in which I spoke out in a forthright manner in support of evolutionist theory in ethnology. When I finished, Ralph Linton, the chairman of the session, remarked that I ought to be given the courtesy extended to horse thieves and shady gamblers in the days of the Wild West, namely, to allow them to get out of town before sundown" (Carneiro 1981, 229).

In a key paper of 1943, White defined the motive force of cultural evolution—energy—and proposed what came to be known as "White's Law": culture evolves as the amount of energy harnessed per capita per year increases. His fully developed theory laid out a model of unilineal evolution based upon the capacity of technologies to capture energy; oddly, however, he excluded environment as a cause (1949). White was a strong proponent of cultural determinism, and he defined culture as phenomena—including objects, acts, ideas, attitudes—that were dependent upon the use of symbols (1959). (Marshall Sahlins would later claim that this was the basis of his own midlife turn to idealism.) Some materialists would find White's definition perverse, given his layer-cake model of cultural causality: in White's model technology, at the base, determined the complexity of social organization, which was the middle layer; ideas and values, the top layer, were epiphenomena of the other levels.

White spent virtually his entire career, from 1930 to 1970, at the University of Michigan, where he taught several generations of students and built up the department to become one of the strongest in the country. He was always getting into trouble at Michigan for his outspoken opinions, including his admiration of Russian socialism (he had visited Russia in 1929) and his scathing views on organized religion. The Catholic diocese even assigned nuns to sit in his classes and take verbatim notes on what he said. White was an inspirational figure for a number of anthropologists, including archaeologists, who came of age in the postwar period, not all of them officially his students. Among this group were Sahlins, Albert Spaulding, Elman Service, Robert Carneiro, Napoleon Chagnon, Lewis Binford (founder of the "new archaeology"), and many others. None, however, pursued White's brand of evolutionism; rather, they merged it with other theoretical strands, particularly ecology.

Steward's career followed a different course. Beginning as an archaeologist in Utah, he carried out ethnological research among the Shoshone of the Great Basin from 1933 to 1935, then joined the Bureau of American Ethnology, where he organized work on the seven-volume *Handbook of South American Indians*. In 1946 he moved to Columbia, succeeding Linton. He remained there for only six years and spent his last years at the University of Illinois.

Steward began writing about environment-culture relationships in his ethnography of the Shoshone (1938), in which he confronted the extreme constraints that environment placed upon their subsistence and social organization. Perhaps reacting against the reluctance of Alfred Kroeber, his teacher, to accord any causal role to environment, he drew a distinction between "core" and "secondary" elements of culture, giving causal priority to the core, which he saw as shaped by environment. He coined the term *cultural ecology* to describe the nexus of resources, technology, and labor: in this nexus available technologies, applied to environmental resources, imposed constraints upon the organization of work, which in turn had a causal influence on other social institutions (1955, 30–42).

Drawing on that theory, Steward also devised an evolutionism of his own. He first developed the idea while working on the *Handbook*. He defined four culture areas of South America but called them culture types, combining criteria of ecological adaptation with an order of complexity to produce an implicitly evolutionary scheme of bands, tribes, chiefdoms, and civilizations (1955, 78–97). Then, under the influence of Karl Wittfogel and V. Gordon Childe, as well as recent archaeology that was uncovering sequences from early settlement to state society in several parts of the world (such as the Viru Valley project in Peru), he drew up a comparison of stages of development in six areas of autochthonous civilization (1949). This comparison showed a key association between irrigation agriculture and the emergence of centralized political power. He labeled this parallel development "multilineal evolution." The opposition between White's unilineal evolution and Steward's multilineal version would trouble those in the next generation who admired both figures. Sahlins attempted to reconcile them by proposing a distinction be-

278 / THE UNITED STATES

tween general evolution—White's—and specific evolution, a rephrasing of Steward (Sahlins 1960).

Steward's relatively short stay at Columbia was momentous. With Linton gone, Ruth Benedict frail (she died in 1948), and Margaret Mead marginalized in the department, the culture-and-personality emphasis was weakening. (When I entered graduate school there a few years later, in 1957, I professed an interest in culture-and-personality. I was told never to say so out loud because that approach had been definitively defeated by the new materialism.) Several descendants of the later Boasians were finishing their PhDs at the time. Under the influence of Alexander Lesser and of the archaeologist William Duncan Strong, who ran an important seminar on "Time Perspective and the Plains," a number of these individuals brought ethnohistory, economy, and class into their analyses of American Indian cultures. Among them were Helen Codere, who showed the relationship between the Kwakiutl potlatch and warfare (1950); Frank Secoy, who wrote on changing military patterns on the Great Plains (1953); and Eleanor Leacock, who argued that property concepts among the Montagnais-Naskapi were consequences of the fur trade (1952).

Steward's materialism and his promise of an anthropology that sought explanation were attractive to the new student cohort—predominantly male, mostly veterans, somewhat older than other graduate students, with leftist political inclinations of one sort or another. Some members of this cohort organized themselves into a discussion group, calling themselves (only partly ironically) the Mundial Upheaval Society (MUS). They taught each other anthropology, read each others' papers, and injected their discussions with their political views and aspirations. The eldest was Elman Service, who had fought in the Spanish Civil War; he went on to work in Paraguay but is better known for his evolutionary model of band, tribe, and state (1962). Stanley Diamond presented to the MUS his work on the Dahomey protostate; he went on from there to launch a continuing critique of Western civilization from the perspective of primitive societies (1974). Morton Fried, a China specialist, became a major theorist of the evolution of political systems; among other things he revised the notion of tribe from its treatment as an ethnological category or an evolutionary stage and showed it to be, instead, a secondary product of state expansion (1975). John Murra, later the key figure in Andean studies, moved in this orbit although he was registered at Chicago. Others in the group were Daniel McCall, Robert Manners, and Rufus Mathewson. Sidney Mintz and Eric Wolf were founding members. Several of these students joined Steward in his ambitious islandwide study of Puerto Rico in 1948. That project proved to be the forcing ground of another wave of materialism.

Slightly younger than the men of the MUS were three other figures who would soon be heard from. Robert Murphy did fieldwork among the Munducurú Indians of Brazil and later the Tuareg of North Africa, and he carved out a theoretical synthesis of cultural ecology, Freudianism, and structuralism (1971). After teaching at Berkeley for a few years, he returned to Columbia in 1963 and became a leader of the department. Sahlins, a student of Fried's, combined the materialisms of Steward and White in his dissertation on stratification in Polynesia 1958), in his book on his fieldwork in Fiji (1962), in his famous contrast of Melanesian "big men" and Polynesian "chiefs" (1968), and in important theoretical works on economic anthropology and tribal society. In 1957 Sahlins joined the Michigan department, to which White had already brought Service; Wolf would move there in 1961, followed by Roy Rappaport, solidifying what was known as the Columbia/Michigan axis. Things changed for Sahlins after a 1967–1969 sojourn in Paris, where he became a structuralist. After his return to Michigan, he found his department moving in the direction of an ecology that was alien to him because it downplayed culture, and the alienation was intensified by the departure of Wolf for the City University of New York in 1971. Soon afterward, Sahlins moved to Chicago.

The third of the younger Columbia group was Marvin Harris. A student of Charles Wagley who was himself a student of Linton and the Boasian Ruth Bunzel, Harris started out by doing a conventional community study in Brazil. In the mid-1950s he spent a year in Mozambique, which politicized him, and when he returned he transformed himself into anthropology's ultramaterialist. He embarked upon a series of ambitious projects to reshape the discipline from the perspective of a techno-eco-demo-determinism.

Among Harris's key efforts was development of the concepts of "etics" and "emics": drawing on the work of linguist Kenneth Pike, he distinguished between cultural phenomena that were objectively observable and those that had to do with meanings and subjectivities. His intention in doing this was to exclude the latter, but the concepts were taken at face value by others, and they endured in many subsequent definitions of culture. Harris developed an extreme behaviorist approach to culture, including an argument that ethnography could be done entirely through the specification of human movements and their physical effects upon objects (1964). Also notable were his forays into sacred cows, pig-eating taboos, cannibalism, and other "riddles" of culture, all of which he solved with straightforward materialist explanations

(1974, 1977). He was a vigorous defender of positivism and constantly railed against "obscurantists"—mentalists of every stripe. Harris was a leader in the 1968 campus uprisings at Columbia; after that difficult year, life in the department became increasingly contentious, with Harris himself usually at the center of the contention. Eventually he moved to the University of Florida, where he remained an active and unrepentant cultural materialist.

Although only White and Harris aimed for totalizing evolutionary theories, the neo-evolutionist challenge to relativism had many repercussions. One manifestation, which came to the fore in the 1950s and 1960s, was the formalist/substantivist debate within economic anthropology. The economic historian Karl Polanyi, who participated in a key seminar at Columbia with anthropologist Conrad Arensberg, economist Harry Pearson, and others (see Polanyi, Arensberg, and Pearson 1957), was the inspiration for a substantivist view of economic systems. Its dispute was with the "formalists" (among them Bronislaw Malinowski, Raymond Firth, and Melville Herskovits), who believed that the principles of formal economics—beginning with the assumption that individuals engaged in rational maximization—applied universally, including (with appropriate modification) to primitive societies. The substantivists argued that formal economics reflected and was valid only for capitalist economies; in studying other systems, therefore, it was necessary to look not for universal economic behavior (capitalism writ small) but for how the economy was embedded in social institutions. They distinguished three types of exchange systems: reciprocity, which governs kin-based societies; redistribution, characteristic of chiefdoms and archaic states; and market economies. Sahlins, Fried, George Dalton, and others expanded on this typology, often invoking Marcel Mauss. The formalists, for their part, saw these efforts merely as old-fashioned evolutionism. Ultimately, the debate ended in a truce as later scholars rejected the polarization between formalism and substantivism. However, the debate had rested upon divergent theoretical stances—individual-centered models as against structural ones—and those differences were to recur in many other contexts.

A parallel to the formalist/substantivist debate was played out in discussions of political systems and law. On one side were those who claimed that there were universal principles of law and politics that could be applied to all societies; modes of social sanction among the Inuit, for example, could be treated as incipient law. On the other side were the political substantivists, such as Fried (1967), who insisted that there was a qualitative difference between such societies and those in which sanctions were backed by institutionalized force; for them, state and nonstate societies were incommensurate, given their definition of the state as an entity based upon a monopoly on force. These positions were elaborated on and argued at length. Those of us at Columbia who were committed to substantivist economics and politics, as well as to the cultural determinism of Kroeber's concept of the superorganic and White's culturology (all liberally laced with cultural ecology), saw ourselves as leading the charge against relativism, individualism, and other unenlightened postures.

Still another variety of materialism had its roots at Columbia. Steward's cultural ecology spawned the ecological approach developed by Andrew Peter Vayda, who in the 1960s set his students to work in Papua New Guinea, the new sexy ethnographic area. The star of this group was Rappaport, who proposed a classic demonstration of the cultural-ecological model, inspired in part by the cybernetics of Gregory Bateson. In his *Pigs for the Ancestors* (1967), Rappaport described a complex ritual cycle among the Tsembaga Maring, which, he argued, had the effect of regulating the pig population: when that population expanded beyond sustainable levels, social tensions and warfare were induced, triggering the rituals that entailed mass slaughter of pigs. In later years Rappaport—in parallel with the transformation of his Michigan colleague Sahlins—became increasingly interested in joining his ecology to notions of belief and sanctity.

Meanwhile, cultural ecology, which Steward had seen as a method for understanding the causal processes in culture, morphed into human ecology, whose central problem was humanity's relation to nature. If the strategic units for Steward had been cultures, now the units were human populations, viewed as integral parts of ecosystems; culture was merely an aspect of the behavioral repertoire of their adaptation. Ecological analyses reinterpreted familiar anthropological topics such as the northwest coast potlatch and Aztec human sacrifice. One criticism of this work was that the emphasis upon systems sometimes took on a functionalist tone. Partly in response to this concern, many human ecologists, led by Vayda himself, shifted toward individual-centered, in some cases cognitivist frameworks. Still later developments, in the 1980s, would bring new varieties of ecology: political ecology, which seeks to marry ecology with political economy, and historical ecology, which aims to historicize ecological processes.

The Context of Postwar American Anthropology

From the 1950s to the mid-1970s there was a widening of opportunities for anthropologists to work in new world areas. The underdeveloped world was of strategic interest to the U.S. government, and money was becoming available for research there. The same impetus led to the creation of area studies centers on many campuses, where anthropologists rubbed shoulders with area specialists of diverse fields. The selection of areas on which to focus was skewed by political priorities, but much of the ethnography that came out of these efforts was of lasting value. Anthropologists contributed to the interdisciplinary mix the benefits of research on the ground and an approach that brought together the disparate domains of social life that other fields parceled out among themselves. In this period work on the so-called Third World generally used a framework of modernization theory. Some anthropologists shared this approach; others contested it.

In the late 1950s, world events conspired to give another boost to the expansion of anthropology and its sources of funding. The fall of 1957 was a turning point. At that time I was taking one of Mead's heavily enrolled evening courses at Columbia. One evening she asked the class: What was the most important thing that happened to you this week? Different people ventured responses: I found an apartment; I got a new job; I broke up with my boyfriend. After hearing all of us out, Mead said: No, the most important thing that happened to you this week was that Sputnik went up. For most of us there was a disconnect between what had happened to us and what was unarguably the most important thing that was happening in to the world. Not for Mead. Her view was not only that we were all profoundly affected and that we were now living in a changed world, but also that anthropology was uniquely equipped to understand that world. She thought that every space flight from then on should carry an anthropologist.

Although that did not happen, what Sputnik did do was to set off a science race between the United States and the Soviet Union. Government agencies were created to fund research and training, and anthropology got itself included in the definition of science. (For that we can thank our coexistence with biological anthropologists and archaeologists, just as the elders of the AAA had foreseen in 1946.) Students were now getting fellowships to go to graduate school, and they could count on funding for their fieldwork. Anthropology became better known and a more attractive field for graduate study than ever before.

A third phenomenon of this time was the fact that the baby boomers were getting close to college age, and there was an urgent need to make room for them in colleges and universities. Existing institutions grew, many new ones were established, and for once there were more jobs than available PhDs. The way in which this growth occurred illustrates the nature of academic life in the United States, which is different from academia in most other countries. On the eve of the expansion, there were fourteen departments awarding significant numbers of PhDs in the United States. Given the relatively small size of the discipline, this was a considerable number. Thus, there were multiple centers of anthropology, a wide range of places that could accommodate differences of theory and approach, and institutions to which people could move if they could not flourish where they were. In contrast to countries where one or a few centers are predominant, and in contrast also to academic systems where the senior professor holds the fate of all juniors in his hands, American anthropology has long had this more open, multicentric structure. Even during Boas's heyday his dominance was never absolute; his own students readily differed with him and could find bases from which to do so.

With the expansion of the 1960s, this pattern became much more pronounced, and by the mid-1970s there were seventy-five departments granting PhDs in anthropology. The prestige order was to some extent disrupted by this growth: in the rankings of departmental reputations, the major old departments were being challenged by new ones, many of them in public-sector universities, and several leading figures chose to leave the prestigious older institutions to carve out their projects in less established, up-and-coming departments. It is not only the large numbers of individuals who came into the discipline after the war that accounts for the great diversity within American anthropology, but also this structure of U.S. academia.

The years from the late 1950s to the mid-1970s were thus a golden age both for the flourishing of new interests and approaches within American anthropology and for anthropological careers. It did come to an end, bringing the difficulties of the academic job market that are still with us. Young PhDs sometimes think they are the first generation to suffer in this way; in fact, the only time when there *were* ample jobs was during this narrow, fifteen-year span.

The postwar period was also a vibrant time for relations among the subfields of anthropology. As I noted in connection with the work of Steward, archaeology was pursuing problems of cultural development and often drawing on the same theories that cultural anthropologists, especially the materialists, were using. In many quarters archaeology was essentially the historical component of a broad-based cultural anthropology that also included linguistic anthropology.

Physical anthropology was revolutionized in this period. Mainly under the leadership of Sherwood Washburn, the long-dominant typological focus gave way to "the new physical anthropology," which drew on the recent synthesis in evolutionary theory to bring together the study of population genetics;

primate behavior and morphology of both extant and fossil primates; and the supposedly unique human behavioral adaptation, culture (Washburn 1951). This development not only changed physical anthropology and brought it closer to all the other subfields; it also led to a spate of new hunter-forager studies, which were invoked in the conceptualization of early human society—as in the model of "Man the Hunter" (the title of a famous synthetic conference in the mid-1960s). In the process a major new specialty was created, field studies of nonhuman primates, today one of the most thriving areas of American anthropology.

The Turn to Mentalism

Something else happened in the 1950s that was to further affect the course of anthropology. The social-science orientation within anthropology was gaining strength, a result of the encouragement of this trend by funding sources since the 1930s, the postwar proliferation of area studies programs, and the increase in interdisciplinary relationships within institutions. In some institutions, interdisciplinary social science became detached from humanistic, biological, and museum-based anthropology.

One place where this happened was at Harvard, through the initiative of Talcott Parsons. Consistent with his theory of social action, Parsons foresaw a division of labor within the social sciences: sociology would study the social system; psychology would cover the individual and the personality system; and anthropology's domain would be the cultural system, defined as ideas and values. The senior anthropologist in Parsons's department, Clyde Kluckhohn, objected to this narrowing of anthropology's traditional range of study. Partly in response to this development, Kluckhohn joined forces with Kroeber to survey all the extant uses of the concept of culture, whose definition had been a matter of dispute since the beginning of American anthropology. Their compendium identified 164 definitions of culture. While they did not try to resolve the differences, they concluded that the most common usage by "social scientists" (they did not say *anthropologists*) was: "patterns . . . of and for behavior acquired and transmitted by symbols" (Kroeber and Kluckhohn 1952, 181). In effect, they conceded to Parsons.

For many, matters were settled in 1958. In a remarkable development, Kroeber and Parsons, the grand old men of their respective disciplines, issued a joint statement about how anthropology and sociology would divide up the social science landscape. (Some have suggested that the making of this pact was like the kings of Spain and Portugal sitting together in 1494 to divide up the New World.) The terms *society* and *social system,* sociology's terrain, would designate relational systems of interaction among individuals and collectivities. *Culture,* left to the anthropologists, would be restricted to "transmitted and created content and patterns of values, ideas, and other symbolic-meaningful systems" (Kroeber and Parsons 1958, 583).

With this definition of culture, Kroeber and Parsons were rejecting the inclusive view that was fundamental to many of the new materialisms and new evolutionisms, so it is not surprising that their agreement failed to receive universal endorsement. Nevertheless, it did profoundly affect the way scholars talked about culture in subsequent years, and Kroeber's and Parsons's definition gradually became the majority position.

This happened, of course, in conjunction with the emergence of new ideational approaches in American anthropology. As these came to the fore, the battleground of the discipline became that of materialists versus mentalists. Harris simplified the conflict as a matter of etics versus emics, but this summation does not serve us. The new mentalisms came in many different forms, and they had different precursors and different effects upon cultural anthropology.

The interest of the later Boasians (especially Edward Sapir and his circle) in mental states, their view of culture or cultural configurations as the personality of a group, and their extreme relativism laid the groundwork for the postwar cultural idealism independently of Parsons's influence. Moreover, linguistics was gaining currency and prestige, and some saw in language a model for culture. Ironically, it was in Sapir's old department at Yale, which had been taken over by George Peter Murdock and others with positivist approaches antipathetic to Sapir, that one of the first language-based movements emerged. A group of linguistic and cultural anthropologists at Yale or with links to it announced that anthropology's future lay in what they called ethnoscience. Language was the model, and formal methods analogous to those of structural linguistics would yield "cultural grammars." Among the key figures in this movement were Floyd Lounsbury, Ward Goodenough, Harold Conklin, and Charles Frake.

With the added refinement of componential analysis, ethnoscience set out to identify culturally specific classifications, or folk taxonomies, in such domains as color categories, kinship, the natural world, illness and disease, and, in principle, every other aspect of social and cultural life. The ethnoscientists spoke of achieving "adequate" ethnography, by which they meant a specification of all the rules used by natives in all domains, or everything one would need to know in order to behave in culturally appropriate ways. In saying this they set for themselves an impossibly high standard, and at the same time they became bogged down in minute classifications of very limited domains (such as the varieties of Tzeltal firewood). The movement soon gave way under its own weight. It was succeeded, however, by a broader cognitive anthropology, which has had a resurgence in recent years.

Another development in anthropological linguistics during the early 1960s looked at language as culturally informed social interaction. As sociolinguistics emerged, especially at Berkeley under the leadership of John Gumperz, it carved out a direction fundamentally different from that of the dominant, Chomskyan model in mainstream linguistics at the time, which construed language as the product of inborn structures of the brain and hence as universal. Sociolinguistics, in contrast, put language variation at the center and opened up new possibilities for a linkage between linguistics and cultural anthropology. A member of the Berkeley group, Dell Hymes, joined this approach to language with the ethnoscientists' search for a more sophisticated microethnography, coining the concept of the "ethnography of communication" (1974). Hymes subsequently took this project to the University of Pennsylvania, bringing together the social interactionist Erving Goffman (who had been with him at Berkeley), the urban folklorist John Szwed, and later the urban sociolinguist William Labov to form the Center for Urban Ethnography.

Although ethnoscience took language as its model, it was not concerned with meaning as such; its semantics consisted of formal relationships among elements within a classificatory system, much like phonemes in a phonemic system. Sociolinguistics, for its part, was concerned with communication in social interaction; meaning was constructed in discourse between the parties but was not itself a central interest. In the Parsons heartland, however, other brands of mentalism were developing that focused squarely upon meaning.

The major figures in this new symbolic anthropology were Clifford Geertz and David Schneider, both Harvard-trained and both having come of age in the theoretical eclecticism that reigned in the 1950s beyond the Columbia/ Michigan axis. Geertz, initially funded for research in Indonesia under one of the Cold War–era programs for the study of strategic "new nations," produced ethnographies of Indonesia and then Morocco that were in the theoretical tradition of Parsons, or more precisely, of Max Weber. However, he increasingly emphasized meaning in his analytic statements, representing the real world as the product of "models of" and "models for" the world in the minds of culture bearers. Schneider, a veteran of combat in the Pacific, had done a conventional study of kinship on the island of Yap, but a few years later he renounced this work, declaring that kinship is nothing more than cultural (that is, mental) models; eventually he denied that kinship exists at all. These new directions in the work of both Geertz and Schneider unfolded during the 1960s, and each of them went on to more elaborated versions after 1970, when they were joined by the converted Sahlins to make up a triumvirate of American symbolic anthropology.

Both Geertz and Schneider moved from Harvard to Berkeley and then, in 1960, to Chicago (along with another Berkeley colleague, Lloyd Fallers). Anthropology at Chicago had long had a sociological bent. Originally anthropology and sociology, including the urban sociology of the Chicago ecological school, formed a joint department, and even after the departments separated, the anthropologists, especially Robert Redfield, maintained close relations with the sociologists. A. R. Radcliffe-Brown's fateful stay at Chicago in the 1930s introduced a view of anthropology as comparative sociology, which was strengthened by the appointment of W. Lloyd Warner (at Radcliffe-Brown's urging). In the postwar years, Chicago also saw the founding of interdisciplinary social science programs in which anthropologists participated, including the Committee on Human Development and the Committee for the Comparative Study of New Nations, which was headed by the Parsonian sociologist Edward Shils.

When Geertz and Schneider arrived at Chicago, they proceeded to shape the anthropology department in the direction of Parsonian systems theory, and as they both moved toward more extreme culturalist positions they urged the department along in that direction. In the process, they undercut the other subfields of anthropology as well as the social-structural tradition of the department, making it a bastion of cultural anthropology of the symbolic variety. It was therefore a congenial home for Sahlins when he came there in 1973. Geertz meanwhile had left, in 1970, for the Institute for Advanced Study at Princeton, a prestigious think tank, where he did no teaching. Schneider stayed at Chicago and wielded a heavy influence over the next generation of students there until about 1985, when he moved to the University of California at Santa Cruz.

Let us take a closer look at these two figures in the early phases of their careers. Geertz entered graduate school in 1949 in Harvard's Department of Social Relations, along with his wife Hildred Geertz. Like his age-mates at Columbia, he was a veteran with a stipend from the GI Bill. The Geertzes both did their initial fieldwork in Java, which they followed with work in Bali, as part of an interdisciplinary project on emerging nations. This research led to Clifford Geertz's monographs on varieties of religion in Java and on the role of religion in social change (1960); on the contrasting roles of Javanese merchants and Balinese aristocrats in modernization (1963b); and on types of agriculture and agricultural cycles, for which he coined the term "agricultural involution," extending Alexander Goldenweiser's concept of involution (1963a). He also collaborated with Hildred Geertz in her research on Balinese kinship (Geertz and Geertz 1975). After they left Indonesia, the Geertzes worked in Morocco along with a number of graduate students, and Clifford then wrote a comparative study of Islam in the two areas of his field experience (1968).

While none of this sounds like a revolutionary new departure, throughout the 1960s Geertz was also writing essays that were laying out his emerging theory of culture as meaning—as constructions that resided in people's minds but were embodied in public symbols and constituted "local knowledge" (1973). His anthropology, he said, was an interpretive one in search of meaning; it was not a science in search of explanation. Increasingly hostile to positivist social science, Geertz turned to hermeneutics and specifically to literary criticism. Culture for him was a text that the ethnographer read over the shoulders of the native. He labeled his method "thick description," through which he would "explicate explications," and he illustrated it with ethnographic examples such as the Balinese cockfight.

All of this pointed to a highly particularistic, relativistic, and aesthetic program for anthropology, one that had much in common with earlier scholars' interest in ethos and was reminiscent of Benedict's notion of the patterning of distinctive, coherent cultural systems. Some critics called it a way of discovering more and more about less and less. Others observed that in ruling out of his analyses real events in the real world, Geertz dealt with the political upheavals and massacres in Indonesia in the 1960s in terms of "structures of meaning."

Schneider's biography and theoretical twists were quite different. He began graduate work before World War II in the School of Human Relations at Yale, an interdisciplinary program like its counterparts at Harvard and Chicago but dominated by behaviorism. Anthropology there was led by Murdock, who created the Human Relations Area Files and introduced a method of cross-cultural comparison that draws ethnographic bits and pieces from the Files and subjects them to elaborate statistical manipulation in a search for cross-cultural regularities. Using this method, Murdock produced a compendium of laws of kinship systems (1949). (The method has come in for heavy criticism over the years, although it still survives in some quarters.) Schneider and Murdock found each other mutually uncongenial.

After the war Schneider returned to graduate school, this time under Parsons and Kluckhohn at Harvard. When he was ready to do his fieldwork, he found his opportunity, ironically, in a cultural survey project that Murdock was organizing for the navy on strategic areas of the Pacific. Micronesia, where he was sent, was the focus at the time of a policy debate over the fate of these occupied islands, which ended in their annexation as trust territories. Schneider's dissertation on kinship in Yap basically followed Murdock, although he injected some criticisms of the senior scholar.

During the 1960s Schneider embarked on a study of kinship in Chicago, which was intended to be part of a comparative project with Firth in London. The experience turned Schneider around theoretically. It was in *American Kinship: A Cultural Account* (1968) that he proposed his idea of kinship as something neither more nor less than a system of symbols, constructs in people's minds, and independent of behavior. He contended that kinship symbols were of two kinds: notions of relationships based upon shared natural substance (such as blood), and codes for conduct. For Schneider anthropology's whole enterprise of treating kinship as a genealogical grid laid over the assumed facts of biology was misguided; instead, it was the "core symbols" that defined what kinship was for a given culture. The symbols he identified for American kinship were, curiously enough, sexual intercourse and love; love came in two varieties, conjugal and cognatic. Schneider's separation of kinship from genealogy and biological relationships and his later denial of kinship had profound effects on American anthropology. And for Schneider what was true of kinship applied to all of culture: behavior and things were cultural constructs and had no objective reality. The purpose of anthropology was to extract the internal logic of systems of symbols.

The development of symbolic anthropology in the United States was shaped also by voices from abroad. Claude Lévi-Strauss's works were talked about as soon as they were published; in the 1960s, translations made them accessible to those who had known them only secondhand. From Britain came the ideas of Victor Turner, Mary Douglas, and Edmund Leach; Turner moved to the United States in the early 1960s, and Douglas was a frequent visitor. These influences brought interests in the mind that did not depend upon the culture concept, and they enriched the stew of mentalisms.

The Vietnam Era

As members of the materialist and mentalist camps battled it out with each other, and among themselves, during the 1960s, American anthropologists were increasingly drawn into the political ferments on their campuses and in public life. Many participated in the civil rights movement, but it was dissension over the Vietnam War and the U.S. government's involvement in counterinsurgency that penetrated into the heart of the universities. Anthropologists were conspicuous in the intensifying antiwar activism. For example, at the University of Michigan Wolf and Sahlins were instrumental in the March 1965 invention of the "teach-in," a phenomenon that spread rapidly across the country. Antiwar protests ignited wider student demands for reforms in the universities, from the free-speech movement at Berkeley to the occupation of administration buildings on many campuses. Faculties were split over whether to support or discipline the students, and the ruptures in some departments would take years to heal.

Within the anthropological profession, crises erupted when it was discovered that social scientists, including anthropologists, were being recruited for counterinsurgency work. The first one hit with Project Camelot, a U.S. Army mission to "assist friendly governments in dealing with active insurgency problems," specifically in Latin America. Protests from academics scuttled the project, but the AAA was moved to pay attention to issues of ethics in research. Though the profession was divided on the war and on the propriety of assisting government efforts in strategic underdeveloped countries, the association was able to agree on some ethical guidelines, and it appointed an ethics committee to explore how they could be implemented.

Matters came to a head in 1970 when members of the ethics committee were presented with evidence that a number of anthropologists might be implicated in counterinsurgency research in Thailand. Eric Wolf, as chair of the committee, invited the individuals named to respond. When the charges were made public (by a student group, not by the committee), the association exploded in controversy. Margaret Mead, the most prominent senior member of the discipline, was appointed to head a special committee to investigate the charges, as well as countercharges that the ethics committee had acted improperly by questioning colleagues. The Mead committee's report in essence chastised the ethics committee while vindicating those originally charged. At the next meeting of the association, the membership roundly rejected Mead's report, in a humiliating repudiation of this epic figure. (See Wakin 1992 for a detailed account of this episode.)

These events created divisions within the profession that to some extent corresponded to theoretical differences, and they had a lasting effect: on the one hand, they raised the level of contentiousness in the expression of disagreements; on the other, they led to a certain skittishness in taking on work with political implications. It has been suggested that they sparked a retreat into trivia, a reference to the revival of relativism and particularism in the 1970s. More generally, the political and cultural upheavals of the 1960s ushered in a series of new developments that in various ways challenged the very premises of anthropology and prompted efforts to "reinvent" the discipline.

3

Bringing Anthropology into the Modern World

A particular concern of American anthropology has been the study of complex societies. Because this interest goes back to the interwar years, I interrupt my chronology here to trace its development and follow it up to the early 1970s. The term *complex societies* has long been used in anthropology to refer to state-organized systems, including those of premodern times (civilizations of the Old and New World), those of the modern industrialized era, and those whose states stem from postcolonial or other recent political transformations. In this context state and nation are distinct concepts: states are institutional apparatuses and are as old as ancient Mesopotamian; *nation* refers to the construction of peoplehood, usually around a political entity, a phenomenon stemming essentially from nineteenth-century Europe.

Because American anthropology began with and for a long time remained concentrated on the American Indians, our venturing out onto new ethnographic terrain marked a definitive transition. In the study of primitive peoples, it was Margaret Mead's trip to Samoa that opened up this expansion. But at about the same time, in the mid-1920s, some anthropologists turned to a different arena: the rural and small-town folk of modern nations. That this occurred so early was due, I believe, to the close association of one segment of anthropology in the United States with sociology, even as the mainstream of American ethnology was still pursuing the program of historical particularism.

Early Community Studies

A convenient beginning point for this story is Robert Redfield's fieldwork in the Mexican village of Tepoztlán in 1926. His study was the most influential early effort to apply to a modern nation the methods and concepts developed in anthropological research on primitive societies. Redfield was a product of the joint sociology and anthropology department at the University of Chicago, which was the seat of the urban ecology school of sociology spearheaded by Robert Park, Redfield's father-in-law. The approach of this school was to look at cities as zones of residence and urban activity laid out in more or less concentric circles, in which the distribution of social groups in space was a corollary of their differential positioning in social relations.

Redfield applied this model to Tepoztlán, seeing it as the outermost zone in a circle around Mexico City. The center of the village was the locus of its political and cultural elite, who had links to the city, while the outlying areas of the village were the domain of the rustic folk. This scheme gave primary place to communication, that is, the flow of cultural messages between zones and between social sectors, but little attention to the grounding of social interaction in material circumstances, in institutional contexts, or in history. To characterize Tepoztlán, Redfield adopted a version of the typological contrast between urban and rural society that has a long pedigree in sociology. Tepoztlán was his prototypical folk society (1930).

Two years before Redfield's fieldwork, the sociologists Robert and Helen Lynd had undertaken a study in much the same vein in Muncie, Indiana, which they called Middletown (1929). From these beginnings a tradition of community studies emerged and was carried forward by anthropologists of sociological bent and by sociologists who, reacting against the armchair theory and macromethods of their discipline, took up fieldwork with anthropological methods. Small communities in the United States and in countries around the world were treated in similar ways, with the underlying assumption that such communities could be seen as microcosms of the larger societies of which they were part.

The impetus for work in the United States came from a number of sources. In the 1920s some American foundations were beginning to address problems of race relations. Franz Boas's student Melville Herskovits was funded to study "race crossing" and other aspects of the lives of blacks in the United States (1928). To aid him, Herskovits recruited Zora Neale Hurston, who went on to do important work on black folklore in Harlem and the South with Boas's encouragement. Several anthropologists were supported to do research in communities in the Deep South. One of them, Hortense Powdermaker, an American who studied under Bronislaw Malinowski in London and then won the sponsorship of Edward Sapir while he was at Yale, had no sooner returned from fieldwork in Melanesia than she set out in 1932 for Indianola, Mississippi, where she produced a novel account of both black and white sectors of the society (1939). John Dollard, Alison Davis, and others followed with their own studies of communities in the Deep South (Dollard 1937; Davis, Gardner, and Gardner 1941). Some of this literature was later cited in arguments in *Brown v. Board of Education,* the landmark Supreme Court case that ended legal public school segregation.

Depression-era programs under the U.S. Bureau of Agricultural Economics underwrote a number of anthropologists' studies of rural communities for the purpose of informing government agencies about conditions in American agriculture. Most of the reports remained unpublished, but a few, such as Carl Withers's study of "Plainville," in the Midwest (1945), became part of the emerging community-study literature. Of special note was Walter Goldschmidt's research on agribusiness in the Central Valley of California (1947), which was surely the first anthropological analysis of rural society to focus on the impact of industrial agricultural production. The study was used by New Dealers to repel an effort by corporate landholders to rewrite law to their own benefit; in the process, Goldschmidt became the target of political attacks.

An important series of community studies was launched at Harvard by W. Lloyd Warner, who had studied under Alfred Kroeber and Robert Lowie but became a protégé of A. R. Radcliffe-Brown. Having done his initial fieldwork among Australian aborigines, soon after coming to Harvard in 1929 Warner embarked on a long-term project in Newburyport, Massachusetts, which he called Yankee City. The project, whose central theme was social class in the United States, resulted in multivolume publications (e.g., Warner and Lunt 1941, 1942) and spawned both offshoots and reactions. One of the offshoots was the work of Conrad Arensberg, who took the community-study approach to Ireland, producing the first published work of this kind in Europe (1937). Another participant in the project, William F. Whyte, carried out an innovative study of an Italian slum in New York City (1943). Both Arensberg and Whyte moved away from the Weberian approach and the Radcliffe-Brownian structuralism that had influenced the Yankee City project, and they ultimately developed an interactionist theory geared to the study of small groups. Members of the Yankee City group must also be credited for the beginnings of anthropological research on industrial organization. Warner joined up with the psychiatrist Elton Mayo, whom he knew at Harvard, to initiate what was perhaps the first anthropological study of industrial work, while Arensberg brought his interest in group behavior to organizational research, partly in collaboration with Eliot Chapple.

The early ethnographic studies of small American communities were not primitivist, as the community-study tradition has sometimes been characterized. Many of them were initiated in order to address problems of contemporary American life, and some had a real impact. For the most part, they did not carry assumptions of homogeneity, or a uniform culture, but were marked by interest in class and race and sometimes in the power structure and economic organization of the communities. This was less true, however, of the research on communities outside the United States at the time.

In 1929 Redfield returned to Mexico, this time to Yucatán, and working with a team of collaborators, he initiated studies of four communities. The four, he proposed, represented points along a "folk–urban continuum" corresponding to their location from southeast to northwest, from a settlement of "tribal" Indians in Quintana Roo to a peasant village (Chan Kom) to a town (Dzitas) to the city of Merida. In *The Folk Culture of Yucatan* (1941) Redfield expanded on the nature of that continuum in terms of several polarities: organization as opposed to disorganization of culture, sacrality as against secularization, and group relations versus individualized ones. His contrast between folk and urban society drew on the sociologist Louis Wirth's notion of "urbanism as a way of life" (1938). This model rested upon ideal types and on polar contrasts familiar to us from Henry Sumner Maine, Ferdinand Tönnies, Émile Durkheim, and others. The model survived long after World War II in the form of modernization theory. It would also provide fuel for a generation of young Turks, and paradoxically it proved to be extremely productive precisely in the reactions it engendered.

During the 1930s Redfield's department at Chicago, which was then also under the influence of Radcliffe-Brown, produced a number of community studies in different countries. Among these were Charlotte Gower Chapman's in Sicily (1935/1981), John Embree's in Japan (1939), and Horace Miner's in Quebec (1939). Anthropologists at other institutions carried out village studies in Peru (Gillin 1947), India (Wiser and Wiser 1930), and China (Fei Hsaio-Tung [1939], a student of Malinowski). In these years Latin America and Asia were the main focus of village studies, which tended to be descriptive and modest in their theoretical aspirations. Some of them did, however, pay attention to the villages' ties to elites and to the state, laying the basis for later definitions of peasants.

National Character

With World War II, a different approach to modern societies came to the fore. As noted above, Ruth Benedict and Margaret Mead, along with Geoffrey

Gorer, Robert Lowie, and other anthropologists, began to work out cultural depictions of national character drawing on the culture-and-personality theory of the 1930s. These analyses were designed to predict the behavior of particular groups, and they had explicit policy aims. As Mead put it, they were intended to aid in the implementation of various governmental programs, to facilitate relationships with allies and partisan groups in occupied countries, to provide estimates of enemy strengths and weaknesses, and to recommend and provide rationales for policies (Mead and Métraux 1953, 397).

The most significant of these studies was Benedict's on Japan, *The Chrysanthemum and the Sword* (1946). Asked in 1944 by the Office of War Information to provide an analysis of "what the Japanese were like" that could help predict how they would behave in the war and afterward, Benedict had applied the ideas she had presented in *Patterns of Culture* (1934) to the Japanese nation. Her assumptions were that each culture has a coherence, that certain dominant themes—a core of values and beliefs—are the expression of that coherence, and that the development of individual personality is constrained by those cultural givens. Her unit of analysis was the whole nation; her method drew evidence from within the culture, emphasizing uniformities to the neglect of internal diversity. This was a functionalist approach that was little concerned with historical development or change. Published at a time when the United States was still puzzling over its defeated enemy, the book was a great popular success. Benedict's analysis, which appeared in reports prior to publication of the book, was the most influential of the national character studies in terms of impact on policy: it was the basis for anthropologists' advice to the government on the likelihood that Japanese soldiers would surrender (they said the soldiers would surrender if the emperor did), and it contributed to the decision to retain the emperor as a figurehead after the war.

At war's end, Benedict and Mead expanded this effort into a large-scale project funded by a grant from the U.S. Office of Naval Research: the Columbia University Research in Contemporary Cultures. Several other nations were brought into the array of cultures studied "at a distance" from New York City. Mead continued the project after Benedict's death in 1948 (Mead and Métraux 1953), and her ambition for it was as grand as her sweep, but it found little resonance with policy makers and soon fell into obscurity.

The Puerto Rico Project

Julian Steward pursued another course in the study of complex societies during his stay at Columbia in the immediate postwar period. He had been involved in community studies earlier while employed at the Bureau of American Ethnology, where he organized fieldwork projects in Mexico and Peru. Villages, not "tribal" Indians, were the focus of research because the goal was to sample the "basic population" of those countries. The most important of these projects was the intensive study of a particular region, the Tarascan area of Mexico, which included several villages with different characteristics. Steward would later criticize the premise of this project: the communities were supposed to represent "variant types of local culture," and each one was treated "as if it were a locally self-contained and integrated whole" (Steward 1950, 60–62).

Steward's Columbia years coincided with the development of area research, including area studies programs that were intended to yield knowledge of the emerging nations strategic to U.S. national interests. In that context, and with funding from the Rockefeller Foundation, Steward embarked on a major investigation of Puerto Rico, then the object of U.S. policy geared toward economic transformation of the island. In planning the project, he was reacting against several trends in the study of complex societies: acculturation studies, which saw a uniform tribal culture confronting a uniform national culture; the treatment of communities as if they were microcosms of a nation; and the national character approach, which took national cultures as undifferentiated wholes and analyzed them as "personalities."

Applying his notion of cultural ecology (which he always spoke of as a method, not a theory), Steward identified various regions of Puerto Rico that were ecologically distinctive and characterized by particular kinds of agricultural regimes. The labor and organizational requirements of each productive complex, he thought, would define certain social and cultural patterns. His theoretical scheme dissected the island in terms of different "vertical" (localized) subgroups, namely the ecologically diverse communities, and "horizontal" subgroups (occupational, class, ethnic, and other divisions) that cut across communities and regions; the whole was linked together by formal national institutions. This complexity, along with Steward's concept of "levels of sociocultural integration" (that is, family, multifamily, community, and nation) marked a major departure from the ideal types of Redfield, as well as from the holism of most other approaches to nations (see Steward 1955, 43–77).

The participants in the project worked in a range of localities with different ecological and productive bases: Eric Wolf in a coffee- and tobacco-growing community in the central highlands, an area of traditional haciendas and small farms; Sidney Mintz in a rural proletarian community in the corporate-owned sugar-producing area of the south coast; Elena Padilla on a government-owned sugar plantation; Robert Manners in a mountain community of small farmers raising subsistence crops and tobacco; and Raymond Scheele among the upper-class families of San Juan (it was rumored that Steward selected him for this assignment because he was the only one of the group who owned a tuxedo). A number of other individuals from the University of Chicago and the University of Puerto Rico were also involved in the project.

Steward, characteristically, lost interest in the enterprise before it was long underway, and it was left mainly to Mintz and Wolf to put together the monograph, which was finally published as *The People of Puerto Rico* (Steward et al. 1956). In the process they found themselves diverging more and more from Steward's views. Steward, they believed, had omitted the crucial role of the market and the implications of Puerto Rico's dependence on the U.S. state. They also felt that it was necessary to delve into history to trace these phenomena and their impact. Thus Mintz and Wolf adopted what they then called a cultural-historical approach, but increasingly their analyses moved them toward the kind of political economy that would come to mark the work of each of them. When they looked back at the Puerto Rico book years later, they thought they had not gone far enough in their departures from Steward; they had not put enough emphasis on the role of the state, Puerto Rico's colonial relationship with the United States, and the growing migratory stream from the island to the mainland (see Wolf 2001, 38–48).

After Puerto Rico, much of Mintz's research focused on workers of different types and their relations to peasants, markets, and the circulation of commodities—interests that were shaped by the proletarian character of his subject community. He went on to do fieldwork in Haiti and Jamaica and then to define differences and commonalities among the islands of the Caribbean as these developed within the history of slavery and sugar production (1974). Wolf's subsequent work took him to Mexico, where in the early 1950s he began to explore processes of nation formation and to carve out an approach to peasantry that differed sharply from Redfield's (see Wolf 2001). Later he went to the South Tyrol in Italy, examining two adjacent villages that were similar in their ecological adaptation but different in their languages and historical trajectories; his problem there was how to account for the development of divergent ethnicities in a context of common ecological imperatives (Cole and Wolf 1974).

Peasants, Folk, and Communities

In the 1950s studies of peasants and small communities around the globe proliferated. At first the theoretical framework most readily at hand was Redfield's folk society and folk-urban continuum, and it dominated the literature through the critiques it generated. Oscar Lewis had done a restudy of Tepoztlán, and his picture was very unlike that of the folk society: he saw the community as riven by conflict, marked by class differences, and much involved in divisive politics (1951). Others contended that many so-called folk were not folklike at all; Sol Tax, for instance, described the Highland Maya (close relatives of the Yucatecans) as pecuniary, secularized, and characterized by individual mobility and impersonality in relationships (1953). Still others chimed in with examples of cities that didn't conform to the urban type, such as those of West Africa. Gideon Sjoberg criticized the folk concept as inaccurately merging tribal societies with those he called feudal (1952). Horace Miner claimed that Redfield focused on form, not process, thus missing the effects of technological change on societal forms (1952). Sidney Mintz observed that the Yucatán project ignored the henequen plantations that were the underpinnings of the economy of the whole region (1953).

Redfield, as always the gentleman, accepted the criticisms with good grace and incorporated them into his synthetic books of the mid-1950s, *The Little Community* (1955) and *Peasant Society and Culture* (1956). This was the time when the "peasant" was established as an analytic category and a subject matter in its own right. Out of numerous debates over definitions of peasants, two approaches emerged. Redfield's focused on "way of life," values and worldview, community cohesion, and tradition. Wolf's began with the material base and with structural relationships—peasants were agricultural producers in effective control of land who aimed at subsistence, not reinvestment. After this beginning, Wolf's work on peasantries increasingly emphasized relations of power, not in contradiction to economic processes but as their counterpart.

Critiques of Redfield eventually ran their course, and research on peasants turned to wider theoretical issues in general anthropology. For example, the dominant model of social organization in the 1950s still took corporate kinship groups as the norm. George Foster, studying a Mexican peasant village, Tzintzuntzan in the Tarascan area, proposed the notion of the dyadic contract: dyadic relationships of different kinds (which he saw as structured, not as an absence of structure) offered alternative models (1961). He followed this effort with the proposal of another concept that found wide resonance (although to my mind it was a less helpful contribution): the "image of limited good," a zero-sum-game idea elevated to a moral imperative (1965).

Other theoretical interests came to the fore out of this work of the 1950s and early 1960s that impacted anthropological thinking well beyond the peasant field. In kinship study diverse forms of nonunilineal descent were revealed, new attention was paid to the multiple functions and flexibility of families, and the analysis of inheritance systems took on strategic significance. Types of labor and labor control, as well as market systems, became standard topics. Social stratification assumed a prominent place on the anthropological agenda, with attention to different kinds of stratification: class, status (prestige), caste, and other dimensions of ranking. The study of peasants led outward to interest in elite sectors of society, processes of nation formation, and societal transformations whereby peasants became proletarians or worker-peasants and rural people became urbanites.

In the 1950s anthropologists also began to develop typologies and taxonomies of peasants and communities. Charles Wagley and Marvin Harris produced one of the first, describing "subcultures" of Latin America (1955). Wolf offered a different approach to defining types of Latin American peasants, one based upon variability in ecological and economic relations; it was a typology of structure rather than of culture content (1955). He also proposed that two of his types—closed corporate peasantries and open cash-crop peasantries—were associated with characteristic community types. He saw the closed corporate community, which he identified in several areas of the world, not just as a cultural form but as a response to specific political-historical processes (1957).

In his later work on peasantry, Wolf emphasized the place of peasants within their larger matrices and the role of the state in guaranteeing claims to peasant "rent" and in maintaining asymmetrical power relations. In the mid-1960s he put together the various strands of his work in *Peasants* (1966). In the book he sought to specify the strategic relations that characterized peasants in general and that accounted for variability among them. He did so by means of a series of typologies: different ecotypes (modes of transferring energy from nature); kinds of marketing and exchange systems; types of "domains," that is, sociopolitical modalities whereby liens were exercised on peasant production; different kinds of funds to meet resource needs (including a subsistence and replacement fund, a ceremonial fund, and a fund of rent); types of domestic groups and their strategies; "coalitions," that is, social relationships that differed according to the number of people involved, the nature of the interests that tied them together, and their relative positions in the social order; and kinds of relations with the ideological order. He discussed each type in terms of its structural implications and, in many instances, its historical context. The book served to systematize the anthropology of peasantry as of the time of writing.

In a role parallel to that played by Wolf in peasant studies, Arensberg became the synthesizer of theory and method in community studies. He defended the validity of the community concept, treating the community as both an "object" and a "sample," that is, as itself the object of study and as a locus of observation of wider social phenomena (1961). However, he had clear criteria for identifying what a community was and for determining what it could and could not reveal about the larger society. For Arensberg, a community was marked by characteristic spatial arrangements, persistence in time, and specifiable complements of personnel, functions, and activities. His approach drew upon his interactionist theory, and his method specified ways of identifying patterns of interaction and their consequences in spatial arrangements, social relationships, and cultural forms (1954, 1972).

Arensberg was probably the key figure in opening up the study of modern Europe for anthropology, beginning with his own pioneering work in Ireland in the 1930s. He encouraged students to work in what was still an anthropologically suspect part of the world. Research on complex societies outside the United States had mostly gone forward in Latin America and Asia, and one need only read E. E. Evans-Pritchard's grudging foreword to Julian Pitt-Rivers's book on Andalusia (1954) to get a sense of mainstream ambivalence about anthropologists working in Europe in the 1950s.

Arensberg, moreover, provided a theoretical framework for this new field. He picked up the old notion of culture areas and turned it to his own ends (1963). For him, culture areas were complexes of ecology, subsistence regimes, settlement patterns, and social interaction distinctive to an area—the areas themselves being open-ended and fluid. For example, he demarcated an area of open-field villages: nucleated settlements whose residents retained corporate rights to the stripped fields and other resources that lay outside the village. What he saw in this was not just a settlement form but a nexus of patterns of resource use, family and household, kinship and marriage, inheritance and land tenure, status and authority, even folklore and religious practice. Like the folk-urban continuum and the closed corporate community, Arensberg's culture areas came under a barrage of criticism, but in the process an anthropology of Europe began to take shape.

By the 1960s, the assumption that the community could be a microcosm of the larger society had fallen by the wayside. Also giving way was the hope that one might comprehend the larger society by placing different kinds of communities side by side. (Still, as late as 1973 Anthony Leeds was moved to say that "even if we had exemplary studies, one each from every category of community in a total-society or macrocosm, we would still not have" a description of the macrocosm [1973, 18].) The central problem became how to grasp relationships among levels, groups, and institutions within the complex society. This problem was usually conceptualized as one of linkages, between local and national levels, for example. A number of researchers focused on mediators, or cultural brokers, who guarded "the crucial junctures . . . that connect the local system to the larger whole" (Wolf 1956) and who negotiated those junctures. There was special interest in patronage, or clientelism, as a mechanism for making such linkages. In another approach to this problem, some scholars were concerned with the symbolic modes whereby nations managed their internal heterogeneity. All these studies were looking "beyond the community" long before that became a slogan of criticism brandished by the next generation.

Modernization and Its Critique

The Cold War profoundly affected the social sciences in this period, as did the emergence of new nations after independence. Area studies programs expanded within universities, at research institutes and think tanks, and in foundation initiatives. Although dominated by political science, these programs created space for anthropologists to carry out local-level fieldwork, greatly enlarging the discipline's geographical reach into the areas of old civilizations. The same strategic interests that yielded research funding selected the areas to be given priority, with a resultant skewing toward favored areas.

This work was dominated by modernization theory. In a revival of unilineal evolutionism combined with the sociological tradition of polar types, modernization theory posed an opposition between traditional and modern societies and an expectation that the traditional would inevitably be transformed into the modern. The focus of research was on the conditions in different settings that aided or impeded that progress. This approach became common currency in public-policy discussions, where it was advanced by the more influential political scientists of the time.

Many anthropologists employed the modernization model during the 1950s and 1960s. It became central to Redfield's later work, which increasingly turned away from study of the folk in villages and toward that of civilizations. Under his guidance and in collaboration with the philosopher Milton Singer, a specialist on India, the University of Chicago became a center for the comparative study of civilizations: Chinese, Islamic, Indian, and others. Redfield's interest here, as it had been from the beginning, was in communication. His notion of the "social organization of tradition" exemplifies his approach. It conceived of civilizations as containing two cultural systems, a "great tradition of the reflective few," that is, the specialists, and a "little tradition of the largely unreflective many . . . in their village communities" (1956, 41–42). The concept envisioned a two-way flow of communication: a process of universalization whereby the little traditions were amplified to become elements of the great tradition, and a counter process of parochialization through which the little traditions adapted and refashioned patterns from the great tradition. As productive as this idea was for a while, Redfield's approach remained locked into typological polarities: the moral order and the technical order, the folk and the elite, tradition and modernity.

Steward too turned to an interest in civilizations in his later years, when he was at Illinois in the 1950s. He organized a comparative project on "contemporary change in traditional societies" that incorporated an ahistorical form of modernization theory (1967). By then his former students, some of whom joined him at Illinois for a time as research associates, had departed from him theoretically and had become his respectful critics.

These critics were among the many anthropologists for whom modernization theory was anathema. They saw it as distorting realities on the ground and as substituting an ideology of progress and modernity for a search for diverse processes of change. They were also concerned about its policy implications, especially in the way it viewed underdevelopment and development programs in the Third World. A good deal of anthropological work on complex societies at the time thus offered critiques of modernization approaches and proposed alternative analyses.

I offer an example from the debate over "amoral familism." In 1958 political scientist Edward C. Banfield published a community study of a southern Italian town, *The Moral Basis of a Backward Society.* He described the people as resistant to cooperation, averse to joining formal organizations, unwilling to engage in political activity for the common good, and in general self-serving and shortsighted. To explain why these southern Italians were unable to modify their behavior and enter the modern world, he proposed that they were hampered by an ethos that had as its rule: "Maximize the material, short-run advantage of the nuclear family; assume that all others will do likewise" (1958, 85). That the Montegranesi were "prisoners" of this ethos, Banfield said, was "a fundamental impediment to their economic and other progress" (1958, 163). Any efforts at reform would have to be aimed at the ethos.

Many anthropologists and others chimed in with objections, on the grounds of both descriptive deficiencies and analytic fallacies in Banfield's account. My own response was to acknowledge that, despite its distortions, amoral familism described some salient realities of southern Italian rural society; it was a reading in moral terms of features of social organization. The problem, as I saw it, was in Banfield's taking an ethos as a cause of or an explanation for behavior. My analysis looked rather at the agricultural system in the region, which I saw as the basis of the social patterns and, in turn, the values that Banfield summarized as amoral familism. The prescription for change, therefore, would be reform of the agrarian system and its associated conditions: the southern Italians were prisoners not of an ethos but of certain objective realities (Silverman 1968).

The political upheavals of the 1960s in the United States—especially the Vietnam War, which dominated national consciousness for a decade after 1964—had profound effects upon anthropology. These were not, however, immediately apparent, and they did not reach into all corners of the discipline. For scholars in peasant studies, the impact of war and revolution on the rural sectors of the societies involved and the increasing engagement of peasants themselves in political movements inevitably called attention to issues of peasant politics. One of the first full-scale studies of these issues was a direct outgrowth of the antiwar protests. Wolf wrote a briefing paper on Vietnam for a teach-in at the University of Michigan. This led him to a comparison of the role of peasants in revolutions in six countries—Mexico, Russia, China, Algeria, and Cuba, as well as Vietnam—which was published as *Peasant Wars of the Twentieth Century* (1969). Peasant protest and revolution became a focus for many other researchers; this interest was stimulated also by the growing prominence of Marxist approaches in the social sciences after 1970.

By the late 1960s anthropologists had become critical of the community-nation model, that is, the "articulation" approach to complex societies, and they were seeking ways to grasp social structures that transcended community boundaries. Some found an alternative in the analysis of regions. One version focused on regional elites whose networks or coalitions forged the integration of their region and whose positions within national and international matrices shaped economic and political change in the region. For example, Peter and Jane Schneider and Edward Hansen (1972) introduced a concept of different kinds of elites: dependence elites and development elites. Drawing a distinction between modernization and development, they showed how western Sicily had experienced modernization but not development; Catalonia, in contrast, had followed a course toward development that was cut short because of opposition from the Spanish state, resulting in, among other things, Catalan nationalism.

A different approach to regional analysis originated in the 1960s with the work of anthropologist G. William Skinner, who developed a model of regional settlement systems in traditional China, tracing out their corollaries in market patterns and social structure (1964–1965). Employing central-place theory from economic geography, he analyzed the distribution of settlements in a region—spatially, as a hierarchy of settlements of different kinds, and as an economic and social system. His student Carol Smith built on his approach in her study of a marketing system in Guatemala. In 1973 she organized an important conference that brought together a number of anthropologists engaged in regional analyses of economic and social systems in different areas of the world; the common denominator was their use of locational theory. The two volumes that resulted set forth a strategy for studying complex societies that was influential in both cultural anthropology and archaeology (C. A. Smith 1976).

While anthropologists were offering critiques of modernization theory from a variety of perspectives, a major alternative came from outside of anthropology, from the economist Andre Gunder Frank. His ideas had precursors in the earlier Marxist literature and in the writings of Gunnar Myrdal and some Latin American development economists, but it was mainly through Frank that dependency theory entered anthropology. With his notion of "the development of underdevelopment," Frank argued that there was not a linear sequence from underdevelopment to development; rather, these were opposite sides of the same coin, manifestations of internal contradictions of capitalism (Frank 1966, 1967). The spread of capitalism turned hinterlands into dependent satellites of metropolitan centers that, by exploiting the material and human resources of their satellites to propel their own development, created underdevelopment. With dependency theory's attention to asymmetrical relations between regions, anthropologists had a panoply of new concepts for thinking about how the areas of their ethnographic interest were constructed: among those concepts were metropolis/satellite relationships, enclaves, internal colonialism, and uneven development.

Looking at dependency in terms of processes that engaged disparate and widely separated regions moved anthropologists toward thinking globally, no longer just with reference to the multiple cultures from around the world, which had always been part of their comparative perspective, but now also in terms of direct and indirect interaction, exchange, and exploitation. For anthropologists of complex societies the translation of Fernand Braudel's great work *The Mediterranean and the Mediterranean World in the Age of Philip II* (1972) offered a powerful model. Even more influential, however, was Immanuel Wallerstein's introduction of the concept of the world-system with the publication of *The Modern World-System* (1974), the first volume of a four-part opus.

Wallerstein, a historical sociologist, differentiated between the world-economy and the world-system. He saw the origin in the sixteenth century of a European world-economy marked by a global market and a global division of labor. He then traced its transformation, under industrial capitalism, into a "modern," worldwide economic and social system. His basic distinction within this world-system was between core countries and the periphery; his typology also made room for a semiperiphery. Anthropologists readily adopted the language of world-system and dependency theories, but many found Wallerstein and Frank as problematic as they were liberating because their treatment of the periphery, or of satellite regions, took insufficient account of diverse ethnographic realities.

Urban Anthropology and Ethnicity

Urban anthropology came into its own during the postwar period. Cities had been on the agenda of American anthropology since as early as Redfield's counterposing of urban society to folk society and his folk-urban continuum. Critiques of these concepts introduced more variegated views of cities, although with only limited empirical research. As peasants came to be defined in relation to the city, or as "part societies with part cultures" (after Kroeber), attention also turned to the urban and elite segments of the whole society or culture.

Urban anthropology in its early years consisted of two strands: studies *in* cities and studies *of* cities. The first took off from the assumption that anthropology was best suited to the study of face-to-face groups; an anthropologist could approach a large, complex entity like a city by concentrating on a neighborhood, an occupational group, a voluntary association, or some other segment. This kind of fieldwork was carried out in the United States and around the world. In the cities of the Third World, migrants from rural areas were of particular interest—this was the "peasants in cities" approach. The key concept was urbanization, in contrast to urbanism. This research owed much to the influence of the Manchester anthropologists working in African cities, who also offered new methods for reaching beyond the limitations of participant observation, such as network analysis.

In the United States, the War on Poverty during the Johnson administration brought anthropologists into the public arena as the "culture of poverty" was invoked by some and criticized by others. That notion had been introduced by Oscar Lewis, who came to it from his studies of families in Mexico City, San Juan, and New York City (1959, 1966a, 1966b). His critics acknowledged that some of the patterns he described were indeed adaptive strategies of the poor, but they argued that to use culture as an explanation for poverty was wrong on theoretical grounds and inimical to good public policy (see Valentine 1968; Leacock 1971).

By this time critiques had mounted of this "anthropology of city streets" (Fox 1972), or of "infra-urban domains" (Leeds 1976), and many hoped that an anthropology of urbanism would come to fruition. What I have referred to as the second strand of urban anthropology, studies *of* cities, had an antecedent in the community studies of the 1930s, which had sought to grasp settlements, including (at least in theory) large ones, as totalities. It also had an impetus from the postwar archaeology that took a problem-oriented approach to early urban civilizations. The archaeologists were concerned with the origin of the state, the "urban revolution," and the nature of cities in the areas of pristine development of civilization in the Near East, pre-Columbian America, India, and China. Their findings not only fed into the revival of evolutionism in cultural anthropology; they also stimulated theoretical interest in urbanism as such and in the diversity of urban forms. A number of anthropologists, in tandem with historians and geographers, answered the call for synthetic urban studies that "cope with the city itself," that delineate the structure of whole cities and trace their relationship to broader societal features (Leeds 1976). This work came mostly from researchers looking at non-Western cities, and it had a strong comparative element.

Research in both strands of urban anthropology accelerated during the 1960s so that by the end of the decade Peter Gutkind was able to put together a bibliography of almost a thousand publications in the field (1973). In subsequent years, as it became routine for anthropologists to work in and on cities, and as urban phenomena were increasingly seen as linked to national and global processes, urban anthropology came to be absorbed into more broadly defined interests. Within the American Anthropological Association, for example, the section on urban anthropology was renamed Urban, National, and Transnational/Global Anthropology.

Ethnicity studies blossomed in American anthropology in the late 1960s and early 1970s, a period that some have described as A.B., "after Barth." In the United States anthropologists were reacting against the long tradition of ethnic group study in sociology, which tended to treat such groups as clearly delimited and marked by specific traits, whose main dynamic consisted in their becoming either more like the dominant society (the assimilationist view) or more like themselves (the separatist view). There was also the baggage of the plural-society concept, which emerged in anthropology during the 1950s to describe the multiplicity of cultural groups that coexisted within national societies in, for example, the West Indies and Indonesia. What Fredrik Barth offered with his focus on "the ethnic *boundary* that defines the group, not the cultural stuff that it encloses" (1969, 15) was a new set of questions at a time when many of the older questions had proven irrelevant.

The early work on the "new ethnicity" employed, for the most part, the language of ecology. Key concepts were adaptive strategy, competition for resources, niche, and the like. One version took the individual as its reference point and adopted a kind of rational formal economics (Bennett 1975). Individuals manipulated ethnic identity as a strategy in pursuit of their interests. The analyses drew on notions of choice, bargaining, tactics, selective use of categories, decision making, boundary defining, and other concepts referring to processes of strategizing. The underlying assumption was that identity was freely chosen.

Another version began with a larger, polyethnic system (a region, nation, or "total society") and moved from there to the ethnic entities within it (e.g., Despres 1975). In this approach the ethnic populations were seen as competing for resources of all kinds, material and nonmaterial, and as strategically employing identity markers, like individuals according to the first version. In the process, ethnic boundaries were drawn and redrawn, interethnic conflict (always present, if latent) often erupted, and the system as a whole was inevitably stratified. An unresolved issue in this work was the relationship between class and ethnicity. Leo Despres argued that class was not the same

thing as ethnicity, but that the two represented entangled systems of stratification (1975, 204). The nature of that entanglement is still a problem for us.

In later years, it was the first of these versions of that became predominant:
ethnicity as individual strategizing. Ethnicity studies have to a large extent
merged with the increasingly pervasive interest in identity in American anthropology. The main theoretical approach in this work has been constructivism of a kind that retains fairly intact the individual-centered, choice-
making premises of the earlier studies of ethnicity. Thus, the problem is
usually phrased as one of how people [i.e., individuals] construct their identity as [fill in the particular ethnic label]. At the same time, identity politics has
superseded class-based politics in many of the areas where anthropologists of
complex societies have worked, or so some political analysts claim. Class analysis has fallen on hard times while work on the representation and construction of ethnic and other political identities proceeds apace.

Not everyone endorses this trend, of course, or accepts that the battle has
been decided. In fact, during the 1970s and 1980s the positions of anthropologists on opposite sides of several theoretical divides—this one among others—diverged even further, and the debates grew more contentious.

4

Rebellions and Reinventions

The political upheavals of the 1960s had a powerful impact on American anthropology. After 1970 there were calls to reinvent anthropology, but there was disagreement on how that should be done. Two different versions emerged. To some extent these continued the earlier division between materialists and mentalists, but now the division took the form of political economy as against interpretive anthropology, with the latter giving rise to a textual humanism. The divergence may be seen in the different meanings attached to the term *critical*. Both sides claimed that label: for one side, the critique it referred to was political; for the other side the model was literary criticism. During the 1970s and 1980s the sides grew more antagonistic to each other, but neither one was monolithic: each covered a range of theoretical and political positions, and each side underwent change over the course of these decades.

To understand what happened after 1970, we need to recall the 1960s. The early years of the decade had seen the civil rights movement, and by 1965 both the Vietnam War and the antiwar protests moved into high gear. Then 1968, the year so critical for academics worldwide, brought the United States the Martin Luther King Jr. assassination and the turn to violence in the civil rights movement; the Robert Kennedy assassination; Lyndon Johnson's concession of defeat by the antiwar demonstrators; student revolts and occupations of campus buildings; the Democratic Party convention in Chicago, where violent clashes with the local police erupted; the flourishing of the new youth culture; and more. For anthropologists the Camelot affair was a recent memory and the specter of clandestine research would soon arise again in the context of Southeast Asia.

All these events were debated within anthropology—in departmental conflicts, in newsletters and journals, and at the annual meetings of the American Anthropological Association (AAA) and the specialty societies, where resolutions concerning political events were argued over heatedly late into the night. These debates spilled over into the intellectual and social interaction among colleagues; it was a time of passionate opinions and hard feelings. Divisions on these issues ran in different directions, but underlying all of them was a fundamental question about the nature of anthropology as a discipline. Was it—should it be—"pure" science, a scholarly enterprise, so that political involvements were the business of anthropologists only as private individuals? Or was it appropriate, even necessary, that anthropology speak to political concerns for which it presumably had special expertise or legitimate interest when the peoples studied by anthropologists were involved? From another perspective, it was a conflict between defenders of traditional authority and challengers to it.

Materialist Responses

The materialists were the first to be heard from, with the publication of *Reinventing Anthropology,* edited by Dell Hymes (1969). The contributors were a diverse group, but they shared the common denominator of a view of anthropology as "unavoidably a political and ethical discipline" (Hymes 1969, 48). This reinvention was by no means a uniform program; each of the writers spoke to problems and solutions according to his or her own lights. Taken as a whole, the essays made a fivefold plea: first, for relevance, for anthropology to speak to problems of the contemporary world; second, for responsibility, both the personal accountability of anthropologists for their professional acts and the social responsibility of the discipline itself; third, for the study of cultures of power, including both the dominant institutions of our own society and wider processes such as imperialism; fourth, for attention to human experience, including the experiential dimensions of anthropological practice; and fifth, for reflexivity, that is, an understanding of how anthropological traditions are contextually situated and culturally mediated. (This reflexivity, inspired by a variety of Marxism, was not quite the same as the version discovered by the dialogic ethnographers a decade later.)

A sampling of the papers in *Reinventing Anthropology* reflects the concerns of the time. Gerald Berreman described the malaise of many anthropologists, including students, that resulted from the "sterile scientism" of anthropology, which led to its failure to confront human issues. Kurt Wolff distinguished two kinds of radical anthropology, the humanly radical and the politically radical. William S. Willis Jr. and John Szwed both spoke to anthropology's explicit or implicit racism and its neglect or distortion of Afro-American cultures. Mina Davis Caulfield proposed anthropological analyses of imperialism that would take account not only of economic but also of cultural imperialism. Richard Clemmer analyzed resistance movements among American Indians, which he argued were obscured by theories of acculturation and culture change. Eric Wolf traced the historical phases in the development of American anthropology as reflections of major societal conditions, and he argued for a more adequate conceptual treatment of power. Laura Nader made a case for anthropologists to "study up" (that is, to do research on the more powerful segments of society) and discussed both the payoff and the methodological problems of doing so. Stanley Diamond, drawing on Rousseau and Marx, called for a renewed perspective on human nature that could come from encounters with primitive cultures. Bob Scholte bade anthropology to turn criticism upon itself and proposed a "critical, phenomenological" approach as an antidote to scientism.

In most cases, the vision the contributors offered was not a radical rejection of anthropological traditions or a plea for a fresh start; their goal was "to revise, not to repudiate." Yet such were the sensitivities of the time that many of the reviews and other responses were ad hominem in the extreme. It was probably the choice of the term *reinventing* for the title (this was in the days before it became a cliché) that set off this kind of reaction, more than the content of the essays, which, in retrospect, seem rather tame.

Because my focus is on American anthropology, I note only in passing the responses of British critics, who denounced the book as a kind of hippie expression of "anachronistic emotion, without intellect or scholarship" (Gluckman 1974) or as dogmatic, paranoiac, and mystical, a case of witch-hunting (Leach 1974). In the pages of the *American Anthropologist* a harshly polemical debate raged between David Kaplan and some of the contributors. According to Kaplan, the "reinventors" denied the possibility of anthropology as a systematic field of inquiry by rejecting objectivity and value-free science and by demanding the deprofessionalization and deinstitutionalization of the discipline, which would leave "everyman his own anthropologist" (1974). Hymes (1975) and some of the other contributors, in turn, accused Kaplan of misunderstanding objectivity and of being "ill equipped to assess radical and dialectical alternatives to analytic scientism" (Diamond, Scholte, and Wolf 1975, 870). Kaplan entered a rejoinder, charging that these enemies of social science wanted to "return to a previous ideological age of oracular wisdom" (1975, 880). Scholte later summed up the portrayal of radical anthropologists such as himself: they were self-indulgent narcissists, anti-institutional to a degree bordering on anarchism, antirational Luddites steeped in emotion and resentment (1981, 158).

Reinventing Anthropology had a counterpart in Britain, *Anthropology and the Colonial Encounter*, edited by Talal Asad (1973), which carried a similar critical view of anthropology's history and future. In France at this time Marxist theory was becoming prominent in anthropology. While there was also a Marxist strand in the United States, it was not yet defined as Marxist anthropology. Thus, Bridget O'Laughlin's overview of Marxist approaches in anthropology in the 1975 *Annual Review of Anthropology* cited French scholars almost exclusively. Maurice Bloch's edited collection of the same year had only two contributors who were Americans by origin, both of whom were based in Europe, Joel Kahn and Jonathan Friedman. A survey of a few years later by Kahn and Joseph Llobera (1981) still equated Marxist anthropology with French versions, but these had an extensive following in Britain as well. The new Marxist scholars were of great interest to anthropologists on the other side of the Atlantic, many of whom drew on them, cited them, and considered them bedfellows.

American anthropologists took an eclectic approach to Marxism. In their self-descriptions, anthropologists of the postwar period who considered themselves leftists have referred to a variety of sources of political influence. A number of them had read Marx from an early age and were involved in a range of political activities. However, partly because of the chilling atmosphere of the McCarthy era and partly because the Marxian concepts did not readily translate into the ethnographic and theoretical frameworks that anthropologists were working with, direct citations of Marx were rare at first. Few American anthropologists identified themselves as Marxists in the 1960s. Notable exceptions were Kathleen Gough, who argued for an anthropology of world imperialism (1968a, 1968b) and was driven out of more than one university for her views, and Eleanor Leacock, who brought Engels into political and feminist anthropology (1972).

The radicalization that many anthropologists experienced during the 1960s coincided with the advent of new publications by both British and American socialist scholars. At the same time, the translation into English of the works by French structural Marxists and by German and Russian Marxist scholars, including Marx's own writings, brought these theoretical currents directly into American anthropology. As the 1970s proceeded, Marxist concepts and citations appeared more frequently. Three of the contributors to *Reinventing Anthropology* described themselves, in a joint statement in 1975, as "critical scientists in the Marxist tradition, engaged in . . . analyzing the salient structures of exploitation" (Diamond, Scholte, and Wolf 1975, 870). Diamond founded a Marxist journal, *Dialectical Anthropology,* at the New School for Social Research in 1975 and at about the same time published a book that Wolf described in the foreword as "the prolegomena for a Marxist ethnology," *In Search of the Primitive, A Critique of Civilization* (Diamond 1974). Scholte placed his phenomenological approach within Marxism, and Wolf was already working with explicitly Marxian concepts in papers leading up to his *Europe and the People without History* (1982). Articles with Marxist orientation could now be found in the standard anthropological journals, and the anthropological literature increasingly dealt with themes of inequality, rebellion, and critical politics. Many anthropologists of this bent were also active in interdisciplinary Marxist journals and organizations, along with historians, sociologists, and scholars of other fields.

Thus a number of materialists evolved into Marxists in the 1970s or used an amalgam of Marxian ideas. However, there was never a "school" of Marxist anthropology in the United States. Perhaps the one thing that most Marxian-inspired anthropologists agreed upon was a rejection of "vulgar Marxism," the crude technological determinism they attributed to Marvin Harris. What emerged was a loose notion of political economy that focused on structures of power based on relations of production. This concept became an umbrella for a range of approaches in anthropology. In addition to their emphasis upon power and its economic foundations, proponents of political economy shared a global perspective, a particular interest in the relationship between large-scale processes and microregions, and a concern to incorporate history. They were therefore much invigorated by both the ascendance of world-systems theory and the rapprochement between anthropologists and historians during the 1970s, as seen, for example, in the field of peasant studies and in journals like *Comparative Studies in Society and History.*

New Voices in the Academy

Other developments on the American scene in the 1970s challenged the established order and contributed to the politicization of anthropologists. First and foremost was the women's movement, which gave birth to feminist anthropology and left its mark even on those who were not feminists. One of the first works in this vein was the 1970 book *Women in the Field,* edited by Peggy Golde, which was part of a budding literature of subjective accounts of anthropological fieldwork. Autobiographical essays by twelve women anthropologists elucidated the fieldwork process as they experienced it, focusing on how their gender affected the conduct of their work and the kinds of data and analysis they produced. Another formative feminist contribution was Eleanor Leacock's introduction to a new edition of Engels's *The Origins of the Family, Private Property, and the State* (1972), in which she underlined the key question of the subjugation of women and its relationship to class society and the state.

The appearance of such works coincided with efforts to raise the consciousness of the profession about the position of women in anthropology. In the early 1970s the AAA passed a series of resolutions on the status of women in anthropology. Under pressure from women members, the association initiated a survey of academic institutions that revealed serious patterns of discrimination. This led to the censure of departments that were shown to have an extreme underrepresentation of women and were not inclined to correct it.

Two books effectively launched feminist anthropology; both of them grew out of university courses—often unofficial ones undertaken by "collectives"—on the theme of women in cross-cultural perspective. Their initial problematic was sexual asymmetry—the questions of whether women inevitably occupied an inferior status, what differences there were among cultures, and how to explain the constants and account for the differences. These two books, *Women, Culture, and Society,* edited by Michelle Rosaldo and Louise Lamphere (1974), and *Toward An Anthropology of Women,* edited by Rayna Reiter (later Rapp) (1975), acknowledged sexual asymmetry to be universal, if variable in degree and form, but questioned biological and evolutionary explanations for it. Both took as a central dynamic the distinction between public and private spheres, which Rosaldo called a universal, structural opposition. The contributors to these collections also sought to convey a liberatory message by bringing attention to the ways in which women have achieved a degree of power and social recognition within male-dominated cultures.

A number of the essays in these two books defined the course of feminist anthropology for the next decade or so. Sally Slocum's "Woman the Gatherer" challenged the dominant model of "Man the Hunter," which held that male hunting was the context for the evolution of culture (in Reiter 1975). Joan Bamberger's "The Myth of Matriarchy: Why Men Rule in Primitive Society" showed how ideologies of female dominance served to sustain masculine rule, while Sherry Ortner's "Is Female to Male as Nature Is to Culture?" analyzed cultural rationales for female subordination (both in Rosaldo and Lamphere 1974). Sacks's "Engels Revisited: Women, the Organization of Production, and Private Property" and Gayle Rubin's "The Traffic in Women: Notes on the 'Political Economy' of Sex" proposed Marxist explanations for sexual asymmetry and women's oppression (both in Reiter 1975).

Ortner's paper was a prelude to another development in feminist anthropology during the late 1970s: a symbolic approach to gender, as represented by the volume *Sexual Meanings: The Cultural Construction of Gender and Sexuality*, edited by Ortner and Harriet Whitehead (1981). These years also saw the publication of ethnographies that demonstrated how the feminist perspective could provide new insights into classic analyses, such as Annette Weiner's revision of Bronislaw Malinowski in her study of women in the Trobriands (1976). At the same time Marxian approaches to gender issues burgeoned. For example, Rapp revisited the public/private distinction in the context of industrial capitalism, arguing that these were not separate domains but were in fact part of the same economically driven system. Increasingly, studies appeared on women's role in the labor force, on domestic economies, and on the intersection of gender, class, and race or ethnicity.

Feminism had an enduring theoretical impact on anthropology. It fundamentally challenged normative assumptions in the study of social structure (asking, for example, how a marriage-exchange system looked from the viewpoint of the wives), and it recast notions of power and resistance. It helped open up new areas of research, among them an anthropology of the body, political approaches to reproduction, an anthropology of work, the study of new forms of kinship, and an expanded interest in sexuality that came to include gay and lesbian studies. Eventually, however, the focus on women and sex roles, soon redefined as gender studies, receded as a subject in its own right and was incorporated into all aspects of anthropological inquiry.

During the 1970s, in parallel with the demand that anthropology make room for women and women's viewpoints, there emerged the voice of the "natives," who had their own critique of anthropology and who also sought entry into the ranks of academia. If the British were concerned with the role of anthropology in their colonies, the counterpart for Americans was our relation to American Indians. Vine Deloria Jr., a Sioux scholar, fired the opening salvo on behalf of all Native Americans with his *Custer Died for Your Sins* (1969), in which he accused anthropology of exoticizing the Indians. His attack raised the hackles of anthropologists but also drew their attention to legitimate concerns, including the need to better incorporate native perspectives into anthropology. A few years later, another nonanthropologist speaking for the subjects of anthropological study, Edward Said, played something of the same role with his *Orientalism* (1978). Said argued that Western academics had essentialized and homogenized the diverse societies of Asia into an image that counterposed a mysterious, sensuous Orient with the rational West. This representation, he maintained, was a process at once of mystification, of domination, and of subjugation to the Western civilizing mission. Later, James Carrier would make the counterargument with a book he called *Occidentalism: Images of the West* (1995).

The politics of the academy increasingly became an ethnic politics. There was an impetus—or, more often, a reluctant concession to demands—to form academic programs focused around various minority groups; anthropologists frequently participated in these programs. Many institutions became riven by conflicting claims of different groups for representation. Consider, for example, programs geared to Spanish-speaking minority groups: were these to be Hispanic, Latino, Chicano, Latin American? Were Caribbeans to be included or merged with African Americans, perhaps in a program of diaspora studies? In California and Texas, Spanish-speaking meant Chicano (from Mexico). In New York, however, Puerto Ricans, who claimed prerogatives because of their U.S. citizenship, were often aligned against Dominicans, the largest Spanish-speaking group in the city. Both of these distinguished themselves from Cubans, who were themselves divided between pro- and anti-Castroites. All the Caribbean groups set themselves apart from Central and South Americans. Of course, many of these groups were overlapping, and alliances to press shared claims were as common as conflict among the groups.

Some of these efforts flourished and produced significant research; others fell by the wayside. Many were subsequently absorbed into a broader movement for multiculturalism. Despite its use of anthropology's signal concept, multiculturalism generally went forward independently of anthropologists, who were critical of the essentialism implicit in it. The new cultural studies, which, much to our annoyance, also preempted anthropology's claim to the culture concept, was its usual home.

Materialists and Culturalists in the 1970s

Each of the major figures who appeared in my discussion of materialists and mentalists entered new phases of their work during the 1970s. To start with the most materialist of materialists, Marvin Harris began the decade with a textbook (1971) that complemented his earlier text for more advanced students, *The Rise of Anthropological Theory* (1968), which rewrote the history of anthropology to show the inevitable ascendance of cultural materialism.

He followed this with two semipopular books that provided thumbnail eco-logical solutions to the "riddles" of cultural behavior (1974, 1977). He ended the decade with his theoretical magnum opus, *Cultural Materialism: The Struggle for a Science of Culture* (1979), in which he exposed the "errors" of his fellow anthropologists, leaving few untouched, and doggedly pursued his "search for verifiable truth" in the evolution of societal systems. At this stage, his techno-eco-demo-determinism remained intact but was couched in a lan-guage of "etic behavioral modes of production and reproduction," "etic be-havioral domestic and political economies," and "behavioral superstructure" (1979, 51–54). This language incorporated Marxian notions even as Harris excoriated dialectics as "obfuscation." Harris had a coterie of students who were inspired by his vision and accepted his dogmatism, but he never achieved the influence on the discipline that he hoped for. Still, he continued to argue the truth as he saw it, applying it to issues of contemporary life, until his death in 2001.

Eric Wolf pursued his interest in peasants, now concentrating on themes of peasant rebellion and protest and exploring the applicability of Marxian concepts, such as rent, class, and "the peasant question," to the analysis of peasantry. Increasingly, however, he "began to think more systematically about the genesis and spread of forces in the world-system as a whole that underwrote the development of sociocultural entities and provided them the capacity to articulate with one another. I saw these forces as acting to build wider-ranging systems based on what I called kin-ordered, tributary, and cap-italist modes of production" (2001, 9). These ideas formed the premise of his *Europe and the People without History* (1982), essentially an anthropological history of the world. It sought to go beyond dependency theory, Wallerstein's world-systems theory, and other depictions of global relationships to examine the processes that had shaped the micropopulations studied by anthropolo-gists. The book found wide resonance in anthropology and in other social sci-ences, and much of its approach and analysis came to be adopted even by some who criticized it for giving too scant attention to the agency of the people im-pacted by the processes Wolf traced. In concert with his work on this book, Wolf became ever more vocal in his criticism of such bounded concepts as cul-ture and society and ever more explicit in his attention to power, especially what he called structural power. He wrote on these themes up to the time of his death in 1999.

The work of Wolf, and particularly his *Europe* book, signaled the crystal-lization in the late 1970s of what became known as political economy. Other figures who were also key to this development published signature works during this period, especially Sidney Mintz, whose *Sweetness and Power* (1985) was an analysis of cultural changes in consumption patterns within the world economy of sugar production, and June Nash, whose *We Eat the Mines and the Mines Eat Us* (1979) dealt with Bolivian tin miners. The anthropological approach to political economy built on but also criticized world-systems theory and French structural Marxism, attending to the local differences and processes within the world economy and to the articulation of capitalism with other modes of production.

A number of ethnographies examined relationships between the global and the local, doing so in diverse ways. Among these were Jane and Peter Schneider's *Culture and Political Economy in Western Sicily* (1976), which analyzed cultural codes, including those associated with the Mafia, in a world-systems framework; Joan Vincent's *Teso in Transformation: The Political Economy of Peasant and Class in Eastern Africa* (1982), an account of the impact of capitalism in Uganda; and William Roseberry's *Coffee and Capitalism in the Venezuelan Andes* (1983), which looked at the changing articulation of noncapitalist and capitalist modes of production. The political-economy approach also gave rise to other currents, such as work that drew inspiration from Antonio Gramsci and Raymond Williams to focus on cultural phenomena as these relate to class and power. An example in this vein was Aihwa Ong's *Spirits of Resistance and Capitalist Discipline* (1987), an analysis of spirit possession among women factory workers in Malaysia.

Marshall Sahlins, the erstwhile evolutionist and cultural ecologist, emerged in the 1970s as a structuralist and thoroughgoing culturalist. He began the decade with a collection of essays from his earlier incarnation, *Stone Age Economics* (1972), a highpoint of sophisticated substantivist economics, despite the fact that opponents of substantivism such as Manning Nash (1967, 250) had already declared its final demise. This book included Sahlins's famous papers "The Original Affluent Society," "On the Sociology of Primitive Exchange," and "The Domestic Mode of Production," which appeared in two parts, one of which drew heavily on A. V. Chayanov. By the time the book came out, however, Sahlins had spent two fateful years in Paris, where he had become immersed in the debates over Marxism and structuralism and had turned his efforts toward bringing them together.

Sahlins's conversion was laid out in his 1976 book, *Culture and Practical Reason,* which in a sense marked another phase in the long-standing opposition between materialism (the "practical reason" of Sahlins's title) and idealism (the "culture") in American anthropology. Sahlins, however, rejected that distinction, which he thought the culture concept (as he defined it) resolved by "not merely mediating the human relation to the world by a social logic of significance, but constituting by that scheme the relevant subjective and objective terms of the relationship" (1976, x). The opposition he wished to transcend was that between historical materialism (Marx) and structuralism (Lévi-Strauss). His approach was to come down squarely on the side of a symbolic, structural interpretation of culture. "It is culture," in the sense of a system of meaning, "which constitutes utility" (1976, viii).

In all of his subsequent work, Sahlins's culturalism has been deeply historical and his history profoundly culturalist. History for him is the working out of a symbolic order; what appears to be change is actually a manifestation of the underlying ideological structure, through which people interpret events. Myths both explain and direct change; Sahlins's concept of "mythopraxis" describes the way myths are constantly reenacted in the context of the present. To deal with the problem of "events," the unpredictable twists of history, he proposed the notion of "the structure of the conjuncture," whereby events are ordered by culture and, in the process, culture itself is reordered. (As he phrased it, "the reproduction of a structure" may "become its transformation.") He developed these ideas in great detail in a series of works reinterpreting the encounter of Captain Cook with the Hawaiians in 1778 and the events that followed (1981, 1985). Not surprisingly, Sahlins was challenged (by the American exile Jonathan Friedman, among others) for reducing social, economic, and other forces of history to cultural codes. Still, as the senior eminence at the University of Chicago, Sahlins influenced a quarter-century of students with his cultural determinism and structuralist history, which nevertheless made room for individual agency.

During the 1970s David Schneider made the transition from a culturalist theory of kinship to a rejection of the anthropological concept of kinship itself, claiming it was nothing more than anthropologists' turning their own, Western symbolic system into a universal theory (1984). He now denied that the Yap, whose supposed kinship he had once described, had a kinship system at all; they had nuclear families (which, as a sociological fact, did not interest him), but their cultural conceptions of relatedness did not conform to the anthropologists' idea of kinship. His basic objection was to the biological assumptions underlying the genealogical grid, and he turned instead to culturally specific concepts such as substance and blood. This approach found followers among his students, who used it in seeking alternatives to standard treatments of kinship, but critics accused him of having killed off kinship study in anthropology.

Clifford Geertz's publication in 1973 of *The Interpretation of Cultures* brought together a number of essays he had written in the 1960s, but with its expanded statement on "thick description" it became a point of departure for his brand of symbolic anthropology. From his prestigious position at the Institute for Advanced Study, Geertz elaborated his interpretive methodology and his relativistic, particularistic approach to cultures as "webs of significance." With his further research in Bali, published in *Negara: The Theater State in Nineteenth-Century Bali* (1980), his treatment of culture became more dramaturgical. In this story the king, who stood at the apex of the status hierarchy, embodied sacred power, leaving secular power to the lower levels of the system; the state cult and the court rituals constituted cultural paradigms for the whole society. Other students of Southeast Asia, such as Stanley Tambiah, questioned his separation of ritual and political power in this analysis. However, because of the resonance Geertz's textual approach found with literary, philosophical, and historical scholars, and because of his frequent writings for the literate public, he has been perhaps the most visible and influential of all American anthropologists to those outside the discipline since Margaret Mead.

If critics of materialist bent took issue with Geertz's cultural interpretations, charging that he ignored the economic and political realities at the heart of his cases, a different kind of critique came from rebels in his own camp. Some of the younger participants in his Morocco project, particularly Paul Rabinow (1977), Vincent Crapanzano (1980), and Kevin Dwyer (1982), rejected his approach to ethnographic description in their own accounts. While Geertz saw culture as "public symbols," a text to be read by the ethnographer "over the shoulder" of the native and interpreted by the ethnographer alone, for these dissidents ethnography was a reflexive encounter with the "Other." It was dialogic—that is, it was constructed collaboratively in the interaction of the anthropologist and the Other—and polyvocal: there were many Others, with different voices. This was only a prelude to the postmodernists' challenge to Geertz, who was their original inspiration. Geertz responded to all the criticisms in kind, and in the exchanges he began to look more like a positivist and a believer in science than his pronouncements of the 1970s would have predicted.

In the developments of the 1970s one can see a widening breach: between the perspectives of materialism, Marxism, and political economy, on the one hand, and those of idealism, symbolism, and interpretivism, on the other. However, there were also efforts to bridge this divide. Sherry Ortner collapsed a number of such efforts under the term *practice theory* (1984). This was not a single paradigm but a concept that brought together actor-oriented and structure-oriented theories—*agency* and *structure* became the preferred terms once Anthony Giddens's work was known. In its various permutations practice entailed activity, interaction, experience, performance, and other action-based phenomena that were located within systemic imperatives (institutional, material, and symbolic) and that, in turn, acted upon the system. Among the unifying themes of the approaches Ortner identified were an emphasis upon asymmetrical relations and domination, a concern with practices of everyday life, an interest in motivational processes underlying action (emotion, self, personhood, and the like), attention to how culture shapes and constrains experiential reality, and a diachronic perspective applied to both microdevelopmental and macrohistorical processes.

In addition to home-grown inspirations like Sahlins's structuralist history and British sources such as Giddens, these approaches drew heavily on the work of Pierre Bourdieu, whose *Outline of a Theory of Practice* was translated into English in 1977. His key concept (at least as the anthropologists read him) was the notion of habitus, the taken-for-granted dispositions of daily life, which he summarized as "a community of dispositions." Bourdieu, who died in 2002, has had a continuing strong influence on American anthropology.

The Postmodern Development

By the 1980s much had changed in American society and in academia. The Reagan victory marked the ascendance of a new conservativism; the revolutionary fervor of the 1960s and the optimism of the left for fundamental social reform were gone. The golden age of university expansion was over, and most departments were now at stable levels or in retrenchment. As new PhDs confronted the job crisis within academia, they increasingly sought employment outside of it. For some anthropologists this trend signified a need for a more inclusive vision of the discipline; for others, including rebels of the past who were now comfortably tenured, it prompted an insistence upon a scholarly, even arcane, conception of anthropology.

It was in that general context that the second reinvention of the period came about. This one took place in the camp of the symbolists of literary turn, who were out-Geertzing Geertz, as it were. It fit into the larger academic and intellectual movement of postmodernism, but the anthropologists identified with it did not all accept that designation. Some saw the new experimental ethnography that they advocated as modernist, in contrast to anthropology's long tradition of realist ethnography (George Marcus), while others considered their project to be late modern (Paul Rabinow). Nevertheless, they and their fellow travelers were readily labeled as postmodernists by others.

The postmodern movement in a broad sense has as its premise that the world changed fundamentally during the 1970s. We were now in a postindustrial, post-Fordist era marked by a new capitalism of flexible accumulation and a shift from the production of commodities to consumption. We were seeing an erasure of political and social boundaries as a result of transnational migration, greatly intensified information flows, and the spread of mass-media culture; a disruption and dislocation of social relationships, which were now all subsumed by capitalism; and new forms of consciousness expressed, among other ways, in global social movements.

The postmodernist response to this new world was marked by several features: a rejection of totalizing metanarratives and foundational theories and an emphasis instead on fragmentation, pastiche, and blurred genres; a denial that truth has an objective reality and an insistence instead that truth is always positional, which entailed a denial also of universal standards; a dissolving of boundaries of all kinds; and a conjunction with the linguistic turn in the human sciences, which locates social practices in how people talk (that is, in discourse) and in how they think and write. Terms that appear frequently in the postmodern literature include *parody, collage, decentering,* and *defamiliarization*. For anthropology, this stance has meant, minimally, reflexivity and a disavowal of any privileged position for the observer or analyst and hence a rejection of the claims of positivism. It also has meant a renewed relativism, this time not just cultural relativism but relativism with respect to all our concepts. The way these ideas can translate into the work of the discipline is suggested by Stephen Tyler's definition of the postmodern ethnography: it is, he says, "a cooperatively evolved text consisting of fragments of discourse intended to evoke . . . an emergent fantasy of a possible world of commonsense reality. . . . It is, in a word, poetry" (in Clifford and Marcus 1986, 125).

This development had continental influences: Michel Foucault, who called attention to knowledge as power, to cultural domination and resistance, and to discourse; Mikhail Bakhtin, who inspired literary readings of ethnography with an emphasis upon multivocality and dialogics; and cultural Marxists like Gramsci. Its definitive impact on American anthropology, however, came with the appearance in 1986 of two key texts: George Marcus and Michael Fischer's *Anthropology as Cultural Critique: An Experimental Moment in the Human Sciences,* and a volume edited by James Clifford and George Marcus, *Writing Culture: The Poetics and Politics of Ethnography.* The 1986 date is a rather arbitrary marker: Marcus had already sketched out his position in a review article on

"Ethnographies as Texts" (Marcus and Cushman 1982), and the Clifford and Marcus volume was based on a seminar held in 1984.

At this time Marcus, Fischer, and Tyler were all at Rice University in Texas, while Clifford, a historian of anthropology, was in the History of Consciousness Program at the University of California at Santa Cruz. Thus, this movement did not come out of the major departments of anthropology. Nevertheless, it found ready adherents at Stanford (for example, Renato Rosaldo), Berkeley, Chicago, and elsewhere, and almost every department now has some members who would associate themselves with it.

These two texts take a number of departures from prevalent understandings of anthropology. Ethnography becomes the core of the discipline, and it becomes equated with writing. There is no separation between fieldwork and write-up or between ethnographic data and theory; writing *is* theory, and the ethnographic experience and its representation in writing are of a piece. (This narrowing of the scope of anthropology to ethnography is one reason for the general antipathy of archaeologists, biological anthropologists, and even linguists to this approach.) Ethnographic authority is deeply questioned; in effect, the whole body of literature of cultural anthropology becomes suspect. Critique and reformation of the discipline are goals, but they translate into experimentation in writing. We are here at the opposite pole from Harris's search for "verifiable truth."

Marcus and Fischer put ethnographic writing at the center because they believe it to be the major concern of contemporary cultural anthropologists—rather than theory, which they think is impoverished. For them critique means counterposing other cultural realities against our own in order to gain more adequate knowledge of them all, but especially to allow self-criticism of our own ways. Experimentation is the play of ideas free of authoritative paradigms and open to diverse influences. Marcus and Fischer acknowledge the origin of their work in interpretive anthropology but see that perspective as having become just one accepted paradigm among all the others; they want to position themselves differently, outside of any paradigm. They begin with what they see as a "crisis of representation" within the human sciences in general since the 1960s, then pursue the crisis as it has developed in anthropology.

Their main focus is the recent experimentation in ethnographic writing. They see two kinds of experimentation. One, which they call "ethnographies of experience," seeks more adequate means of representing "the authentic differences of other cultural subjects." The other is concerned with how the penetration of large-scale processes has shaped the cultures of subjects; these ethnographies may incorporate themes of political economy, not as the central problem but to elucidate subjectivities. Finally, Marcus and Fischer consider how these experiments provide cultural critique through strategies of defamiliarization. Their goal, they conclude, is "a historically and politically sensitive interpretive anthropology, preserving relativism as the method of engaged inquiry" (1986, 166).

The Clifford and Marcus collection concentrates on writing too, but with a somewhat different, more radical emphasis; its aim is "to introduce a literary consciousness to ethnographic practice by showing the various ways in which ethnographies can be read and written" (1986, 262). Clifford's overarching concern is with the literary forms that anthropologists use to establish their authority. Rabinow helpfully distinguishes Clifford's project from Geertz's in this way: "Geertz . . . is still directing his efforts to reinvent an anthropological science with the help of textual mediations. The core activity is still social description of the other. . . . The other for Clifford is the anthropological representation of the other" (in Clifford and Marcus 1986, 242). The participants in the original seminar (Clifford, Marcus, Fischer, Tyler, Rosaldo, Rabinow, Crapanzano, Asad, Mary Louise Pratt, and Robert Thornton) were selected because each had "contributed significantly to the analysis of ethnographic textual forms" and was "opening up . . . ethnographic writing possibilities." The papers all revisit the ethnographic literature, and each one takes up a problem of ethnographic rhetoric, a mode of representation, or a textual strategy of authorization. We hear about the rhetoric of objectivity (Rosaldo); the use of allegory (Clifford); ethnic autobiography, or "the postmodern arts of memory" (Fischer); occult documents (Tyler); and other literary devices. The hope of the group is that such self-critique will clear the way for a reconceptualization of anthropological practice.

Both these volumes came under ferocious attack. They were charged with being intellectually irresponsible; with lacking predictability, replicability, verifiability, and law-generating capacity; with indulging in mystification and fabrication unaccountable to any challenge of logic or fact; with being navel-gazing; with misrepresenting the activity of ethnography; and other bad things (see Watson in Fox 1991, 73–74). Harris referred to the group as "untrained would-be novelists and ego-tripping narcissists afflicted with congenital logo-diarrhea" (1994, 64), and even Geertz chimed in with warnings about "epistemological hypochondria." The rejoinders to these attacks were equally polemical.

Much of the discipline became embroiled in the conflict between the proponents and opponents of postmodernism. Some hailed the development as a breakthrough and a welcome triumph of the reflexive turn. Others saw it as a retreat into the ivory tower; this reinvention invoked power and politics as well as text, the critics acknowledged, but in it *struggle* referred to debates over words. The charge of elitism was not always disputed. In the mid-1980s a group from the postmodern camp attempted to establish a new scholarly society with membership to be by invitation only. While this project did not materialize, the move yielded a new journal, *Cultural Anthropology,* which has since become more inclusive than it was at its founding.

Despite the furor, many anthropologists, including those critical of postmodern excesses, accepted the basic message of postmodernism and tried to integrate it with other approaches. An example is a collection edited by Richard Fox, *Recapturing Anthropology: Working in the Present* (1991, from a seminar in 1989). Fox sees the postmodern critique as a recognition of anthropology's difficulties in working within the contemporary world, but he rejects the textualist strategy. The contributors to his book criticize postmodernism but also use postmodern insights as they seek various modes of gaining "reentry" into the real world and of "recapturing" anthropology's authority. Thus Michel-Rolph Trouillot considers the "savage slot," which anthropology did not create but inhabited and thereby confirmed. Joan Vincent cautions that texts always exist in a political, historical context that cannot be discerned from the texts alone. Graham Watson claims that the postmodern critique does not go far enough in that it leaves realist notions of representation intact; he argues for "rewriting culture" by adopting some key ideas from the British constructivist sociologists and from ethnomethodology as developed by Harold Garfinkel. Lila Abu-Lughod, in contrast, wants to write "against culture"; from her stance as a feminist (a position excluded from the "writing culture" fest) and a "halfie" (part Western, part "Other"), she advocates "ethnographies of the particular," which she sees as part of a strategy for "disturbing" the culture concept. Arjun Appadurai outlines a transnational anthropology that focuses on "global ethnoscapes," ethnographies of how everyday life is lived out globally.

Thus, while not many anthropologists became avowed postmodernists, aspects of the postmodern approach were widely, if selectively, adopted. This happened, in part, through convergence with other trends in cultural anthropology that had been gaining ground for some time: the move toward treating culture as representation and the shift toward constructionism (the idea that culture is constructed rather than something fixed). As for the two reinventions that dominated anthropological discourse during the 1970s and 1980s, it was not long before both reached the limits of their extremes. By the early 1990s, each had made its point and had protested the caricatures made of it by the other; each had spawned many divergent offshoots; and the major insights of both had been absorbed into mainstream anthropological thinking.

5

American Anthropology at the End of the Century

The history of anthropology as a professional discipline in the United States nearly coincides with the span of the twentieth century, if we mark its formal beginnings by the awarding in 1901 of the first PhD and by the founding in 1902 of the American Anthropological Association (AAA). What can we say of the state of the discipline at its centennial?

The 1990s were challenging years for anthropology in the United States. The decade began with the redrawing of the map of Eastern Europe, the display of American force in the Gulf War, and an economic recession that helped bring about the Clinton victory in 1992. From that point on, it was a decade of unprecedented prosperity, but academia, for the most part, did not reap the rewards. Universities (except for the most privileged ones) were forced into cost-accounting administration, which, among other things, looked to the employment of low-paid part-time faculty in the classrooms and the magic of distance learning to help balance the books. Thus, despite the retirement of professors of the postwar generation, the academic job market did not greatly improve. Academia took the form of a three-tier system: a few stars enjoyed the benefits of bidding wars among institutions, while the heavy lifting of university life was carried out by the relatively secure middle tier of tenured professors and, increasingly, by those at the bottom rung, the part-time and temporary teaching faculty.

With limited numbers of university jobs, employment outside the academy continued to rise. Over half of new PhDs were now "practicing anthropologists," bringing the long-standing tension between academic anthropology (which fancied itself "theoretical") and applied anthropology into a new phase. The tension did not disappear, but the academics had to make room—in their institutions and in their professional societies—for a new brand of colleague.

Of all the subfields, archaeology experienced this change most profoundly. Historical-preservation legislation during the 1970s and 1980s and then, in 1990, the National Graves Protection and Repatriation Act (NAGPRA) gave impetus to the new specialty of cultural resource management (CRM). Increasing numbers of archaeologists were employed in this survey and salvage work, shifting the center of gravity of the field away from academia and anthropological archaeology. Biological anthropology too moved farther away from general anthropology, prompted by the revolution in genetics and other catalysts of intensified specialization. Cultural anthropology was also pulled away from the other subfields by new interdisciplinary affiliations, especially in the case of the interpretive wing, which moved closer to the humanities. Linguistic anthropology, for its part, suffered from its small size and its marginal status in both anthropology and linguistics, not fully belonging to either discipline. Thus, the traditional integration of American anthropology was called into question, if not utterly rejected by many.

The decade brought other problems too. More and more ethnographic areas were closed off to anthropological research, because of either political instability or the locals' unwillingness to be the targets of foreigners' scrutiny. Tensions in relations with American Indians ran high, with growing demands for repatriation of skeletal, archaeological, and cultural materials and for intellectual-property compensation. NAGPRA put the museums on notice and most took steps to fulfill their obligations, but rarely were both sides in the negotiations satisfied with the outcome. To add insult to injury, other academic disciplines were encroaching on anthropology's heritage of concepts and methods. Cultural studies had seized the terrain of American anthropology's most treasured intellectual possession, the culture concept; programs of multiculturalism were proceeding blissfully indifferent to anthropology's claim to special expertise in their subject matter; and everyone in the social sciences and humanities, it seemed, was doing fieldwork and calling it ethnography.

Nevertheless, American anthropology thrived in the 1990s. The long period of postwar growth had been followed by a phase of decline in the 1980s; but then the demographic profile of the discipline stabilized in terms of the number of PhDs granted (now at close to five hundred a year) and the number of card-carrying members of the professional associations. College students still clamored for anthropology classes, and graduate students perversely insisted on pursuing their studies, even though the holy grail of a job in teaching research was more elusive than ever. Above all, the spirit of the discipline was strong, and anthropologists' belief in the intellectual value and public benefit of their work was unshaken. The missionary fervor was undiminished.

The face of cultural anthropology had changed in the prior decades. Its practitioners were now more diverse (for one thing, women made up the majority of new PhD holders), and the contexts in which they plied their trade were more varied. Social networks changed too as anthropologists, equipped with e-mail and the Internet, interacted as much with colleagues around the country and abroad who shared their special interests as with those in the next office, and usually more than with other members of their own institutions.

The sectionalism of the discipline, especially in cultural anthropology, had been institutionalized in the reorganization of the AAA in 1983. Specialty societies and groups with common research or professional concerns could now petition to be incorporated as sections of the association. At last count there were thirty-four sections, and more were seeking official recognition.

Most of the association's sections are within cultural anthropology or are made up predominantly of cultural anthropologists. A listing of the sections' names suggests the range of interests they cover. Ethnology and cultural anthropology each has a society of its own, the American Ethnological Society, which goes back to the mid-nineteenth century, and the Society for Cultural Anthropology born out of the recent interpretive thrust. Other sections are: Africanist Anthropology; Anthropology and Education; Anthropology and Environment; Anthropology of Consciousness; Anthropology of Europe; Anthropology of North America; Anthropology of Religion; Anthropology of Work; Culture and Agriculture; Feminist Anthropology; Humanistic Anthropology; Latin American Anthropology; Medical Anthropology; Middle East; Museum Anthropology; Nutritional Anthropology; Political and Legal Anthropology; Practicing Anthropology (NAPA); Psychological Anthropology; Urban, National, and Transnational/Global Anthropology; and Visual Anthropology. There are also sections for black anthropologists; Latina and Latino anthropologists; lesbian, gay, and bisexual/transgender anthropologists; senior anthropologists; students; and anthropologists in community colleges. Finally, there are a general anthropology division; archaeology, biological anthropology, and linguistic anthropology sections; and some regional societies that have the status of sections.

The total membership of the AAA is around eleven thousand, but some of the preexisting professional organizations did not opt to merge with it in 1983; thus, there are also large numbers of anthropologists in the Society for American Archaeology, the American Association of Physical Anthropologists, and the Society for Applied Anthropology, many of whom do not belong to the AAA.

The AAA reorganization was an acknowledgement of a process that was already under way. In an article for the *New York Times* in 1980, Eric Wolf discussed this segmentation and its threat to a common theoretical framework for the discipline; the editor added the title, "They Divide and Subdivide, and Call It Anthropology." To many it seemed that anthropology was flying apart as a result of centrifugal forces; to others this trend signaled a healthy diversification that did not preclude the continued unity of the discipline.

Fault Lines

The issue of disciplinary segmentation was one of a number of fault lines that marked American anthropology during the 1990s and that are still with us; though they cut across all the subfields, I will emphasize their impact on cultural anthropology. The fault line involving the question of fragmentation versus integration is usually phrased as the four-field issue: can and should anthropology retain its inclusive nature, keeping all the subfields within a single discipline, or should the trend toward specialization be acknowledged and accommodated through other institutional structures? This question is debated in many departments. In a few cases, the outcome has been divorce. In more than a few others (among them those of Berkeley, Columbia, and Chicago), a compromise has been reached with a modification of graduate-student requirements to allow for specialization without a demand for competence in the four fields.

European anthropologists may be mystified about why Americans have clung for so long to the four-field structure and why so many of us continue to support it. It goes without saying that its creation was a historical accident, a result of how American anthropology first became institutionalized. That story includes the early reaction against conjectural history and consequently the concern with uncovering the actual historical processes of nonliterate cultures—above all, those of Native America. Whatever the origin of the structure, the close association among the four fields has proven to be a productive one. Recall, for example, the neo-evolutionist development of the period after World War II, which was greatly vitalized by the links between cultural anthropology and archaeology, to the benefit of both fields. Or the emergence of the "new physical anthropology" in the same period, which revolutionized human evolutionary studies through a collaboration of biological anthropology, field primatology, hunter-forager ethnography, and other specialties. Or the development of linguistic anthropology from the 1920s on, in which the relationship with cultural anthropology made possible the forging of a different kind of linguistics than existed before or has existed since in mainstream linguistics.

More recently, the historical turn in cultural anthropology both impelled and was impelled by its linkage with archaeology and ethnohistory. Major research areas were transformed by those subfields working in conjunction with one another and incorporating the contributions of biological and linguistic anthropology as well. Some prime cases are Maya and Andean studies, but there are also examples from North America, the Pacific, and indeed practically every arena of research. One might investigate, for instance, the nature of social inequality or violence in a society no longer extant by drawing on the data of archaeology and ethnohistory; the evidence for diet, disease, and lifestyle that can be read through skeletal remains; and the interpretive insights of ethnographic comparison.

The bringing together of these different perspectives has led to a reevaluation of several of the classic ethnographic cases, such as those of the Kung Bushmen, the Kwakiutl, and the Hopi, allowing us to rethink the conclusions that had become received knowledge about human nature and culture. Consider, for example, Amazonia. Recent archaeology that has extended the prehistoric record back to twelve thousand years ago has revealed much greater early complexity than had been expected, casting doubt on theories based on the assumption that this was a marginal environment with low productive capacity (Roosevelt 1994). Similarly, the uncovering through ethnohistory of the demographic and ecological impact of European conquest on human organization in Amazonia has called into question prevalent ethnographic analyses on topics from warfare to myth. This range of evidence and these modes of interpretation are proving as useful for understanding the complex and contemporary societies on which cultural anthropology is now more often focused, as for comprehending societies of traditional anthropological interest.

My argument is not that all four fields are relevant to all problems, but rather that they are linked differently to one another and that the linkages depend on the problem at hand. Thus, symbolic anthropology cannot do without linguistics, while human evolutionary studies require not only biological anthropology and archaeology, but also linguistic and cultural anthropology for some problems; but it is the case, as critics of the four-field structure argue, that much of anthropological research does not necessitate venturing out of one's own field. Nevertheless, it cannot always be predicted in advance when and where cross-field collaboration will be productive. For that reason, I think it is important for American anthropology as a whole to keep the lines of communication open and to ensure that new generations are trained with enough understanding of all the fields to be able to benefit from the contributions of specialties other than their own when the need or opportunity arises.

The heart of the issue, however, is the very definition of anthropology. For many in the American tradition, that definition takes in the full scope of understanding of the human species, including its development and trajectory in all times and places. Those who define anthropology more narrowly—as the study of modernities, for instance—would beg to differ, as would those who would allocate the physical species and its behavior to different disciplines. That's what the argument is about.

I have described the throes of the debate between advocates and critics of postmodernism, and before that the debate over political economy versus interpretivism, and before that the debate over materialism versus mentalism. With each turn to a new opposition, the earlier ones were declared to be outdated, and in each phase too there were efforts to transcend the differences. In the 1990s we were faced with yet another epistemological division within the discipline, which formed a second fault line: that between positivism and constructivism. In a sense, this was a continuation of the argument about postmodernism, but those who accept the premises of social constructivism cover a much wider range of theoretical positions than just textualist postmodernism. What is at stake is the difference between, on the one hand, the belief that the external world consists of an objective reality that can be grasped with the use of procedures shared by a scientific community, and, on the other hand, the idea that all of social life and culture is constructed within a given historical context and that cultural codes shape the way people, including scientists, perceive and make sense of the world. This divergence has ripped institutions apart; in one famous case, Stanford's anthropology department split into two—one embracing "anthropological science" and the other skeptical of anthropology as science—not because of an argument about the four fields, but because it had run aground on this issue of epistemology.

A third fault line in American anthropology today involves views of the culture concept: whether to scuttle it or reform it. For many Americans, and for perhaps most anthropologists in other countries, the concept has become counterproductive, particularly in its assumptions of boundedness and congruence and in the expectation that cultures correspond to similarly bounded and homogeneous social groups. *Culture* has also taken on an ominous political meaning in some contexts. Proponents of retaining the culture concept acknowledge these difficulties but believe that its strengths merit its redefinition and rehabilitation. Interestingly, the anticulture contingent is made up largely of cultural anthropologists, while archaeologists, biological anthropologists, primatologists, and linguists are among the strongest advocates of the value of the concept (see Fox and King 2002).

A fourth fault line of recent years is found in a theoretical division of a different kind. It emerged with the introduction of Darwinian theory into anthropology that came with sociobiology after publication of the book with that title by E. O. Wilson in 1975. This was the latest phase of the long-standing debate over nature versus nurture. One of the controversies this argument generated erupted when Derek Freeman "unmasked" what he called the hoaxing of Margaret Mead, a challenge that was at bottom an attack on cultural determinism from the viewpoint of a crude sociobiology. In some quarters, the premises of sociobiology joined with individual-centered maximization theory to yield a variety of neo-Darwinism. In this approach, all features of social and cultural life are understood as having evolved through a process of natural selection, ultimately determined by differential reproductive success. This stance has had an influence on all the subfields of anthropology, but its more extreme form is represented by those who call themselves evolutionary psychologists, a group made up primarily of psychologists and popular-science writers, along with a few anthropologists. This form of neo-Darwinism employs a fundamental reductionism, which, the critics say, erases all the social and cultural patterns that anthropologists have described in a century of ethnography. On analytic grounds, and because of the political implications of this approach and its potential for mischief, it has met with powerful opposition from cultural anthropologists and others.

Finally, there are several issues concerning the practice of anthropology that constitute other fault lines. Among these issues are different views about anthropology's involvement in public affairs ("politics," the critics call this); about the relationship of anthropologists to the "natives" they study, including the role of indigenous anthropologists; and about the contradictions raised by the practice of anthropology outside the academy.

Current Debates

As examples of what American anthropologists have been arguing about, I refer to three of the prominent debates of the last years of the century. Although fought out between individuals, they reflect underlying theoretical and epistemological divisions in the discipline. The differences between the opposing sides correspond to the fault lines described above, but these debates all involve more than one fault line, and they combine them in different ways.

My first example is the debate that emerged in 1992 with the challenge by the Sri Lankan, Princeton-based anthropologist Gananath Obeyesekere to Marshall Sahlins in a book called *The Apotheosis of Captain Cook: European Mythmaking in the Pacific.* A few years later Sahlins responded with his own book, *How "Natives" Think: About Captain Cook, for Example* (1995). The argument had to do with Sahlins's interpretation of Captain Cook's encounter with the Hawaiians, which he had presented in terms of the "mythopraxis" of the natives. Obeyesekere countered with the claim that the relevant myths were not the natives' but those of Cook's sailors, Western illusions that Sahlins took at face value, according to Obeyesekere. An underlying issue was whether non-Western intellectuals have a privileged perspective. It may seem paradoxical that it was the anthropologist from the West who offered a culturally embedded analysis, while the spokesman for the natives argued that the Hawaiians were acting in terms of a universalistic rationality. The division has echoes of the debate over Orientalism, although in this instance the protagonists shared a common anthropological frame of reference.

A second mano a mano debate of the mid-1990s engaged Roy D'Andrade (1995) and Nancy Scheper-Hughes (1995). This one reflected the epistemological divide over the issue of objectivity and positivist science, as well as differences concerning the place of morality in anthropological practice. D'Andrade, a cognitive anthropologist, made a strong case for anthropology as science, answering all those who would deny the possibility of objectivity. He insisted that scientific models, our access to "truth," be kept separate from moral models, which are based on individual anthropologists' subjective views of the world and are an expression of their personal and political values.

Scheper-Hughes is best known for drawing attention to child hunger and death in northeastern Brazil; she charged that this tragedy is papered over both by anthropologists whose fascination with the symbols of culture blind them to suffering and by well-meaning practitioners who treat the problem medically (1992). Her argument in the debate with D'Andrade was for a deeply engaged, militant anthropology, one based on a morality that demands struggle against injustice and oppression. Interestingly, both D'Andrade and Scheper-Hughes attacked postmodernism and relativism, but for opposite reasons. Scheper-Hughes also came down hard on the "hot pursuit of a transnational, borderless anthropology," which she suggested was a tactic for distancing oneself from local realities. This debate provoked a barrage of heated responses from other anthropologists, who took issue with either or both combatants on a variety of grounds. Clearly, the lines that divide our field run in many crosscutting (and sometimes contradictory) directions.

A third recent, very public debate in American anthropology engaged the fault line concerning neo-Darwinism, as well as a number of ethical issues. In 2000 the journalist Patrick Tierney levied charges against Napoleon Chagnon, the ethnographer of the Yanomami (whom he had made famous as "the fierce people") in a book called *Darkness in El Dorado: How Scientists and Journalists Devastated the Amazon*. Tierney accused Chagnon of both ethical misconduct in his own research and complicity with the geneticist James Neel in practices that Tierney claimed had caused a measles epidemic during the 1960s. Terry Turner, an anthropologist working with the Kayapo, used the Tierney book to press his own attack on Chagnon, long an opponent of his on both theoretical and political grounds. Among other things, Turner has taken an active role in assisting the Kayapo to modernize in defense of their own interests, while Chagnon has treated Amazonia as a natural laboratory for testing his neo-Darwinian theories.

In the debate that ensued, anthropologists aligned partly according to their views of Chagnon's theoretical bent and partly according to their readiness to believe the charges about the ethical violations attributed to him. The argument over ethics elicited another alignment: one side focusing on the conduct of the researchers, the other side accusing Tierney of manipulating what he purported to be evidence. The AAA appointed a committee to investigate all charges; a year later it issued a report that criticized Tierney's book but also acknowledged the importance of some of the ethical issues it raised. The debate remains unresolved.

Transcending the Divides

Despite these fault lines and arguments, there have been developments in recent anthropology that hold promise of transcending the oppositions. Consider, first, the polarity between political economy and interpretivism—and postmodernism, its descendant—that marked the 1970s and 1980s. One of the enduring effects of the mentalist program, as it moved from symbolic to interpretive to postmodern anthropology, was to make culture, in many quarters, more or less synonymous with representation. In this view culture is no longer what people do, but instead what they think; it is no longer the objective conditions of existence but images of it. Cultural difference is no longer a framework for comparison but a matter of identity. The redefinition of culture as representation was accepted by most but not all of those on the political economy side as well; for them, however, culture is not an autonomous realm but is grounded in relations of production and their political manifestations.

By the late 1980s, however, the two poles began to come together as the limitations of the extreme versions of each became apparent. Within each camp there was new work that approached or incorporated the position of the other. The political economy contingent developed interest in the formation and agency of human subjects at the intersection of global and local histories. Moreover, inspired by cultural Marxism, a number of anthropologists who were identified with political economy focused on cultural themes in the context of class, work, and power. From the reflexive/interpretive side, George Marcus and Michael Fischer hailed ethnographies that specifically addressed "the meshing of political economy and interpretive concerns in anthropology" (1986, 84). One of their two main categories of "experimental ethnographies" consisted of those that try to describe how "subjects are implicated in broader processes of historical political economy" (1986, 44). In fact, in published overviews of each of these trends, the same anthropologists turn up as examples of both.

The concern to find a compromise between political economy and postmodernism appears also in the language with which some anthropologists are trying to define their stance. For Marcus and Fischer it is *engaged relativism,* by which they mean a mode of inquiry about communication within and between cultures that recognizes global structures of political and economic power (1986, 32). For Lila Abu-lughod it is *tactical humanism—humanism* because that term gives human equality moral force, *tactical* because she seeks a strategy for exposing the dominance implicit in the notion of cultural difference (in Fox 1991, 158–59). For Bruce Knauft the key term is *critically humanist sensibilities.* What he means by this is "the self-conscious application of . . . competing humanist perspectives to keep their respective excesses in check" (1996, 48). Specifically, "appreciations of cultural diversity and critiques of inequality provide checks and balances on each other" (1996, 53). This two-pronged approach, Knauft believes, maintains "objectivism as a rigorous and progressive tool" (1996, 61) for engaging cultural difference while avoiding the "hyperrelativism of postmodernism" (1996, 105).

Knauft suggests that the polarity between political economy and postmodernism is being resolved in contemporary American anthropology. He sees a trilogy of interest in culture, power, and history as a dominant trend in institutions across the country, with a west-to-east gradient: culture (reflexivity and representation) being emphasized on the west coast and power and history (political economy) on the east coast (1996, 129, 301). Midwestern institutions like Chicago and Michigan occupy an intermediate position. Presumably balmy California breeds flights of fancy, while gritty New York is never far removed from material realities.

There are, in fact, several trends in recent research that are breaking down barriers of the past, both within cultural anthropology and in its relationship with other fields. These trends engage the opposition between different epistemologies; they also expose the tension between particularism and comparison, and between local and global perspectives. They suggest some of the ways that anthropologists are finding to use these tensions productively or to move beyond them. In identifying these trends, I am drawing mainly on my experience with some twenty international symposia sponsored by the Wenner-Gren Foundation during the 1990s. Because each symposium was designed to address a cutting-edge problem or issue within contemporary anthropology, in their totality they provide a window on the state of the discipline during this period.

My first case comes from human evolutionary studies. Social-cultural anthropologists might think this field is not their concern, but they would be wrong, for it is here that the basic questions about human nature are most directly addressed. I will not discuss the explosion of new fossil discoveries and the revolution in genetics that have changed the evidentiary base of the field. Rather, I want to look at how specialties and disciplines across a wide range are being brought together around evolutionary problems of common interest.

My example is a 1990 symposium we called "Tools, Language, and Intelligence: Evolutionary Implications," which was co-organized by American biological anthropologist Kathleen Gibson and British social anthropologist Tim Ingold. The symposium was tackling the long-intractable question of the origin of language, which goes to the heart of how we think about humanity and culture. It took off from the hypothesis that tool use, language, and cognition rest on common neurological substrates. To pursue that hypothesis, as well as alternatives to it, an extraordinarily diverse group of researchers was put together: biological anthropologists with interest in brain evolution; linguists concerned with the biological basis of language and the clues to be gleaned from studies of brain damage; archaeologists expert in the emergence of tool use in the Lower Paleolithic; developmental psychologists who could speak to cognitive processes in human children (including one who focuses on deaf children); field primatologists and an ape-language psychologist who are documenting object manipulation and communication in chimpanzees and other primates; a social anthropologist working with foragers; a neurobiologist; and a comparative animal behaviorist.

This mixed group quickly found a common project to which, with their varied expertise, they could all contribute in different but complementary ways. Even the divide between the primatologists and those linguists and psychologists who knew only humans (and who began on a note of amused skepticism about what chimpanzees had to do with it all) was bridged as the evidence pointed to strong ape-human continuities in most cognitive and communicative domains. The general conclusion was that while there is no simple relationship among tool use, language, and culturally shaped social behavior, they appear to have common neural bases and are likely to have evolved in mutuality with one another. More importantly, the symposium opened up a range of new research directions on human cognitive evolution that require collaboration among specialists from all the subfields and related disciplines. The implications of this new research are as profound for cultural anthropology as they are for evolutionary studies as such (see Gibson and Ingold 1993).

This kind of multidisciplinary approach is encouraging, but it is hardly the norm in the study of human evolution. As in this field, in the areas of physical anthropology concerned with processes of human biology and variation there has been a trend toward increasing specialization and closer affiliation with the biological sciences. But here too some efforts are being made to recast the relationship with other subfields of anthropology in order to address a wide range of problems at the intersection of biology and culture.

Within physical anthropology, now more often called biological anthropology, the domination of evolutionary and adaptationist models up to the 1990s left little room for social, economic, or political factors or contexts, which tended to be collapsed into "environmental conditions" or excluded as "noise." Interest in those conditions in their own right—as processes that impact human biology, including the forces of global change that often have devastating biological consequences—was ruled out. The organizers of a 1992 symposium on "Political-Economic Approaches in Biological Anthropology," Alan Goodman and Thomas Leatherman, hoped to reverse this trend. They wanted to foster the study of biological capacities and well-being in the "context of local cultures and histories, which in turn are shaped by and interact with interregional and global processes." They are among a small number of biological anthropologists who are beginning to see that stressors move through a cultural filter and are intimately linked with social inequality. The mainstream of the subdiscipline has tended to discount such views as inappropriately injecting politics into science.

The participants in the symposium were divided about equally between biological anthropologists selected for their openness to political-economic perspectives and scholars from other subfields working within those perspectives. The symposium had two major components: critical analyses of the history of theory in biological anthropology (especially of the adaptation concept) and a series of case studies linking biology to political-economic processes. Thus several cases examined how global forces, such as capitalist transformations, were transmitted and reshaped locally into the material conditions that impact human biology. Despite the disciplinary and other differences among the conferees, they found common ground and came to see themselves as the advance guard of an effort to encourage a more socially conscious and reflexive biological anthropology. The symposium did not change the prevailing currents in the subdiscipline, but it opened up new research directions and gave credibility to politically informed approaches to the study of human biology (see Goodman and Leatherman 1998).

I turn now to more familiar ground in cultural anthropology. One of the most striking trends of the late 1980s and the 1990s was the growing attention to globalization and transnational processes. This trend was manifested in a variety of interests: in migration, especially the kind in which populations maintain social ties to their place of origin; in state responses to both immigrants and emigrants; in cultural flows and cultural production, including the "ethnoscapes" and "bricolage" of the postmodern world; in economic globalization and the emergence of global cities; in diaspora studies, which emphasize issues of identity; in multisited ethnography; and in other interests. A symposium in 1994 had as its goal to develop a more coherent framework for understanding such processes and to explore their contexts and implications. The strategy was to bring together proponents of the various current approaches to transnationalism, as well as researchers working in a wide range of ethnographic settings. The group included anthropologists, sociologists, political scientists, a political economist, a historian, and a scholar of cultural studies.

The symposium defined a central problem: Given that increasing numbers of people are living their lives across borders and given that capital accumulation is becoming more global, why are some states closing their borders, others trying to incorporate past citizens, and small territorial units constituting themselves as new nation-states? And why in the midst of intensive economic and cultural globalization is there a growth of nationalism and of social movements organized around particularistic identities? This problem spoke to the prevailing debate over whether transnationalism presaged the dissolution of the nation-state. The group's answer was that nation-states not only were not being weakened but were responding with intensified nation-building projects.

The major conclusion of the symposium was that analysis of cultural production and identity requires taking account of global capitalism, class, and multiple structures of power. In retrospect, the organizers saw the symposium as having straddled a first and second wave of transnational anthropology (Glick Schiller, Szanton Blanc, and Basch 1999). The first wave was marked by a fascination with various kinds of flows across state borders, by a predominance of postmodern language, and by an emphasis on cultural hybridity and homogenization. Much of this work was ahistorical and strongly culturalist. The second wave, which the symposium foreshadowed, takes a more critical and historical stance on globalization, seeing it as a political program and attending to the ways in which nation-states have reasserted their power so as to control it. This wave of scholarship is concerned less with homogenization than with inequalities and regional differences within the global system and with processes of domination and resistance.

Another recent trend in cultural anthropology has been a new kind of interest in reproduction, stimulated in part by the rapid advances in reproductive technologies and in part by the politicization of reproduction in many contexts. In 1991 Rayna Rapp and Faye Ginsburg organized a symposium to highlight this emerging interest and to move the topic of reproduction out of its marginal status as a woman's domain and to the center stage of contemporary theory. "The Politics of Reproduction" proposed to examine reproductive issues from two perspectives simultaneously: the practices associated with human reproduction over the life cycle as these are embedded in particular cultures (the local lens); and the larger, more distant power relations that shape reproductive experiences (the global lens). The approach was simultaneously discursive, biologically embedded, and attuned to political-economic forces.

This symposium brought together cultural anthropologists (the majority), medical anthropologists, biological anthropologists, a demographer, a sociologist, a political scientist, and a historian. The treatment of reproduction encompassed a range of topics, from the one-child policy in China to the banning of abortion in Romania, from prenatal diagnostic screening to in-vitro fertilization, from the politics of birth and birth control to the politics of parenting. Each case study showed the links between culturally specific, local practices and the processes at work at the levels of the state and of global political economy.

The symposium succeeded in carving out what has since become a lively, growing field for anthropology and in providing some guideposts for it. The symposium did not invent the subject, of course, but it brought to bear on it developments in several related domains, including feminist theory, interests in childhood and in new forms of kinship, the politics of the body, and political demography, as well as research on new reproductive technologies and their cultural implications. By bringing together these developments, the symposium gave shape to a political anthropology of reproduction (see Ginsburg and Rapp 1995).

In close parallel to the redefinition of anthropological approaches to reproduction has been the emergence of new directions in the study of kinship. It had become clear that reproductive technologies were affecting kinship systems, which raised questions about other ways in which kinship practices and kinship studies were changing. A symposium in 1998 assessed the new work on kinship; the organizers were Sarah Franklin, who came out of British cultural studies, and Susan McKinnon, who had been a student of David Schneider and Marshall Sahlins. The organizers challenged the widely pronounced claim that kinship, so long at the very heart of anthropology, was moribund in the post-Schneider era, having given way to interests in gender and sexuality, ethnicity, identity, and other trendy topics. Kinship had not disappeared, they argued; it had just been backgrounded in these and other contexts so that it no longer constituted a discrete domain. In the process, the new approaches to kinship had been redefining the concept itself.

In addition to social and cultural anthropology, the participants in the kinship symposium came from biological anthropology, medical anthropology, and science studies. They examined a series of new sites where kinship was being rediscovered: transcultural adoption; the medical clinic; the laboratory, where technological innovations in biology and genetics were altering the "natural facts" of reproduction, bodies, and species; the use of kinship representations in notions of knowledge and property; the invocation of genealogy in biomedical contexts and political projects; and the implication of "blood" and "shared substance" (Schneider's concepts) in definitions of similarity and difference in several arenas, including gender, race, and nationalism.

The organizers summed up the symposium's work as addressing two questions: What comes to signify kinship, and what does kinship come to signify (Franklin and McKinnon 2000)? This formulation reflects the enduring influence of Schneider's culturological approach to kinship, although the symposium was intended to go beyond his nihilistic stance. The achievement of the symposium and the research it considered was to open up ways of re-thinking the familiar ground of kinship and to extend that ground into new areas that have not traditionally been thought of as kinship topics (see Franklin and McKinnon 2002).

Of these symposia, the three that were primarily within the scope of cultural anthropology included participants from both political-economic and interpretive persuasions. In general, because they were focusing on a common set of problems, their differences came to be expressed as complementary rather than mutually exclusive modes of analysis. All three engaged the opposition between positivism and constructivism and succeeded, to a large extent, in transcending it.

Two other symposia made those opposing positions their central issue. These two were inspired by a final trend that I want to point to: a growing anthropological interest in science as a topic in its own right. This trend is linked to the emergence of the new field of science studies, to which anthropology's special contribution has been ethnographies and cultural analyses of science practices. The interest in science as an object of study has brought into high relief the contrasting views of science held by anthropologists: a belief in positivist science as the route to truth and the understanding of science as constructed, like any other cultural practice. These symposia, however, offered hints that the divergent views may not be irretrievably at odds with each other.

In 1996 two biological anthropologists who study monkeys, Shirley Strum and Linda Fedigan, organized a symposium to look at the history of primatology as a case study of how science works. They were originally interested in the question of whether the entrance of large numbers of women into this field had affected how our views of primate societies have changed. Their larger goal was to examine the interplay among theory, method, the social organization of a science, and the wider societal and cultural context in which the science was practiced. About half of the group they assembled were primatologists, men and women of different generations and from several national traditions, and the other half included scholars of science studies, feminist studies, and popular culture. Among the latter group was Donna Haraway, who had enraged primatologists with her interpretive history of the field, *Primate Visions* (1989); she, along with Bruno Latour, who had written about laboratory life (1987; Latour and Woolgar 1986), were regarded by most of the primatologists present as incarnations of extreme postmodernism.

What the symposium did, therefore, was to bring together the primatologists, who believed that what they were doing was objective, testable, "normal" science, with those who had studied them and who treated their science as historically, socially, and culturally situated. Conflict was inevitable, but the two groups worked through many of the issues dividing them. In the process, which continued beyond the week of meetings into an eighteen-month-long exchange of e-mails, caricatures were set aside and a richer understanding of science practice emerged. No one's mind was greatly changed, but the questions that the symposium began with were transformed in ways that opened up possibilities for collaboration rather than dissension (see Strum and Fedigan 2000).

During the 1990s the revolution in genetics deeply impacted anthropology. New genetic methods and data infused all the subfields, opening up novel research problems and inviting reexamination of old ones, but also raising an array of ethical, legal, and policy issues. Not only was biological anthropology being transformed, but cultural anthropologists were doing ethnographies of genetic practices and discourses in a range of contexts—in laboratories, clinics, the popular media, and everyday life. To address the question of how the advances in genetics were affecting anthropology and to consider their implications for the future, in 1999 I organized a symposium on "Anthropology in the Age of Genetics" in collaboration with biological anthropologist Alan Goodman and cultural anthropologist Deborah Heath.

This topic was particularly intriguing for me, as one who grew up in the four-field tradition, because it brought into conjuncture anthropologists from opposite poles on the spectrum of subfields: at one end the most "scientific" and specialized of the biological anthropologists, and at the other end the social-cultural anthropologists doing cultural studies of science, who favored interpretive approaches and worked in nontraditional sites—some of them were even postmodern. The symposium was, in a sense, a test of whether anthropologists at these two poles could speak to each other and find common purpose; if they could, we would have reason to hope that anthropology has a future as an integrated discipline.

The participants were drawn, one-third each, from biological anthropology, cultural anthropology, and a number of related disciplines (evolutionary biology, genetics, science studies, and history of science). The discussions revealed how much biological and cultural issues interpenetrated, and it became abundantly clear that each specialist needed to take account of that interpenetration in his or her own work. The symposium was a testament to the possibility and the value of dissolving boundaries—between subdisciplines of anthropology and between the sciences and the humanities more generally.

Like all the symposia I have described, it not only crossed anthropological subfields and reached out to other disciplines, but it also gave voice to theoretical fault lines in anthropology and to some extent transcended them (see Goodman, Heath, and Lindee 2003).

Anthropology in the United States as a National Tradition

At the conclusion of these discussions of four kinds of anthropology, we might ask whether what we have described constitute national traditions. The discussions traced internal debates and transformations but also highlighted distinctive brands of anthropology, each with its own historical trajectory. At the same time, they documented cross-currents and mutual influences among the four. Such interactions are particularly important for the American case given the late arrival of the United States on the international academic scene and the critical role that foreign-born scholars played in that country. In what sense, then, might anthropology in the United States be a national tradition, and what is distinctive about it?

As we have seen, Franz Boas brought from Germany the elements of a concept of culture, but he redefined it in the American context: setting it against biological determinism, giving it a pluralist meaning, and using it as a touchstone for recording the lifeways of native peoples and tracing their histories. Culture then became the unifying rationale for a four-field approach. The Boasian paradigm, elaborated and reshaped by his students over three generations, dominated American anthropology until mid-century. Many of the leading Boasian figures, especially in the first cohort, were European-born, some having emigrated after receiving higher education abroad. However, they too adapted ideas derived from other traditions to the exigencies of the United States, where the predominant concerns were issues of race and cultural difference and where the natives whose cultures were at stake were the American Indians.

I would suggest that in this early period, and to some extent in later periods as well, a characteristic of American anthropology was a pattern of infusion of outside influences and then an absorption and Americanization of those influences. Concepts originating with German, French, and British social theorists, in particular, were digested and re-formed in a framework that was distinctively American and responsive to the social and political context of the United States. Thus, the ideas of Bronislaw Malinowski and A. R. Radcliffe-Brown were translated into an American functionalism that, joined with Boasian cultural relativism, engendered not only academic innovations such as the culture-and-personality school but also a political program and an ongoing commentary on American life.

After World War II American cultural anthropology was marked by the tension between materialisms and mentalisms; each of these underwent shifts over time, but the tension continued into the 1990s. Although much influenced by the contributions of foreign-born scholars from Karl Wittfogel and Karl Polanyi to Eric Wolf and Victor Turner, this was primarily a homegrown development, and it became a singularly American argument. For example, both sides reacted to the political upheavals of the 1960s and to the entry of new voices into the academy, but they did so with different kinds of reinventions of anthropology.

For anthropologists who came of age during the postwar expansion, Karl Marx, Max Weber, and Émile Durkheim were required reading; everything that came out of British social anthropology during its heyday was followed closely; and Marcel Mauss and Claude Lévi-Strauss were read at least in translation. Later, the French and British Marxists became reference points for American anthropologists of the left, and of course today Pierre Bourdieu and Michel Foucault are universally cited, if not always read. Americans have always had a hypervaluation of European scholarship, even a kind of inferiority complex with regard to it. Yet our diffidence coexists with our brashness—our readiness to adopt outside influences and make them our own, often erasing their history in the process.

Around 1970 something changed: with the waning of British dominance, the United States became hegemonic in anglophone anthropology. At the same time, the streams of cross-national influence intensified, with people moving back and forth, with many more works published in translation, and with much expanded mechanisms of international communication—professional societies, conferences, and the like, and increasingly in later decades, electronic modes of rapid communication. In this situation no national tradition can remain insulated or entirely hegemonic. We are moving toward an international community of anthropology that is itself linked to other international academic communities, but we are not there yet.

In following the development of ideas in our four anthropological traditions, I was struck by a peculiar quality of the American experience. Unlike traditions in which there is a sequence of influence from teachers to students, American anthropologists have consistently reacted against their teachers and other precursors, and new ideas have usually emerged as they were counterposed against old ones. I believe this quality is related to the institutional structure of academia in the United States. The multicentricity, the limited degree of hierarchy, and the diversity of settings available for academic careers make it possible for renegades to survive—until they become victims of the next generation's revisionism. This structure also means that no paradigm can remain dominant for very long without challenges from both within and without.

In view of what some see as the fragmentation of American anthropology today and the questioning of its foundational tenets, such as the four-field structure and the culture concept, can we say that it still constitutes a national tradition? My opinion is that although the configuration of American anthropology is an accident of history, it gives the U.S. version of the discipline a certain coherence of outlook despite its diversity. While not all practitioners in the United States would agree with that judgment, they nevertheless share underlying assumptions and research questions about humans and their engagement with the world. That shared framework keeps American anthropology both distinctively American and distinctively anthropological—even as we argue about what exactly that means. The future will surely see an accelerating internationalization of anthropology, but that might well encompass the continuation (for a time, at least) of different traditions—different ways of defining our discipline and of going about our work.

Abélès, M. 1991. *Quiet Days in Burgundy: A Study of Local Politics.* Cambridge, U.K.: Cambridge University Press.

———. 1992. *La vie quotidienne au Parlement européen.* Paris: Hachette.

———. 1996. "La Communauté européene: Une perspective anthropologique." *Social Anthropology* 4:33–45.

———. 1999. "How the Anthropology of France Has Changed Anthropology in France: Assessing New Directions in the Field." *Current Anthropology* 14:404–8.

———. 2000. *Un ethnologue l'Assemblée.* Paris: Odile Jacob.

Aborigines Protection Society. 1837. *Regulations of the Society.* London: W. Ball.

Adams, W. Y. 1998. *The Philosophical Roots of Anthropology.* Stanford, Calif.: Center for the Study of Language and Information.

Adorno, T. W. 1969. *Der Positivismusstreit in der deutschen Soziologie.* Berlin: Neuwied.

Allen, N. J. 1985. "The Category of the Person: A Reading of Mauss's Last Essay." In *The Category of the Person: Anthropology, Philosophy, History,* ed. M. Carrithers, S. Collins, and S. Lukes. Cambridge: Cambridge University Press.

———. 1998. "Louis Dumont (1911–1998)." *Journal of the Anthropological Society of Oxford* 29:1–4.

Ankermann, B. 1905. "Kulturkreise und Kulturschichten in Afrika." *Zeitschrift für Ethnologie* 37:54–84.

Arendt, H. 1958. *The Human Condition.* Chicago: University of Chicago Press.

Arensberg, C. M. 1937. *The Irish Countryman: An Anthropological Study.* New York: P. Smith.

———. 1954. "The Community-Study Method." *American Journal of Sociology* 60:109–24.

———. 1961. "The Community as Object and as Sample." *American Anthropologist* 63:241–64.

———. 1963. "The Old World Peoples: The Place of European Cultures in World Ethnography." *Anthropological Quarterly* 36:75–99.

————. 1972. "Culture as Behavior: Structure and Emergence." *Annual Review of Anthropology* 1:1–26.

Aron, R. 1968. *Main Currents in Sociological Thought*. Harmondsworth: Penguin.

Asad, T., ed. 1973. *Anthropology and the Colonial Encounter*. Atlantic Heights, N.J.: Humanities Press.

Augé, M. 1982. *The Anthropological Circle: Symbol, Function, History*. Cambridge: Cambridge University Press.

————. 1995. *Non-Places: Introduction to an Anthropology of Supermodernity*. New York: Verso.

————. 1999. *An Anthropology for Contemporaneous Worlds*. Stanford, Calif.: Stanford University Press.

Bachelard, G. 1934. *Le nouvel esprit scientifique*. Paris: Presses Universitaires de France.

————. 1953. *Le matérialisme rationnel*. Paris: Presses Universitaires de France.

Badcock, C. R. 1975. *Lévi-Strauss: Structuralism and Sociological Theory*. London: Hutchinson.

Balandier, G. 1966. *Ambiguous Africa: Cultures in Collision*. London: Chatto & Windus.

————. 1968. *Daily Life in the Kingdom of the Kongo from the Sixteenth to the Eighteenth Century*. London: Allen & Unwin.

————. 1970a. *Political Anthropology*. London: Allen Lane the Penguin Press.

————. 1970b. *The Sociology of Black Africa: Social Dynamics in Central Africa*. London: André Deutsch.

Banfield, E. C. 1958. *The Moral Basis of a Backward Society*. Glencoe: Free Press.

Barnes, J. A. 1962. "African Models in the New Guinea Highlands." *Man* 62:5–9.

————. 1966. "Durkheim's Division of Labour in Society." *Man*, n.s. 1:158–75.

Barnes, R. H., D. de Coppet, and R. J. Parkin. 1985. *Contexts and Levels: Anthropological Essays on Hierarchy*. Oxford: Jaso.

Barraud, C. 1981. *Tanebar-Evav: Une société de maisons tournée vers le large*. Cambridge: Cambridge University Press.

Barraud, C., D. de Coppet, A. Iteanu, and R. Jamous. 1994. *Of Relations and the Dead: Four Societies Viewed from the Angle of their Exchanges*. Oxford: Berg.

Barth, F. 1959. *Political Leadership among Swat Pathans*. London: University of London Athlone Press.

————, ed. 1969. *Ethnic Groups and Boundaries: The Social Organization of Culture Difference. (Results of a Symposium Held at the University of Bergen, 23rd to 26th February 1967)*. Bergen: Universitetsforlaget.

Barthes, R. 1974. *S/Z*. New York: Hill and Wang.

————. 1975. *The Pleasure of the Text*. New York: Hill and Wang.

Barthes, R., and A. Lavers. 1972. *Mythologies*. London: Jonathan Cape.

Bastide, R. 1950. *Sociologie et psychoanalyse*. Paris: Presses Universitaires de France.

————. 1958. *Le condomblé de Bahia, rite nago*. Paris: Mouton.

————. 1972. *Le reve, la transe, et la folie*. Paris: Flammarion.

———. 1973. *Applied Anthropology*. London: Croom Helm.

Bataille, G. 1970. *Oeuvres complétes*. Paris: Gallimard.

———. 1997. *The Bataille Reader*. Oxford: Blackwell.

Bateson, G. 1936. *Naven, a Survey of the Problems Suggested by a Composite Picture of the Culture of a New Guinea Tribe Drawn from Three Points of View*. Cambridge: Cambridge University Press.

Baudler, G. 1970. *Im Worte sehen. Das Sprachdenken Johann Georg Hamanns*. Bonn: Bouvier.

Baudrillard, J. 1968. *Le système des objets*. Paris: Gallimard.

———. 1970. *La société de consommation: Ses mythes, ses structures*. Paris: Denoël.

———. 1975. *The Mirror of Production*. St Louis, Mo.: Telos Press.

———. 1988a. *America*. London: Verso.

———. 1988b. *Selected Writings*. Stanford: Stanford University Press.

———. 1993. *Symbolic Exchange and Death*. London: Sage.

Bauer, K. J. 1989. *Alois Musil: Wahrheitssucher in der Wüste*. Vienna: Böhlau.

Baumann, H. 1934. "Die afrikanischen Kulturkreise." *Africa* 7:127–39.

Bekombo, M. 1998. "Celui qui va là-bas ne parle pas." *L'Homme* 148:11–14.

Bellier, I. 1995. "Moralité, language et pouvoirs dans les institutions européenes." *Social Anthropology* 3:235–50.

Bellier, I., and T. M. Wilson, eds. 2000. *An Anthropology of the European Union: Building, Imagining, and Experiencing the New Europe*. Oxford: Berg.

Belmont, N. 1979. *Arnold van Gennep: The Creator of French Ethnography*. Chicago: University of Chicago Press.

———. 1991. "Van Gennep." In *Dictionnaire de l'ethnologie et de l'anthropologie*, ed. P. Bonte and M. Izard. Paris: Presses Universitaires de France.

Benedict, R. 1934. *Patterns of Culture*. Boston: Houghton Mifflin.

———. 1946. *The Chrysanthemum and the Sword: Patterns of Japanese Behavior*. Boston: Houghton Mifflin.

Bennett, J. W., ed. 1975. *The New Ethnicity: Perspectives from Ethnology*. 1973 Proceedings of the American Ethnological Society. St. Paul, Minn.: West Publishing.

Benveniste, E. 1973. *Indo-European Language and Society*. London: Faber and Faber.

Berg, E. 1990. "Johann Gottfried Herder." Pp. 51–68 in *Klassiker der Kulturanthropologie: Von Montaigne bis Margaret Mead*, ed. W. Marschall. München: Beck.

Bergson, H. 1960. *Creative Evolution*. London: Macmillan & Company.

———. 1986. *Matter and Memory*. London: Macmillan.

Bernatzik, H. A., and E. Bernatzik. 1936. *Die Geister der gelben Blätter: Forschungsreisen in Hinterindien*. München: Union.

Berndt, R. M. 1977. "Anthropologiocal Research in British Colonies: Some Personal Accounts." Special issue, *Anthropological Forum* 4.

Bernot, L. 1967a. *Les Cak: Contribution et l'étude ethnographique d'une population de langue loi*. Paris: Editions du Centre National de la Recherche Scientifique.

————. 1967b. *Les paysans arakanais du Pakistan oriental: L'histoire, le monde végétal et l'organisation sociale des réfugise Marma (Mog). [École pratique des hautes Études, Sorbonne. 6me section: sciences économiques et sociales].* Paris: Mouton.

————. 1986. "Hommage à André Leroi-Gourhan." *L'Homme* 100:7–20.

Bernot, L., and D. Bernot. 1958. *Les Khyang des collines de Chittagong (Pakistan oriental): Matériaux pour l'étude linguistique des Chin.* Paris: Plon.

Bernot, L., and R. Blancard. 1953. *Nouville: Un village français.* Paris: Institut d'Ethnologie.

Biardeau, M. 1989. *Hinduism: The Anthropology of a Civilization.* Delhi: Oxford University Press.

Biardeau, M., and C. Malamoud. 1976. *Le sacrifice dans l'Inde ancienne.* Paris: Presses Universitaires de France.

Bing, F. 1964. "Entretiens avec Alfred Métraux." *L'Homme* 4:20–32.

Bloch, M. 1983. *Marxism and Anthropology: The History of a Relationship.* Oxford: Clarendon.

————, ed. 1975. *Marxist Analysis and Social Anthropology.* London: Malahy.

Bloch, M., and J. Parry, eds., 1982. *Death and the Regeneration of Life.* Cambridge: Cambridge University Press.

Bloch, M., and D. Sperber. 2002. "Kinship and Evolved Psychological Dispositions: The Mother's Brother Controversy Reconsidered." *Current Anthropology* 43:723–48.

Boas, F. 1896/1940. "The Limitations of the Comparative Method in Anthropology." Pp. 270–80 in F. Boas, *Race, Language, and Culture.* New York: Macmillan.

————. 1911a. *Change in Bodily Form of Descendants of Immigrants.* New York: Columbia University Press.

————. 1911b. *The Mind of Primitive Man.* New York: Macmillan.

————. 1928. "Foreword." In M. Mead, *Coming of Age in Samoa: A Psychological Study of Primitive Youth for Western Civilization.* New York: New American Library.

————. 1934. "Introduction." Pp. xiii–xv in R. Benedict, *Patterns of Culture.* Boston: Houghton Mifflin.

Bonte, P., and M. Izard, eds. 1991. *Dictionnaire de l'ethnologie et de l'anthropologie.* Paris: Presses Universitaires de France.

Boschetti, A. 1985. *Sartre et "Les Temps modernes": Une entreprise intellectuelle.* Paris: Editions de Minuit.

Boserup, E. 1970. *The Conditions of Agricultural Growth. The Economics of Agrarian Change under Population Pressure.* London: Allen & Unwin.

Bouez, S. 1985. *Réciprocité et hiérarchie: L'alliance chez les Ho et les Santal de l'Inde.* Paris: Société d'Ethnographie: Service du Publication du Laboratoire d'Ethnologie et de Sociologie Comparative Université de Paris X.

————. 1992. *La déesse apaisé: Norme et transgression dans l'hindouisme au Bengale.* Paris: Éditions de l'École des Hautes Études en Sciences Sociales.

Bouglé, C. C. A. 1899. *Les idées égalitaires: Etude sociologique.* Paris: Alcan.

———. 1903. *La démocratie devant la science: Études critiques sur l'hérèdité, la concurrence et la différenciation.* Paris: Alcan.

———. 1912. *La sociologie de Proudhon.* Paris: Armand Colin.

———. 1969. *The Evolution of Values: Studies in Sociology with Special Applications to Teaching.* New York: A. M. Kelley.

———. 1971. *Essays on the Caste System.* Cambridge: Cambridge University Press.

Bouquet, M. 2000. "Figures of Relations: Reconnecting Kinship Studies and Museum Collections." In *Cultures of Relatedness: New Approaches to the Study of Kinship,* ed. J. Carsten. Cambridge: Cambridge University Press.

Bourdieu, P. 1962. *The Algerians.* Boston: Beacon.

———. 1977. *Outline of a Theory of Practice.* Cambridge: Cambridge University Press.

———. 1979. *Algeria 1960: The Disenchantment of the World; The Sense of Honour; The Kabyle House, or, the World Reversed: Essays.* Cambridge: Cambridge University Press.

———. 1984. *Distinction: A Social Critique of the Judgement of Taste.* London: Routledge & Kegan Paul.

———. 1988. *Homo Academicus.* Cambridge, U.K.: Polity Press.

———. 1990a. *In Other Words: Essays Towards a Reflexive Sociology.* Cambridge, U.K.: Polity Press.

———. 1990b. *The Logic of Practice.* Cambridge, U.K.: Polity Press.

Bourdieu, P., et al. 1999. *The Weight of the World: Social Suffering in Contemporary Society.* Cambridge, U.K.: Polity Press.

Bourdieu, P., and J.-C. Passeron. 1979. *The Inheritors: French Students and Their Relation to Culture.* Chicago: University of Chicago Press.

Bourgin, H. 1925. *Cinquante ans d'expérience démocratique, 1874–1924.* Paris: Nouvelle Librairie Nationale.

———. 1970. *De Jaurès à Léon Blum: L'école normale et la politique.* Paris: Gordon & Breach.

Bowman, G. 1994. "Xenophobia, Fantasy, and the Nation: The Logic of Ethnic Violence in Former Yugoslavia." In *The Anthropology of Europe: Identities and Boundaries in Conflict,* ed. V. Goddard et al. Oxford: Berg.

Brandewie, E. 1990. *When Giants Walked the Earth: The Life and Times of Wilhelm Schmidt, SVD.* Fribourg: University Press.

Braudel, F. 1972. *The Mediterranean and the Mediterranean World in the Age of Philip II.* New York: Harper & Row.

Brauen, M. 2000. *Traumwelt Tibet: Westliche Trugbilder.* Bern: Haupt.

Braukämper, U. 2001. "Gustav Nachtigal." Pp. 332–37 in *Hauptwerke der Ethnologie,* ed. C. F. Feest and K.-H. Kohl. Stuttgart: Kröner.

Braun, J. 1995. *Eine deutsche Karriere: Die Biographie des Ethnologen Hermann Baumann (1902–1971).* München: Akademischer Verlag.

Brooke, M. Z. 1970. *Le Play: Engineer and Social Scientist: The Life and Work of Frédéric Le Play*. London: Longmans.

Bucher, G. 2002. "'Unterricht, was bey Beschreibung der Völker, absonderlich der Sibirischen in acht zu nehmen.' Die Instruktionen Gerhard Friedrich Müllers und ihre Bedeutung für die Geschichte der Ethnologie und der Geschichtswissenschaft." Stuttgart: Steiner.

Buchheit, K. P., and K. P. Köpping. 2001. "Adolf Philipp Wilhelm Bastian." Pp. 19–25 in *Hauptwerke der Ethnologie*, ed. C. F. Feest and K.-H. Kohl. Stuttgart: Kröner.

Bunzl, M. 1996. "Franz Boas and the Humboldtian Tradition: From Volksgeist and Nationalcharakter to an Anthropological Concept of Culture." Pp. 17–78 in *Volksgeist as Method and Ethic: Essays on Boasian Ethnography and the German Anthropological Tradition*, ed. G. W. Stocking Jr. Madison: University of Wisconsin Press.

Burguière, A. 1975. *Bretons de Plozévet*. Paris: Flammarion.

Burke, P. 1989. "French Historians and Their Cultural Identities." In *History and Ethnicity*, ed. E. Tonkin, M. McDonald, and M. Chapman. London: Routledge.

Byer, D. 1999. *Der Fall Hugo Bernatzik: Ein Leben zwischen Ethnologie und Öffentlichkeit 1897–1953*. Köln: Böhlau.

Caillois, R. 1950. *L'homme et le sacré*. Paris: Gallimard.

Calame-Griaule, G. 1965/1986. *Words and the Dogon World*. Philadelphia: Institute for the Study of Human Issues.

Carneiro, R. 1981. "Leslie White." Pp. 209–52 in *Totems and Teachers: Perspectives on the History of Anthropology*, ed. S. Silverman. New York: Columbia University Press.

Carrier, J. 1995. *Occidentalism: Images of the West*. Oxford: Oxford University Press.

Carrin-Bouez, M. 1986. *La fleur et l'os: Symbolisme et rituel chez les Santal*. Paris: Ecole des Hautes Etudes en Sciences Sociales.

Carsten, J. 2000. "Introduction: Cultures of Relatedness." In *Cultures of Relatedness: New Approaches to the Study of Kinship*, ed. J. Carsten. Cambridge: Cambridge University Press.

Casajus, D. 1985. "Why Do the Tuareg Veil Their Faces?" In *Contexts and Levels: Anthropological Essays on Hierarchy*, ed. R. H. Barnes, D. de Coppet, and R. J. Parkin. JASO Occasional Papers 4. Oxford: JASO.

———. 1996. "Claude Lévi-Strauss and Louis Dumont: Media Portraits." In *Popularizing Anthropology*, ed. J. MacClancy and C. McDonaugh. London: Routledge.

Cazeneuve, J. 1972. *Lucien Lévy-Bruhl*. Oxford: Basil Blackwell.

Chapman, C. G. 1935/1981. *Milocca, a Sicilian Village*. Cambridge, Mass.: Schenkman.

Charachidzé, G. 1991. "Georges Dumézil." In *Dictionnaire de l'ethnologie et de l'anthropologie*, ed. P. Bonte and M. Izard. Paris: Presses Universitaires de France.

Chevron, M.-F. 2003. *Anpassung und Entwicklung in Evolution und Kulturwandel: Ein Paradigmenstreit in der beginnenden deutschsprachigen Ethnologie und seine Folgen*. Berlin: LIT.

Cladis, M. S. 1999. *Durkheim and Foucault: Perspectives on Education and Punishment.* Oxford: Durkheim Press.

Clarke, S. 1981. *The Foundations of Structuralism: A Critique of Lévi-Strauss and the Structuralist Movement.* Brighton, U.K.: Harvester.

Clastres, P. 1972/1998. *Chronicle of the Guayaki Indians.* New York: Zone Books.

———. 1987. *Society against the State: Essays in Political Anthropology.* New York: Zone Books.

Clifford, J. 1982. *Person and Myth: Maurice Leenhardt in the Melanesian World.* Berkeley: University of California Press.

———. 1983. "Power and Dialogue in Ethnography: Marcel Griaule's Initiation." In *Observers Observed: Essays on Ethnographic Fieldwork,* ed. G. W. Stocking Jr. Madison: University of Wisconsin Press.

———. 1991. "Maurice Leenhardt." In *Dictionnaire de l'ethnologie et de l'anthropologie,* ed. P. Bonte and M. Izard. Paris: Presses Universitaires de France.

Clifford, J., and G. E. Marcus, eds. 1986. *Writing Culture: The Poetics and Politics of Ethnography.* Berkeley: University of California Press.

Codere, H. 1950. *Fighting with Property: A Study of Kwakiutl Potlatching and Warfare, 1792–1930.* New York: J. J. Augustin.

Colchester, M. 1982. "Les Yanomami, Sont-Ils Libres? Les Utopias Amazoniennes, Une Critique: A Look at French Anarchist Anthropology." *Journal of the Anthropological Society of Oxford* 13:147–64.

Cole, D. 1999. *Franz Boas: The Early Years, 1858–1906.* Toronto.

Cole, J. 1977. "Anthropology Comes Part-Way Home: Community Studies in Europe." *Annual Review of Anthropology* 6:349–78.

Cole, J. W., and E. R. Wolf. 1974. *The Hidden Frontier: Ecology and Ethnicity in an Alpine Valley.* New York: Academic Press.

Comte, A. 1973. *System of Positive Polity.* New York: Hill.

———. 1988. *Introduction to Positive Philosophy.* Indianapolis: Hackett.

Condominas, G. 1965. *L'exotique est quotidien: Sar Luk, Viêtnam central.* Paris: Plon.

———. 1977. *We Have Eaten the Forest: The Story of a Montagnard Village in the Central Highlands of Vietnam.* New York: Hill and Wang.

———. 1980. *L'espace social à propos de l'Asie du Sud-Est.* Paris: Flammarion.

Conte, E. 1987. "Wilhelm Schmidt: Des letzten Kaisers Beichtvater und das neudeutsche Heidentum." Pp. 261–278 in *Volkskunde und Nationalsozialismus,* ed. H. Gerndt. Edited special edition, *Münchner Beiträge zur Volkskunde* 7.

Conte, E., and C. Essner, eds. 1995. *La quête de la race: Une anthropologie du Nazisme.* Paris: Hachette.

Crapanzano, V. 1980. *Tuhami, Portrait of a Moroccan.* Chicago: University of Chicago Press.

Cresswell, R. 1991. "André Leroi-Gourhan." In *Dictionnaire de l'ethnologie et de l'anthropologie,* ed. P. Bonte and M. Izard. Paris: Presses Universitaires de France.

Crocker, J. C. 1985. *Vital Souls: Bororo Cosmology, Natural Symbolism, and Shamanism.* Tucson: University of Arizona Press.

Culler, J. D. 1976. *Saussure.* Glasgow: Fontana/Collins.

Current Anthropology. 1980. "Anthropology in France, Present and Future." *Current Anthropology* 21:479–89.

Dam Bo [Dournes, J]. 1950. "Les populations montagnardes du Sud-Indo-Chinois (Pémsiens)." *France-Asie* 49–50:931–1203.

Dampierre, É. d. 1963. *Poètes nzakara.* Paris: Juilliard.

———. 1984. *Penser au singulier: Étude nzakara.* Paris: Société d'ethnographie Universite de Paris X.

D'Andrade, R. 1995. "Moral Models in Anthropology." *Current Anthropology* 36:399–408, 433–36.

Danforth, L. M. 1982. *The Death Rituals of Rural Greece.* Princeton, N.J.: Princeton University Press.

Darnell, R. 2001. *Invisible Genealogies: A History of Americanist Anthropology.* Lincoln: University of Nebraska Press.

Davis, A., B. B. Gardner, and M. R. Gardner. 1941. *Deep South: A Social Anthropological Study of Caste and Class.* Chicago: University of Chicago Press.

de Coppet, D. 1985. "Land Owns People." In *Contexts and Levels: Anthropological Essays on Hierarchy,* ed. R. H. Barnes, D. de Coppet, and R. J. Parkin. JASO Occasional Papers 4. Oxford: JASO.

de Coppet, D., and A. Iteanu, ed. 1995. *Cosmos and Society in Oceania.* Oxford: Berg.

Delafosse, M. 1922. *Les noirs de l'Afrique.* Paris: Payot & Cie.

Delamont, S. 1995. *Appetites and Identities: An Introduction to the Social Anthropology of Western Europe.* London: Routledge.

Deleuze, G., and F. Guattari. 1984. *Anti-Oedipus: Capitalism and Schizophrenia.* London: Athlone.

———. 1988. *A Thousand Plateaus: Capitalism and Schizophrenia.* London: Athlone Press.

Deliège, R. 1985. *The Bhils of Western India: Some Empirical and Theoretical Issues in Anthropology in India.* New Delhi: National.

———. 1997. *The World of the "Untouchables": Paraiyars of Tamil Nadu.* Delhi: Oxford University Press.

———. 1999. *The Untouchables of India.* Oxford: Berg.

Deloria, V. 1969. *Custer Died for Your Sins.* London: Collier-Macmillan.

Deluz, A. 1991a. "Georges Devereux." In *Dictionnaire de l'ethnologie et de l'anthropologie,* ed. P. Bonte and M. Izard. Paris: Presses Universitaires de France.

———. 1991b. "Roger Bastide." In *Dictionnaire de l'ethnologie et de l'anthropologie,* ed. P. Bonte and M. Izard. Paris: Presses Universitaires de France.

Derrida, J. 1976. *Of Grammatology.* Baltimore: Johns Hopkins University Press.

———. 1978. *Writing and Difference.* Chicago: University of Chicago Press.

Descola, P. 1994. *In the Society of Nature: A Native Ecology in Amazonia*. Cambridge: Cambridge University Press.

————. 1996. *The Spears of Twilight: Life and Death in the Amazon Jungle*. London: HarperCollins.

Despres, L. A., ed. 1975. *Ethnicity and Resource Competition in Plural Societies*. The Hague: Mouton.

Devereux, G. 1937. "Functioning Units in Hä(rh)ndea(ng) Society." *Primitive Man* 10:1–7.

————. 1961. *Mohave Ethnopsychiatry and Suicide: The Psychiatric Knowledge and the Psychic Disturbances of an Indian Tribe*. Washington, D.C.: United States Government Printing Office.

————. 1967. *From Anxiety to Method in the Behavioral Sciences*. Paris: Mouton.

————. 1970. *Essais d'ethnopsychiatrie générale*. Paris: Gallimard.

Diamond, S. 1974. *In Search of the Primitive: A Critique of Civilization*. New Brunswick, N. J.: Transaction Books.

Diamond, S., B. Scholte, and E. Wolf. 1975. "Anti-Kaplan: Defining the Marxist Tradition." *American Anthropologist* 77:870–76.

Dias, N. 1991. "Musées." In *Dictionnaire de l'ethnologie et de l'anthropologie*, ed. P. Bonte and M. Izard. Paris: Presses Universitaires de France.

Dias, N., and J. Jamin. 1991. "Origines de l'anthropologie: Du début du xixe siècle à 1860." In *Dictionnaire de l'ethnologie et de l'anthropologie*, ed. P. Bonte and M. Izard. Paris: Presses Universitaires de France.

Dibie, P. 1991. "André Georges Haudricourt." In *Dictionnaire de l'ethnologie et de l'anthropologie*, ed. P. Bonte and M. Izard. Paris: Presses Universitaires de France.

Dieterlen, G. 1951. *Essai sur la religion bambara*. Paris: Presses Universitaires de France.

————, ed. 1973. *La notion de personne en Afrique noire, Paris 11–17 octobre 1971*. Paris: Editions du Centre National de la Recherche Scientifique.

Dollard, J. 1937. *Caste and Class in a Southern Town*. New York: Harper.

Dostal, W., ed. 1975. *Die Situation der Indios in Südamerika: Grundlagen der interethnischen Konflikte der nichtandinen Indianer*. Wuppertal: Peter Hammer.

————. 1994. "Silence in the Darkness: An Essay on German Ethnology during the National Socialist Period." *Social Anthropology/Anthropologie Sociale* 2/3:251–62.

Dostal, W., and A. Gingrich. 1996. "German and Austrian Anthropology." Pp. 263–65 in *Encyclopedia of Social and Cultural Anthropology*, ed. A. Barnard and J. Spencer. London: Routledge.

Dournes, J. 1951. "Nri (Coutumier Srê: Extraits)." *France-Asie* 73:1232–41.

————. 1972. *Coordonnées: Structures Jörai familiales et sociales*. Paris: Institut d'Ethnologie.

————. 1977. *Pötao: Une théorie du pouvoir chez les Indochinois Jörai*. Paris: Flammarion.

Dousset-Leenhardt, R. 1977. "Maurice Leehardt." *L'Homme* 17:105–15.

Dresch, P. 1998. "Mutual Deception: Totality, Exchange, and Islam in the Middle East." In *Marcel Mauss: A Centenary Tribute,* ed. W. James and N. J. Allen. New York: Berghahn.

Dreyfus, S. 1991. "Alfred Métraux." In *Dictionnaire de l'ethnologie et de l'anthropologie,* ed. P. Bonte and M. Izard. Paris: Presses Universitaires de France.

Dumézil, G. 1968–1973. *Mythes et épopées.* Paris: Gallimard.

———. 1988. *Mitra-Varuna: An Essay on Two Indo-European Representations of Sovereignty.* New York: Zone Books.

Dumont, L. 1951. *La Tarasque: Essai de description d'un fait local d'un point de vue ethnographique.* Paris: Gallimard.

———. 1966/1980. *Homo Hierarchicus: The Caste System and Its Implications.* Chicago: University of Chicago Press.

———. 1983. *Affinity as a Value: Marriage Alliance in South India, with Comparative Essays on Australia.* Chicago: University of Chicago Press.

———. 1986. *A South Indian Subcaste: Social Organization and Religion of the Pramalai Kallar.* Delhi: Oxford University Press.

———. 1992. *Essays on Individualism: Modern Ideology in Anthropological Perspective.* Chicago: University of Chicago Press.

———. 1994. *German Ideology: From France to Germany and Back.* Chicago: University of Chicago Press.

Durkheim, É. 1893/1984. *The Division of Labour in Society.* London: Macmillan.

———. 1894/1951. *Suicide: A Study in Sociology.* Glencoe: Free Press.

———. 1895/1982. *The Rules of Sociological Method: And Selected Texts on Sociology and Its Method.* London: Macmillan.

———. 1897/1997. "On the Work of Taine." In *Montesquieu: Quid secundatus politicae scientiae instituendae contulerit,* ed. É. Durkheim. Oxford: Durkheim Press.

———. 1912/1995. *The Elementary Forms of Religious Life.* New York: Free Press.

———. 1979. *Durkheim: Essays on Morals and Education.* London: Routledge and Kegan Paul.

———. 1997. *Montesquieu: Quid secundatus politicae scientiae instituendae contulerit.* Oxford: Durkheim Press.

Durkheim, É., and M. Mauss. 1903/1963. *Primitive Classification.* Chicago: University of Chicago Press.

Dwyer, K. 1982. *Moroccan Dialogues: Anthropology in Question.* Baltimore: Johns Hopkins University Press.

Ehl, S. 1995. "Ein Afrikaner erobert die Mainmetropole: Leo Frobenius in Frankfurt (1924–1938)." Pp. 121–140 in *Lebenslust und Fremdenfurcht: Ethnologie im Dritten Reich,* ed. T. Hauschild. Frankfurt: Suhrkamp.

Elias, N. 1969. *Über den Prozess der Zivilisation: Soziogenetische und psychogenetische Untersuchungen.* Bern: Francke.

Elphinstone, M. 1839/1972. *An Account of the Kingdom of Caubul.* Karachi: Oxford University Press.

Embree, J. 1939. *Suye Mura, A Japanese village.* Chicago: University of Chicago Press.

Enzensberger, U. 1979. *Georg Forster: Weltumsegler und Revolutionär.* Berlin: Wagenbach.

Eriksen, T. H., and F. S. Nielsen. 2001. *A History of Anthropology.* London: Pluto Press.

Evans, A. D. 2003. "Anthropology at War: Racial Studies of POWs during World War I." Pp. 198–229 in *Worldly Provincialism: German Anthropology in the Age of Empire,* ed. H. G. Penny and M. Bunzl. Ann Arbor: University of Michigan Press.

Evans-Pritchard, E. E. 1937. *Witchcraft, Oracles, and Magic among the Azande.* Oxford: Clarendon.

———. 1940. *The Nuer: A Description of the Modes of the Livelihood and Political Institutions of a Nilotic People.* Oxford: Clarendon.

———. 1949. *The Sanusi of Cyrenaica.* Oxford: Clarendon.

———. 1951. *Kinship and Marriage among the Nuer.* Oxford: Clarendon.

———. 1954. "Foreword." Pp. ix–xi in J. A. Pitt-Rivers, *The People of the Sierra.* London: Weidenfeld & Nicolson.

———. 1962. *Essays in Social Anthropology.* London: Faber and Faber.

———. 1965. *Theories of Primitive Religion.* Oxford: Clarendon.

———. 1981. *A History of Anthropological Thought,* ed. A. Singer and E. Gellner. New York: Basic Books.

Fauconnet, P. 1920. *La responsibilité: Étude de sociologie.* Paris: Alcan.

Favret-Saada, J. 1980. *Deadly Words: Witchcraft in the Bocage.* Cambridge: Cambridge University Press.

Feest, C. F. 1976. *Das rote Amerika: Nordamerikas Indianer.* Wien: Europaverlag.

Fei, H.-T. 1939. *Peasant Life in China.* London: Kegan Paul, Trench, Trubner.

Ferrell, R. 1996. *Passion in Theory: Conceptions of Freud and Lacan.* London: Routledge.

Firth, R. W. 1929. *Primitive Economics of the New Zealand Maori.* London: G. Routledge.

———. 1936. *We, the Tikopia: A Sociological Study of Kinship in Primitive Polynesia.* London: G. Allen & Unwin.

———. 1975. "An Appraisal of Modern Social Anthropology." *Annual Review of Anthropology* 4:1–25.

———, ed. 1957. *Man and Culture: An Evaluation of the Work of Malinowski.* London: Routledge and Kegan Paul.

Fischer, H. 1981. *Die Hamburger Südsee-Expedition: Über Ethnographie und Kolonialismus.* Frankfurt: Syndikat.

———. 1990. *Völkerkunde im Nationalsozialismus: Aspekte der Anpassung, Affinität und Behauptung einer wissenschaftlichen Disziplin.* Berlin: D. Reimer.

Forster, J. R. 1777. *A Voyage Round the World.* London: B. White.

Förster, T. 2001. "Heinrich Barth." Pp. 15–19 in *Hauptwerke der Ethnologie,* ed. Christian F. Feest and Karl-Heinz Kohl. Stuttgart: Kröner.

Fortes, M. 1945. *The Dynamics of Clanship among the Tallensi: Being the First Part of an Analysis of the Social Structure of a Trans-Volta Tribe.* London: Oxford University Press.

———. 1949a. "Time and Social Structure: An Ashanti Case Study." Pp. 54–84 in *Social Structure: Studies Presented to A. R. Radcliffe-Brown,* ed. M. Fortes. Oxford: Clarendon..

———. 1949b. *The Web of Kinship among the Tallensi: The Second Part of an Analysis of the Social Structure of a Trans-Volta Tribe.* London: Oxford University Press.

———. 1953. "The Structure of Unilineal Descent Groups." *American Anthropologist* 55:17–41.

———. 1959. "Descent, Filiation, and Affinity: A Rejoinder to Dr. Leach." *Man* 59:193–97, 206–12.

———, ed. 1949. *Social Structure: Studies Presented to A. R. Radcliffe-Brown.* Oxford: Clarendon.

Fortes, M., and E. E. Evans-Pritchard, eds. 1940. *African Political Systems.* London: Oxford University Press for the International African Institute.

Fortune, R. 1935. *Manus Religion.* Philadelphia: American Philosophical Society.

Foster, G. M. 1961. "The Dyadic Contract: A Model for the Social Structure of a Mexican Peasant Village." *American Anthropologist* 65:1280–94.

———. 1965. "Peasant Society and the Image of Limited Good." *American Anthropologist* 67:293–315.

Foucault, M. 1978. *The History of Sexuality.* Vol. 1. New York: Pantheon.

———. 1979. *Discipline and Punish: The Birth of the Prison.* New York: Vintage.

———. 1984. *The History of Sexuality.* Vol. 2. New York: Pantheon.

———. 1985. *The History of Sexuality.* Vol. 3. New York: Pantheon.

———. 1997. *Madness and Civilization: A History of Insanity in the Age of Reason.* London: Routledge.

Fournier, M. 1994. *Marcel Mauss.* Paris: Fayard.

Fox, R. G. 1972. "Rationale and Romance in Urban Anthropology." *Urban Anthropology* 1:205–33.

———, ed. 1991. *Recapturing Anthropology: Working in the Present.* Santa Fe: School of American Research Press.

Fox, R. G., and B. J. King, eds. 2002. *Anthropology beyond Culture.* Oxford: Berg.

Frank, A. G. 1966. "The Development of Underdevelopment." *Monthly Review* (September), 17–31.

———. 1967. *Capitalism and Underdevelopment in Latin America.* New York: Monthly Review Press.

Franklin, S., and S. McKinnon. 2000. "New Directions in Kinship Study: A Core Concept Revisited." *Current Anthropology* 41:275–79.

———, eds. 2002. *Relative Values: Reconfiguring Kinship Studies.* Durham, N.C.: Duke University Press.

Frazer, J. G. 1911–1936. *The Golden Bough: A Study in Magic and Religion.* 12 vols. London: Macmillan.

Freedman, M. 1975. "Introduction." In M. Granet, *The Religion of the Chinese People.* Oxford: Blackwell.

Freeman, D. 1983. *Margaret Mead and Samoa: The Making and Unmaking of an Anthropological Myth.* Cambridge, Mass.: Harvard University Press.

Fricke, C. 1993. "Die Deutschen Gesellschaften des 18. Jahrhunderts—ein Forschungsdesiderat." Pp. 77–98 in *Sprachwissenschaft im 18. Jahrhundert: Fallstudien und Überblicke,* ed. K. D. Dutz. Münster: Nodus.

Fried, M. H. 1967. *The Evolution of Political Society: An Essay in Political Anthropology.* New York: Random House.

———. 1975. *The Notion of Tribe.* Menlo Park, Calif.: Cummings.

Frobert, L. 1997. "Sociologie juidique et socialisme réformiste: Note sur le projet d'Emmanuel Lévy." *Durkheimian Studies* 3:27–42.

Fustel de Coulanges, N. D. 1864/1882. *The Ancient City: A Study on the Religion, Laws, and Institutions of Greece and Rome.* Garden City: Doubleday.

Gaborieau, M. 1978. *Le Népal et ses populations.* Bruselles: Editions Complexe.

Galey, J.-C. 1982. "A Conversation with Louis Dumont, Paris, 12 December 1979." In *Way of Life: King, Householder, Renouncer: Essays in Honour of Louis Dumont,* ed. T. N. Madan. Paris: Maison des Sciences de l'Homme.

———. 1989. "Reconsidering Kingship in India: An Ethnological Perspective." *History and Anthropology* 4:123–87.

Gane, M. 1992. "Introduction: Emile Durkheim, Marcel Mauss, and the Sociological Project." In *The Radical Sociology of Durkheim and Mauss,* ed. M. Gane. London: Routledge.

Garber, K. 1996. "Sozietät und Geistesadel: Von Dante zum Jakobiner-Club. Der frühneuzeitliche Diskurs de vera nobilitate und seine institutionelle Ausformung in der gelehrten Akademie." In *Europäische Sozietätsbewegung und demokratische Tradition: Die europäischen Akademien der Frühen Neuzeit zwischen Frührenaissance und Spätaufklärung,* ed. K. Garber, H. Wismann, and W. Siebers. Tübingen: M. Niemeyer.

Gardt, A. 1999. *Geschichte der Sprachwissenschaft in Deutschland. Vom Mittelalter bis ins 20. Jahrhundert.* Berlin: Walter de Gruyter.

Geertz, C. 1960. *The Religion of Java.* Glencoe: Free Press.

———. 1963a. *Agricultural Involution: The Process of Ecological Change in Indonesia.* Berkeley: University of California Press.

————. 1963b. *Peddlers and Princes: Social Change and Economic Modernization in Two Indonesian Towns.* Chicago: University of Chicago Press.

————. 1968. *Islam Observed: Religious Development in Morocco and Indonesia.* New Haven: Yale University Press.

————. 1973. *The Interpretation of Cultures.* New York: Basic Books.

————. 1980. *Negara: The Theatre State in Nineteenth-Century Bali.* Princeton, N.J.: Princeton University Press.

Geertz, H., and C. Geertz. 1975. *Kinship in Bali.* Chicago: University of Chicago Press.

Geisenhainer, K. 2000. "Rassenkunde zwischen Metaphorik und Metatheorie—Otto Reche." Pp. 83–100 in *Ethnologie und Nationalsozialismus,* ed. B. Streck. Gehren: Escher.

————. 2002. *"Rasse ist Schicksal": Otto Reche (1879–1966)—ein Leben als Anthropologe und Völkerkundler.* Leipzig: Evangelische Verlagsanstalt.

Gellner, E. 1959. *Words and Things.* London: Gollancz.

Gennep, Arnold van. 1909/1960. *The Rites of Passage.* London: Routledge.

Gephart, W. 1997. *Symbol und Sanktion: Zur Theorie der kollektiven Zurechnung von Paul Fauconnet.* Opladen: Leske & Budrich.

Gibson, K., and T. Ingold, eds. 1993. *Tools, Language, and Cognition in Human Evolution.* Cambridge: Cambridge University Press.

Gillin, J. P. 1947. *Moche: A Peruvian Coastal Community.* Washington, D.C.: U.S. Government Printing Office.

Gilsenbach, R. 1988a. "Die Verfolgung der Sinti—ein Weg, der nach Auschwitz führte." *Feinderklärung und Prävention: Beiträge zur Nationalsozialistischen Gesundheits—und Sozialpolitik* 6:11–42.

————. 1988b. "Wie Lolitschai zur Doktorwürde kam." *Feinderklärung und Prävention: Beiträge zur Nationalsozialistischen Gesundheits—und Sozialpolitik* 6:101–34.

Gingrich, A. 1999a. *Erkundungen: Themen der ethnologischen Forschung.* Wien: Böhlau.

————. 1999b. "Marxismus und Ethnologie." Pp. 245–246 in *Wörterbuch der Völkerkunde (begründet von Walter Hirschberg).* Berlin: Reimer.

————. Forthcoming. "Gebrochene Kontexte einer prekären Ethnographie: Einleitende Überlegungen zum Frühwerk von Christoph Fürer-Haimendorf." Introduction to H. Schäffler, *Begehrte Köpfe: Zum ethnographischen Werk von Christoph Fürer-Haimendorf.* Vienna: Boehlau.

Gingrich, A., and S. Haas. 1999. "Vom Orientalismus zur Sozialanthropologie: Ein Überblick zu österreichischen Beiträgen für die Ethnologie der islamischen Welt." *Mitteilungen der Anthropologischen Gesellschaft in Wien* 125/126:115–34.

Ginsburg, F. D., and R. Rapp, eds. 1995. *Conceiving the New World Order: The Global Politics of Reproduction.* Berkeley: University of California Press.

Girard, R. 1972. *La violence et le sacré.* Paris: B. Grasset.

Girtler, R. 2001. "Franz Boas. Burschenschaftler und Schwiegersohn eines öster-reichischen Revolutionärs von 1848." *Anthropos* 96:572.

Glick Schiller, N., C. Szanton Blanc, and L. Basch. 1999. "On the Way Towards Trans-national Anthropology: The 1994 Wenner-Gren Symposium on Transnationalism, Nation-State Building, and Culture." Paper prepared for Wenner-Gren Interna-tional Symposium 125, "Anthropology at the End of the Century," October 30–November 5, 1999, Cabo San Lucas, Mexico.

Gluckman, M. 1963. *Order and Rebellion in Tribal Africa.* London: Cohen & West.

———. 1974. "Report from the Field." *New York Review of Books* 21 (19): 43–44.

Godelier, M. 1977. *Perspectives in Marxist Anthropology.* Cambridge: Cambridge Uni-versity Press.

———. 1986. *The Making of Great Men: Male Domination and Power among the New Guinea Baruya.* Cambridge: Cambridge University Press.

———. 1999. *The Enigma of the Gift.* Cambridge, U.K.: Polity Press.

———. 2000. "Is Social Anthropology Still Worth the Trouble? A Response to Some Echoes from America." *Ethnos* 65:301–16.

Godelier, M., and M. Panoff, eds. 1998. *La production du corps: Approches anthro-pologiques et historiques.* Amsterdam: Gordon & Breach.

Godelier, M., and M. Strathern, eds. 1991. *Big Men and Great Men: Personifications of Power in Melanesia.* Cambridge: Cambridge University Press.

Godelier, M., T. R. Trautmann, and F. E. Tjon Sie Fat, eds. *Transformations of Kin-ship.* Washington, D.C.: Smithsonian Institution Press.

Golde, P., ed. 1970. *Women in the Field: Anthropological Experiences.* Chicago: Aldine.

Goldenweiser, A. 1917. "Review of Emile Durkheim, *Les Formes Elementaires de la Vie Religieuse.*" *American Anthropologist* 17:719–35.

Goldschmidt, W. 1947. *As You Sow: Three Studies in the Social Consequences of Agri-business.* New York: Harcourt, Brace.

Goodman, A., D. Heath, and S. Lindee, eds. 2003. *Genetic Nature/Culture: Anthropol-ogy and Science beyond the Two Culture Divide.* Berkeley: University of California Press.

Goodman, A., and T. Leatherman, eds. 1998. *Building a New Biocultural Synthesis: Political Economic Perspectives on Human Biology.* Ann Arbor: University of Michi-gan Press.

Goody, J., ed. 1958. *The Developmental Cycle in Domestic Groups.* London: Cambridge University Press.

———. 1977. *The Domestication of the Savage Mind.* Cambridge: Cambridge Univer-sity Press.

———. 1995. *The Expansive Moment: The Rise of Social Anthropology in Britain and Africa, 1918–1970.* Cambridge: Cambridge University Press.

Gothsch, M. 1983. *Die deutsche Völkerkunde und ihr Verhältnis zum Kolonialismus: Ein*

Beitrag zur kolonialideologischen und kolonialpraktischen Bedeutung der deutschen Völkerkunde in der Zeit von 1870 bis 1975. Baden-Baden: Nomos.

Goudineau, Y. 1991. "Marcel Granet." In *Dictionnaire de l'ethnologie et de l'anthropologie,* ed. P. Bonte and M. Izard. Paris: Presses Universitaires de France.

Gough, K. 1968a. "Anthropology: Child of Imperialism." *Monthly Review* 19:12–27.

———. 1968b. "New Proposals for Anthropologists." *Current Anthropology* 9:405–35.

Gräbner, F. 1905. "Kulturkreise und Kulturschichten in Ozeanien." *Zeitschrift für Ethnologie* 37:28–53.

Granet, M. 1930. *Chinese Civilization.* London: Routledge & Kegan Paul.

Granet, M. 1939. *Catégories matrimoniales et relations de proximité dans la Chine ancienne.* Paris: Alcan.

———. 1953. *Études sociologiques sur la Chine.* Paris: Presses Universitaires de France.

———. 1975. *The Religion of the Chinese People.* Oxford: Blackwell.

Griaule, M. 1938. *Masques dogons.* Paris: Institut d'Ethnologie.

———. 1957. *Méthode de l'ethnographie.* Paris: Presses Universitaires de France.

———. 1948/1965. *Conversations with Ogotemmêli: An Introduction to Dogon Religious Ideas.* Oxford: Oxford University Press for the International African Institute.

Griaule, M., and G. Dieterlen. 1965. *Le renard pâle.* Paris: Institut d'Ethnologie.

Guilleminet, P. 1952. *Coutumier de la tribu bahnar des Sedang et des Jarai de la province de Kontum.* Paris: E. de Boccard: École Française d'Extrême-Orient.

Gumperz, J., and S. Levinson, eds. 1996. *Rethinking Linguistic Relativity.* Cambridge: Cambridge University Press.

Gutkind, P. C. W. 1973. "Bibliography of Urban Anthropology." Pp. 425–89 in *Urban Anthropology: Cross-Cultural Studies of Urbanization,* ed. A. Southall. New York: Oxford University Press.

Habinger, G. 2003. *Eine Wiener Biedermeierdame erobert die Welt: Die Lebensgeschichte der Ida Pfeiffer (1797–1858).* Wien: Promedia.

Haddon, A. C., ed. 1901–1935. *Reports of the Cambridge Anthropological Expedition to Torres Straits.* Cambridge: Cambridge University Press.

———. 1910. *History of Anthropology.* London: Watts.

Hahn, H. P. 2001. "Fritz Graebner/Bernhard Ankermann." Pp. 137–142 in *Hauptwerke der Ethnologie,* ed. C. F. Feest and K.-H. Kohl. Stuttgart: Kröner.

Halbwachs, M. 1912. *La classe ouvrière et les niveaux de vie: Recherches sur la hiérarchie des besoins dans les société industrielles contemporaines.* Paris: Alcan.

———. 1930. *Les causes du suicide.* Paris: Alcan.

———. 1933. *L'évolution des besoins dans les classes ouvrières.* Paris: Alcan.

———. 1999. *On Collective Memory.* Chicago: University of Chicago Press.

Hallpike, C. R. 1979. *The Foundations of Primitive Thought.* Oxford: Clarendon.

Hammond-Tooke, W. D. 1997. *Imperfect Interpreters: South Africa's Anthropologists, 1920–1990.* Johannesburg: Witwatersrand University Press.

Haraway, D. J. 1989. *Primate Visions: Gender, Race, and Nature in the World of Modern Science.* New York: Routledge.

Harbsmeier, M. 1992. "Die Rückwirkungen des europäischen Ausgreifens auf Übersee auf den deutschen anthropologischen Diskurs um 1800." Pp. 422–42 in *Frühe Neuzeit - frühe Moderne? Forschungen zur Vielschichtigkeit von Übergangsprozessen,* ed. R. Vierhaus. Göttingen: Vandenhoeck & Ruprecht.

———. 1995. "Towards a Prehistory of Ethnography: Early Modern German Travel Writing as Traditions of Knowledge." Pp. 19–38 in *Fieldwork and Footnotes: Studies in the History of European Anthropology,* ed. H. Vermeulen and A. A. Roldán. London: Routledge.

Harms, V. 2001. "Karl von den Steinen." In *Hauptwerke der Ethnologie,* ed. C. F. Feest and K.-H. Kohl. Stuttgart: Kröner.

Harris, M. 1964. *The Nature of Cultural Things.* New York: Random House.

———. 1968. *The Rise of Anthropological Theory: A History of Theories of Culture.* New York: Thomas Crowell.

———. 1971. *Culture, Man, and Nature: An Introduction to General Anthropology.* New York: Thomas Crowell.

———. 1974. *Cows, Pigs, Wars and Witches: The Riddles of Culture.* New York: Random House.

———. 1977. *Cannibals and Kings: The Origins of Cultures.* New York: Random House.

———. 1979. *Cultural Materialism: The Struggle for a Science of Culture.* New York: Thomas Crowell.

———. 1994. "Cultural Materialism Is Alive and Well and Won't Go Away until Something Better Comes Along." Pp. 62–76 in *Assessing Cultural Anthropology,* ed. R. Borofsky. New York: McGraw-Hill.

Harstick, H.-P., ed. 1977. *Karl Marx über Formen vorkapitalistischer Produktion: Vergleichende Studien zur Geschichte des Grundeigentums, 1879–80.* Frankfurt: Campus Verlag.

Haudricourt, A. G. 1943. *L'homme et les plantes cultivées.* Paris: Gallimard.

———. 1987. *La technologie science humaine: Recherches d'histoire et d'ethnologie des techniques.* Paris: Editions de la Maison des Sciences de l'Homme.

Hauschild, T. 1995. "'Dem lebendigen Geist': Warum die Geschichte der Völkerkunde im "Dritten Reich" auch für Nichtethnologen von Interesse sein kann." Pp. 13–61 in *Lebenslust und Fremdenfurcht: Ethnologie im Dritten Reich,* ed. T. Hauschild. Frankfurt: Suhrkamp.

Hauser-Schäublin, B., ed. 1991. *Ethnologische Frauenforschung*: Ansätze, Methoden, Resultate. Berlin: Reimer.

Hegel, G. W. F. 1956. *The Philosophy of History.* New York: Dover.

Heinrichs, H.-J., ed. 1975. *Materialien zu Bachofens "Das Mutterrecht."* Frankfurt: Suhrkamp.

Heintze, D. 1990. "Georg Forster." Pp. 69–87 in *Klassiker der Kulturantropologie: Von Montaigne bis Margaret Mead*, ed. W. Marschall. München: C. H. Beck.

Herder, J. G. 1772/1960. "Abhandlung über den Ursprung der Sprachen." Pp. 3–87 in J. G. Herder, *Sprachphilosophische Schriften*, ed. E. Heintel. Hamburg: F. Meiner.

Héritier, F. 1981. *L'exercice de la parenté*. Paris: Gallimard.

———. 1999. *Two Sisters and Their Mother: The Anthropology of Incest*. New York: Zone Books.

Herrenschmidt, O. 1989. *Les meilleurs dieux sont hindous*. Lausanne: L'Age de l'Homme.

Herrnstein, R. J., and C. Murray. 1994. *The Bell Curve: Intelligence and Class Structure in American Life*. New York: Free Press.

Herskovits, M. J. 1928. *The American Negro: A Study in Racial Crossing*. New York: Alfred A. Knopf.

Hertz, R. 1907/1960. "A Contribution to the Study of the Collective Representation of Death." In *Death and the Right Hand*, ed. R. Hertz. London: Cohen & West.

———. 1909/1973. "The Pre-Eminence of the Right Hand: A Study in Religious Polarity." In *Right and Left: Essays in Dual Symbolic Classification*, ed. R. Needham. Chicago: University of Chicago Press.

———. 1910. *Socialisme et dépopulation*. Paris: Librairie du Parti Socialiste.

———. 1913/1983. "St. Besse: A Study of an Alpine Cult." In *Saints and Their Cults: Studies in Religious Sociology*, ed. S. Wilson. Cambridge: Cambridge University Press.

———. 1917. "Contes et dictons recueillis sur le front parmi les poilus de la Mayenne et d'ailleurs." *Revue des Traditions Populaires* 32:32–45; 74–91.

———. 1922/1994. *Robert Hertz: Sin and Expiation in Primitive Societies*. Oxford: British Centre for Durkheimian Studies.

Heusch, L. d. 1981. *Why Marry Her? Society and Symbolic Structures*. Cambridge; Paris: Cambridge University Press.

———. 1982. *The Drunken King, or the Origin of the State*. Bloomington: Indiana University Press.

———. 1985. *Sacrifice in Africa: A Structuralist Approach*. Manchester, U.K.: Manchester University Press.

Heuzé, G. 1996. *Workers of Another World: Miners, the Countryside, and Coalfields in Dhanbad*. Delhi: Oxford University Press.

Hildebrandt, H.-J. 1983. *Der Evolutionismus in der Familienforschung des 19. Jahrhunderts: Ansätze einer allgemeinen, historisch orientierten Theorie der Familie bei Johann Jakob Bachofen, John Ferguson McLennan und Lewis Henry Morgan*. Berlin: Reimer.

Hirschberg, W., C. F. Feest, and A. Janata, eds. 1966/1989. *Technologie und Ergologie in der Völkerkunde*. Berlin: Reimer.

Hohmann, J. S. 1996. *Handbuch zur Tsiganologie*. New York: P. Lang.

Holder, P. 1951. "The Role of Caddoan Horticulturalists in Culture History on the Great Plains." PhD diss., Columbia University.

Hollier, D., and G. Bataille, eds. 1995. *Le Collége de sociologie: 1937–1939.* Paris: Gallimard.

Horowitz, I. L. 1968. *Radicalism and the Revolt against Reason: The Social Theories of Georges Sorel.* Carbondale: Southern Illinois University Press.

Hubert, H. 1905/1999. *Essay on Time: A Brief Study of the Representation of Time in Religion and Magic.* Oxford: Durkheim Press.

———. 1950. *Les Celtes depuis l'époque de La Téne et la civilisation celtique.* Paris: A. Michel.

———. 1952. *Les Germains: Cours professé à l'école du Louvre en 1924–1925.* Paris: A. Michel.

Hubert, H., and M. Mauss, ed. 1964. *Sacrifice: Its Nature and Function.* London: Cohen & West.

———. 1972. *A General Theory of Magic.* London: Routledge and K. Paul.

Hugh-Jones, C. 1979. *From the Milk River.* Cambridge: Cambridge University Press.

Hugh-Jones, S. 1979. *The Palm and the Pleiades.* Cambridge: Cambridge University Press.

Hunter, M. 1936. *Reaction to Conquest: Effects of Contact with Europeans on the Pondo of South Africa.* Oxford: Oxford University Press.

Hymes, D., ed. 1969. *Reinventing Anthropology.* New York: Random House.

———. 1974. *Foundations in Sociolinguistics: An Ethnographic Approach.* Philadelphia: University of Pennsylvania Press.

———. 1975. "Reinventing Anthropology: Response to Kaplan and Donald." *American Anthropologist* 77:869–70.

Icke-Schwalbe, L. 1972. "Die sozial-politische Rolle der Oberhäupter bei Adivasi-Gruppen in Zentralindien im Prozess der Industrialisierung." *Jahrbuch des Museums für Völkerkunde zu Leipzig* 28:211–17.

Israel, H. 1969. *Kulturwandel grönländischer Eskimo im 18. Jahrhundert—Wandlungen in Gesellschaft und Wirtschaft unter dem Einfluss der Herrenhuter Brüdermission.* Special issue, *Adhandlungen und Berichte des Staatlichen Museums für Völkerkunde Dresden* 29.

Iteanu, A. 1983. *La ronde des échanges: De la circulation aux valeurs chez les Orokaiva.* Cambridge: Cambridge University Press.

Izard, M. 1991. "Germaine Dieterlin." In *Dictionnaire de l'ethnologie et de l'anthropologie,* ed. P. Bonte and M. Izard. Paris: Presses Universitaires de France.

Jablow, J. 1951. *The Cheyenne in Plains Indian Trade Relations, 1795–1840.* New York: J. J. Augustin.

Jakobson, R., and C. Lévi-Strauss. 1962. "Les chats de Charles Baudelaire." *L'Homme* 2:5–21.

James, W., and N. J. Allen. 1998. *Marcel Mauss: A Centenary Tribute*. New York: Berghahn Books.

Jamin, J. 1991a. "Denise Paulme." In *Dictionnaire de l'ethnologie et de l'anthropologie*, ed. P. Bonte and M. Izard. Paris: Presses Universitaires de France.

———. 1991b. "France: L'anthropologie française." In *Dictionnaire de l'ethnologie et de l'anthropologie*, ed. P. Bonte and M. Izard. Paris: Presses Universitaires de France.

———. 1991c. "Lucien Lévy-Bruhl." In *Dictionnaire de l'ethnologie et de l'anthropologie*, ed. P. Bonte and M. Izard. Paris: Presses Universitaires de France.

———. 1991d. "Marcel Mauss." In *Dictionnaire de l'ethnologie et de l'anthropologie*, ed. P. Bonte and M. Izard. Paris: Presses Universitaires de France.

———. 1991e. "Michel Leiris." In *Dictionnaire de l'ethnologie et de l'anthropologie*, ed. P. Bonte and M. Izard. Paris: Presses Universitaires de France.

Jamous, R. 1981. *Honneur et Baraka: Les structures sociales traditionnelles dans le Rif.* Cambridge: Cambridge University Press.

———. 1991. *La relation frère-soeur: Parenté et rites chez les Meo de l'Inde du Nord.* Paris: Editions de l'École des Hautes Études en Sciences Sociales.

Jenkins, A. 1979. *The Social Theory of Claude Lévi-Strauss*. London: Macmillan.

Johnson, C. 2003. *Claude Lévi-Strauss: The Formative Years*. Cambridge: Cambridge University Press.

Jouin, B. Y. 1949. *La mort et la tombe: L'abandon de la tombe, les cérémonies, priéres et sacrifices se rapportant à ces trés importantes manifestations de la vie des autochtones du Darlac.* Paris: Institut d'Ethnologie.

Juillerat, B. 1971. *Les bases de l'organisation sociale chez les Mouktélé (Nord-Cameroun): Structures lignagères et mariage.* Paris: Institut d'Ethnologie.

———. 1991. *Oedipe chasseur: Une mythologie du sujet en Nouvelle-Guinée.* Paris: Presses Universitaires de France.

———. 1993. *La révocation des Tambaran: Les Banaro et Richard Thurnwald revisités.* Paris: CNRS.

———. 1995. *L'avènement du père: Rite, representation, fantasme, dans un culte mélanésien.* Paris: CNRS.

———. 1996. *Children of the Blood: Society, Reproduction, and Cosmology in New Guinea.* Oxford: Berg.

———. 2001. *Penser l'imaginaire: Essays d'anthropologie psychanalytique.* Lausanne: Payot & Cie.

Kahn, J. S., and J. R. Llobera. 1981. "Towards a New Marxism or a New Anthropology?" Pp. 263–329 in *The Anthropology of Pre-Capitalist Societies*, ed. J. S. Kahn and J. R. Llobera. London: Macmillan.

Kahveci, E. 1995. "Durkheim's Sociology in Turkey." *Durkheimian Studies* 1:51–57.

Kaplan, D. 1974. "The Anthropology of Authenticity: Everyman His Own Anthropologist." *American Anthropologist* 76:824–39.

———. 1975. "The Idea of Social Science and Its Enemies: A Rejoinder." *American Anthropologist* 77:876–81.

Karady, V. 1981. "French Ethnology and the Durkheimian Breakthrough." *Journal of the Anthropological Society of Oxford* 12:165–76.

Kautsky, K. 1899. *Die Agrarfrage: Eine Übersicht über die Tendenzen der modernen Landwirthschaft und die Agrarpolitik der Sozialdemokratie.* Stuttgart: Dietz.

Kilborne, B. 1982. "Anthropological Thought in the French Revolution: The Société des Observateurs de l'Homme." *European Journal of Sociology* 23:73–91.

Kirchhoff, P. 1931. "Die Verwandtschaftsorganisation der Urwaldstämme Südamerikas." *Zeitschrift für Ethnologie* 63:85–193.

Knauft, B. M. 1996. *Genealogies for the Present in Cultural Anthropology.* New York: Routledge.

Köcke, J. 1979. "Some Early German Contributions to Economic Anthropology." *Research in Economic Anthropology* 2:119–67.

Kohl, P., and J. A. P. Gollan. 2002. "Religion, Politics, and Prehistory: Reassessing the Lingering Legacy of Oswald Menghin." *Current Anthropology* 43: 561–86.

König, W. 1962. *Die Achal-Teke: Zur Wirtschaft und Gesellschaft einer Turkmenen-Gruppe im XIX. Jahrhundert.* Berlin: Akademie-Verlag.

Köpping, K. P. 1995. "Enlightenment and Romanticism in the Work of Adolf Bastian: The Historical Roots of Anthropology in the Nineteenth Century." Pp. 75–91 in *Fieldwork and Footnotes: Studies in the History of European Anthropology,* ed. by H. Vermeulen and A. A. Roldán. London: Routledge.

Köstlin, K. 2002. "Volkskunde: Pathologie der Randlage." Pp. 369–414 in *Geschichte der österreichischen Humanwissenschaften,* ed. K. Acham. Wien: Passagen.

Krader, L., ed. 1976. *Karl Marx. Die ethnologischen Exzerpthefte.* Frankfurt: Suhrkamp.

Kramer, F., and C. Sigrist. 1978. *Gesellschaften ohne Staat.* Frankfurt: Syndikat.

Krauskopf, G. 1989. *Maîtres et possedés: Les rites et l'ordre sociale chez les Tharu de dang (Népal).* Paris: CNRS.

Kristeva, J. 1980. *Desire in Language: A Semiotic Approach to Literature and Art.* New York: Columbia University Press.

———. 1988. *Étrangers à nous-mêmes.* Paris: Fayard.

———. 1993. *Nations without Nationalism.* New York: Columbia University Press.

Kroeber, A. L. 1917. "The Superorganic." *American Anthropologist* 19:163–213.

———. 1939. *Cultural and Natural Areas of Native North America.* Berkeley: University of California Press.

———. 1944. *Configurations of Culture Growth.* Berkeley: University of California Press.

———. 1957. *Style and Civilization.* Ithaca, N.Y.: Cornell University Press.

Kroeber, A. L., and C. Kluckhohn. 1952. *Culture: A Critical Review of Concepts and Definitions.* Cambridge, Mass.: Harvard University Press.

Kroeber, A. L., and T. Parsons. 1958. "The Concepts of Culture and of Social System." *American Sociological Review* 23:582–83.

Kuhn, T. S. 1970. *The Structure of Scientific Revolutions*. Chicago: University of Chicago Press.

Kuklick, H. 1991. *The Savage Within: The Social History of British Anthropology, 1885–1945*. Cambridge: Cambridge University Press.

Kulick-Aldag, R. 2000. "Hans Plischke in Göttingen." In *Ethnologie und Nationalsozialismus*, ed. B. Streck. Gehren: Escher.

Kuper, A. 1973. *Anthropology and Anthropologists: The British School, 1922–1972*. London: Allen Lane.

———. 1999. *Culture: The Anthropologist's Account*. Cambridge, Mass.: Harvard University Press.

Kurzweil, E. 1980. *The Age of Structuralism: Lévi-Strauss to Foucault*. New York: Columbia University Press.

Labouret, H. 1941. *Paysans d'Afrique occidentale*. Paris: Gallimard.

Lacan, J. 1968. *The Language of the Self: The Function of Language in Psychoanalysis*. Baltimore: Johns Hopkins University Press.

———. 1977. *Écrits: A Selection*. London: Routledge.

Lafont, P.-B. 1963. *Toloi djuat: Coutumier de la tribu Jarai*. Paris: École Française d'Extrême-Orient.

Lane, E. W. 1836. *An Account of the Manners and Customs of the Modern Egyptians: Written in Egypt during the Years 1833, –34, and –35, Partly from Notes Made during a Former Visit to that Country in the Years 1825, –26, –27, and –28*. London: C. Knight.

Lane, M., ed. 1970. *Structuralism: A Reader*. London: Cape.

Latour, B. 1987. *Science in Action: How to Follow Scientists and Engineers through Society*. Cambridge, Mass.: Harvard University Press.

———. 1993. *We Have Never Been Modern*. London: Harvester Wheatsheaf.

Latour, B., and S. Woolgar. 1986. *Laboratory Life: The Construction of Scientific Facts*. Princeton, N.J.: Princeton University Press.

Leach, E. 1952. "The Structural Implications of Matrilateral Cross-Cousin Marriage." *Journal of the Royal Anthropological Institute* 81.

———. 1954. *Political Systems of Highland Burma: A Study of Kachin Social Structure*. London: G. Bell.

———. 1961. *Pul Eliya, a Village in Ceylon: A Study of Land Tenure and Kinship*. Cambridge: Cambridge University Press.

———. 1967. "Introduction." In *The Structural Study of Myth and Totemism*, ed. Edmund Leach. London: Tavistock.

———. 1974. "Anthropology Upside Down." *New York Review of Books* 21(5):33–35.

———. 1982. *Social Anthropology*. Glasgow: Fontana Paperbacks.

———. 1984. "Glimpses of the Unmentionable in the History of British Social Anthropology." *Annual Review of Anthropology* 13:1–23.

Leacock, E. B. 1952. "The Montagnais-Naskapi 'Hunting Territory' and the Fur Trade." PhD diss., Columbia University.

———. 1972. "Introduction and Notes." Pp. 7–67 in F. Engels, *The Origin of the Family, Private Property, and the State, in the Light of the Researches of Lewis H. Morgan.* New York: International Publishers.

———, ed. 1971. *The Culture of Poverty: A Critique.* New York: Simon and Schuster.

Le Bon, G. 1995. *The Crowd.* New Brunswick: Transaction Publishers.

Leeds, A. 1973. "Locality Power in Relation to Supralocal Power Institutions." Pp. 15–41 in *Urban Anthropology,* ed. A. Southall. New York: Oxford University Press.

———. 1976. *Cities, Classes, and the Social Order.* Ithaca: Cornell University Press.

Leenhardt, M. 1902/1976. *Le mouvement éthiopien au sud de l'Afrique de 1896 à 1899.* Paris: Academie des Sciences d'Outre-Mer.

———. 1937. *Gens de la Grande Terre.* Paris: Gallimard.

———. 1947/1979. *Do Kamo: Person and Myth in the Melanesian World.* Chicago: University of Chicago Press.

Leiris, M. 1934. *L'Afrique fantôme.* Paris: Gallimard.

———. 1950. "L'ethnographie devant le colonialisme." *Les Temps Modernes* 58:357–74.

———. 1968. *Manhood: The Autobiographer as Torero.* London: Cape.

Le Play, F. 1982. *Frédéric Le Play on Family, Work, and Social Change.* Chicago: University of Chicago Press.

Leroi-Gourhan, A. 1943–1945. *L'homme et la matière.* Paris: Albin Michel.

———. 1946. *Archéologie du Pacifique-nord: Matériaux pour l'étude des relations entre les peuples riverains d'Asie et d'Amérique.* Paris: Institut d'Ethnologie.

———. 1983. *Le fil du temps: Ethnologie et préhistoire (1935–1970).* Paris: Fayard.

Le Roy Ladurie, E. 1978. *Montaillou: Cathars and Catholics in a French village, 1294–1324.* London: Scholar Press.

———. 1982. *The Peasants of Languedoc.* Urbana: University of Illinois Press.

Lesser, A. 1933. *The Pawnee Ghost Dance Hand Game: A Study of Cultural Change.* New York: Columbia University Press.

———. 1961. "Social Fields and the Evolution of Society." *Southwestern Journal of Anthropology* 17:40–48.

———. 1981. "Franz Boas." Pp. 1–33 in *Totems and Teachers: Perspectives on the History of Anthropology,* ed. S. Silverman. New York: Columbia University Press.

Lévine, D. 1991. "Paul Rivet." In *Dictionnaire de l'ethnologie et de l'anthropologie,* ed. P. Bonte and M. Izard. Paris: Presses Universitaires de France.

Lévi-Strauss, C. 1949/1969. *The Elementary Structures of Kinship.* Boston: Beacon Press.

————. 1963. *Totemism*. Boston: Beacon.

————. 1964. *Mythologiques*. Paris: Plon.

————. 1966. *The Savage Mind*. London: Weidenfeld & Nicolson.

————. 1967. "The Story of Asdiwal." In *The Structural Study of Myth and Totemism*, ed. E. Leach. London: Tavistock.

————. 1973. *Tristes tropiques*. London: Jonathan Cape.

————. 1987. *Introduction to the Work of Marcel Mauss*. London: Routledge & Kegan Paul.

Lévi-Strauss, C., et al. 1964. "In Memoriam: Alfred Métraux." *L'Homme* 4:5–19.

Lévy, E. 1903. *L'affirmation du droit collectif.* Paris: Societe Nouvelle de Librairie et d'Edition.

————. 1926. *La vision socialiste du droit*. Paris: M. Giard.

————. 1933. *Les fondements du droit*. Paris: Alcan.

Lévy-Bruhl, L. 1912/1926. *How Natives Think*. London: Allen & Unwin.

————. 1923. *Primitive Mentality*. London: Allen & Unwin.

————. 1949/1975. *The Notebooks on Primitive Mentality*. Oxford: Basil Blackwell.

Lewis, I. M. 2000. "Germaine Dieterlin." *Anthropology Today* 16:25–26.

Lewis, O. 1942. *The Effects of White Contact upon Blackfoot Culture: With Special Reference to the Role of the Fur Trade*. New York: J. J. Augustin.

————. 1951. *Life in a Mexican Village: Tepoztlán Restudied*. Urbana: University of Illinois Press.

————. 1959. *Five Families: Mexican Case Studies in the Culture of Poverty*. New York: Basic Books.

————. 1966a. "The Culture of Poverty." *Scientific American* 215:19–25.

————. 1966b. *La Vida: A Puerto Rican Family in the Culture of Poverty*. New York: Random House.

Le Wita, B. 1994. *French Bourgeois Culture*. Cambridge: Cambridge University Press.

Lienhardt, G. 1974. "E-P: A Personal View." *Man* 9:299–304.

Linimayr, P. 1994. *Wiener Völkerkunde im Nationalsozialismus: Ansätze zu einer NS-Wissenschaft*. Frankfurt: P. Lang.

Linton, R. 1936. *The Study of Man*. New York: Appleton-Century.

Lips, J. E. 1937. *The Savage Hits Back: The White Man through Native Eyes*. New Haven: Yale University Press.

————. 1953. *Die Erntevölker: Eine wichtige Phase in der Entwicklung der menschlichen Wirtschaft [Rektoratsrede gehalten am 31. Oktober 1949 in der Kongresshalle zu Leipzig]*. Berlin: Akademie-Verlag.

Lizot, J. 1985. *Tales of the Yanomami: Daily Life in the Venezuelan Forest*. Cambridge: Cambridge University Press.

————. 1994. "Words in the Night: the Ceremonial Dialogue, One Expression of

Peaceful Relationships among the Yanomami." In *The Anthropology of Peace and Nonviolence*, ed. Leslie Sponsel and Thomas Gregor. Boulder, Colo.: Lynne Rienner.

Llobera, J. 1985. "A Note on a Durkheimian Critic of Marx: The Case of Gaston Richard." *Journal of the Anthropological Society of Oxford* 16:35–41.

———. 1996. "The Fate of Anthroposociology in *l'Année Sociologique*." *Journal of the Anthropological Society of Oxford* 27:235–51.

Lösch, N. C. 1997. *Rasse als Konstrukt: Leben und Werk Eugen Fischers*. Frankfurt: Peter Lang.

Lowie, R. H. 1920. *Primitive Society*. New York: Liveright.

———. 1937. *The History of Ethnological Theory*. New York: Holt, Rinehart and Winston.

———. 1945. *The German People: A Social Portrait to 1945*. New York: Farrar and Rinehart.

Lukes, S. 1973. *Émile Durkheim, His Life and Work: A Historical and Critical Study*. London: Allen Lane.

Lynd, R. S., and H. M. Lynd. 1929. *Middletown: A Study in American Culture*. New York: Harcourt Brace.

Lyotard, J.-F. 1984. *The Postmodern Condition: A Report on Knowledge*. Manchester, U.K.: Manchester University Press.

MacDonald, A. W. 1983. *Essays on the Ethnology of Nepal and South Asia*. Vol. 1. Kathmandu: Ratna Pustak Bhandar.

———. 1987. *Essays on the Ethnology of Nepal and South Asia*. Vol. 2. Kathmandu: Ratna Pustak Bhandar.

Maitre, H. 1912. *Les jungles moi: Exploration et histoire des hinterlands moi du Cambodge, de la Cochinchine, de l'Annam et du bas Laos*. Paris: E. Larose.

Malamoud, C. 1989. *Cuire le monde: Rite et pensée dans l'Inde ancienne*. Paris: Editions La Decouverte.

Malinowski, B. 1922. *Argonauts of the Western Pacific: An Account of Native Enterprise and Adventure in the Archipelagoes of Melanesian New Guinea*. London: G. Routledge & Sons.

———. 1927. *Sex and Repression in Savage Society*. London: International Library of Psychology, Philosophy, and Scientific Method.

———. 1929. *The Sexual Life of Savages in North-Western Melanesia: An Ethnographic Account of Courtship, Marriage, and Family Life among the Natives of the Trobriand Islands, British New Guinea*. London: G. Routledge & Sons.

———. 1935. *Coral Gardens and Their Magic: A Study of the Methods of Tilling the Soil and of Agricultural Rites in the Trobriand Islands*. London: G. Allen & Unwin.

———. 1967/1989. *A Diary in the Strict Sense of the Term*. London: Athlone.

Maquet, J. 1972. *Africanity: The Cultural Unity of Black Africa*. New York: Oxford University Press.

————. 1979. *Introduction to Aesthetic Anthropology*. Malibu, Calif.: Undena Publications.

————. 1986. *The Aesthetic Experience: An Anthropologist Looks at the Visual Arts*. New Haven: Yale University Press.

Maranda, P. 1974. *French Kinship: Structure and History*. Paris: Mouton.

Marcel, J.-C. 2001a. "Georges Bataille: L'enfant illégitime de la sociologie durkheimienne." *Durkheimian Studies n.s.* 7:37–52.

————. 2001b. *Le durkheimisme dans l'entre-deux-guerres*. Paris: Presses Universitaires de France.

Marchand, S. 2003. "Priests among the Pygmies: Wilhelm Schmidt and the Counter-Reformation in Austrian Ethnology." Pp. 283–316 in *Worldly Provincialism: German Anthropology in the Age of Empire*, ed. H. G. Penny and M. Bunzl. Ann Arbor: University of Michigan Press.

Marcus, G. E., and D. Cushman. 1982. "Ethnographies as Texts." *Annual Review of Anthropology* 11:25–69.

Marcus, G. E., and M. M. J. Fischer. 1986. *Anthropology as Cultural Critique: An Experimental Moment in the Human Sciences*. Chicago: University of Chicago Press.

Massin, B. 1996. "From Virchow to Fischer: Physical Anthropology and 'Modern Race Theories' in Wilhelmine Germany." Pp. 79–154 in *Volksgeist as Method and Ethic: Essays on Boasian Ethnography and the German Anthropological Tradition*, ed. G. W. Stocking Jr. Madison: University of Wisconsin Press.

Mauss, M. 1909/2003. *On Prayer*. Oxford: Berghahn.

————. 1925. "In Memoriam." *L'Année Sociologique* 1:7–29.

————. 1938/1985. "A Category of the Human Mind: The Notion of Person, the Notion of Self." In *The Category of the Person: Anthropology, Philosophy, History*, ed. M. Carrithers, S. Collins, and S. Lukes. Cambridge: Cambridge University Press.

————. 1954. *The Gift: Forms and Functions of Exchange in Archiac Societies*. London: Routledge & Kegan Paul.

————. 1968–1969. *Oeuvres*. 3 vols. Paris: Les Editions de Minuit.

————. 1979. *Sociology and Psychology: Essays*. London: Routledge & Kegan Paul.

————. 1999. "Paul Fauconnet." *Durkheimian Studies* 5:24–28.

Mauss, M., and H. Beuchat. 1979. *Seasonal Variations of the Eskimo: A Study in Social Morphology*. London: Routledge & Kegan Paul.

Mauss, M., and P. Fauconnet. 1901. "Sociologie." *La grande encyclopédie* 30:165–76.

McLennan, J. F. 1865. *Primitive Marriage: An Inquiry into the Origin of the Form of Capture in Marriage Ceremonies*. Edinburgh: Black.

Mead, M. 1928. *Coming of Age in Samoa: A Psychological Study of Primitive Youth for Western Civilization*. New York: New American Livrary.

Mead, M., and R. Métraux, eds. 1953. *The Study of Culture at a Distance*. Chicago: University of Chicago Press.

Meillassoux, C. 1981. *Maidens, Meal, and Money: Capitalism and the Domestic Community*. Cambridge: Cambridge University Press.

Melk-Koch, M. 1989. *Auf der Suche nach der menschlichen Gesellschaft: Richard Thurnwald*. Berlin: Reimer.

———. 2001. "Richard Thurnwald." Pp. 480–84 in *Hauptwerke der Ethnologie*, ed. C. F. Feest and K.-H. Kohl. Stuttgart: Kröner.

Mellor, C. 1998. "Sacred Contagion and Social Vitality: Collective Effervescence in Les Formes Élémentaires de la Vie Religieuse." *Durkheimian Studies* 4:87–114.

———. 2002. "In Defence of Durkheim: Sociology, the Sacred and 'Society.'" *Durkheimian Studies* 8:15–34.

Merker, M. 1904. *Die Masai: Ethnographische Monographie eines ostafrikanischen Semitenvolkes*. Berlin: Reimer.

Merleau-Ponty, M. 1962. *Phenomenology of Perception*. London: Routledge & Kegan Paul.

Métraux, A. 1940. *Ethnology of Easter Island*. Honolulu: Bishop Museum.

———. 1942. *The Native Tribes of Eastern Bolivia and Western Matto Grosso*. Washington, D.C.: U.S. Government Printing Office.

———. 1958. *Le Vaudou haïtien*. Paris: Gallimard.

———. 1959. "The Ancient Civilizations of the Amazon: The Present Status of the Question of their Origins." *Diogenes* 28:91–106.

Michel, U. 1991. "Wilhelm Emil Mühlmann (1904–1988)—ein deutscher Professor. Amnesie und Amnestie: Zum Verhältnis von Ethnologie und Politik im Nationalsozialismus." In *Jahrbuch für Soziologiegeschichte* 2:69–118.

———. 1995. "Neue ethnologische Forschungsansätze im Nationalsozialismus? Aus der Biographie von Wilhelm Emil Mühlmann (1904–1988)." Pp. 141–67 in *Lebenslust und Fremdenfurcht: Ethnologie im Dritten Reich*, ed. T. Hauschild. Frankfurt: Suhrkamp.

———. 2000. "Ethnopolitische Reorganisationsforschung am Institut für Deutsche Ostarbeit in Krakau." Pp. 149–66 in *Ethnologie und Nationalsozialismus*, ed. B. Streck. Gehren: Escher.

Miner, H. M. 1939. *St. Denis, a French-Canadian Parish*. Chicago: University of Chicago Press.

———. 1952. "The Folk-Urban Continuum." *American Sociological Review* 17:529–37.

Mintz, S. 1953. "The Folk-Urban Continuum and the Rural Proletarian Community." *American Journal of Sociology* 59:136–43.

———. 1974. *Caribbean Transformations*. Chicago: Aldine.

———. 1981. "Ruth Benedict." Pp. 141–68 in *Totems and Teachers: Perspectives on the History of Anthropology*, ed. S. Silverman. New York: Columbia University Press.

———. 1985. *Sweetness and Power: The Place of Sugar in Modern History*. New York: Viking.

Mischek, U. 2000. "Autorität außerhalb des Fachs. Diedrich Westermann und Eugen Fischer." Pp. 69–82 in *Ethnologie und Nationalsozialismus*, ed. B. Streck. Gehren: Escher.

———. 2002. *Leben und Werk Günter Wagners (1908–1952)*. Gehren: Escher.

Mishkin, B. 1940. *Rank and Warfare among the Plains Indians*. New York: J. J. Augustin.

Montesquieu, C. d. 1949. *The Spirit of the Laws*. New York: Hafner Press.

Montoya, M. V. I. 1992. *Trabajos científicos y corresondencia de Tadeo Haenke*. Madrid: Coleccion Synopsis.

Morgan, L. H. 1851. *League of the Ho-dé-no-sau-ne, or Iroquois*. Rochester: Sage and Broa.

———. 1870. *Systems of Consanguinity and Affinity of the Human Family*. Washington D.C.: Smithsonian Institution.

———. 1877. *Ancient Society, or, Researches in the Lines of Human Progress from Savagery, through Barbarism to Civilization*. New York: World Publishing.

Morin, E. 1977. *Plodemet*. London: Allen Lane.

Mosen, M. 1991. *Der koloniale Traum: Angewandte Ethnologie im Nationalsozialismus*. Bonn: Mundus.

Mühlfried, F. 2000. "R. Bleichsteiners "Kaukasische Forschungen"—ein kritischer Beitrag zur Ethnologie des Kaukasus." Unpublished thesis, University of Hamburg.

Mühlmann, W. E., and A. M. Dauer. 1961. *Chiliasmus und Nativismus: Studien zur Psychologie, Soziologie und historischen Kasuistik der Umsturzbewegungen*. Berlin: Reimer.

Murdock, G. P. 1949. *Social Structure*. New York: Macmillan.

Murphy, R. F. 1971. *The Dialectics of Social Life: Alarms and Excursions in Anthropological Theory*. New York: Basic Books.

Musil, A. 1928. *The Manners and Customs of the Rwala Bedouins*. New York: American Geographical Society.

Nadel, S. F. 1952. "Witchcraft in Four African Societies." *American Anthropologist* 54:18–29.

Nash, J. C. 1979. *We Eat the Mines and the Mines Eat Us: Dependency and Exploitation in Bolivian Tin Mines*. New York: Columbia University Press.

Nash, M. 1967. "Reply to Review of Primitive and Peasant Economic Systems, by Manning Nash." *Current Anthropology* 8:249–50.

Needham, R. 1967. "Introduction." In *The Semi-Scholars*, ed. A. van Gennep. London: Routledge & Kegan Paul.

Neocleous, M. 1997. *Fascism*. Buckingham: Open University Press.

Niebuhr, C. 1969. *Beschreibung von Arabien*. Graz: Akademische Verlagsanstaet.

Obeyesekere, G. 1982. *The Apotheosis of Captain Cook: European Mythmaking in the Pacific*. Princeton, N.J.: Princeton University Press.

O'Laughlin, B. 1975. "Marxist Approaches in Anthropology." *Annual Review of Anthropology* 4:341–70.

Ong, A. 1987. *Spirits of Resistance and Capitalist Discipline: Factory Women in Malaysia.* Albany: State University of New York Press.

Ôno, M. 1996. "Collective Effervescence and Symbolism." *Durkheimian Studies* 2:79–98.

Ortner, S. B. 1984. "Theory in Anthropology since the Sixties." *Comparative Studies in Society and History* 26:126–66.

Ortner, S. B., and H. Whitehead, eds. 1981. *Sexual Meanings: The Cultural Construction of Gender and Sexuality.* Cambridge: Cambridge University Press.

Otto, R. 1917. *Das Heilige: Über das Irrationale in der Idee des Göttlichen und sein Verhältnis zum Rationalen.* Breslau: Trewendt und Granier.

Parkin, R. J. 1996. *The Dark Side of Humanity: The Work of Robert Hertz and Its Legacy.* Amsterdam: Harwood Academic Publishers.

———. 1997. "Durkheimians and the Groupe d'Etudes Socialistes." *Durkheimian Studies* 3:43–58.

———. 1998. "'From Science to Action': Durkheimians and the Groupe d'Études Socialistes." *Journal of the Anthropological Society of Oxford* 29:81–90.

———. 2001. *Perilous Transactions: Papers in General and Indian Anthropology.* Orissa, India: Sikshasandhan.

———. 2003. *Louis Dumont and Hierarchical Opposition.* Oxford: Berghahn.

Parry, J. 1986. "The Gift, the Indian Gift and the 'Indian Gift.'" *Man* 21:453–73.

Paulme, D. 1940/1988. *Organisation sociale des Dogon de Sanga.* Paris: Jean-Michel Place.

———. 1984. *La statue du commandeur: Essays d'ethnologie.* Paris: Le Sycomore.

Penny, H. G. 2002. *Objects of Culture: Ethnology and Ethnographic Museums in Imperial Germany.* Chapel Hill: University of North Carolina Press.

Penny, H. G., and Matti Bunzl. 2003. "Introduction: Rethinking German Anthropology, Colonialism, and Race." Pp. 1–30 in *Worldly Provincialism: German Anthropology in the Age of Empire,* ed. H. G. Penny and M. Bunzl. Ann Arbor: University of Michigan Press.

———, eds. 2003. *Worldly Provincialism: German Anthropology in the Age of Empire.* Ann Arbor: University of Michigan Press.

Peters, E. L. 1960. "The Proliferation of Segments in the Lineage of the Bedouin of Cyrenaica." *Journal of the Royal Anthropological Institute* 90:29–53.

———. 1967. "Some Structural Aspects of the Feud among the Camel-Herding Bedouin of Cyrenaica." *Africa* 37:261–82.

———. 1990. *The Bedouin of Cyrenaica: Studies in Personal and Corporate Power.* Cambridge: Cambridge University Press.

Piaget, J. 1971. *Structuralism.* London: Routledge & Kegan Paul.

Picone, M. 1982. "Observing 'Les Observateurs de l'Homme': Impressions of Contemporary French Anthropology in Context." *Journal of the Anthropological Society of Oxford* 13:292–99.

Pignède, B. 1993. *The Gurungs: A Himalayan Population of Nepal*. Kathmandu: Ratna Pustak Bhandar.

Pina-Cabral, J. d. 1980. "Cults of Death in Northwestern Portugal." *Journal of the Anthropological Society of Oxford* 11:1–14.

Polanyi, K., C. M. Arensberg, and H. W. Pearson, eds. 1957. *Trade and Market in the Early Empires*. Glencoe: Free Press.

Poster, M., and J. Baudrillard. 1988. "Introduction." In *Selected Writings, Jean Baudrillard*. Stanford, Calif.: Stanford University Press.

Powdermaker, H. 1939. *After Freedom: A Cultural Study in the Deep South*. New York: Viking.

———. 1966. *Stranger and Friend: The Way of an Anthropologist*. New York: Norton.

Putzstück, L. 1995. *"Symphonie in Moll": Julius Lips und die Kölner Völkerkunde*. Pfaffenweiler: Centaurus-Verlagsgesellschaft.

Rabinow, P. 1977. *Reflections on Fieldwork in Morocco*. Berkeley: University of California Press.

Radcliffe-Brown, A. R. 1913. "Three Tribes of Western Australia." *Journal of the Royal Anthropological Institute* 43:143–94.

———. 1922/1948. *The Andaman Islanders: A Study in Social Anthropology Anthony Wilkin Studentship Research, 1906*. Glencoe, Ill.: Free Press.

———. 1930–1931. "The Social Organization of Australian Tribes." *Oceania* 1:34–63, 207–46, 322–41, 426–56.

———. 1952. *Structure and Function in Primitive Society: Essays and Addresses*. London: Cohen & West.

———. 1956/1964. *A Natural Science of Society*. New York: Free Press.

Radcliffe-Brown, A. R., and C. D. Forde, eds. 1950. *African Systems of Kinship and Marriage*. London: Oxford University Press.

Radin, P. 1920. *The Autobiography of a Winnebago Indian*. Berkeley: University of California Publications in American Archaeology and Ethnology.

———. 1927. *Primitive Man as Philosopher*. New York: Dover.

Raheja, G. G. 1988. *The Poison in the Gift: Ritual, Prestation, and the Dominant Caste in a North Indian Village*. Chicago: University of Chicago Press.

Rappaport, R. A. 1967. *Pigs for the Ancestors: Ritual in the Ecology of a New Guinea People*. New Haven: Yale University Press.

Raum, J. W. 2001. "Peter Kolb." Pp. 192–196 in *Hauptwerke der Ethnologie*, ed. C. F. Feest and K.-H. Kohl. Stuttgart: Kröner.

Redfield, R. 1930. *Tepoztlán, a Mexican Village*. Chicago: University of Chicago Press.

———. 1941. *The Folk Culture of Yucatan*. Chicago: University of Chicago Press.

————. 1955. *The Little Community: Viewpoints for the Study of a Human Whole.* Chicago: University of Chicago Press.

————. 1956. *Peasant Society and Culture.* Chicago: University of Chicago Press.

Reed-Danahay, D. 1996. *Education and Identity in Rural France: The Politics of Schooling.* Cambridge: Cambridge University Press.

Reemtsma, K. 1996a. *Sinti und Roma: Geschichte, Kultur, Gegenwart.* München: C.H. Beck.

————. 1996b. *"Zigeuner" in der ethnographischen Literatur: Die "Zigeuner" der Ethnographen.* Frankfurt: Fritz Bauer Institut.

Reiniche, M. L. 1979. *Les dieux et les hommes: Étude des cultes d'un village du Tirunelveli, Inde du Sud.* Paris: Mouton.

Reiter, R. R., ed. 1975. *Toward an Anthropology of Women.* New York: Monthly Review Press.

Rey, P. P. 1971. *Colonialisme, néo-colonialisme et transition au capitalisme: Exemple de la Comilog au Congo-Brazzaville.* Paris: Maspéro.

Richards, A. I. 1932. *Hunger and Work in a Savage Tribe: A Functional Study of Nutrition among the Southern Bantu.* London: G. Routledge.

Richardson, J. 1940. *Law and Status among the Kiowa Indians.* New York: J. J. Augustin.

Richardson, J., and A.L. Kroeber. 1940. *Three Centuries of Women's Dress Fashion: A Quantitative Analysis.* Berkeley: University of California press.

Richman, M. H. 2002. *Sacred Revolutions: Durkheim and the Collège de Sociologie.* Minneapolis: University of Minnesota Press.

Ricoeur, P. 1974. *The Conflict of Interpretations: Essays in Hermeneutics.* Evanston: Northwestern University Press.

————. 1977. *The Rule of Metaphor: Multi-Disciplinary Studies of the Creation of Meaning in Language.* Toronto: University of Toronto Press.

Riese, B. 1995. "Während des Dritten Reiches (1933–1945) in Deutschland und Österreich verfolgte und von dort ausgewanderte Ethnologen." Pp. 210–20 in *Lebenslust und Fremdenfurcht: Ethnologie im Dritten Reich,* ed. T. Hauschild. Frankfurt: Suhrkamp.

————. 2001. "Konrad Theodor Preuß." Pp. 366–371 in *Hauptwerke der Ethnologie,* ed. Christian F. Feest and Karl-Heinz Kohl. Stuttgart: Kröner.

Rivers, W. H. R. 1906. *The Todas.* London: Macmillan.

————. 1914. *The History of Melanesian Society.* Cambridge: Cambridge University Press.

Rivet, P. 1912. *Ethnographie ancienne de l'équateur.* Paris: Gauthier-Villars.

Rivière, C. 1991. "Georges Balandier." In *Dictionnaire de l'ethnologie et de l'anthropologie,* ed. P. Bonte and M. Izard. Paris: Presses Universitaires de France.

Robbins, D. 2003. "The Responsibility of the Ethnographer: An Introduction to Pierre Bourdieu on 'Colonialism and Ethnography.'" *Anthropology Today* 19:11–12.

Robey, D., ed. 1973. *Structuralism: An Introduction*. Oxford: Clarendon.

Rödiger, I. 2001. "Gustav Friedrich Klemm." Pp. 188–92 in *Hauptwerke der Ethnologie*, ed. C. F. Feest and K.-H. Kohl. Stuttgart: Kröner.

Rogers, S. C. 2001. "Anthropology in France." *Annual Review of Anthropology* 30:481–504.

Roosevelt, A. C., ed. 1994. *Amazonian Indians from Prehistory to the Present: Anthropological Perspectives*. Tucson: University of Arizona.

Rosaldo, M. Z., and L. Lamphere, eds. 1974. *Woman, Culture, and Society*. Stanford, Calif.: Stanford University Press.

Roseberry, W. 1983. *Coffee and Capitalism in the Venezuelan Andes*. Austin: University of Texas Press.

Rousseau, J.-J. 1762/1993. *Emile*. Londont: J. M. Dent.

Royal Anthropological Institute. 1874. *Notes and Queries on Anthropology, for the Use of Travellers and Residents in Uncivilized Lands*. London: Royal Anthropological Institute.

Sabatier, L. 1930. *Palabre du serment au Darlac: Assemblée des chefs de tribus 1. janvier 1926*. Hanoi: EFEO.

Sabatier, L., and D. Antomarchi. 1940. *Recueil des coutumes rhadées du Darlac*. Hanoi: Imprimerie d'Extreme-Orient.

Sahlins, M. D. 1958. *Social Stratification in Polynesia*. Seattle: University of Washington Press.

———. 1960. "Evolution: Specific and General." Pp. 12–44 in *Evolution and Culture*, ed. M. S. Sahlins and E. R. Service. Ann Arbor: University of Michigan Press.

———. 1962. *Moala: Culture and Nature on a Fijian Island*. Ann Arbor: University of Michigan Press.

———. 1968. *Tribesmen*. Englewood Cliffs, N.J.: Prentice-Hall.

———. 1972. *Stone Age Economics*. Chicago: Aldine.

———. 1976. *Culture and Practical Reason*. Chicago: Aldine.

———. 1981. *Historical Metaphors and Mythical Realities*. Ann Arbor: University of Michigan Press.

———. 1985. *Islands of History*. Chicago: University of Chicago Press.

———. 1995. *How "Natives" Think: About Captain Cook, for Example*. Chicago: University of Chicago Press.

Said, E. W. 1978. *Orientalism*. New York: Pantheon.

Saint-Simon, Henri, Comte de. 1975. *Henri Saint-Simon (1760–1825): Selected Writings on Science, Industry and Social Organisation*, ed. and trans. K. Taylor. London: Croom Helm.

Salemink, O. 1991. "Mois and Maquis: The Invention and Appropriation of Vietnam's Montagnards from Sabatier to the CIA." In *Colonial Situations: Essays in the Contextualization of Ethnographic Knowledge*, ed. G. W. Stocking Jr. Madison: University of Wisconsin Press.

———. 2003. *The Ethnography of Vietnam's Central Highlanders: A Historical Contextualization, 1850–1990*. London: Routledge Curzon.

Sales, A. d. 1991. *Je suis né de vos jeux de tambours: La religion chamanique des Magar du nord*. Nanterre: Société d'Ethnologie.

Sapir, E. 1917. "Do We Need the Superorganic?" *American Anthropologist* 19:441–47.

———. 1924. "Culture, Genuine and Spurious." *American Journal of Sociology* 29:401–29.

Sartre, J. P. 1948. *Qu'est-ce que la literature*. Paris: Gallimard.

Saussure, F. d. 1983. *Course in General Linguistics*. London: Duckworth.

Schäffler, H. 2001. "Ethnologisches Wissen, Objekte und koloniale Macht: Eine kritische Bearbeitung der von Christoph Fürer-Haimendorf gesammelten Objekte aus Nagaland." Unpublished thesis, University of Vienna.

Scheper-Hughes, N. 1992. *Death without Weeping: The Violence of Everyday Life in Brazil*. Berkeley: University of California Press.

———. 1995. "The Primacy of the Ethical: Propositions for a Militant Anthropology." *Current Anthropology* 36:409–20; 436–38.

Schimmel, A. 1987. *Friedrich Rückert: Lebensbild und Einführung in sein Werk*. Freiburg im Breisgau: Herder Taschenbuch Verlag.

Schippers, T. K. 1995. "A History of Paradoxes: Anthropologies of Europe." In *Fieldwork and Footnotes: Studies in the History of European Anthropology*, ed. H. Vermeulen and A. A. Roldán. London: Routledge.

Schlegel, F. 1808. *Über die Sprache und Weisheit der Indier. Ein Beitrag zur Begründung der Alterthumskunde*. Heidelberg: Mohr und Zimmer.

Schmidt, J. 1985. *Maurice Merleau-Ponty: Between Phenomenology and Structuralism*. Basingstoke: Macmillan.

Schneider, D. M. 1968. *American Kinship: A Cultural Account*. Englewood Cliffs, N.J.: Prentice Hall.

———. 1984. *A Critique of the Study of Kinship*. Ann Arbor: University of Michigan Press.

Schneider, J., and P. Schneider. 1976. *Culture and Political Economy in Western Sicily*. New York: Academic Press.

Schneider, P., J. Schneider, and E. Hansen. 1972. "Modernization and Development: The Role of Regional Elites and Non-Corporate Groups in the European Mediterranean." *Comparative Studies in Society and History* 14:328–50.

Scholte, B. 1981. "Critical Anthropology since Its Reinvention." Pp. 148–84 in *The Anthropology of Pre-Capitalist Societies*, ed. J. S. Kahn and J. R. Llobera. London: Macmillan.

Schröter, S. 2001. "Johann Jakob Bachofen." Pp. 8–10 in *Hauptwerke der Ethnologie*, ed. C. F. Feest and K.-H. Kohl. Stuttgart: Kröner.

Schweitzer, P. 2001. "Siberia and Anthropology: National Traditions and Transnational Moments in the History of Research." Unpublished *venia docendi* thesis, University of Vienna.

Scott, J. C. 1985. *Weapons of the Weak: Everyday Forms of Peasant Resistance.* New Haven: Yale University Press.

Secoy, F. R. 1953. *Changing Military Patterns on the Great Plains: 17th Century through Early 19th Century.* New York: J. J. Augustin.

Segalen, M. 1983. *Love and Power in the Peasant Family: Rural France in the Nineteenth Century.* Oxford: Blackwell.

———. 1985. *Quinze générations de Bas-Bretons: Parenté et société dans le pays bigouden Sud, 1720–1980.* Paris: Presses Universitaires de France.

———. 1986. *Historical Anthropology of the Family.* Cambridge: Cambridge University Press.

———. 1989. *L'autre et le semblable: Regards sur l'ethnologie des sociétés contemporaines.* Paris: Presses du CNRS.

Seidler, C. 2003. *Wissenschaftsgeschichte nach der NS-Zeit: des Beispiel der Ethnologie. Die beiden deutschen Ethnologen Wilhelm Mühlmann (1904–1988) und Hermann Baumann (1902–1970).* Contemporary history thesis: Freiburg University.

Seligman, C. G. 1910. *The Melanesians of British New Guinea.* Cambridge: Cambridge University Press.

Seligman, C. G., and B. Z. Seligman, eds. 1911. *The Veddas.* Cambridge: Cambridge University Press.

———. 1932. *Pagan Tribes of the Nilotic Sudan.* London: G. Routledge & Sons.

Service, E. R. 1962. *Primitive Social Organization: An Evolutionary Perspective.* New York: Random House.

Sharp, J. S. 1980. "Two Separate Developments: Anthropology in South Africa." *Royal Anthropological Institute News* 36:4–5.

Shilling, C., and P. A. Mellor. 2001. *The Sociological Ambition: Elementary Forms of Social and Moral Life.* London: Sage.

Sigaud, L. 2002. "The Vicissitudes of The Gift." *Social Anthropology* 10:335–58.

Silverman, S. 1968. "Agricultural Organization, Social Structure, and Values in Italy: Amoral Familism Reconsidered." *American Anthropologist* 70:1–20.

———. 1981. *Totems and Teachers: Perspectives on the History of Anthropology.* New York: Columbia University Press.

Simiand, F. 1903. "Méthode historique et sciences socials: Étude critique." *Review de Synthèse Historique* 6:1–22; 129–57.

———. 1934–1942. *De l'échange primitif à l'économie complexe.* Paris: La Pensée Ouvrière.

Sjoberg, G. 1952. "Folk and Feudal Societies." *American Journal of Sociology* 58:231–39.

Skinner, G. W. 1964–1965. "Marketing and Social Structure in Rural China." *Journal of Asian Studies* 24:3–43, 195–228, 363–99.

Smith, C. A. 1976. *Regional Analysis*. 2 vols. New York: Academic Press.

Smith, D. N. 1995. "Ziya Gölkap and Emile Durkheim: Sociology as an Apology for Chauvinism?" *Durkheimian Studies* 1:45–50.

Smith, W. R. 1885. *Kinship and Marriage in Early Arabia*. Cambridge: Cambridge University Press.

———. 1889. *Lectures on the Religion of the Semites: First Series; The Fundamental Institutions*. Edinburgh: Black.

Sperber, D. 1975. *Rethinking Symbolism*. Cambridge: Cambridge University Press.

———. 1985. *On Anthropological Knowledge: Three Essays*. Cambridge: Cambridge University Press.

———. 1996. *Explaining Culture: A Naturalistic Approach*. Oxford: Blackwell.

Sperber, D., and D. Wilson. 1986. *Relevance: Communication and Cognition*. Oxford: Basil Blackwell.

Spivak, G. C. 1976. "Translator's Preface." In J. Derrida, *Of Grammatology*. Baltimore: Johns Hopkins University Press.

Srinivas, M. N. 1952. *Religion and Society among the Coorgs of South India*. Oxford: Clarendon.

Stagl, J. 1995. *A History of Curiosity: The Theory of Travel, 1550–1800*. Chur: Harwood Academic Publishers.

———. 1999. "Theodor Koch-Grünberg." Pp. 208 in *Wörterbuch der Völkerkunde (begründet von Walter Hirschberg)*. Berlin: Reimer.

Stedman-Jones, S. 2001. "Durkheim and Bataille: Constraint, Transgression, and the Concept of the Sacred." *Durkheimian Studies* 7:53–64.

Stein, L. 1967. *Die Šammar-Ǧerba: Beduinen im Übergang vom Nomadismus zur Sesshaftigkeit*. Berlin: Akademie-Verlag.

Steiner, G. 1977. *Georg Forster*. Stuttgart: Metzler.

Steward, J. H. 1938. *Basin-Plateau Aboriginal Sociopolitical Groups*. Washington, D.C.: U.S. Government Printing Office.

———. 1949. "Cultural Causality and Law: A Trial Formulation of the Development of Early Civilizations." *American Anthropologist* 51: 1–27.

———. 1950. *Area Research: Theory and Practice*. New York: Social Science Research Council.

———. 1955. *Theory of Culture Change: The Methodology of Multilinear Evolution*. Urbana: University of Illinois Press.

———, ed. 1967. *Contemporary Change in Traditional Societies*. 3 vols. Urbana: University of Illinois Press.

Steward, J. H., et al. 1956. *The People of Puerto Rico: A Study in Social Anthropology*. Urbana: University of Illinois Press.

Stocking, G. W., Jr. 1964. "French Anthropology in 1800." *Isis* 4/2:134–50.

———. 1971. "What's in a Name? The Origins of the Royal Anthropological Institute (1837–1871)." *Man* 6:369–90.

———. 1987. *Victorian Anthropology.* New York: Free Press.

———. 1996a. *After Tylor: British Social Anthropology, 1888–1951.* London: Athlone Press.

———, ed. 1996b. *Volksgeist as Method and Ethic: Essays on Boasian Ethnography and the German Anthropological Tradition.* Madison: University of Wisconsin Press.

———, ed. 1974. *The Shaping of American Anthropology, 1883–1911: A Franz Boas Reader.* New York: Basic Books.

Strathern, M. 1992. "Parts and Wholes: Refiguring Relationships in a Post-Plural World." Pp. 75–104 in *Conceptualizing Society,* ed. A. Kuper. London: Routledge.

Straube, H. 1990. "Leo Frobenius (1873–1938)." Pp. 151–170 in *Klassiker der Kultur-antropologie: Von Montaigne bis Margaret Mead,* ed. W. Marschall. München: C. H. Beck.

Streck, B., ed. 2000. *Ethnologie und Nationalsozialismus.* Gehren: Escher.

———. 2001a. "Theodor Waitz." Pp. 503–8 in *Hauptwerke der Ethnologie,* ed. C. F. Feest and K.-H. Kohl. Stuttgart: Kröner.

———. 2001b. "Wilhelm Maximilian Wundt." Pp. 524–31 in *Hauptwerke der Ethnologie,* ed. C. F. Feest and K.-H. Kohl. Stuttgart: Kröner.

Striedter, K. H. 2001. "Fritz Graebner." Pp. 142–147 in *Hauptwerke der Ethnologie,* ed. C. F. Feest and K.-H. Kohl. Stuttgart: Kröner.

Strum, S. C., and L. M. Fedigan, eds. 2000. *Primate Encounters: Models of Science, Gender, and Society.* Chicago: University of Chicago Press.

Swingewood, A. 1984. *A Short History of Sociological Thought.* London: Macmillan.

Tambiah, S. J. 2002. *Edmund Leach: An Anthropological Life.* Cambridge: Cambridge University Press.

Tauxier, L. 1924. *Nègres Gouro et Gagou: Centre de la Cote d'Ivoire.* Paris: Librairie Orientaliste P. Geuthner.

Tax, S. 1953. *Penny Capitalism: A Guatemalan Indian Economy.* Washington, D.C.: U.S. Government Printing Office.

Tcherkézoff, S. 1987. *Dual Classification Reconsidered: Nyamwezi Sacred Kingship and Other Examples.* Cambridge: Cambridge University Press.

Terray, E. 1972. *Marxism and "Primitive" Societies: Two Studies.* London: Monthly Review Press.

Thurnwald, H. 1950. "Thurnwald-Lebensweg und Werk." Pp. 9–19 in *Beiträge zur Gesellungs- und Völkerwissenschaft. Professor Dr. Richard Thurnwald zum achtzigsten Geburtstag gewidmet.* Berlin: Mann.

Tierney, P. 2000. *Darkness in El Dorado: How Scientists and Journalists Devastated the Amazon.* New York: Norton.

Toffin, G. 1984. *Société et religion chez les Néwar du Népal.* Paris: Editions du C.N.R.S.

———. 1993. *Le palais et le temple: La fonction royale dans la vallée du Népal.* Paris: CNRS.

———. 1995. "Lucien Bernot (1919–1993)." *L'Homme* 133:5–8.

———. 1999. "Louis Dumont (1911–1998)." *L'Homme* 150:7–14.

Turner, V. 1965. "Colour Classification in Ndembu ritual: A Problem in Primitive Classification." In *Anthropological Approaches to the Study of Religion*, ed. M. Banton. London: Tavistock.

———. 1967. *The Forest of Symbols: Aspects of Ndembu ritual*. Ithaca, N.Y.: Cornell University Press.

———. 1968. *The Drums of Affliction: A Study of Religious Processes among the Ndembu of Zambia*. Oxford: Clarendon Press.

———. 1969. *The Ritual Process: Structure and Anti-Structure*. London: Routledge & Kegan Paul.

Tylor, E. B. 1865. *Researches into the Early History of Mankind and the Development of Civilization*. London: J. Murray.

———. 1871. *Primitive Culture: Researches into the Development of Mythology, Philosophy, Religion, Art, and Custom*, 2 vols. London: John Murray.

Ulrich, M. 1987. "Heinrich Cunow." Unpublished PhD thesis, University of Vienna.

Vacher de Lapouge, G. 1896. *Les selections socials*. Paris: Fontemoing.

———. 1909. *Race et milieu social: Essais d'anthroposociologie*. Paris: Riviere.

Valentine, C. A. 1968. *Culture and Poverty: Critique and Counter-Proposals*. Chicago: University of Chicago Press.

Van Gennep, A. 1907/1967. *The Semi-Scholars*. London: Routledge & Kegan Paul.

———. 1920. *L'état actuel du problème totémique*. Paris: E. Leroux.

———. 1937–1953. *Manuel d'ethnographie français contemporain*. Paris: A. et J. Picard.

———. 1909/1960. *The Rites of Passage*. London: Routledge & Kegan Paul.

Vermeulen, H. 1995. "Origins and Institutionalization of Ethnography and Ethnology in Europe and the USA, 1771–1845." In *Fieldwork and Footnotes: Studies in the History of European Anthropology*, ed. H. Vermeulen and A. A. Roldán. London: Routledge.

Vermeulen, H., and A. Alvarez Roldán. 1995. *Fieldwork and Footnotes: Studies in the History of European Anthropology*. London: Routledge.

Vernier, B. 1991. *La Genése sociale des sentiments: Ainés et cadets dans l'île grecque de Karpathos*. Paris: École des Hautes Études en Sciences Sociales.

Vidal, D. 1997. *Violence and Truth: A Rajasthani Kingdom Confronts Colonial Authority*. Delhi: Oxford University Press.

Vincent, J. 1982. *Teso in Transformation: The Political Economy of Peasant and Class in Eastern Africa*. Berkeley: University of California Press.

Wacquant, L. 1989. "Towards a Reflexive Sociology: A Workshop with Pierre Bourdieu." *Social Theory* 7:26–63.

Wagley, C. 1964. "Alfred Métraux." *American Anthropologist* 66:603–7.

Wagley, C., and M. Harris. 1955. "A Typology of Latin American Subcultures." *American Anthropologist* 57:428–51.

Wagner, G. 1940. "The Political Organization of the Bantu of Kavirondo." Pp. 197–

236 in *African Political Systems*, ed. M. Fortes and E. E. Evans-Pritchard. London: Oxford University Press for the International African Institute.

Waitz, T. 1863. *Introduction into Anthropology*. London: Longman, Green, Longman, and Roberts.

Wakin, E. 1992. *Anthropology Goes to War: Professional Ethics and Conterinsurgency in Thailand*. Madison: University of Wisconsin Center for Southeast Asian Studies.

Wallerstein, I. 1974. *The Modern World-System*, vol. 1: *Capitalist Agriculture and the Origins of the European World-Economy of the Sixteenth Century*. New York: Academic Press.

Warner, W. L., and P. S. Lunt. 1941. *The Social Life of a Modern Community*. New Haven: Yale University Press.

———. 1942. *The Status System of a Modern Community*. New Haven: Yale University Press.

Washburn, S. L. 1951. "The New Physical Anthropology." *Transactions of the New York Academy of Sciences* 13:298–304.

Weber, F. 2001. "Settings, Interactions and Things: A Plea for Multi-Integrative Ethnography." *Ethnos* 2:475–99.

Weiner, A. B. 1976. *Women of Value, Men of Renown: New Perspectives in Trobriand Exchange*. Austin: University of Texas Press.

White, L. A. 1943. "Energy and the Evolution of Culture." *American Anthropologist* 45:335–56.

———. 1949. *The Science of Culture, a Study of Man and Civilization*. New York: Grove Press.

———. 1959. "The Concept of Culture." *American Anthropologist* 61:227–51.

Whyte, W. F. 1943. *Street Corner Society: The Social Structure of an Italian Slum*. Chicago: University of Chicago Press.

Williams, E. A. 1985. "Art and Artefact at the Trocadero: *Ars Americana* and the Primitivist Revolution." In *Objects and Others: Essays on Museums and Material Culture*, ed. G. W. Stocking. Madison: University of Wisconsin Press.

Wilson, E. O. 1975. *Sociobiology: The New Synthesis*. Cambridge, Mass.: Harvard University Press.

Windisch, E. 1992. *Geschichte der Sanskrit-Philologie und indischen Altertumskunde*. Berlin: De Gruyter.

Winkelmann, I. 1966. *Die bürgerlich Ethnographie im Dienste der Kolonialpolitik des Deutschen Reiches (1870–1918)*. Unpublished PhD thesis, Humboldt University, Berlin.

Wirth, L. 1938. "Urbanism as a Way of Life." *American Journal of Sociology* 144:1–24.

Wiser, W. H., and C. V. Wiser. 1930. *Behind Mud Walls*. New York: Richard R. Smith.

Wissler, C. 1917. *The American Indian: An Introduction to the Anthropology of the New World*. New York: D. C. McMurtrie.

Withers, C. 1945. *Plainville, U.S.A.* New York: Columbia University Press.

Wittfogel, K. A. 1931. *Wirtschaft und Gesellschaft Chinas: Versuch der wissenschaftlichen Analyse einer grossen asiatischen Agrargesellschaft.* Leipzig: Hirschfeld.

———. 1970. *Marxismus und Wirtschaftsgeschichte.* Frankfurt: Junius.

———. 1981. *Oriental Despotism: A Comparative Study of Total Power.* New York: Vintage.

Wolf, E. R. 1955. "Types of Latin American Peasantry: A Preliminary Definition." *American Anthropologist* 57:452–71.

———. 1956. "Aspects of Group Relations in a Complex Society: Mexico." *American Anthropologist* 58:1065–78.

———. 1957. "Closed Corporate Peasant Communities in Mesoamerica and Central Java." *Southwestern Journal of Anthropology* 13:1–18.

———. 1966. *Peasants.* Englewood Cliffs, N.J.: Prentice-Hall.

———. 1969. *Peasant Wars of the Twentieth Century.* New York: Harper & Row.

———. 1980. "They Divide and Subdivide, and Call It Anthropology." *New York Times* (November 30).

———. 1982. *Europe and the People without History.* Berkeley: University of California Press.

———. 1999. *Envisioning Power Ideologies of Dominance and Crisis.* Berkeley: University of California Press.

———. 2001. *Pathways of Power: Building an Anthropology of the Modern World.* Berkeley: University of California Press.

Xanthakou, M. 1995. "De la mémoire à méthode: Georges Devereux, tell qu'en nous-mêmes." *L'Homme* 134:179–90.

Yalman, N. 1967. *Under the Bo Tree: Studies in Caste, Kinship, and Marriage in the Interior of Ceylon.* Berkeley: University of California Press.

Yans-McLaughlin, V. 1986. "Science, Democracy, and Ethics: Mobilizing Culture and Personality for World War II." Pp. 184–217 in *Malinowski, Rivers, Benedict, and Others: Essays on Culture and Personality,* ed. G. W. Stocking Jr. History of Anthropology, vol. 4. Madison: University of Wisconsin Press.

Zammito, J. H. 2002. *Kant, Herder, and the Birth of Anthropology.* Chicago: University of Chicago Press.

Zimmermann, A. 2001. *Anthropology and Antihumanism in Imperial Germany.* Chicago: University of Chicago Press.

Zitelmann, T. 1999. *Des Teufels Lustgarten. Themen und Tabus der politischen Anthropologie Nordostafrikas.* Unpublished *venia docendi* thesis, Free University, Berlin.

Zonabend, F. 1984. *The Enduring Memory: Time and History in a French Village.* Manchester. U.K.: Manchester University Press.

———. 1991. "France 2: Les recherches sur la France." In *Dictionnaire de l'ethnologie et de l'anthropologie,* ed. P. Bonte and M. Izard. Paris: Presses Universitaires de France.

———. 1993. *The Nuclear Peninsula.* Cambridge: Cambridge University Press.